VCP6-NV
Official Cert Guide

(Exam #2V0-641)

VMware Press is the official publisher of VMware books and training materials, which provide guidance on the critical topics facing today's technology professionals and students. Enterprises, as well as small- and medium-sized organizations, adopt virtualization as a more agile way of scaling IT to meet business needs. VMware Press provides proven, technically accurate information that helps them meet their goals for customizing, building, and maintaining their virtual environment.

VMware Press provides proven, technically accurate information that will help you achieve your goals for customizing, building, and maintaining a virtual environment— from the data center to mobile devices to the public, private, and hybrid cloud.

With books, certification and study guides, video training, and learning tools produced by world-class architects and IT experts, VMware Press helps IT professionals master a diverse range of topics on virtualization and cloud computing and is the official source of reference materials for preparing for the VMware Certified Professional certification.

VMware Press is also pleased to have localization partners that can publish its products in more than 42 languages, including, but not limited to, Chinese (Simplified), Chinese (Traditional), French, German, Greek, Hindi, Japanese, Korean, Polish, Russian, and Spanish.

For more information about VMware Press, please visit **vmwarepress.com.**

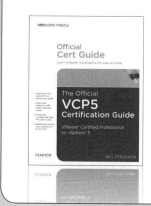

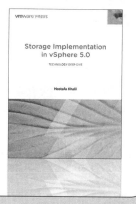

VCP6-NV
Official Cert Guide
(Exam #2V0-641)

Elver Sena Sosa

vmware® PRESS

Hoboken, NJ • Boston • Indianapolis • San Francisco
New York • Toronto • Montreal • London • Munich • Paris • Madrid
Cape Town • Sydney • Tokyo • Singapore • Mexico City

VCP6-NV Official Cert Guide (Exam #2V0-641)

Copyright © 2017 VMware, Inc.

Published by Pearson Education, Inc.

Publishing as VMware Press

ISBN-10: 0-7897-5480-0

ISBN-13: 978-0-7897-5480-6

Library of Congress Control Number is on file.

Printed in the United States of America

1   16

All terms mentioned in this book that are known to be trademarks or service marks have been appropriately capitalized. The publisher cannot attest to the accuracy of this information. Use of a term in this book should not be regarded as affecting the validity of any trademark or service mark.

VMware terms are trademarks or registered trademarks of VMware in the United States, other countries, or both.

Warning and Disclaimer

Special Sales

For information about buying this title in bulk quantities, or for special sales opportunities (which may include electronic versions; custom cover designs; and content particular to your business, training goals, marketing focus, or branding interests), please contact our corporate sales department at corpsales@pearsoned.com or (800) 382-3419.

For government sales inquiries, please contact governmentsales@pearsoned.com.

For questions about sales outside the United States, please contact intlcs@pearson.com.

EDITOR IN CHIEF
Mark Taub

PRODUCT LINE MANAGER
Brett Bartow

EXECUTIVE EDITOR
Mary Beth Ray

VMWARE PRESS PROGRAM MANAGER
Karl Childs

DEVELOPMENT EDITOR
Christopher Cleveland

MANAGING EDITOR
Sandra Schroeder

PROJECT EDITOR
Mandie Frank

TECHNICAL EDITORS
William Grismore, Richard Hackman, Jon Hall

COPY EDITOR
Geneil Breeze

PROOFREADER
The Wordsmithery LLC

INDEXER
Ken Johnson

EDITORIAL ASSISTANT
Vanessa Evans

DESIGNER
Chuti Prasertsith

COMPOSITOR
TnT Design

Contents at a Glance

Contents

Dedication

I am dedicating this book to my father, who told me when I was still in high school to learn as much about computers as I could. He convinced me to take a Lotus 1-2-3 class and later an A+ class! Thanks, Dad!

About the Author

Elver Sena Sosa, CCIE 7321 Emeritus (R&S), VCDX-NV (#154), CCSI, VCI. Elver has been working in IT since the late 1990s. Elver started his IT career as an intern network engineer in Appleton, Wisconsin, later moving to Columbus, Ohio, to work with AT&T Solutions. Over the years Elver continued to learn more about different technologies and how these technologies could help solve business problems. Feeling constrained and limited working in a siloed environment, Elver decided to become an independent contractor so that he could help provide technical solutions for as many different clients as possible. Elver currently is the data center infrastructure architect at Hydra 1303, Inc. You can follow Elver on Twitter @ElverS_Opinion, or his blog, http://blog.senasosa.com.

Acknowledgments

I have a lot of people to thank for making this first book a reality. The biggest and most important are my wife, Katy, and son, Danilo. Katy served as my non-technical English editor, reading chapters while having no idea about what she was reading and somehow translating and fixing what she read from Elver to English. They both endured my physical and emotional absence throughout this process, at times encouraging me to keep going when I wanted to quit (did I allude to how hard it is to write a book?). Although at times it looked as if they were more pleased than not that I was locked in my office, their support is what made this project possible.

I also want to thank those at VMware (Chris McCain, Jenny Lawrence, Quang Nguyen) who provided the opportunities that put me on the path to writing this book. I want to thank those at Pearson (Mary Beth Ray, Chris Cleveland) who took a chance on me and provided me guidance along the way to get this done.

Special thanks goes to my editors (Richard Hackman, William Grismore, Jon Hall) for going through the pain of reading my drafts. I know it wasn't easy, but your feedback was very valuable (well, most of the feedback ☺).

I want to save the last thanks to those who kept asking me "when is the book coming out?" Every few weeks someone would ask me this, and although I didn't say it, it was encouraging that someone out there was interested in reading what I wrote. Muchas gracias.

We Want to Hear from You!

As the reader of this book, *you* are our most important critic and commentator. We value your opinion and want to know what we're doing right, what we could do better, what areas you'd like to see us publish in, and any other words of wisdom you're willing to pass our way.

We welcome your comments. You can email or write us directly to let us know what you did or didn't like about this book—as well as what we can do to make our books better.

Please note that we cannot help you with technical problems related to the topic of this book.

When you write, please be sure to include this book's title and author as well as your name, email address, and phone number. We will carefully review your comments and share them with the author and editors who worked on the book.

Email: VMwarePress@vmware.com

Mail: VMware Press
           ATTN: Reader Feedback
           800 East 96th Street
           Indianapolis, IN 46240 USA

Reader Services

Register your copy of *VCP6-NV Official Cert Guide (Exam #2V0-641)* at www.pearsonitcertification.com for convenient access to downloads, updates, and corrections as they become available. To start the registration process, go to www.pearsonitcertification.com/register and log in or create an account*. Enter the product ISBN, 9780789754806, and click Submit. Once the process is complete, you will find any available bonus content under Registered Products.

*Be sure to check the box that you would like to hear from us in order to receive exclusive discounts on future editions of this product.

Introduction

Hola y bienvenidos. I'm grateful that you have decided to pick up a copy of the *VCP6-NV Official Cert Guide (Exam #2V0-641)* and read it. Or if the book was given to you, I'm grateful that you decided to keep the book and read it instead of donating it to someone else. Why am I grateful? I'm grateful because I understand that your time is valuable, and out of all the available sources of information about NSX for vSphere, you chose my book as one of your study sources. Thank you.

About This Book

I was lucky to be in the right place at the right time when NSX for vSphere came out. I was one of the few folks around who knew vSphere, vRealize Automation (formerly VCAC), and vCloud Director well enough, and also had a better than average understanding of networking and network security. Being one of the few folks who fit the mold, it was a natural progression for me to get involved with NSX and thus I took the plunge. Over the last three years I have been traveling the world educating about NSX for vSphere and software defined networks, including delivering the first week of training to the first group of NSX Ninja candidates. I have also served as a mentor to many of the current NSX professionals and instructors, some of whom have grown to be way more competent than me in the subject. Before plunging into NSX, I was already working as an independent consultant as well as a VMware and Cisco instructor (and at one time a high school math teacher in the Bronx). I have delivered many courses over the years and have met many people.

Before writing the book I was heavily involved in writing the *NSX for vSphere: Install, Configure, Manage* and *NSX for vSphere: Fast Track* courses, one of which must be attended before you can be certified as a VMware Certified Professional 6 - Network Virtualization (VCP6-NV) (if you don't already have a VCP from another VMware solution track). Having now done both I can attest that writing a course is a cakewalk compared to writing a certification book. From time to time I try to pen some stuff in my blog, http://blog.senasosa.com/, as well as give talks at VMUGs, which I greatly enjoy.

This is my first book, so I'm really hoping you like it and find it useful. Although VMware puts out an exam blueprint to help students prepare for the exam, located in this site www.vmware.com/go/vcp6nv, this book does not follow the layout of the blueprint. The book's layout is designed to help the student fully understand what NSX is, the problems it solves, and the different features it provides. You will notice the book starts with a short trip down memory lane on how data center networking used to be and how it evolved to what it is today, followed by the introduction to NSX and its components. In Chapters 6 and 8 I opted for walking the reader through different packet walks so as to better illustrate how logical switches and logical routers work. While the book covers all the objects in the blueprint (as of January 2016), it is possible that the blueprint could be modified at VMware's discretion at any time.

In writing the book I assumed that you know what a virtual machine is and not much more. I assumed that your knowledge of the vSphere switches and basic networking is limited, thus I spent some time covering those basics where needed in the book. If you feel that you are above average in those topics, feel free to skip over them. If you are not sure how to rate yourself in those topics, the material is here for you to read; it should be a quick read anyway.

I also strongly advise you to get your hands on an NSX lab as part of your studies. There is nothing like having practical experience beyond reading and memorizing. If you can't get yourself your own lab, you can try the ones provided by VMware (for free) at the Hands On Labs, http://labs.hol.vmware.com.

And with that said, I wish you best of luck in your studies, and let's set sail.

Who Should Read This Book

If you work in the data center as a network administrator, storage administrator or vSphere administrator, this book is for you. By now you should have noticed that infrastructure components you work with in the data center have been prepended with a "Software Defined" term in front of it. The days of having a strict silo where you only knew one aspect of the data center infrastructure are numbered as all those Software Defined *whatever* have a strong co-dependency with each other. In the data center, infrastructure will be automated but to get us there (and for you to have a job in the data center) you must understand how each of those silos work. This book is one of the steps in the ladder to get you there by helping you become VCP6-NV certified.

Book Features

To help you customize your study time using this book, the core chapters have several features that help you make the best use of your time:

- **"Do I Know This Already?" quiz:** Each chapter begins with a quiz that helps you determine how much time you need to spend studying that chapter.

- **Foundation Topics:** These are the core sections of each chapter. They explain the concepts for the topics in that chapter.

- **Exam Preparation Tasks:** After the "Foundation Topics" section of each chapter, the "Exam Preparation Tasks" section lists a series of study activities that you should do at the end of the chapter. Each chapter includes the activities that make the most sense for studying the topics in that chapter:

  - **Review All the Key Topics:** The Key Topic icon appears next to the most important items in the "Foundation Topics" section of the chapter. The "Review All the Key Topics" section lists the key topics from the chapter, along with their page numbers. Although the contents of the entire chapter could be on the exam, you should definitely know the information listed in each key topic, so you should review these.

  - **Complete Tables and Lists from Memory:** To help you memorize some lists of facts, many of the more important lists and tables from the chapter are included in a document on the book's website. This document lists only partial information, allowing you to complete the table or list.

  - **Define Key Terms:** Although the exam may be unlikely to ask a question such as "Define this term," the VCP-NV exam does require that you learn and know a lot of terminology. This section lists the most important terms from the chapter, asking you to write a short definition and compare your answer to the glossary at the end of the book.

  - **Web-based practice exam:** The companion website includes the Pearson Cert Practice Test engine that allows you to take practice exam questions. Use these to prepare with a sample exam and to pinpoint topics where you need more study.

How to Use This Book

The book is organized by chapters that cover a topic that I believe is needed to fully understand NSX. Some chapters should be read sequentially, such as Chapters 4, 5, and 6, while other chapters can be read in any order, such as Chapters 15 and 18. Be aware that I do make references throughout the book to previously covered chapters.

The core chapters, Chapters 1 through 20, cover the following topics:

- **Chapter 1, "Introduction to VMware NSX:"** This chapter covers some of the history behind the data center network infrastructure, the challenges (Ethernet, IP, and security) that must be designed for, and how VMware NSX attempts to handle these challenges by eliminating them outright.

- **Chapter 2, "Network and VMware vSphere Requirements for NSX:"** This chapter covers the different types of data center infrastructure designs, the NSX underlay requirements, and the vSphere requirements for NSX.

- **Chapter 3, "NSX Architecture and NSX Manager:"** This chapter introduces the architecture of NSX and NSX Manager, describing its functions as well as how to deploy it.

- **Chapter 4, "VXLAN, NSX Controllers, and NSX Preparation:"** This chapter introduces VXLAN, one of the control planes of NSX, NSX Controllers, and how to prepare the vSphere environment for NSX.

- **Chapter 5, "NSX Switches:"** This chapter introduces logical switches, both global logical switches and universal logical switches.

- **Chapter 6, "Logical Switch Packet Walks:"** This chapter describes multiple step-by-step scenarios of the flow of virtual machine frames over logical switches.

- **Chapter 7, "Logical Router:"** This chapter introduces logical routers, including distributed logical routers and universal logical routers.

- **Chapter 8, "Logical Router Packet Walks:"** This chapter describes multiple step-by-step scenarios of the flow of virtual machine frames over logical routers.

- **Chapter 9, "NSX Edge Services Gateway:"** This chapter introduces the NSX Edge Services Gateway, describes its characteristics, and lists the features it supports.

- **Chapter 10, "Layer 2 Extensions:"** This chapter explains the ways in which NSX allows for a broadcast domain to be extended between a logical switch and a VLAN.

- **Chapter 11, "Layer 3 Connectivity Between Virtual and Physical Networks:"** This chapter explains how traffic between a virtual machine and a physical entity can take place when the virtual machine is connected to a logical switch.

- **Chapter 12, "Routing Protocols:"** This chapter describes the routing protocols supported by NSX: OSPF, BGP, and ISIS.

- **Chapter 13, "NSX Edge VPN Services:"** This chapter explains the virtual private network features supported by the NSX Edge.

- **Chapter 14, "NSX Edge Network Services and Security:"** This chapter explains the NSX Edge features of Network Address Translation, load balancer, and logical firewall.

- **Chapter 15, "Distributed Logical Firewall:"** This chapter introduces the distributed logical firewall (as well as the universal logical firewall), integration with LDAP/AD, and SpoofGuard.

- **Chapter 16, "Security Services:"** This chapter covers Security Composer, its components (security groups, security services), and the types of security services that can be offered by NSX.

- **Chapter 17, "Additional NSX Features:"** This chapter covers Layer 7 and Application security services, and troubleshooting tools native to NSX such as VMware Data Security, Activity Monitoring, and Traceflow.

- **Chapter 18, "NSX Automation:"** This chapter introduces RESTful APIs and how NSX APIs are used to create various NSX objects. There is a discussion of integration between NSX and vRealize Automation.

- **Chapter 19, "Upgrade to NSX for vSphere 6.2:"** This chapter covers how to upgrade a vCloud network and security or pre-NSX 6.2 installation to NSX 6.2.

- **Chapter 20, "Final Preparation:"** This chapter identifies tools for final exam preparation and helps you develop an effective study plan. It contains tips on how to best use the web-based material to study.

Certification Exam and This Preparation Guide

As mentioned earlier, this book is written in a way that best helps you understand NSX, which doesn't always make it clear as to which blueprint objectives are being covered in a particular chapter. Some objectives are covered over multiple chapters. Table I-1 lists the VCP6-NV Exam Blueprint Objectives and the chapters in the book that covers them.

Table I-1   VCP6-NV Exam Topics and Chapter References

Exam Section/Objective	Chapter Where Covered
Section 1—Understand VMware NSX Technology and Architecture	
Objective 1.1—Compare and Contrast the Benefits of a VMware NSX Implementation	Chapters 1, 15
Objective 1.2—Understand VMware NSX Architecture	Chapter 3
Objective 1.3—Differentiate Physical and Virtual Network Technologies	Chapters 2, 15
Objective 1.4—Understand VMware NSX Integration with Third-Party Products and Services	Chapter 10
Objective 1.5—Understand VMware NSX Integration with vRealize Automation (vRA)	Chapter 18
Section 2—Understand VMware NSX Physical Infrastructure Requirements	
Objective 2.1—Compare and Contrast the Benefits of Running VMware NSX on Physical Network Fabrics	Chapter 2
Objective 2.2—Determine Physical Infrastructure Requirements for a VMware NSX Implementation	Chapter 2
Section 3—Configure and Manage vSphere Networking	
Objective 3.1—Configure and Manage vSphere Distributed Switches (vDS)	Chapter 2
Objective 3.2—Configure and Manage vDS Policies	Chapter 2
Section 4—Install and Upgrade VMware NSX	
Objective 4.1—Configure Environment for Network Virtualization	Chapter 2
Objective 4.2—Deploy VMware NSX Components	Chapters 3, 4
Objective 4.3—Upgrade Existing vCNS/NSX Implementation	Chapter 19
Objective 4.4—Expand Transport Zone to Include New Cluster(s)	Chapter 4

Exam Section/Objective	Chapter Where Covered
Section 5—Configure VMware NSX Virtual Networks	
Objective 5.1—Create and Administer Logical Switches	Chapters 5, 6
Objective 5.2—Configure VXLAN	Chapters 4, 5
Objective 5.3—Configure and Manage Layer 2 Bridging	Chapter 10
Objective 5.4—Configure and Manage Logical Routers	Chapters 7, 8, 9, 11, 12
Section 6—Configure and Manage NSX Network Services	
Objective 6.1—Configure and Manage Logical Load Balancing	Chapter 14
Objective 6.2—Configure and Manage Logical Virtual Private Networks (VPN)	Chapters 4, 10, 13
Objective 6.3—Configure and Manage DHCP/DNS/NAT	Chapter 14
Objective 6.4—Configure and Manage Edge Services High Availability	Chapter 9
Section 7—Configure and Administer Network Security	
Objective 7.1—Configure and Administer Logical Firewall Services	Chapter 14
Objective 7.2—Configure Distributed Firewall Services	Chapter 15
Objective 7.3—Configure and Manage Service Composer	Chapter 16
Section 8—Deploy a Cross-vCenter NSX Environment	
Objective 8.1—Differentiate Single and Cross-vCenter NSX Deployments	Chapters 3, 5, 7, 15
Objective 8.2—Determine Cross-vCenter Requirements and Configurations	Chapters 3, 4, 5, 7
Section 9—Perform Operations Tasks in a VMware NSX Environment	
Objective 9.1—Configure Roles, Permissions, and Scopes	Chapter 17
Objective 9.2—Understand NSX Automation	Chapter 18
Objective 9.3—Monitor a VMware NSX Implementation	Chapter 17
Objective 9.4—Perform Auditing and Compliance	Chapter 17
Objective 9.5—Administer Logging	Chapters 12, 13, 14, 15
Objective 9.6—Backup and Recover Configurations	Coming Soon. Check Appendix B on the book website

Exam Section/Objective	Chapter Where Covered
Section 10—Troubleshoot a VMware Network Virtualization Implementation	
Objective 10.1—Compare and Contrast Tools Available for Troubleshooting	Chapter 17
Objective 10.2—Troubleshoot Common NSX Installation/Configuration Issues	Coming Soon. Check Appendix B on the book website
Objective 10.3—Troubleshoot Common NSX Component Issues	Chapters 3, 4, 7, 10
Objective 10.4—Troubleshoot Common Connectivity Issues	Chapter 4
Objective 10.5—Troubleshoot Common vSphere Networking Issues	Coming Soon. Check Appendix B on the book website

Book Content Updates

Since VMware occasionally updates exam topics without notice, VMware Press might post additional preparatory content on the web page associated with this book at http://www.pearsonitcertification.com/title/9780789754806. It is a good idea to check the website a couple of weeks before taking your exam, to review any updated content that might be posted online. We also recommend that you periodically check back to this page on the Pearson IT Certification website to view any errata or supporting book files that may be available.

Companion Website

Register this book to get access to the Pearson IT Certification test engine and other study materials plus additional bonus content. Check this site regularly for new and updated postings written by the author that provide further insight into the more troublesome topics on the exam. Be sure to check the box that you would like to hear from us to receive updates and exclusive discounts on future editions of this product or related products.

To access this companion website, follow these steps:

Step 1.   Go to www.pearsonITcertification.com/register and log in or create a new account.

Step 2.   Enter the ISBN: **9780789754806**

Step 3.   Answer the challenge question as proof of purchase.

Step 4.   Click on the **Access Bonus Content** link in the Registered Products section of your account page to be taken to the page where your downloadable content is available.

Please note that many of our companion content files can be very large, especially image and video files.

If you are unable to locate the files for this title by following the preceding steps, please visit www.pearsonITcertification.com/contact and select the **Site Problems/ Comments** option. Our customer service representatives will assist you.

Pearson IT Certification Practice Test Engine and Questions

The companion website includes the Pearson IT Certification Practice Test engine—software that displays and grades a set of exam-realistic multiple-choice questions. Using the Pearson IT Certification Practice Test engine, you can either study by going through the questions in Study Mode, or take a simulated exam that mimics real exam conditions. You can also serve up questions in a Flash Card Mode, which displays just the question and no answers, challenging you to state the answer in your own words before checking the actual answers to verify your work.

The installation process requires two major steps: installing the software and then activating the exam. The website has a recent copy of the Pearson IT Certification Practice Test engine. The practice exam (the database of exam questions) is not on this site.

NOTE   The cardboard sleeve in the back of this book includes a piece of paper. The paper lists the activation code for the practice exam associated with this book. Do not lose the activation code. On the opposite side of the paper from the activation code is a unique, one-time-use coupon code for the purchase of the Premium Edition eBook and Practice Test.

Install the Software

The Pearson IT Certification Practice Test is a Windows-only desktop application. You can run it on a Mac using a Windows virtual machine, but it was built specifically for the PC platform. The minimum system requirements are as follows:

- Windows 10, Windows 8.1, or Windows 7

- Microsoft .NET Framework 4.5 Client

- Pentium-class 1 GHz processor (or equivalent)

- 512 MB RAM

- 650 MB disk space plus 50 MB for each downloaded practice exam

- Access to the Internet to register and download exam databases

The software installation process is routine as compared with other software installation processes. If you have already installed the Pearson IT Certification Practice Test software from another Pearson product, there is no need for you to reinstall the software. Simply launch the software on your desktop and proceed to activate the practice exam from this book by using the activation code included in the access code card sleeve in the back of the book.

The following steps outline the installation process:

Step 1. Download the exam practice test engine from the companion site.

Step 2. Respond to Windows' prompts as with any typical software installation process.

The installation process gives you the option to activate your exam with the activation code supplied on the paper in the cardboard sleeve. This process requires that you establish a Pearson website login. You need this login to activate the exam, so please do register when prompted. If you already have a Pearson website login, there is no need to register again. Just use your existing login.

Activate and Download the Practice Exam

Once the exam engine is installed, you should then activate the exam associated with this book (if you did not do so during the installation process) as follows:

Step 1. Start the Pearson IT Certification Practice Test software from the Windows Start menu or from your desktop shortcut icon.

Step 2. To activate and download the exam associated with this book, from the My Products or Tools tab, click the **Activate Exam** button.

Step 3.   At the next screen, enter the activation key from the paper inside the cardboard sleeve in the back of the book. Once entered, click the **Activate** button.

Step 4.   The activation process downloads the practice exam. Click **Next**, and then click **Finish**.

When the activation process completes, the My Products tab should list your new exam. If you do not see the exam, make sure that you have selected the **My Products** tab on the menu. At this point, the software and practice exam are ready to use. Simply select the exam and click the **Open Exam** button.

To update a particular exam you have already activated and downloaded, display the **Tools** tab and click the **Update Products** button. Updating your exams ensures that you have the latest changes and updates to the exam data.

If you want to check for updates to the Pearson Cert Practice Test exam engine software, display the **Tools** tab and click the **Update Application** button. You can then ensure that you are running the latest version of the software engine.

Activating Other Exams

The exam software installation process, and the registration process, only has to happen once. Then, for each new exam, only a few steps are required. For instance, if you buy another Pearson IT Certification Cert Guide, extract the activation code from the cardboard sleeve in the back of that book; you do not even need the exam engine at this point. From there, all you have to do is start the exam engine (if not still up and running) and perform steps 2 through 4 from the previous list.

Assessing Exam Readiness

Exam candidates never really know whether they are adequately prepared for the exam until they have completed about 30 percent of the questions. At that point, if you are not prepared, it is too late. The best way to determine your readiness is to work through the "Do I Know This Already?" quizzes at the beginning of each chapter and review the foundation and key topics presented in each chapter. It is best to work your way through the entire book unless you can complete each subject without having to do any research or look up any answers.

Premium Edition eBook and Practice Tests

This book also includes an exclusive offer for 70% off the Premium Edition eBook and Practice Tests edition of this title. See the coupon code included with the cardboard sleeve for information on how to purchase the Premium Edition.

This chapter covers all or part of the following VCP6-NV exam blueprint topics:

- **Objective 1.1**—Compare and Contrast the Benefits of a VMware NSX Implementation

CHAPTER 1

Introduction to VMware NSX

A network engineer, an application developer, and a vSphere administrator walk into a bar with a network security engineer as the bartender. The application developer tells the other two, "I need to securely deploy multitier applications that have tier-dependent requirements for CPU and memory. Some tiers have Ethernet dependencies, and all the applications' tiers have to be deployed with physical diversity to provide for survivability and recoverability." Overhearing the conversation, the bartender tells the application developer, "That will take a lot of man hours and cost money to set up the infrastructure to support it." The application developer responds, "I refuse to accept that answer," and turning to his two companions says, "I'll pay for drinks inversely proportional to the number of days that it would take you to deliver the services that I need." The vSphere administrator gave her answer and had her drinks paid for all night. The network engineer gave her answer and ended up paying for the application developer's drinks.

Bad jokes aside, we all are familiar with the challenges faced by businesses when trying to deploy new applications in data centers or simply scale up the ones they already have. Over the last decade or so, many of those challenges have been addressed in the data center by virtualizing the compute and, more recently, the storage. Data center networks, however, are still being designed, provisioned, and managed more or less the same way they have been over the last 10 or so years—with the exception of the introduction of some network technologies that could be classified as patching the challenges rather than eliminating them. In this chapter, we discuss the reasons why data center physical networks are challenged to provide the network and security services to virtual workloads in an automated and timely manner that meet the most rigorous of business requirements.

Do I Know This Already?

The "Do I Know This Already?" quiz allows you to assess whether you should read this entire chapter or simply jump to the "Exam Preparation Tasks" section for review. If you are in doubt, read the entire chapter. Table 1-1 outlines the major headings in this chapter and the corresponding "Do I Know This Already?" quiz questions. You can find the answers in Appendix A, "Answers to the 'Do I Know This Already?' Quizzes."

Table 1-1   Headings and Questions

Foundation Topic Section	Questions Covered in This Section
Physical Network Challenges	1-4
Ethernet Challenges	5-6
IP Network Challenges	7
Security Challenges	8
VMware NSX	9-10

1. An application developer has a network requirement for a feature not currently supported by the physical IP network.

   Which option could not be used to meet the application requirements?

   a. Upgrade the code of the network devices.

   b. Turn the network feature on.

   c. Install a new network just for the application.

   d. Do a network refresh.

2. What is one challenge of implementing network security on a physical network?

   a. Firewalls require additional network resources to operate.

   b. Firewall rules sprawl.

   c. Firewalls are expensive.

   d. Firewalls provide only 98% security.

3. Which of the following is not a characteristic of a physical network?

   a. A workload can be moved anywhere at any time.

   b. A Layer 3 segment can be separated by other Layer 3 segments.

   c. A Layer 2 domain must be contiguous.

   d. Systems in the same broadcast domain must be within 100 meters.

4. Which constraint is not encountered when deploying services with network dependencies?

   a. The variable time to prepare the network for the service(s)

   b. The manual involvement of a network engineer to configure the network

   c. Potential procurement of new network equipment

   d. The ability of a service owner to have IP connectivity between different tiers of the service

5. What is the maximum number of usable VLANs that can be deployed in the same Ethernet switch?

  a. 4094

  b. 4095

  c. 4096

  d. 4097

6. Which statement accurately describes an Ethernet constraint that impacts the ability of virtual workloads to be deployed in separate racks?

  a. There is a maximum number of VLANs that can't be exceeded in the data center.

  b. A broadcast domain can't be divided by a Layer 3 segment.

  c. A MAC address can only be associated with one Ethernet port at a time.

  d. All end systems in the VLAN must belong to the same subnet.

7. What is a typical constraint virtual workloads face because of the physical network?

  a. Different workloads residing in different subnets

  b. Hairpinning of the default gateway

  c. NAT configuration for virtual workloads in different subnets

  d. Routing protocols configured for virtual workloads in different subnets

8. Which of these features is not feasibly provided to virtual workloads by physical firewalls?

  a. Layer 2 security

  b. Layer 3 security

  c. Layer 4 security

  d. Layer 7 security

9. Which of the following is not an NSX use case for data center automation?

  a. Speeding up network provisioning

  b. Streamlining demilitarized zones

  c. Maximizing hardware sharing among tenants

  d. Simplification of service insertion

10. Which NSX component is the focal entity for the automation of NSX?

  a. NSX Controller

  b. NSX Manager

  c. NSX Edge

  d. Service Composer

Foundation Topics

Physical Network Challenges

It is often said that networking and security are hard, and there is some truth to that. A physical network has traditionally been responsible for providing many services to applications, including

- Layer 2 connectivity

- Layer 3 connectivity

- Packet delivery

- Network security

- Load balancing

- Virtual private networks

The physical network does a really good job in providing these and other services to applications that run in bare-metal servers (physical workloads). This is because the physical network is deployed and configured to support the applications *before* the applications are put in production, and physical workloads don't just relocate at 2 p.m. without notice. It takes time for the application developer to stand up the physical server(s) to run the application. For one, the physical servers need to be procured, racked and stacked, and configured. While the application developer gets her servers ready, the network engineer does some of her work in parallel. In our story at the beginning of the chapter, the network engineer didn't get any free drinks because she knew she would have to touch many network devices to ensure the application developer's applications could get the network services they needed. She also knows that if the application requirements include a network feature not currently supported in the network, she would have to do code upgrades or network refreshes, which would entail replacing an untold number of network devices. In some cases where replacing network equipment is not an option, a new parallel network would have to be installed to support the application. This will delay the deployment of the applications, add costs to the project, and potentially delay the go-to-market strategy of the business.

The bartender (the network security engineer) scoffed at the amount of time it would take to provide the security services because he knows that adding and configuring security policies to the network requires coordination and planning. There is an inherent risk of manually updating firewall rules because of the firewall rule sprawls that are the norm in many organizations. There is a saying that goes something like this: Once a firewall rule goes in, it never comes out. Well, that's actually a saying I just came up with after watching *The Godfather III*; but there is a level of truth to it.

Virtualization substantially reduces the amount of time it takes to stand up an application and remove the physical boundaries where the application can run. The physical network is, however, ill-equipped to provide many of these services to applications running in virtual machines (virtual workloads). Physical networks, including physical security appliances, have been designed and put together with the following core assumptions: Layer 2 domains and Layer 3 segments will be contiguous, meaning there is a logical path between any two devices in the Layer 2 domain or Layer 3 segment. A direct result of this is that physical networks were built assuming limited or no physical movement of the physical workloads, creating a rigid and mostly static network topology where the Layer 2 and Layer 3 addresses of physical workloads stay in one place.

If you connect a physical workload to a port in an Ethernet switch, the MAC address associated with that physical workload remains associated with that port. The default gateway router for the workload will always be the same router or the same pair of routers if using a redundancy router protocol such as Virtual Router Redundancy Protocol, VRRP. You couldn't just take the physical workload and move it from one rack to a rack on the other side of the data center. If you did, chances are pretty good that the physical workload will lose all network connectivity. The irony of this example is that by losing all network connectivity you make the physical workload very secure ☺.

Virtual workloads turn the physical network's core assumptions on their head. Virtual workloads move to different physical locations, taking their MAC and IP addresses with them. There is no efficient way for the physical network to continue to provide to the virtual workloads the Layer 2, Layer 3, security, and other network services the virtual workloads need as they relocate.

There is also the cloud and its native capability to deploy virtual workloads on demand in any location. As already mentioned, the physical network needs to be deployed and configured before applications are placed in production. How is the cloud to do its job of deploying on demand if it must wait for the physical network to be ready for the workload?

Ethernet Challenges

Ethernet is a standard for connecting end systems in a local area network (LAN). End systems connecting to an Ethernet domain, also called Ethernet broadcast domain, use a Media Access Control (MAC) address to locate each other. Ethernet assumes that two end systems in the same broadcast domain will not share the same MAC address. Ethernet also assumes that if two systems are in the same broadcast domains, then there exists a contiguous Layer 2 path for the two systems to communicate with each other. Ethernet is thus designed to provide unrestricted access between end systems in the same broadcast domain. You should interpret that last sentence as meaning Ethernet has no built-in security features.

Ethernet switches keep a MAC table to map MAC addresses with the egress switch port where the MAC address should be located. The MAC table keeps one egress port per MAC address. Switches populate their MAC tables by doing MAC learning. MAC learning is the process of reading the source MAC address of an Ethernet frame as well as the ingress switch port where the Ethernet frame arrived, and then adding the information to the MAC table. If a source MAC is not received by the switch during a period of time, the MAC address is removed from the MAC table. When a switch processes ingress Ethernet frames, it reads the destination MAC address of the frames and tries to find an egress port by searching the MAC table. If no entry is found in the MAC table, the switch sends a copy of the frame out of every switch port, except the ingress port of the frame. This process of sending a copy of a frame out of every port, except the ingress port in which the frame came, when the destination MAC address is not in the MAC table is called *flooding*. Figure 1-1 shows a switch receiving the first frame from MAC address 00:73:21:01:54:FA. The switch will do MAC learning from the frame and flood the frame out of the non-ingress ports if it doesn't have the destination MAC address in the MAC table.

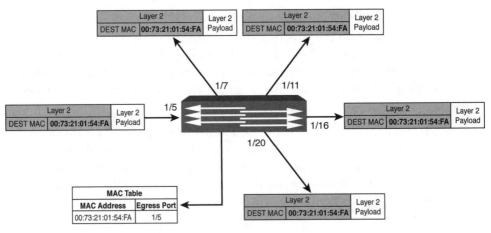

Figure 1-1   MAC learning and flooding

When a switch receives a unicast frame that does not have an entry for the destination MAC address in the MAC table, the Ethernet frame is called an *unknown unicast*. Every end station in the same Ethernet broadcast domain receives the same unknown unicasts. Every end station also receives all broadcasts in the same Ethernet broadcast domain. If the unknown unicast or the broadcast is not meant for a particular end system, the end system simply drops the frame when it receives it. As the number of end stations increases in the Ethernet broadcast domain, the number of unknown unicasts and broadcasts increases. This increase of unknown unicasts and broadcasts causes the end systems to process increasing numbers of frames that would be dropped by them and adds additional load on the Ethernet switches to process the frames.

Virtual LANs (VLANs), were introduced to reduce the size of Ethernet broadcast domains. A VLAN is a number that represents an Ethernet broadcast domain. Each port in the switch gets assigned a number, VLAN number, from 1 through 4094, and when an ingress frame arrives in the ports the VLAN number is also added to the MAC table entry. When the switch processes an unknown unicast or a broadcast, the switch only floods or broadcasts the frame out of those ports with the same VLAN number. In addition, when the switch processes an ingress frame, it only searches the MAC table for those egress ports that have the same VLAN number as the ingress port. These features of VLANs have the added benefit of providing a level of security between two Ethernet broadcast domains. No longer can an end system talk to another end system via Layer 2 unless they are in the same contiguous VLAN. Figure 1-2 shows a switch processing an unknown unicast in VLAN 20 and flooding the frame only out of the ports in VLAN 20.

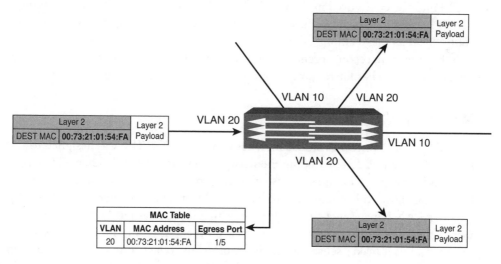

Figure 1-2   VLAN unknown unicast flooding

VLANs are not a standard. VLANs are mentioned in the 802.1Q standard, which defines a method of transporting multiple Ethernet broadcast domains over the same port. A port configured to support 802.1Q is called a *trunk*. The 802.1Q standard extends the Ethernet frame by adding 4 bytes to the frame. Of those 4 bytes, 12 bits are reserved for VLAN numbers. That means there are a maximum of 4096 VLAN numbers defined by 802.1Q. VLAN number 0 is not used to identify broadcast domains and VLAN number 4095 is reserved for internal switch use. That leaves VLANs 1 through 4094 as usable VLANs, as mentioned in the previous paragraph.

4094 different broadcast domains seems like a big number but in today's data centers that number does not scale. Not even close. Multitier applications require some level of security, which is typically provided by the network. It is price-prohibited to deploy Ethernet switches that can provide Layer 2 security (also referred to as inline firewalls), thus it is more practical to place different application tiers in their own broadcast domains. Virtual workloads multiply like rabbits. As the number of virtual applications grows, as well as the number of tiers between those applications, 4094 broadcast domains evaporate rather quickly.

The cap on the number of broadcast domains that VLANs support and the restraint of Ethernet to have a contiguous path between broadcast domains are debilitating factors in restricting the provisioning, deployment, and scaling of virtual workloads and the cloud.

A solution typically used to extend Ethernet broadcast domains for virtual workloads is to extend VLANs between different racks, each rack with its own Ethernet switch, in the data center. This solution, however, implies that Spanning Tree Protocol (STP) must be configured in the physical switches. STP's goals are well-meaning, but STP has the nasty side effect that it eliminates Ethernet path redundancy by disabling the data plane among all paths between two switches except for one. There is also the latency in reconvergence when there are Ethernet topology changes, which impact even switches far removed from where the topology changes occurred.

IP Network Challenges

The Transport Control Protocol/Internet Protocol (TCP/IP), was designed to make it easy to find IPs by finding the network to which the IP belongs. TCP/IP assumes that a group of end systems will reside in the same LAN (nowadays Ethernet), and those end systems will all have an IP from the same network subnet. By having a LAN dependency, TCP/IP expects that all end systems in the same network subnet be within close proximity to each other. After all, the L in LAN stands for *local*. Thus it makes sense for physical workloads to have one router, maybe two, acting as default gateways. In most cases the routers act as default gateways for many different subnets.

In a virtual network, having one or two routers as default gateways for workloads might not make as much sense. Virtual workloads don't conform to physical topology for placement. Virtual workloads in the same subnet could be running in different racks, which don't necessarily have to be in close proximity to the default gateways. This would cause all egress traffic from the subnet to be hairpinned to where the default gateway is before it can be routed. *Hairpinning*, or *pinning*, is the forcing of traffic though a single point. Pinning can also impact traffic in the case of traffic between virtual workloads running in the same ESXi host but in different subnets. Figure 1-3 shows examples of traffic from a virtual workload being pinned to the default gateway, which is somewhere in the data center network.

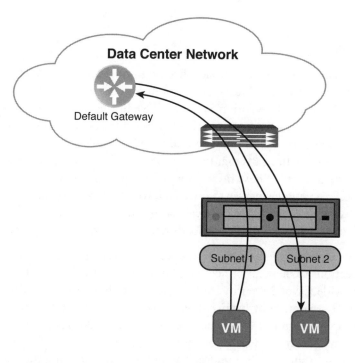

Figure 1-3   Pinning traffic to the physical default gateway

While pinning is an impediment to virtual workloads, perhaps a bigger challenge is the lack of flexibility in creating subnets on demand. Network engineers need to be careful when adding new subnets to the environment. One thing network engineers really dread is to deploy duplicate subnets without having Network Address Translation (NAT) in place. Unintentionally having duplicate subnets in a network will cause network outages. To ensure no duplicate subnets are deployed, or if duplicate subnets will be deployed it is done with NAT, some IP Address Management (IPAM) platform should be available. Even with IPAMs in place, it is still the network engineer's responsibility to use the IPAM to get new subnets and, in the case where a subnet is removed from the network, to reclaim the subnet and put it back in the pool of available subnets in the IPAM platform. IPAMs are not as common an occurrence as they should be (not counting Excel files), and there have been cases where there is an IPAM for the data center, yet it is not used by everyone (we are human after all).

This manual interaction for getting new subnets does not scale for the cloud, where virtual workloads are created and destroyed dynamically all the time. It is common practice for application developers to create many replicas of their virtual workloads, do work on them, destroy them, and recreate them again. All this could happen in the span of 30 minutes.

Security Challenges

Network security is primarily enforced by physical firewalls. Firewalls can provide Layer 3, Layer 4, and Layer 7 security. Next-generation firewalls provide additional security services such as Intrusion Prevention Systems (IPS); however, all these firewalls have something in common—they require that workload traffic be pinned. Just like in the case of the default gateway, firewalls can't do their job unless workload traffic goes their way. There are firewalls that think they are a switch, which allows them to also offer Layer 2 security. These firewalls with dual personality can be pricey. It is not feasible for many businesses to provide Layer 2 firewalls to all their physical workloads. It is challenging to use physical Layer 2 firewalls to provide security for virtual workloads because virtual workloads tend not to stay in one place.

This has an interesting consequence in application development. Application developers want their applications to be secure (most do), but knowing that it is not financially feasible to provide Layer 2 security, they are forced to build their multitier applications with Layer 3 separation by having at least a subnet per tier. By having Layer 3 separation the application traffic between tiers can be forced through the security appliance. By having Layer 3 separation, however, the number of Ethernet broadcast domains needed to support the application goes up thus depleting the number of available VLANs for everyone else.

VMware NSX

VMware NSX is a software defined network (SDN) solution that redefines some assumptions about network and security, freeing it to deliver those services to virtual workloads without restricting virtual workloads placement and mobility. NSX has no hardware dependency and reproduces the network model for virtual workloads in software. The vSphere administrator got free drinks because she moved away from hardware dependency years ago and has been able to provision virtual workloads without placement and mobility restrictions. As long as there is enough compute and storage capacity available to support the application, she can have virtual workloads up and running in seconds. NSX is a solution that mimics the virtual machine deployment model by programmatically reproducing complex networks and security in a matter of seconds to minutes. This flexibility allows the application developer to deploy applications at will and on demand, and without the need to buy anyone drinks. Table 1-2 shows some use cases where NSX can be used to make the virtual network more efficient.

Table 1-2   NSX Use Cases

Use Case	Benefits
Data center automation	Speed up network provisioning
	Simplify service insertion
	Enforcement of network and security policies
	Streamlined demilitarized zones (DMZ)
Self-service enterprise IT	Quick application deployment
	Isolated test, development, and production environment
Multitenant clouds	Automated tenant network provisioning
	Tenant network separation
	Maximize hardware sharing among tenants

The last paragraph was partially marketing that I'm contractually obligated to include in the book. (I'm kidding.) NSX allows for networking and security to be done in software without any dependency on hardware. The software part is similar to the way virtual machines have been implemented. Instead of virtualizing the CPU and memory (and storage), NSX virtualizes the network and security functions.

VMware provides two versions of NSX:

- **NSX for vSphere (NSX-V):** Supports hypervisors running ESXi

- **NSX for Multi-Hypervisor (NSX-MH):** Supports multiple hypervisors including ESXi, XEN Server, Redhat KVM, and Hyper-V

This book is based on the VCP6-NV exam blueprint, which is centered on NSX-V. For the remainder of this book we cover NSX-V and refer to it as simply NSX.

NSX requires a vSphere environment with vCenter to coordinate changes, including the deploying, configuring, and removing NSX components and services. NSX and vCenter have a tight integration, which we start discussing in Chapter 3, "NSX Architecture and NSX Manager."

Let us use an example to explain what NSX can do. Imagine you have the topology shown in Figure 1-4, which has a switch and a router that is the default gateway for the physical workloads.

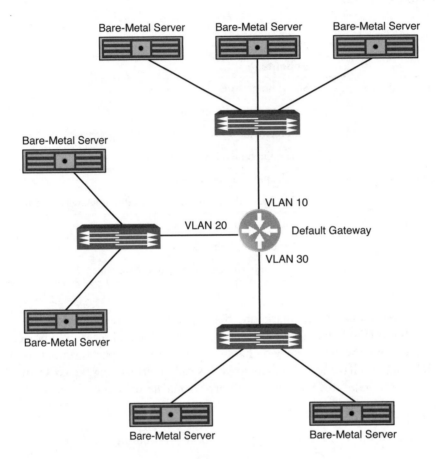

Figure 1-4   Physical network function

Now think of the network services the switch and the router are providing to the physical workloads. The services are switching and routing. NSX allows you to take those services, sometimes referred to as *network functions*, and virtualize them. The services can then be made available to virtual workloads without introducing the caveats native to Ethernet and IP networks that we discussed earlier in this chapter. When a network function is offered without dependency on hardware, or is virtualized, it is called *network function virtualization (NFV)*. Figure 1-5 shows NSX providing switching and routing services to virtual workloads. The virtual workloads are shown in the figure in multiple broadcast domains and running in different racks separated by a Layer 3 network.

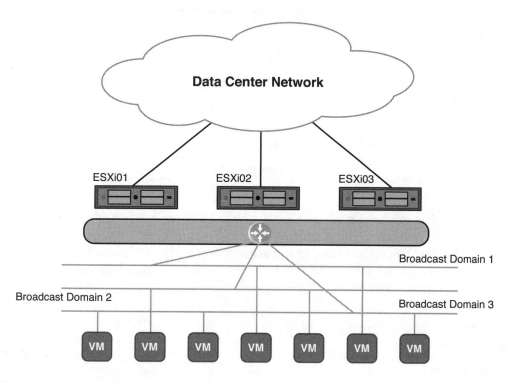

Figure 1-5   NSX virtualizing network functions

If all NSX did was deploy a virtual switch and a virtual router I probably wouldn't have written this book. Table 1-3 has a list of the network and security functions that NSX provides and the NSX component or feature that provides that function. Each NSX component and feature in Table 1-3 is independent of the other. You choose which components and features to use when deploying a virtual machine in an NSX environment.

Table 1-3   NSX Network and Security Functions

Function	NSX Component or Feature
Switching	Logical switch
VLAN extensions	NSX Edge
VXLAN-VLAN bridging	Distributed logical router
	NSX Edge
Routing	Distributed logical router
	NSX Edge

Function	NSX Component or Feature
Security	Distributed firewall
	NSX Edge
Service Chaining	Service Composer
Load Balancer	NSX Edge
VPN	NSX Edge
Automation	NSX Manager
Monitoring	NSX Manager

Now that you have an idea of the network and security functions that NSX can provide, let's review the NSX components and features. Table 1-4 provides a list of the NSX components and features and a description of the capabilities they have. The table also includes the first chapter where we start the detailed discussion on what the component or feature does.

Table 1-4   NSX Components and Features

NSX Component or Feature	Description	Chapter
Logical switch	A virtual Ethernet switch that runs in the kernel of the ESXi host. The logical switch has a built-in mechanism to allow for the extension of virtual Ethernet segments across physical Layer 3 networks.	5
Distributed logical router	A virtual router that runs in the kernel of the ESXi host. Its distributed nature allows the distributed logical router to provide default gateway services locally to all virtual workloads without pinning.	7
Distributed firewall	A virtual firewall that runs in the kernel of the ESXi host. The distributed firewall takes security out of the network and enforces it in a separate plane.	15
NSX Edge	A virtual network and security appliance. The NSX Edge can provide multiple network and security functions such as VPN, load balancing, and routing.	9
Service Composer	A feature of NSX to integrate network and security services that augment the functionality of the virtual environment. The network and security services can be provided by VMware technology partners.	16
NSX Controller	The entity that handles the control planes for the logical switches and the distributed logical router.	4

NSX Component or Feature	Description	Chapter
NSX Manager	The central point for NSX preparation, automation, and management. NSX Manager handles the automation of NSX services, the interaction of NSX with external entities, and the deployment of components and features.	3

Let me make a quick point on NSX and NFV to end the chapter. NSX is not an NFV solution but an SDN solution. NSX does virtualize network and security functions, but it does so by using a methodology that goes beyond just replicating the functionality, and all the caveats, the physical network or security appliance provides. Chapter 3 delves further into how NSX does what it does.

Exam Preparation Tasks

Review All the Key Topics

Review the most important topics from inside the chapter, noted with the Key Topic icon in the outer margin of the page. Table 1-5 lists these key topics and the page numbers where each is found.

Table 1-5 Key Topics for Chapter 1

Key Topic Element	Description	Page Number
Paragraph	802.1Q only supports 4094 usable VLANs.	9
Paragraph	The physical network and many IPAMs are not well suited to allow the dynamic creation of new subnets to support virtual workloads.	11
Paragraph	The lack of physical Layer 2 security results in an increase in the number of VLANs required in multitier applications.	12
Table 1-2	NSX Use Cases.	13
Paragraph	NSX requires a vCenter.	13
Table 1-4	NSX Components and Features	16

Complete Tables and Lists from Memory

Download and print a copy of Appendix C, "Memory Tables" (found on the book's website), or at least the section for this chapter, and complete the tables and lists from memory. Appendix D, "Memory Tables Answer Key," also on the website, includes the completed tables and lists so you can check your work.

Define Key Terms

Define the following key terms from this chapter and check your answers in the glossary:

802.1Q, software defined network, network function virtualization, NSX for vSphere, NSX for Multi-Hypervisors

This chapter covers all or part of the following VCP6-NV exam blueprint topics:

- **Objective 1.3**—Differentiate Physical and Virtual Network Technologies

- **Objective 2.1**—Compare and Contrast the Benefits of Running VMware NSX on Physical Network Fabrics

- **Objective 2.2**—Determine Physical Infrastructure Requirements for a VMware NSX Implementation

- **Objective 3.1**—Configure and Manage vSphere Distributed Switches (vDS)

- **Objective 3.2**—Configure and Manage vDS Policies

- **Objective 4.1**—Configure Environment for Network Virtualization

CHAPTER 2

Network and VMware vSphere Requirements for NSX

You read Chapter 1, "Introduction to VMware NSX," and concluded that you like NSX or at a minimum you want to try it out. NSX will virtualize your network allowing network programmability to finally come to virtual workloads, but the physical network will continue to provide some basic network services. After all, if a virtual machine in one ESXi host wants to communicate with another virtual machine in a different ESXi host, that traffic will traverse some part of the physical network (there are some unconfirmed reports that VMware is working in new technology to enable telepathy between ESXi hosts to make physical networks obsolete).

NSX simplifies the data center network by eliminating some of the design compromises taken to support virtual workloads. NSX also has a dependency on the vSphere Distributed Switch to support the logical switch. In this chapter we cover the vSphere virtual switch features that can be leveraged by NSX, some common data center network designs used to support virtual workloads, and how NSX can eliminate the need to compromise when designing the data center network.

Do I Know This Already?

The "Do I Know This Already?" quiz allows you to assess whether you should read this entire chapter or simply jump to the "Exam Preparation Tasks" section for review. If you are in doubt, read the entire chapter. Table 2-1 outlines the major headings in this chapter and the corresponding "Do I Know This Already?" quiz questions. You can find the answers in Appendix A, "Answers to the 'Do I Know This Already?' Quizzes."

Table 2-1 Headings and Questions

Foundation Topic Section	Questions Covered in This Section
Physical Network Infrastructure	1-2
POD Design	3
Collapsed Access Layer	4
Spine and Leaf Design	5
NSX and Physical Network Infrastructure	6
NSX and vSphere	7
vSphere Distributed Switch	8
Configure LACP	9
Configure QoS Marking	10

1. What are two challenges faced when providing network services to virtual workloads using a physical network infrastructure? (Choose two.)

   a. Inability to provide router redundancy

   b. Restrictions when migrating virtual workloads to ESXi hosts

   c. Managing the amount of access switches required for large-scale vSphere environments

   d. Inability for access switches to provide isolation of uplink failures to virtual workloads

   e. Managing the size of routing tables

2. What are two network design options available to minimize the impact of Spanning Tree Protocol on virtual workloads? (Choose two.)

   a. Collapse the Access Layer.

   b. Disable STP in all access switch uplinks.

   c. Replace Ethernet in the access switch uplinks with a protocol like TRILL.

   d. Reduce the size of the MAC tables on Top of Rack switches.

3. What is an advantage of utilizing a POD design?

   a. It increases the number of available Ethernet broadcast domains.

   b. It increases the mobility diameter of virtual workloads.

   c. It reduces the number of access routers needed to support a vSphere deployment.

   d. It increases the number of MAC addresses that can be stored in the MAC tables.

4. What is a disadvantage of the collapsed Access Layer design?

   a. It moves Layer 3 routing to the Distribution Layer.

   b. It limits the migration of virtual workloads.

   c. It allows for Ethernet broadcast domain extensions.

   d. It increases the number of access routers needed to support a vSphere deployment.

5. What is a design goal of the Spine and Leaf design?

   a. It increases the number of available default gateways for the virtual workloads.

   b. It maximizes the use of uplinks for Top of Rack switches.

   c. It increases the number of available Ethernet broadcast domains.

   d. It increases the size of the MAC table on the Top of Rack switches.

6. Which is not an impact of using NSX with a physical network infrastructure?

   a. The reduction in the size of the MAC table in Top of Rack switches.

   b. The elimination of the need to run STP on the Top of Rack switch to support virtual workloads.

   c. The elimination of the need to have a Distribution Layer.

   d. The reduction in the number of Ethernet broadcast domains needed to support virtual workloads.

7. Which two are vSphere features required for an NSX implementation? (Choose two.)

   a. vSphere Standard Switch

   b. vSphere vMotion

   c. vSphere Distributed Switch

   d. vSphere vCenter

8. How does a vSphere Distributed Switch learn MAC addresses?

    a. The vSphere Distributed Switch learns MAC addresses by MAC learning.

    b. vCenter provides virtual machine MAC addresses to the vSphere Distributed Switch.

    c. The vSphere Distributed Switch learns MAC addresses by flooding every Ethernet frame it processes.

    d. The vSphere Distributed Switch learns MAC addresses by reading the vmx file of virtual machines at power on.

9. Which is not a step in configuring LACP on a vSphere Distributed Switch?

    a. Add VMNICs to the LACP link.

    b. Configure the vSphere Distributed Switch to use the LACP link.

    c. Create an LACP link on the vSphere Distributed Switch.

    d. Configure the dvPortgroup to use the LACP link.

10. Which QoS related action is not supported by vSphere Distributed Switches?

    a. Rewriting the DSCP marking of virtual machine traffic to 51

    b. Adding a CoS value of 2 to ESXi host management traffic

    c. Classifying DSCP or CoS values for traffic coming from the physical network

    d. Assigning a CoS value of 34 to vMotion traffic

Foundation Topics

Physical Network Infrastructure

To understand the positive impact NSX can bring to the data center network infrastructure we need to understand how the infrastructure design has evolved over the years. Data center network design has evolved from the simple idea of having dedicated network switches that provide Ethernet network connectivity to end systems. The network switches, referred to as Top of Rack (ToR) switches, have uplinks to network routers that provide the Layer 3 routing function, as shown in Figure 2-1. In this design, the routers are strictly for Layer 3 and have their IPs and subnets configured in the physical interfaces.

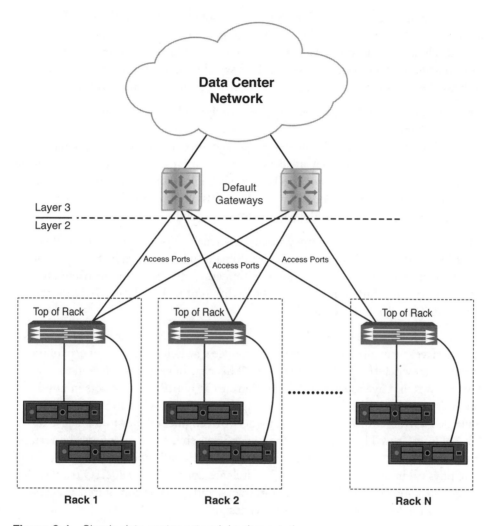

Figure 2-1 Simple data center network implementation

The ToR switches are often called the *access switches* because they provide the network access to the end systems. The routers are called the *access routers* because they are the default gateways for the end systems. These switches and routers are collectively called the *Access Layer*. The Access Layer always includes the entities providing the switching and routing functions for the end systems.

The simplicity of the design in Figure 2-1 is that there is no need for Spanning Tree Protocol (STP) in the switch uplinks (YAY!). Well, there *is* STP, but the ToR uplink ports are configured as access ports, all STP negotiations disabled and the ports are in an STP forwarding state. Without STP in the ToR uplinks, all uplinks are active thus maximizing the amount of bandwidth available and providing for quick failover in case of an uplink failure. Without STP in the uplinks additional Ethernet broadcast domains and racks can be added to the default gateways without impacting existing segments. A link failure in any broadcast domain will be constrained to the affected broadcast domain. Another benefit is that the ToR switches only need to learn the MAC address of end systems in their rack, thus requiring a relatively small MAC table.

There are two fatal scaling problems with this design. The first is the physical limitation of the number of interfaces the routers can have. If the routers' physical size and configuration limits the routers to say, 30 interfaces each, they would each support a maximum of 29 of the physical workload's broadcast domains, with each rack in the design having its own Ethernet broadcast domain. The second problem is that each router creates an Ethernet broadcast domain boundary at the router's physical interfaces, thus preventing the extending of the broadcast domain to other racks and switches.

These problems are a direct impediment for virtualization. First, it forces all virtual machines in the same Ethernet broadcast domain to be in the same rack. Second, it limits the mobility of virtual machines, with features like vMotion restricted to the rack. A virtual machine can't be moved to a different rack with this design without having its IP and subnet changed.

The solution for these two problems is straightforward. Switches have many physical interfaces, way more than routers. Introduce a switch with routing capabilities and let this switch be the default gateway. This type of switch is referred to as a Layer 3 switch. Layer 3 switches do not have to assign IPs and subnets in physical interfaces. IPs and subnets may be assigned to a new logical interface called a Switched Virtual Interface (SVI). Many network engineers refer to SVIs just as VLAN interfaces. That is because the Layer 3 switches can have a logical interface for every VLAN they are aware of and assign the IPs and subnets to that interface. The physical interfaces of the Layer 3 switch are configured as 802.1Q trunks, although in some designs the physical interfaces could also be configured as access ports. Figure 2-2 shows a diagram of this design.

This design removes one of the two scaling problems of the design in Figure 2-1— reduces the impact of the second scaling problem and allows for virtual machine mobility between racks. There are no physical interface limitations restricting the number of broadcast domains that can be supported, and broadcast domains can be extended among different racks. However, the design in Figure 2-2 trades some problems for others. The first one is that we still have a limitation in the number of broadcast domains of 4094, which is an 802.1Q standard limitation. The second is the requirement that STP be configured in the switch uplinks to prevent Ethernet broadcast domain loops (No YAY). No longer will all available data paths from the ToR be active. In the most common configurations for this design, STP blocks one of the uplinks from the ToR to the routers. Now every time a topology change takes place (a rack is added or a link fails) almost every other rack is impacted by it.

A third problem is the MAC table size of each ToR needs to be larger as each ToR learns the MAC address of each end system in all other racks if the ToR has been also configured with the Ethernet broadcast domains, via VLANs, that exist in the other racks. Although this last problem can be remedied by using ToR switches and Layer 3 switches with large MAC table capacity, this tends to increase the cost of procuring network hardware.

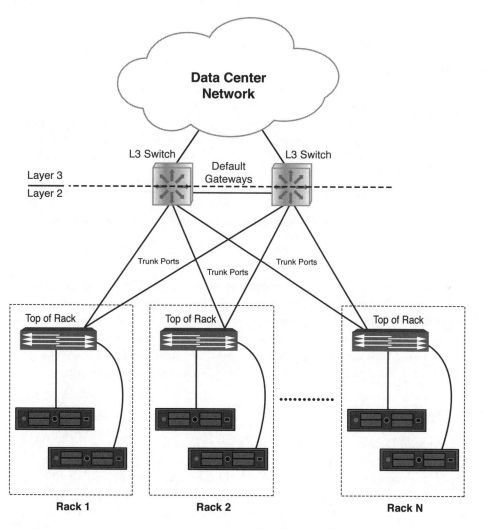

Figure 2-2   Layer 3 switch data center network implementation

Link Aggregation Control Protocol (LACP) can be used between an access switch and the Access Layer 3 switch to maximize bandwidth capacity and link redundancy. LACP benefits the point-to-point connection between the switch and the Layer

3 switch by making all links between the switch and the Layer 3 switch look like a single data path. However, STP still is required to run over the LACP links in this design, thus the other STP problems remain.

While on the topic of LACP, let me mention that when LACP is done between a switch and a server, it is common from the server side to refer to the connection as *NIC teaming*. Also let me take a quick detour to touch on the three modes in which LACP can be configured. Table 2-2 lists the three LACP modes and their description.

Table 2-2   LACP Modes

VLAN Setting	Description
Static	The LACP links are ready to load shared traffic using the configured hash algorithm. No negotiation takes place with the peer switch.
Active	The LACP links are configured and are actively sending and listening for hello packets to negotiate LACP parameters. LACP links come up after successful LACP negotiation. Traffic flows using the hashing algorithm configured in each side of the link.
Passive	The LACP links are configured and are only listening for hello packets to negotiate LACP parameters. LACP links come up after successful LACP negotiation. Traffic flows using the hashing algorithm configured in each side of the link.

Now we return to our regular programming. As you probably suspect, other network design solutions address the problems we have mentioned. Each one makes trade-offs, and none of them provides a nirvana of a solution. We cover three designs that can be used with NSX. Each of these designs addresses the scalability of Ethernet broadcast domains, the MAC table size of switches, and/or the STP problems of single data path availability and topology changes failure domain.

POD Design

The Point of Delivery (POD) network design is intended to address the problem of broadcast domain scalability. With this design, multiple Access Layers are deployed, each one in a container called a POD and capable of supporting 4094 Ethernet broadcast domains. This is possible because the Access Layers do not have any Layer 2 connectivity with each other. They only have Layer 3 connectivity via a separate pair of routers as shown in Figure 2-3.

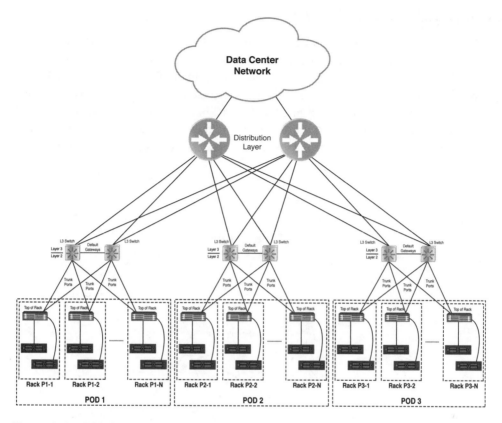

Figure 2-3 POD Design

The distribution plane is the name given to the routers that provide the Layer 3 connectivity to the Access Layers.

The POD design allows for as many PODs as there are interfaces in the Distribution Layer. It can scale even further by adding additional pairs of distribution routers. The POD design comes with a bonus: It partially isolates the impact of STP. A topology change in one POD will not have STP repercussions in another POD. However, the POD design does not address the STP impacts within a POD. The POD design does not address the size of the MAC table in the ToR switches within a POD either. Another limitation of the POD design is that an Ethernet broadcast domain in one POD can't be expanded to another POD. This constrains virtual machine mobility to a single POD. A virtual machine in one POD can't be migrated to a different POD without having its IP and subnet changed.

Collapsed Access Layer

The collapsed Access Layer design goes after STP head on. Instead of having two different entities (the access switch and the access router) in the Access Layer, it merges them both into a single entity, the ToR. The ToR becomes a Layer 3 switch by providing Layer 2 Ethernet connectivity to the end systems as well as being their default gateway. All ports configured as Layer 2 have all STP negotiations disabled and set in an STP forwarding state. Each rack now has its own Access Layer, and all racks connect with each other via the Distribution Layer, as shown in Figure 2-4.

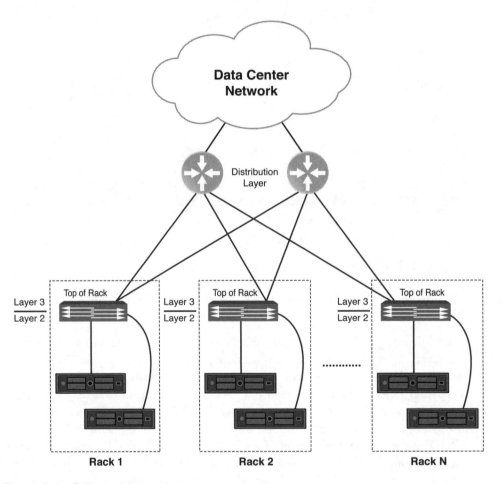

Figure 2-4   Collapsed Access Layer

The upsides of this design: small MAC table size, no STP (YAY again!!), and Ethernet broadcast domain scalability. All uplinks from the racks will be used, and each rack is now capable of having 4094 broadcast domains. It is like the POD design but with each POD consisting of a single rack. The downsides of this design: no virtual machine mobility and no Layer 2 extensions. Virtual machines will be constrained to the rack they are in. With this design it won't be possible to have multitier applications in multiple racks if the application has Layer 2 dependencies.

Spine and Leaf Design

The third design is the Spine and Leaf design, which tackles STP. This design adds a new component to the Access Layer. It renames the access switches as Leafs and adds switches called Spines that are used to provide Layer 2 connectivity between the Leafs. A new protocol called Transparent Interconnection of Lots of Links (TRILL) replaces Ethernet over the links connecting the Leafs and the Spines. TRILL has built-in Layer 2 loop avoidance mechanisms that eliminate the need for having STP at all in the Access Layer. By not having STP, all uplinks are back to being fully utilized, and the topology change failure domain is greatly reduced. TRILL works by transparently extending Ethernet broadcast domains among the end systems, as shown in Figure 2-5. End systems connect to the Leafs via Ethernet, and the Leafs inject the Ethernet broadcast domains, as VLANs, into TRILL thus advertising them to other Leafs via the Spines. The access routers connect to Leafs with 802.1Q Trunks containing all VLANs in the racks.

NOTE   TRILL is an open standard that replaces STP. Most network hardware vendors have developed their own-flavored technology to replace STP. To name a few, Cisco has FabricPath, Brocade has VCS, and Juniper has QFabric. Covering those other STP-replacing technologies is outside the scope of the VCP-NV exam.

The huge benefit of the Spine and Leaf design is the complete elimination of STP while allowing the extension of Ethernet broadcast domains across different racks. The limitation of the Spine and Leaf design is that it doesn't allow for more than 4094 Ethernet broadcast domains. Another current disadvantage to TRILL (and other STP-replacing technologies) is that the network equipment that supports it carries a cost premium.

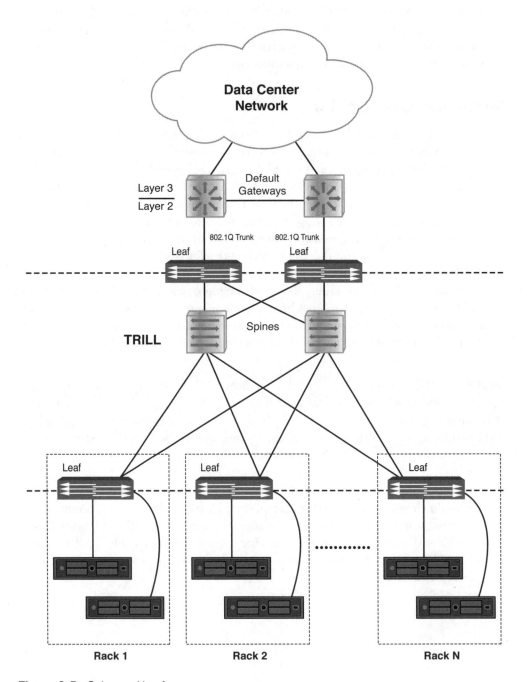

Figure 2-5   Spine and Leaf

NSX and Physical Network Infrastructure

At the end of the day, what NSX does from a network perspective is take the network Access Layer and virtualize it. The network functions the Access Layer provides the virtual machines are now provided by NSX. By virtualizing the Access Layer, NSX removes the trade-offs that the physical network has to make. NSX allows for Ethernet broadcast domain extensions, a huge number of Ethernet broadcast domains, and virtual machine mobility. NSX does this while removing the need for any physical switch to learn the MAC address of the virtual machine, thus keeping the size of the MAC table small, and without the need of STP…and the network engineer sheds a tear while giving a standing ovation.

There are only two requirements from NSX of the network infrastructure if it virtualizes the Access Layer: IPv4 connectivity among the ESXi hosts and jumbo frame support if the virtual machines are using the default MTU size of 1500. The Ethernet MTU must be set to 1600 bytes end-to-end between all ESXi hosts that participate in NSX and use logical switches. To be completely honest, the MTU requirement of 1600 is more of a VMware recommendation than a hard-set requirement. The ESXi hosts use an IP header without extensions, thus an MTU of 1550 is the actual hard-set requirement if the virtual machines are *not* doing VLAN Guess Tagging (VGT), nor Layer 2 Class of Service (CoS), or 1554 otherwise. In practice, VGT won't be used much in an NSX environment. Regardless, the default network infrastructure's default Ethernet MTU of 1500 will need to be changed. We cover this more in Chapter 4, "VXLAN, NSX Controllers, and NSX Preparation."

Figure 2-6 shows a diagram of a data center with an NSX Access Layer. The ToR switches are Layer 3 switches, and they connect to the Distribution Layer via Layer 3 links. Figure 2-6's physical network is identical to Figure 2-4's physical network. In Figure 2-4, Layer 2 domains were constrained to a rack, which limited the span of vMotion. In Figure 2-6, NSX allows Layer 2 domains to span across multiple racks separated by Layer 3 boundaries; the virtual machines shown can be running in any of the ESXi hosts and can vMotion to any ESXi host participating in NSX.

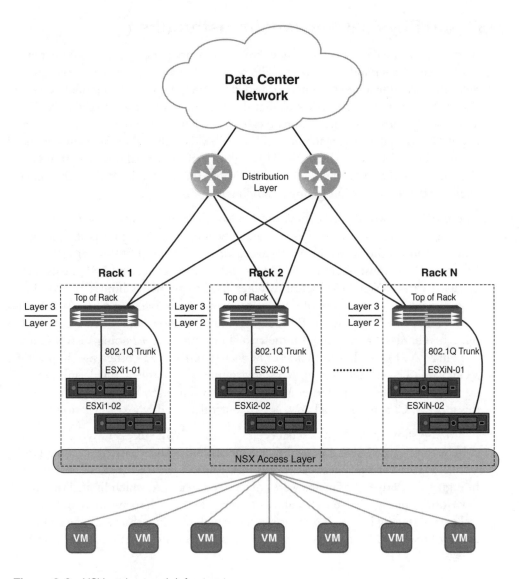

Figure 2-6   NSX and network infrastructure

NSX and vSphere

NSX requires that vSphere be deployed and configured. To be specific, these are the vSphere components that should be deployed before NSX is configured:

- **vCenter**: NSX communicates with vCenter to get access to the vSphere infrastructure and to provide NSX related configuration to vSphere components, including migrating virtual machines to logical switches. vCenter 5.5 or later is needed for single vCenter NSX support. vCenter 6.0 or later is needed for cross-vCenter NSX support. If configuring cross-vCenter NSX support, all NSX participating vCenters must be configured in Enhanced Linked Mode with the Platform Services Controller (PSC).

- **ESXi hosts**: NSX installs some of its components in the kernel of the ESXi hosts so they can provide NSX services to the virtual machines. ESXi 5.5 or later is needed for single vCenter NSX support. ESXi 6.0 or later is needed for cross-vCenter NSX support.

- **ESXi host clusters**: NSX requires that every ESXi host that participates in NSX be a member of a cluster. NSX does not communicate with ESXi hosts that are not in clusters.

- **vSphere Standard Switch**: NSX doesn't require the vSphere Standard Switch (vSS), but the ESXi hosts that participate in NSX and the NSX Edge may have connections to vSphere Standard Switches.

- **vSphere Distributed Switch**: To virtualize the Access Layer, NSX requires that all ESXi hosts in a cluster be part of the same vSphere Distributed Switch, vDS. Different clusters can use the same vDS or different vSphere Distributed Switches.

ESXi Host Network Connectivity

An ESXi host is a server running the vSphere hypervisor as the operating system. The ESXi hosts are the ones that power on and run virtual machines. The ESXi host can be managed remotely via IP by vCenter. Something that makes ESXi hosts different from other servers is that the IP of the ESXi host is not configured in the physical NICs of the host but in a logical interface called VMkernel port. VMkernel ports are almost exactly like SVIs in the sense that both are logical interfaces that get an IP and subnet. The ESXi hosts can have multiple VMkernel ports, and the VMkernel ports can be configured in the same or different subnets. It is common to deploy ESXi hosts with multiple VMkernel ports to provide the following functions, typically in a different subnet per function:

- ESXi host management

- vMotion

- IP storage

VMkernel ports get connected to virtual switches, and the virtual switches have the path to the physical network. The physical NICs in the ESXi hosts are called VM-NICs. It is through the VMNICs that the ESXi host's network traffic reaches the physical network. All network traffic in and out of the ESXi hosts goes through one of the VMNICs. VMNICs almost always connect to the ToR switches or another switch providing Layer 2 access. Inside the ESXi host, the VMNICs are the uplink ports of the virtual switch(es) in the ESXi host. A VMNIC can only be assigned to a single virtual switch. The virtual switch that owns the VMNICs makes the decision of which VMNIC is used for egress traffic from the ESXi host. The decision as to which VM-NIC to use for ingress traffic for the ESXi host is made by the ToR switch based on its MAC table and hashing algorithm (if using Link Aggregation, such as LACP).

Figure 2-7 shows an ESXi host with two VMNICs and multiple VMkernel ports connected to a ToR switch.

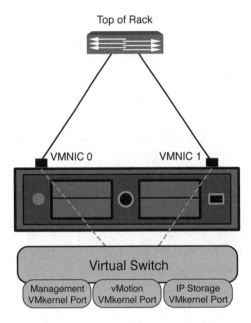

Figure 2-7   ESXi host VMkernel ports

vSphere Standard Switch

The vSphere Standard Switch (vSS) is the default virtual switch of the ESXi hosts that runs in the kernel. Matter of fact, when you install ESXi in a host a vSS gets deployed automatically. Each host manages its own vSS with vCenter ownership of its configuration. An ESXi host may have multiple vSSes. Virtual machines connect their Virtual NIC, vNIC, to a vSS virtual port. Actually, that's kind of half-true. The virtual machine has a vNIC that it uses for Ethernet traffic, but it doesn't quite connect to the vSS. Instead, the vNIC connects to a component of the vSS called a *portgroup*. A portgroup is a logical grouping of ports in the vSS that contains the configuration that is applied to the virtual ports that connect to the virtual machines' vNICs. A portgroup can have multiple vNIC connections from multiple virtual machines. Although the virtual machine's vNIC has a virtual port assigned in the vSS, the connection takes place via the portgroup. In the case of VMkernel ports, the portgroup the VMkernel port connects to only has a single connection, that of the VMkernel port. Figure 2-8 shows multiple virtual machines in an ESXi host with multiple VMkernel ports.

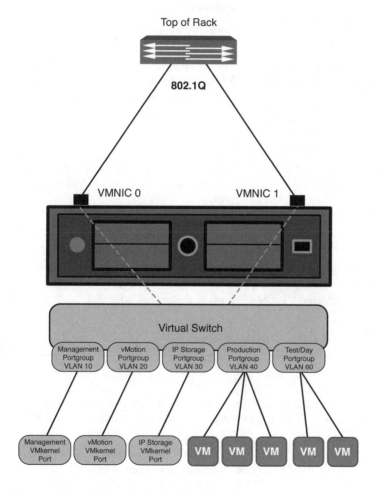

Figure 2-8   vSphere Standard Switch

The vSS is a non-MAC learning switch that does not keep a traditional MAC table. It only knows about the MAC addresses configured in the vmx file of the virtual machines connected to the vSS or the VMkernel port's MAC address. The vmx file is the instruction set that tells the ESXi host the configuration and features that need to be provided to the virtual machine when it powers on. Lacking a MAC learning capability, the vSS follows the rules listed in Table 2-3. The vSS does not support STP, and the second and third rules in Table 2-3 are the reason why it doesn't have to. The vSS won't allow looped traffic from the physical network to be sent back in (rule 2 in Table 2-3) nor can it cause a Layer 2 loop (rule 3 in Table 2-3).

Table 2-3   vSphere Standard Switch Forwarding Decision Rules

Ingress Port	Criteria	Action
All	Destination MAC known	Forward to corresponding virtual machine's virtual port.
Virtual port	Broadcast, Destination MAC Unknown (Unknown Unicast), or Multicast (BUM)	Forward out of all virtual ports in the same VLAN and the uplink port assigned to portgroup in Load Balancing configuration.
Uplink port	Source MAC address is from a virtual machine or VMkernel port in the vSS in the same VLAN	Drop.
Uplink port	Broadcast, Destination MAC Unknown (Unknown Unicast), or Multicast (BUM)	Forward out of all virtual ports in the same VLAN. Do not send out of another uplink port.

The vSS portgroup is also called a *standard portgroup*. One of the configuration options the standard portgroup provides is the assignment of a VLAN. The VLAN configured in the portgroup is the Ethernet broadcast domain that the vNICs, or VMkernel port, will have. The vSS supports three VLAN settings, as shown in Table 2-4.

Table 2-4   vSphere Standard Switch Portgroup VLAN Settings

VLAN Setting	Description
None or 0	No VLAN is assigned to this portgroup. All BUM traffic coming from virtual machines or the VMkernel port is forwarded to the physical switch without 802.1Q tag.
VLAN	The equivalent of a switch access port with a VLAN number from 1 through 4094. All BUM traffic coming from virtual machines or the VMkernel port is forwarded to the physical switch with an 802.1Q tag that includes the VLAN number.
4095	The equivalent of an 802.1Q trunk to the virtual machines, allowing VLANs 1-4094. All traffic coming from virtual machines has an 802.1Q tag. If a non-tagged BUM frame is received from the virtual machine, it is forwarded to the physical switch without an 802.1Q tag.

If you select VLAN or 4095 in any portgroup in the vSS, the vSS automatically enables 802.1Q, trunking, on the uplinks.

Another configuration that can be done in the vSS is load balancing. The load balancing configuration tells the vSS how to decide which uplink port to use to send BUM traffic to the physical network. An uplink port in the vSS maps to a single VMNIC. If the vSS only has a single uplink port, it is not much of a decision which uplink port to use. If the vSS has multiple uplink ports, it follows the rules in Table 2-5 based on what is configured in the portgroup that ingresses the traffic. The uplink port that gets selected does not alter the Ethernet header in any way, passing along the frame with any 802.1Q tags it may have.

Table 2-5   vSphere Standard Switch Portgroup VLAN Settings

VLAN Setting	Description
Route Based on Originating Virtual Port	Each vSS virtual port in the portgroup is pinned to a VMNIC, and all external egress traffic is sent out this VMNIC.
Route Based on Source MAC Hash	A hash is calculated for each source MAC, and BUM traffic is then sent out a VMNIC based on the hash.
Route Based on IP Hash	A hash is calculated for each source and destination IP pair, and BUM traffic is then sent out a VMNIC based on the hash. This requires the physical switch to be configured for static LACP.
Use Explicit Failover Order	Each active uplink port is assigned an order number, and this portgroup uses the highest numbered uplink port from the qualifying VMNICs to egress BUM traffic.

Broadcast, Unknown Unicast, and Multicasts (BUM) traffic also is sent to all virtual machines in the same VLAN in the vSS.

In the next section, and later in this chapter, we go over some of the configurations that would be needed to support NSX. I show you how to configure some vSS settings in case you want to use a vSS to connect the VMkernel ports. The vSphere Client can be used to do many of the configuration steps that I show; however, VMware has announced that the vSphere Web Client will be the one that supports newer features of vSphere, thus I use the vSphere Web Client to document configuration steps.

vSS Configuration

To add or remove a VMNIC in a vSS, follow these steps:

Step 1.   Connect to the vSphere Web Client and log in with an administrator account.

Step 2.   Select the Host and Clusters view.

Step 3.   Select the ESXi host where the vSS is.

Step 4.   Select **Manage > Networking > Virtual Switches**.

Step 5.   Select the vSS where the uplink port changes will take place.

Step 6.   Click the Physical Network Adapters icon and wait for the Manage Physical Network Adapters Wizard to open.

Step 7.   If adding a new uplink interface:

    a. Click the green + icon.

    b. Select the VMNIC to add.

    c. In the Failover Order Group drop-down menu select the adapter order.

    d. Click **OK**.

Step 8.   If removing an existing uplink port:

    a. Select the uplink port.

    b. Click the red X icon.

Step 9.   Click **OK**.

About the only change that can be made to a VMNIC is to configure the speed/duplex setting and enable Single Root I/O Virtualization, SR-IOV. To change the speed/duplex settings for a VMNIC, or change its SR-IOV status, follow these steps:

NOTE   SR-IOV as a topic is outside the scope of the VCP-NV exam.

Step 1.   Connect to the vSphere Web Client and log in with an administrator account.

Step 2.   Select the Host and Clusters view.

Step 3.   Select the ESXi host where the vSS is.

Step 4.   Select **Manage > Networking > Physical Adapters**.

Step 5.   Select the VMNIC you want to edit.

Step 6.   Click the pencil icon and wait for the Edit Settings Wizard to open.

Step 7.   In the Configured Speed, Duplex drop-down menu, choose the speed/duplex setting for the VMNIC.

Step 8.   In the SR-IOV Status drop-down menu, choose to enable or disable SR-IOV.

     a. In the Number of Virtual Functions enter the number of virtual functions to enable.

     b. Changes to the SR-IOV status require the ESXi host be rebooted.

Step 9.   Click **OK**.

If the VMNIC supports TCP Segmentation Offload (TSO), the virtual machines can be configured to leverage it by adding a VMXNET2 or VMXNET3 vNIC to the virtual machine and installing VMware Tools. VMware Tools is code installed in the virtual machine to update the OS drivers in the virtual machine and allow the ESXi host to get some level of direct access to the OS of the virtual machine.

To add a VMkernel port in a vSS you must create a VMkernel portgroup. To add a VMkernel portgroup to a vSS, follow these steps:

Step 1.   Connect to the vSphere Web Client and log in with an administrator account.

Step 2.   Select the Host and Clusters view.

Step 3.   Select the ESXi host where the vSS is.

Step 4.   Select **Manage > Networking > Virtual Switches**.

Step 5.   Click the Add Host Networking icon and wait for the Add Networking Wizard to pop up.

Step 6.   In the Select Connection Type window. Select VMkernel Network Adapter and click **Next**, as shown in Figure 2-9.

     In this window you can choose to create a virtual machine standard portgroup or add an uplink port to an existing vSS.

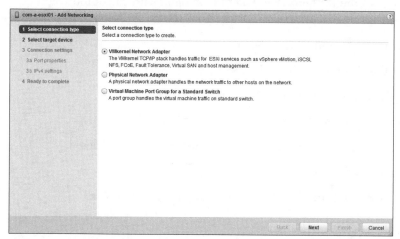

Figure 2-9   Add a VMkernel port to a vSS

Step 7.   In the Select Target Device window, select the vSS where the VMkernel port will be added and click **Next**.

Step 8.   In the Connection Settings Port Properties window, enter the following information:

a. A name for the VMkernel port.

b. The VLAN number for the VMkernel port, per the options in Table 2-4.

c. Choose whether the VMkernel port will use IPv4, IPv6 or both.

d. Check the functions the VMkernel will offer. Choose one or more of the following:

- vMotion Traffic

- Fault Tolerance Logging

- Management Traffic

- Virtual SAN Traffic

e. Click **Next**.

Step 9.   In the IPv4/IPv6 windows, enter the IP information for the VMkernel port and click **Next**.

Step 10. In the Ready to Complete window, review the information entered and click **Finish**.

To delete a standard portgroup, follow these steps:

Step 1.   Connect to the vSphere Web Client and log in with an administrator account.

Step 2.   Select the Host and Clusters view.

Step 3.   Select the ESXi host where the vSS is.

Step 4.   Select **Manage > Networking > Virtual Switches**.

Step 5.   Select the vSS that has the portgroup to be deleted.

Step 6.   In the Standard Switch view, select the portgroup to be deleted.

Step 7.   Click the red X icon.

Step 8.   In the Remove Port Group warning that pops up, click **Yes**.

As mentioned earlier in the chapter, the vSS is not a requirement for NSX. However, a deployment option is to use a vSS to connect the VMkernel ports of the ESXi hosts while moving the virtual machines to NSX logical switches. It is worth mentioning that the VMNICs assigned to the vSS will not be used by NSX's logical switches or distributed logical routers.

vSphere Distributed Switch

If it looks as if the vSS doesn't have many features to offer, that's because it doesn't. Enter the vSphere Distributed Switch (vDS). Compared to the vSS, vDS is feature rich. The vDS is managed by vCenter. All vDS configurations are done via vCenter, which then pushes down a copy of the configuration to each ESXi host that has been added to the vDS. vCenter can support many vDSes, up to 128, and each ESXi host can be part of many vDSes. For NSX to virtualize the Access Layer we need to deploy a vDS, which does not have to be dedicated for just NSX. Each ESXi host in the clusters that will participate in NSX needs to be a member of a vDS, with all the ESXi hosts in the same cluster belonging to the same vDS. Different clusters can be members of a different vDS.

The vDS is a virtual switch like the vSS that runs in the kernel. It is a non-MAC learning switch that follows the same forwarding rules from Table 2-3. Just like the vSS the vDS does not support STP. The vSS also has a portgroup, called a distributed portgroup or dvPortgroup. The vDS also has virtual ports called distributed ports or dvPorts. Virtual machines' vNICs connect to dvPortgroups. With the VMkernel ports it is a bit different; they no longer have a separate portgroup. VMkernel ports can share a portgroup with other virtual machines or other VMkernel ports. Virtual machine vNICs and VMkernel ports get assigned dvPorts.

Uplink ports, called dvUplinks, are set up a bit differently in the vDS. Each dvUplink connects to a single VMNIC in an ESXi host, but from vCenter you add multiple VMNICs to the dvUplink, one from each ESXi host added to the vDS. When vCenter pushes down the vDS configuration to the ESXi host, it only tells the ESXi host about the association of its VMNICs to the dvUplinks. Figure 2-10 shows the dvUplinks of the vDS COM-A_vDS showing two dvUplinks, each one with a VMNIC from ESXi hosts COM-A-ESXi01 and COM-A-ESXi02.

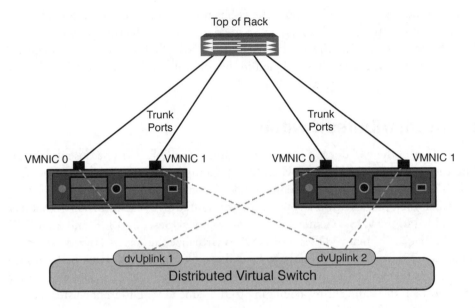

Figure 2-10 vSphere Distributed Switch dvUplinks

VLAN options in the vDS are also slightly different from the vSS. The vDS has support for private VLANs and selective 802.1Q trunking to virtual machines. Table 2-6 shows the VLAN settings available in a distributed portgroup.

Table 2-6 vSphere Distributed Switch Portgroup VLAN Settings

VLAN Setting	Description
None	No VLAN is assigned to this portgroup. All BUM traffic coming from virtual machines or the VMkernel port is forwarded to the physical switch without an 802.1Q tag.
VLAN	A VLAN is assigned. All BUM traffic coming from virtual machines or the VMkernel port is forwarded to the physical switch with an 802.1Q tag that includes the VLAN number.
VLAN Trunking	Enables 802.1Q to the virtual machines. All traffic coming from virtual machines has an 802.1Q tag for the VLANs identified here. If a non-tagged BUM frame is received from the virtual machine, it is forwarded to the physical switch without an 802.1Q tag.
Private VLANs	Enables the use of private VLANS.

If you select VLAN, VLAN Trunking, or Private VLANs in any dvPortgroup in the vDS, the vDS automatically enables 802.1Q trunking on the dvUplinks.

So why does NSX require a vDS instead of a vSS? Or better yet, why does it even require the vDS? After all, NSX has a logical switch that also runs in the ESXi host kernel. The reason has to do with an architecture decision VMware made. The vDS already supports a number of network features, listed in Table 2-7, and instead of reinventing the wheel and coding those features in the logical switch's code, they decided to build the logical switch to tap on the existing features of the vDS.

Table 2-7   vSphere Distributed Switch Features Used by NSX

vDS Feature	Description	vDS Version
Read MAC address from vmx file	Learn the MAC address of the virtual machines at power on by reading the vmx file.	5.1 or higher
Enhanced load balancing	Load share egress traffic from virtual machines and VMkernel ports based on the load of the dvUplinks.	5.5
Jumbo frame	Support for MTU size of 9000.	5.1 or higher
Network I/O control	Proportionally assign traffic shares of the bandwidth capacity of the dvUplinks by use of Network Resource Pools.	5.1 or higher
Traffic shaping	Assign cap and constrain in the amount of traffic a virtual machine or VMkernel port can consume.	5.1 or higher
LACP	Configure active and passive LACP.	5.1 or higher
QoS marking	Change the Class of Service (CoS) and Differentiated Service Code Point (DSCP) values of ingress and egress traffic.	5.5 or higher
Netflow	Capture traffic metadata for monitoring and troubleshooting.	5.1 or higher

Create vSphere Distributed Switch

Creating a vDS is simple. To create a vDS, follow these steps:

Step 1.   Connect to the vSphere Web Client and log in with an administrator account.

Step 2.   Select the Networking view.

Step 3.   Right-click the data center where the vDS will be created and choose **New Distributed Switch**.

Step 4. When the New Distributed Switch Wizard pops up, enter the name for the new vDS, as shown in Figure 2-11. Click **Next**. The name must be unique in vCenter.

Figure 2-11   New vSphere Distributed Switch

Step 5. From **Select Version**, choose the appropriate version for the vDS and click **Next**.

If deploying the vDS for NSX, reference Table 2-6 to decide the minimum version needed based on the features desired for NSX.

Step 6. From **Edit Settings**, make the following selections:

    a. Number of Uplinks: The number of VMNICs, per ESXi host, that will be added to the vDS. Collectively, the vDS dvUplinks are part of the Uplink portgroup.

    b. Network I/O Control: Enable Network I/O Control in the vDS. If enabled, default Network Resource Pools will be assigned to portgroups.

    c. Default Portgroup: Check the box if you want a default portgroup created and assign a name to the default portgroup.

    d. Click **Next**.

Step 7. In the Ready to Complete window, review the information entered and click **Finish**.

It is also simple to create a distributed portgroup; however, there are more options to consider as the portgroups have the bulk of the configuration. To create a distributed portgroup, follow these steps:

Step 1.   Connect to the vSphere Web Client and log in with an administrator account.

Step 2.   Select the Networking view.

Step 3.   Right-click the vDS where the new portgroup will be created and choose **New Distributed Port Group**.

Step 4.   In the New Distributed Port Group Wizard, enter a name for the portgroup and click **Next**.

Step 5.   In the Configure Settings window, complete the following fields:

   a. **Port binding**: Choose how the portgroup will treat the dvPorts. The options are

   - **Static Binding**: Once a dvPort is assigned, the connection remains until the virtual machine is deleted or the vNIC is moved to another connection.

   - **Dynamic Binding**: This option is deprecated.

   - **Ephemeral - No Binding**: The connection to the dvPort is severed when the virtual machine is powered off and the dvPort could be used by another entity.

   b. **Port Allocation**: How to assign dvPorts to this portgroup. The options are

   - **Fixed**: When the portgroup runs out of dvPorts, no new connections to dvPorts can be made.

   - **Elastic**: When the portgroup is about to run out of dvPorts, new dvPorts are given to the portgroup.

   c. **Number of Ports**: The number of dvPorts to reserve for this portgroup.

   d. **Network Resource Pool**: Change the Resource Pool from the default.

   e. **VLAN**: Select the VLAN per the options in Table 2-6.

   f. Check the box under Advanced to customize additional portgroup settings, as shown in Figure 2-12. The additional settings include

- **Security**: Configure restrictions of communications between virtual machines and forging MAC addresses.

- **Traffic Shaping**: Configure average and peak bandwidth for ingress and egress traffic, and burst size.

- **Teaming and Failover**: Select the load balancing mechanism for the portgroup.

- **Monitoring**: Enable NetFlow. NetFlow should be configured at the vDS level first.

g. Click **Next.**

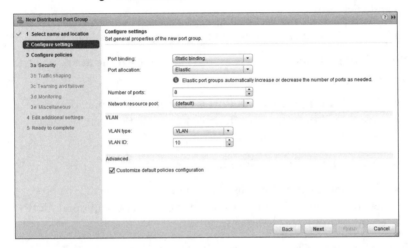

Figure 2-12   Additional portgroup settings

Step 6.   In the Edit Additional Settings window, you can change the default settings of the portgroup ports. Make any desired changes and click **Next**.

Step 7.   In the Ready to Complete window, review the information entered and click **Finish**.

To delete a distributed portgroup, follow these steps:

Step 1.   Connect to the vSphere Web Client and log in with an administrator account.

Step 2.   Select the Networking view.

Step 3.   Right-click the portgroup to be removed and choose **All Actions > Remove from Inventory**.

Step 4.   In the Remove Distributed Port Group warning that pops up, click **Yes**.

Migrate to vSphere Distributed Switch

When an ESXi host is added to a vDS it is typical to also migrate the VMNICs and VMkernel ports from the ESXi host to the vDS. You can choose to migrate one ESXi host at a time or to migrate multiple ESXi hosts at a time. We cover in this section a full migration of multiple ESXi hosts to a vDS.

To migrate multiple ESXi hosts to a vDS follow these steps:

Step 1. Connect to the vSphere Web Client and log in with an administrator account.

Step 2. Select the Networking view.

Step 3. Right-click the vDS where the new ESXi hosts will be added and choose **Add and Manage Hosts**.

Step 4. In the Add and Manage Hosts Wizard that opens, select **Add Hosts** as shown in Figure 2-13 and click **Next**.

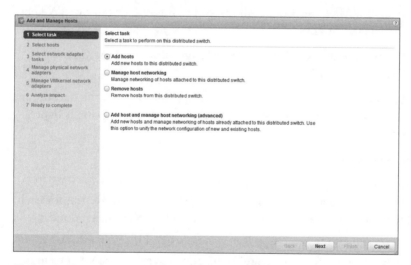

Figure 2-13   Add ESXi hosts to vSphere Distributed Switch

Step 5. In the Select Hosts window, click the green + icon and select all the ESXi hosts that will be migrated, as shown in Figure 2-14. Click **OK**; then click **Next**.

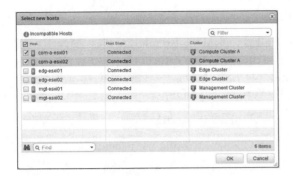

Figure 2-14   Selecting ESXi hosts for vDS

Step 6.   In the Select Network Adapter Tasks window, select the box of each option you want to configure:

- **Manage Physical Adapters**: Allows you to add VMNICs to dvUplinks.

- **Manage VMkernel Ports**: Allows you to migrate or remove VMkernel ports to the vDS.

- **Migrate Virtual Machine Networking**: Allows you to migrate vNICs to the vDS.

- **Manage Advance Host Settings**: Allows you to tweak the maximum number of dvPorts available in each ESXi host. This option is deprecated in vDS 5.5.

Click **Next** when done.

Step 7.   In the Manage Physical Network Adapters window, select the VMNIC to add to the vDS and select the dvUplink to assign it to. Repeat for each VMNIC of each ESXi host being added and click **Next** when done.

Step 8.   In the Manage VMkernel Network Adapters window, select the VMkernel ports you want to migrate to the vDS and select the portgroup to connect them.

  a. If removing the VMkernel port, select the VMkernel port to remove and click **Remove**.

  b. Repeat as necessary and click **Next** when done.

Step 9.   In the Analyze Impact window, review the information and click **Next** if no issues.

Step 10. In the Migrate VM Networking window, select the vNIC for each virtual machine you want to migrate, assign them to a distributed portgroup, and click **Next**.

This step is not necessary if the Virtual Machine will be later on migrated to NSX.

Step 11. In the Ready to Complete window, review the information entered and click **Finish**.

If all goes well, you should have all vDS topology looking similarly to vDS MGT-A1 in Figure 2-15 with all ESXi hosts, VMkernel ports, VMNICs, and virtual machines, if any, migrated.

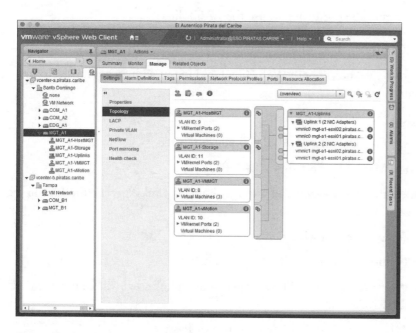

Figure 2-15 Topology view of the vDS

We end the chapter configuring two of the features that should see a lot of use when deploying NSX. They are LACP and QoS markings. When configuring LACP, it is critical that the ToR switches be configured correctly or the LACP link won't come up. For QoS markings, you should ensure that the ToR switch honors the CoS settings and the first hop physical router is configured to trust DSCP.

Configure LACP

When LACP is configured in the vDS, the vDS instructs each ESXi host to start LACP negotiations (if active) or respond to LACP negotiation requests (if passive) over the VMNICs mapped to the dvUplinks in the LACP links. Part of the LACP configuration is to select the VMNICs that will connect to the same physical switch or Multi-Chassis Link Aggregation (MLAG). Two physical switches that present themselves as the same physical switch for the purpose of forming LACP are said to form an MLAG.

The process of creating and using LACP involves three steps:

Step 1.   Create the LACP link.

Step 2.   Add VMNICs to the LACP link.

Step 3.   Configure the portgroup to use the LACP link.

To enable LACP in the vDS, follow these steps:

Step 1.   Connect to the vSphere Web Client and log in with an administrator account.

Step 2.   Select the Networking view.

Step 3.   Select the vDS where LACP will be configured.

Step 4.   Go to **Manage > Settings > LACP**.

Step 5.   Select the green + icon and wait for the New Link Aggregation Group Wizard to pop up.

Step 6.   Complete the following fields:

- **Name**: The name of the LACP link.

- **Number of Ports**: The number of dvUplinks that will be members of the LACP link.

- **Mode**: The LACP mode of Active or Passive.

- **Load Balancing Mode**: The hashing algorithm the vDS will use for egress traffic over the LACP links.

- VLAN Type and NetFlow are available only if overriding the policies set at the vDS Uplink Portgroup.

Step 7.   The configuration should be similar to the one in Figure 2-16. Click **OK**.

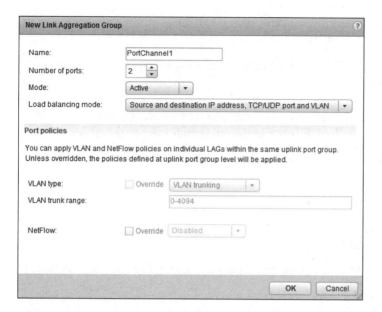

Figure 2-16 LACP vDS configuration

This concludes the first task in configuring and using LACP. Let's move on to the second task, to add VMNICs to the LACP links.

Step 1.   Connect to the vSphere Web Client and log in with an administrator account.

Step 2.   Select the Networking view.

Step 3.   Right-click the vDS where the LACP links were created and select **Add and Manage Hosts**.

Step 4.   In the Add and Manage Hosts Wizard that opens, select **Manage Host Networking** and click **Next.**

Step 5.   In the Select Hosts window, click the green + icon and select all the ESXi hosts that will be participating in the LACP. Click **OK** and click **Next.** LACP is negotiated individually by each ESXi host.

Step 6.   In the Select Network Adapter Tasks window, check the box for Manage Physical Adapters and click **Next.**

Step 7.   In the Manage Physical Network Adapters window, select the VMNIC to add to the LACP and select the LACP port to assign it. Repeat for each VMNIC of each ESXi host being added to the LACP link and click **Next** when done.

Step 8.   In the Analyze Impact window, review the information and click **Next** if no issues.

Step 9.   In the Ready to Complete window, review the information entered and click **Finish**.

For the final step, we need to go to each portgroup that we want using the LACP link and configure it so the LACP is the preferred path for network traffic:

Step 1.   Connect to the vSphere Web Client and log in with an administrator account.

Step 2.   Select the Networking view.

Step 3.   Right-click the portgroup in the vDS where the LACP links were created and select **Edit Settings**.

Step 4.   When the Edit Settings Wizard opens up, select **Teaming and Failover**.

Step 5.   Select the LACP link under the **Failover Order** and move all the way up to the **Active Uplinks**. You should move any VMNICs in the **Active Uplinks** list down to the **Unused Uplinks**, as shown in Figure 2-17.

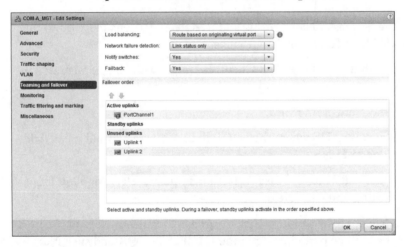

Figure 2-17   Adding the LACP link to a portgroup

Step 6.   Click **OK**.

Step 7.   Repeat steps 3 through 6 for all portgroups that should be using the LACP link.

Configure QoS Marking

The vDS has the flexibility of enabling Quality of Service (QoS) marking for traffic in the portgroup that matches a certain predefined criteria. The QoS marking settings are configured in each portgroup individually in the **Traffic Filtering and Marking** section of the portgroup settings. You can also configure the portgroup to honor QoS markings received from the virtual machine. To configure QoS markings, perform the following steps:

Step 1.   Connect to the vSphere Web Client and log in with an administrator account.

Step 2.   Select the Networking view.

Step 3.   Right-click the portgroup in the vDS where the LACP links were created and select **Edit Settings**.

Step 4.   When the Edit Settings Wizard opens, select **Traffic Filtering and Marking**.

Step 5.   In Status, select **Enable** to activate the QoS marking feature.

Step 6.   Click the green + icon to create a new QoS marking rule, as shown in Figure 2-18.

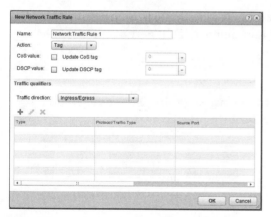

Figure 2-18   Create new QoS marking rule

Step 7.   In the New Network Traffic Rule window, complete the following fields:

- **Name**: Enter the name of the rule.

- **Action**: Select Tag.

- **CoS Value**: Check the box if you want to mark the Class of Service (CoS) value of the interesting traffic. CoS is the Layer 2 QoS marking and requires that the frame have an 802.1Q tag. If the frame does not have an 802.1Q tag, the vDS adds one with a VLAN ID matching the one configured in the portgroup. Select a value from 0-7 to tag the interesting traffic.

- **DSCP Value**: Check the box if you want to mark the Differentiated Service Code Point (DSCP) value of the interesting traffic. DSCP is the Layer 3 QoS marking. Select a value from 0-63 to tag the interesting traffic.

- **Traffic Direction**: Select the direction of the interesting traffic that will be tagged.

    - Click the green + icon to qualify the interesting traffic. The qualifying options are

        - **New System Traffic Qualifier**: Interesting traffic is/is not defined as being from the ESXi host or any virtual machine.

        - **New MAC Qualifier**: Interesting traffic is/is not defined based on the MAC address and/or VLAN number.

        - **New IP Qualifier**: Interesting traffic is/is not defined based on IP address, IP port number, TCP port number, and/or UDP port number.

Click **OK**.

Step 8.   Repeat steps 6 and 7 for new QoS marking rules. The configuration should look similar to Figure 2-19.

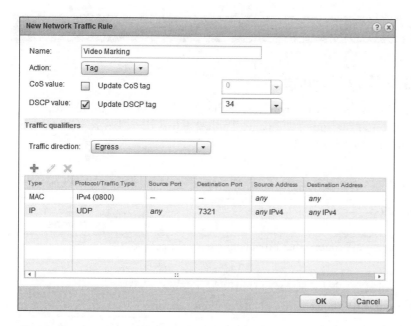

Figure 2-19   QoS marking rule

Step 9.   Click **OK** when done.

Step 10.   Repeat steps 3 through 8 for any additional portgroups.

Exam Preparation Tasks

Review All the Key Topics

Review the most important topics from inside the chapter, noted with the Key Topic icon in the outer margin of the page. Table 2-8 lists these key topics and the page numbers where each is found.

Table 2-8   Key Topics for Chapter 2

Key Topic Element	Description	Page Number
Paragraph	The switches and routers that provide the network access to the end systems.	25
Paragraph	Routers that provide Layer 3 connectivity to the Access Layers.	29
Paragraph	NSX requires IP connectivity and jumbo frame support.	33
Paragraph	NSX depends on vSphere and some of its features.	34
Paragraph	All network traffic in and out of the ESXi goes through a VMNIC.	35
Table 2-3	vSphere Standard Switch Forwarding Decision Rules.	38
Paragraph	802.1Q is enabled when a VLAN or 4095 is assigned to a standard portgroup	39
Paragraph	BUM traffic is sent to all VMs connected to the same VLAN in the same vSS	39
Paragraph	A virtual machine needs a VMXNET2 or VMXNET3 vNIC to leverage TSO.	41
Paragraph	802.1Q is enabled when a VLAN, VLAN trunking or private VLANs is assigned to a dvPortgroup	45
Table 2-7	vSphere Distributed Switch Features used by NSX.	45
Paragraph	The physical network needs to be set up to match and honor the LACP and QoS markings configured in the vDS.	51

Complete Tables and Lists from Memory

Download and print a copy of Appendix C, "Memory Tables" (found on the book's website), or at least the section for this chapter, and complete the tables and lists from memory. Appendix D, "Memory Tables Answer Key," also on the website, includes the completed tables and lists so you can check your work.

Define Key Terms

Define the following key terms from this chapter and check your answers in the glossary:

ToR, STP, SVI, TRILL, ESXi host, vSS, vDS, VMkernel port, VMNIC, vNIC, portgroup, virtual port, uplink port, vmx file, VMware Tools, MLAG

This chapter covers all or part of the following VCP6-NV exam blueprint objectives:

- **Objective 1.2**—Understand VMware NSX Architecture
- **Objective 4.2**—Deploy VMware NSX Components
- **Objective 8.1**—Differentiate Single and Cross-vCenter NSX Deployments
- **Objective 8.2**—Determine Cross-vCenter Requirements and Configurations
- **Objective 10.3**—Troubleshoot Common NSX Component Issues

CHAPTER 3

NSX Architecture and NSX Manager

The term *virtual networks* has been around for many years, and it has basically meant replicating in a virtual environment such as vSphere a physical network device's function or role. VMware's NSX is more than a virtual network. It is a software defined network. To understand what a software defined network is we first need to understand network planes, an architecture that is helpful in understanding how network devices process traffic between end systems. In this chapter we review what network planes are, so we can better define software defined networks. After we have defined software defined networks, we review the networking architecture of NSX and end the chapter with a discussion on NSX Manager, its role, and how to deploy it.

Do I Know This Already?

The "Do I Know This Already?" quiz allows you to assess whether you should read this entire chapter or simply jump to the "Exam Preparation Tasks" section for review. If you are in doubt, read the entire chapter. Table 3-1 outlines the major headings in this chapter and the corresponding "Do I Know This Already?" quiz questions. You can find the answers in Appendix A, "Answers to the 'Do I Know This Already?' Quizzes."

Table 3-1 Headings and Questions

Foundation Topic Section	Questions Covered in This Section
Network Planes	1-2
NSX Architecture	3-4
NSX Manager	5-7
Cross vCenter NSX	8-10

1. An end user at a remote office has an SNMP session open with a router located at the data center. The traffic is routed via the remote office's router.
   From the remote office's router perspective, in which plane does this traffic
   reside?

   a. Management plane

   b. Cloud management plane

   c. Control plane

   d. Data plane

2. An end user at a remote office has an SNMP session open with a router located at the data center. The traffic is routed via the remote office's router.
   From the data center's router perspective, in which plane does this traffic reside?

   a. Cloud management plane

   b. Management plane

   c. Control plane

   d. Data plane

3. Which two are not components of VMware NSX? (Choose two.)

   a. vCenter

   b. Distributed firewall

   c. Edge gateway

   d. vSphere Distributed Switch

4. What port number is used by NSX Manager to communicate with vCenter?

   a. TCP 80

   b. TCP 443

   c. UDP 902

   d. UDP 9443

5. What is the minimum required version number of vCenter to integrate with
   NSX Manager in a Standalone role?

   a. 5.0

   b. 5.1

   c. 5.5

   d. 6.0

6. Where can the integration of NSX Manager and vCenter be configured?

    a. vSphere Client

    b. vSphere Web Client

    c. With the vSphere APIs

    d. NSX Manager user interface

7. How many vCPUs are needed for NSX Manager in a large-scale deployment?

    a. 2

    b. 4

    c. 6

    d. 8

8. Which of the following objects cannot be part of a universal security group?

    a. Universal security group

    b. Universal IP sets

    c. Universal services

    d. Universal MAC sets

9. A Universal Firewall Rule is created on the Primary NSX Manager. Afterward, the Primary NSX Manager's role is changed to Standalone. Which of the following is true?

    a. The Universal Firewall Rule is deleted when the Primary NSX Manager's role is changed to Standalone.

    b. A Primary NSX Manager's role can't be changed while there are Universal Firewall Rules configured. The Universal Firewall Rule must be deleted first.

    c. The Primary NSX Manager communicates its role change to other NSX Managers before transitioning to Standalone. The remaining NSX Managers elect a new Primary manager.

    d. The Primary NSX Manager transitions to the Transit role. While in the Transit role, the NSX Manager does not accept new Universal Firewall Rules.

10. How many Secondary NSX Managers are supported in cross vCenter NSX?

    a. 6

    b. 7

    c. 8

    d. 10

Foundation Topics

Network Planes

There is a layered architecture in networking that is employed by network devices to deliver traffic between end systems. The layers of this architecture are referred to as *planes*. Each plane is a category used to label the activities executed by network devices in support of the delivery of traffic between end systems. These planes are the management, control, and data planes as illustrated in Figure 3-1. As we go over the description of each of the planes, it helps to be mindful of the following: the control plane exists to support the data plane, and the management plane provides the instructions to the control plane on how it will provide support to the data plane. Or put another way, the data plane is on top of a pyramid, with the control and management planes providing the foundations to support it. To be honest and fair, the plane definitions we cover next are from a high level point of view, which is all we need to understand software-defined networks and NSX's networking features.

Before we get a good grasp of what each plane is, let's be clear on this point: If you do not understand the differences between these three planes and what they are, you will be challenged to understand software-defined networks nor would you fully understand what NSX is and does.

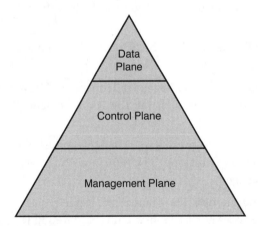

Figure 3-1   Network plane dependencies; the data plane relies on the control plane, which relies on the management plane.

The management plane includes configuration and management of the network device. If you have ever configured a VLAN in a Layer 2 switch or configured OSPF in a router, you have interacted with the management plane of that network device.

Whether you connect to the network device via the console interface, via SSH or APIs, your interaction with the network device is categorized as belonging in the management plane. The management plane does not require that a user be the one interacting with the network device. For example, Simple Network Management Protocol (SNMP) is considered management plane traffic, yet SNMP interactions can and do take place without any human interactions. SNMP may be used to apply configurations to network devices as well as to monitor and manage them.

I find it more valuable to explain the control plane after explaining the data plane. Processing data plane traffic is the primary activity of every network device. Let's review some of the traffic that can be considered as belonging to the data plane from the perspective of a router with three interfaces. Imagine traffic arriving in one of the three interfaces in the router. The router makes a decision and forwards the traffic out of a second interface. This traffic passing through the router is in the data plane of our router. Now instead of forwarding the traffic out of the second interface, the router could've decided to send the traffic out of the third interface, send it back to the first interface the traffic came in, or just drop the traffic. In these three other cases the traffic will also be in the data plane of our router. Are you still there? In all cases, the router processed ingress traffic, made a routing decision, and executed that decision. A Layer 2 switch makes similar forwarding decisions (except that it never sends the traffic back to the ingress port).

But how did our router come about the forwarding decision that it made for the ingress traffic? How did it know what to do with the ingress data plane traffic? That's where the control plane comes in. The control plane facilitates the information the network device needs to make a forwarding decision for ingress data plane traffic. In our router the routing table is in the control plane. In the case of a Layer 2 switch, the MAC table is part of the control plane. Routing protocols, such as OSPF and BGP, are considered part of the control plane, as their sole purpose is to seek out information to populate the routing table. OSPF neighbor exchanges, hello packets, and link state exchanges are all part of the control plane.

So there you have it. The management, control, and data planes are the categories to separate the different activities executed by network devices that ultimately allow for User A to communicate with User B over the network. The management plane tells the network device *what* it will be doing. The control plane tells the network device *how* it is going to do it. The network device then *executes* it in the data plane.

Now ask yourself "did I get this?" If you have a shred of doubt that you might not understand the difference between the planes, stop reading this and step away from the book. Better yet, go jogging or do some push-ups—anything to get your mind off this topic and cleared up. Then come back. Be sure to mark your place in this chapter before you go.

Now that you are back, start reading from the beginning of this chapter and be sure to get the difference between the three planes. Remember the three key words: *what*, *how*, and *execute*.

In traditional physical networks, each network device executes all three functions for their corresponding layer, Layer 2 or Layer 3. This architecture, as discussed in Chapter 1, "Introduction to VMware NSX," can lead to ineffective use of time by network administrators and added network complexity, which brings us to a formal definition of a software defined network (SDN). An SDN is any network solution that separates the control plane function from the network device performing the data plane function. In SDN solutions, it is typical for the management plane function to also be separated from the network device performing the data plane function.

NSX Architecture

The architecture for NSX is based on the three planes we discussed, with different components existing in one of the three planes, as shown in Figure 3-2. The exception to this rule is the NSX Edge and the distributed firewall. The NSX Edge handles both its control and data planes. The distributed firewall's control plane is handled by NSX Manager.

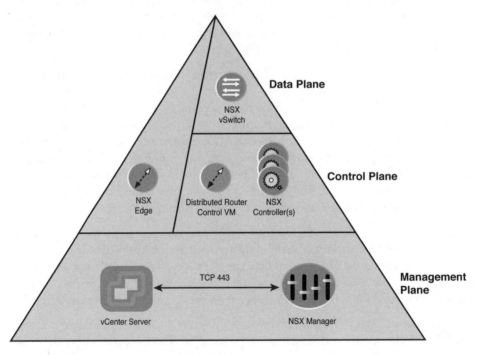

Figure 3-2   NSX components and vCenter

The components of NSX are

- NSX Manager

- NSX Controller

- NSX vSwitch

- NSX Edge Services Gateway

NSX Manager resides in the management plane. vCenter Server is shown in Figure 3-2 to illustrate that it too resides in the management plane and communicates directly with NSX Manager via HTTPS (SSL, TCP port 443). NSX is designed so that an outage in the management plane will not impact the data plane. No configuration changes can be made while the NSX Manager is down or unavailable; however, data plane traffic continues to flow unaffected.

The NSX Controller(s) reside in the control plane as well as an entity called the Distributed Router Control VM. The NSX Controller is the overseer of the Layer 2 control plane, and with the help of the Control VM, it handles the Layer 3 control plane. Both the NSX Controller(s) and the control VM get their configuration information from the NSX Manager. NSX is designed to have minimal impact to the data plane if the entire control plane goes down. We review this further in Chapter 5, "NSX Switches."

The NSX vSwitch resides in the data plane by integrating itself in the kernel code of participating ESXi hosts. It handles Layer 2 (logical switch), Layer 3 (distributed logical router), and security (distributed firewall). The NSX vSwitch gets Layer 2 and Layer 3 control plane information from the NSX Controller(s). The NSX vSwitch receives security information directly from NSX Manager.

Although VMware's official position is that the NSX vSwitch resides in the data plane, it also executes some activities of the control plane. The logical switch partially owns its control plane in conjunction with the NSX Controllers, in some instances owning 100% of its control plane. We cover logical switches in Chapter 5. The distributed firewall, DFW, doesn't quite conform to the network plane categories, as the role of security is *not* to deliver traffic between end systems so much as to *allow* approved traffic between end systems. We cover the DFW in Chapter 15, "Distributed Logical Firewall."

The NSX Edge is a virtual appliance that provides network services not available with the NSX vSwitch's distributed logical router, such as IPsec VPN, NAT, and load balancing. The NSX Edge can also act as a router, stretch Layer 2 domains across Layer 3 segments, and function as a Layer 4 stateful firewall. The NSX Edge never communicates with the NSX Controller(s).

From Figure 3-2, it is important to note that neither the NSX Manager, the NSX Controllers, nor the distributed router control VM are in the data path. NSX is designed so that the failure of any of these components has minimal to no impact to the data plane. We learn more about the NSX Manager later in this chapter. We learn about the NSX Controllers in Chapter 4, "VXLAN, NSX Controllers, and NSX Preparation." We learn about the distributed router control VM in Chapter 7, "Logical Router."

As NSX is an SDN solution that decouples networking and security from the physical hardware and its tight integration with vSphere, NSX offers network and security features not readily available in your traditional network, such as true distributed routing and microsegmentation. We explore this and other features later in the book. For the remainder of this chapter, we discuss NSX Manager.

NSX Manager

NSX Manager is the component of NSX that resides in the management plane. In that role, NSX Manager is responsible for the following tasks:

- Installs the Network and Security vSphere Web Client plugin. Note that NSX Manager does not have a plugin for the vSphere Client.

- Deployment of NSX components in the control and data planes.

- Autogenerates certificates for secure communication with NSX components.

- Owns the configuration for the NSX domain.

- Pushes configurations to the NSX Controllers, the distributed router control VM, the NSX Edges, and the NSX vSwitch.

- Provides external access for management and configuration via the NSX APIs. We learn about the NSX APIs in Chapter 18, "NSX Automation."

- Provides access for management and configuration via the vSphere Web Client User Interface.

All configurations that you implement in the NSX domain are done via the NSX Manager. NSX Manager then contacts other entities, such as vCenter and EXSi hosts, to help apply and execute those configurations. Do not confuse this with the vSphere preparation that needs to take place prior to having a fully functional NSX domain. We cover NSX preparation in Chapter 4.

NSX Manager is provided by VMware as an Open Virtualization Appliance (OVA) that can be deployed in a vSphere environment. You need the appropriate vCenter permissions to install the NSX Manager OVA, and this is the only installation that you need to do for NSX. Every other NSX component needed to support the NSX domain comes preloaded with NSX Manager and gets installed by NSX Manager. Prior to deploying NSX Manager, you should have documented the ESXi host or host cluster where you want NSX Manager to run and the subnet it will connect to. VMware Tools is included in the virtual appliance, and VMware does not support the user updating VMware Tools in NSX Manager.

The NSX Manager virtual appliance has the following requirements:

- Four vCPUs prior to NSX 6.2 and NSX 6.2 for normal deployments, or eight vCPUs prior for large-scale deployments

- 12 GB of memory prior to NSX 6.2, or 16 GB of memory for NSX 6.2 normal deployments, or 24 GB of memory for NSX 6.2 large-scale deployments

- 60 GB of disk space

A large-scale deployment is any NSX deployment with one or more of the following conditions:

- 100 ESXi hosts or more

- 100 NSX Edges or more

- 1,000 or more Universal Distributed Firewall rules

- 10,000 or more Global Distributed Firewall rules

To deploy NSX Manager, obtain the OVA from VMware and connect to the vSphere Web Client or the vSphere Client to access vCenter and deploy NSX Manager. This vCenter may be a totally different vCenter from the one you integrate with NSX Manager, which we discuss after learning how to deploy NSX Manager. The vCenter where you deploy NSX Manager can be version 5.5 or higher. In the examples and screen captures in this book, I use the same vCenter to deploy and integrate with NSX Manager. Although you can use the vSphere Client to deploy the OVA for NSX Manager, you cannot use the vSphere Client for UI access to NSX Manager. Figure 3-3 shows the start of the process to deploy NSX Manager with a vCenter 6.0.

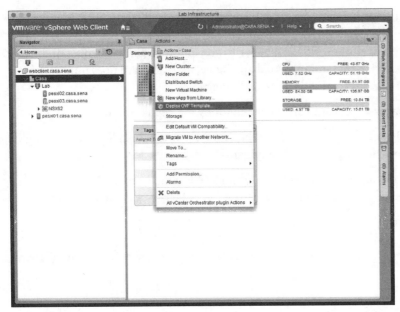

Figure 3-3   Deploying NSX Manager OVF from the vSphere Web Client in a vCenter 6.0 environment

After selecting the location where the OVA is and clicking **Next**, you need to check the box that says **Accept Extra Configuration Options**, as shown in Figure 3-4, which enables step **2d Customize Template** where you can add the NSX Manager passwords, IP configuration, and NTP settings.

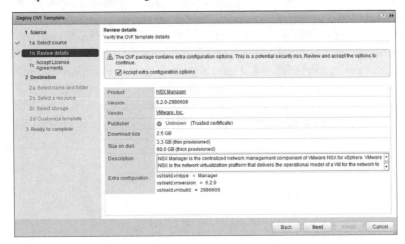

Figure 3-4   NSX Manager OVF deployment details

In the next window you see the End User License Agreement (EULA). Read it, click **Accept**, which grays out the Accept button, and click **Next**.

In the following four windows you give the virtual appliance a name and select the folder or data center, select the compute resource where it will run, select the data-store where it will be deployed, and select the portgroup to connect the Appliance. I gave NSX Manager a name of NSXMGR-B, as shown in Figure 3-5, because I have already deployed an NSXMGR-A to use in a cross vCenter deployment. It is recommended that NSX Manager be deployed in a cluster configured with DRS and HA to provide it with high availability. Although you could use fault tolerance for NSX Manager in vSphere 6.0, this solution may only be used in non-large-scale deployments and, per Knowledge Base Article 2110197, it could lead to unexpected results. Finally, NSX Manager needs a single Ethernet connection, which typically is the same Ethernet broadcast domain as the vCenter with which it will integrate. NSX Manager can be connected to a standard portgroup or a distributed portgroup. NSX Manager is not supported connecting to a logical switch.

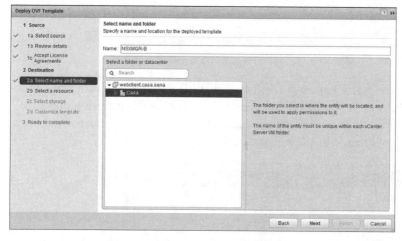

Figure 3-5   Giving the NSX Manager a name and location where NSX Manager will be placed

The last configuration settings are done in the Customize Template window as shown in Figure 3-6. This is where you enter the NSX Manager password for the default admin account as well as a password for CLI privilege mode. You also enter the hostname that will be given to the NSX Manager (think DNS, although you would still need to make sure the FQDN entry gets added to DNS), the IP settings for the virtual appliance, NTP servers, and you have the option to enable SSH. It is worth noting that NSX Manager supports both IPv4 and IPv6 for management.

As of NSX 6.2, VMware expanded the available CLI commands in NSX Manager. Many of the CLI commands allow you to do many of the NSX Manager configurations and queries (show commands) you can do with the API and the UI. The NSX Manager CLI commands are divided into two categories:

- **NSX commands**: Geared to making changes in NSX Manager

- **NSX central commands**: Allow you to get information about the state of NSX components, such as logical switch

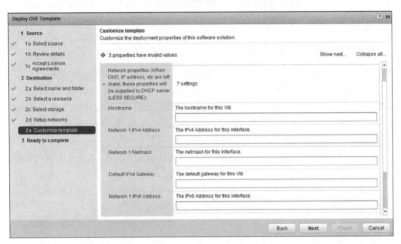

Figure 3-6   Adding the NSX Manager hostname and IP configuration

Take a moment to review Figure 3-7 and note that NSX Manager has deployed successfully with the number of CPUs and memory for a normal installation plus disk size of 60 GB. If you need to increase the number of CPUs and memory to support a large-scale deployment, edit the settings of the appliance.

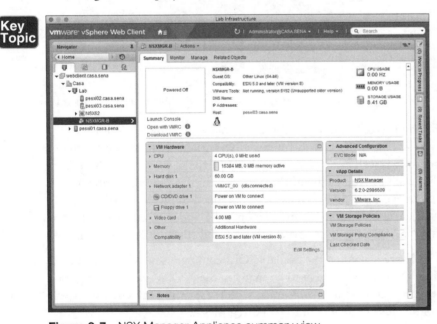

Figure 3-7   NSX Manager Appliance summary view

NSX Manager Base Configuration

I just remembered I have not quite explained this yet: NSX Manager communicates, for management plane purposes, with a single vCenter, and a vCenter only communicates with a single NSX Manager. You can't have an NSX Manger communicate with two vCenters, nor can you have a vCenter communicate with two NSX Managers.

NSX Manager needs to communicate with a vCenter running version 5.5 or higher if you will not be doing cross vCenter NSX, also referred to as the Standalone role. If you intend to do cross vCenter NSX, vCenter must be running 6.0 or higher. We cover cross vCenter NSX later in this chapter.

There are a few reasons why NSX Manager needs to communicate on the management plane with vCenter. For one, the NSX vSwitch has a dependency on the vSphere Distributed Switch, vDS, whose management plane is owned by vCenter. There is also this *minor* detail that virtual machines will be connecting to logical switches, which for now we can think of as NSX virtual switches. This configuration is done via NSX Manager, and since vCenter owns the management of the virtual machines (here is the management plane again), NSX Manager needs to let vCenter know about these connections. Finally, NSX Manager does not acknowledge an ESXi host that is not part of a cluster, and because clusters are a vCenter object, vCenter is required.

Now that the NSX Manager virtual appliance is deployed, we need to start the process of integrating NSX Manager with vCenter. The integration of NSX Manager with vCenter allows NSX Manager to see the vSphere infrastructure inventory, such as hosts and vSphere Distributed Switches. This integration also triggers NSX Manager to install the Network and Security plugin in the vSphere Web Client, which enables NSX Manager to be managed via the vSphere Web Client.

To integrate NSX Manager with vCenter, first connect to the NSX Manager home page using the hostname or the IP for NSX Manager, which you provided during installation as shown previously in Figure 3-6. The IP address would be the one you assigned during the deployment of the OVA. If you elect to use the hostname to connect, the hostname has to have been entered in your DNS system. The address to connect to NSX Manager is https://[NSX Manager Hostname or IP]/, and the credentials are *admin* for the username and the password you assigned during the deployment of the OVA, as shown in Figure 3-8.

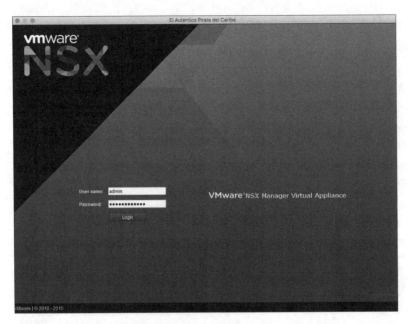

Figure 3-8 NSX Manager login screen

In the NSX Manager home page, shown in Figure 3-9, you find six options:

- View Summary

- Manage Appliance Settings

- Manage vCenter Registration

- Download Tech Support Log

- Backup & Restore

- Upgrade

Clicking **View Summary** allows you to see the NSX Manager version number, processes running (vPostgres, RabbitMQ, and NSX Management Service), and the NSX Manager resource consumption (CPU, memory, and disk).

vPostgres is the database used by NSX Manager, and it is run internally. NSX Manager cannot be configured to use an external database. RabbitMQ is the messaging broker used by NSX Manager to communicate with the ESXi hosts. NSX Manager uses this message bus to communicate, over TCP port 5671, with the VSFW daemon (not demon) running in the ESXi host.

Figure 3-9   NSX Manager home page

Manage vCenter Registration, **Backup & Restore**, and **Upgrade** are shortcuts to configuring settings in the **Manage Appliance Settings** option. Clicking **Download Tech Support Log** opens a window that allows you to download the NSX Manager log files that can be used by VMware support to assist in troubleshooting.

Clicking **Manage Appliance Settings** takes you to the settings window where you can configure or make changes:

- NTP Server, which is required for SSO communication with NSX Manager to work correctly

- Syslog Server

- NSX Manager IP settings

- SSL certificates for external connectivity to NSX Manager, such as NSX APIs

- Backup and restore the NSX Manager

- Update the NSX Manager

- Register NSX Management Service with a Lookup Service

- Integrate NSX Manager with vCenter Server

Integrating NSX Manager with vCenter is straightforward as shown in Figure 3-10: Click **NSX Management Service**, and then click **Edit** in the vCenter Server session, enter the vCenter hostname or IP and the credentials for the administrator account, and click **OK**. Additionally you could check the **Modify Plugin Download Script Location** to choose another NSX Manager from which to download the Network and Security **vSphere** Web Client plugin.

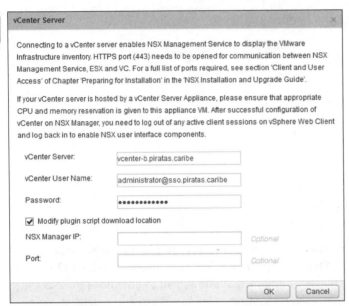

Figure 3-10   Integrating vCenter with NSX Manager

Wait for the vCenter Status to say **Connected**, *as shown in Figure 3-11*, and exit NSX Manager. Similar to when configuring the vCenter Appliance, once you have finished integrating NSX Manager with vCenter and you have modified any additional settings as you see fit, you will have limited reasons to connect to the NSX Manager again.

Figure 3-11   NSX Manager has successfully connected with vCenter.

Now return to the vSphere Web Client and log in using the same administrator account you used to integrate NSX Manager to vCenter; otherwise, you won't see your NSX Manager in the vSphere Web Client. If you were already logged in, you need to log out and log in again. Chapter 17, "Additional NSX Features," covers how to configure additional accounts that can manage NSX Manager from the vSphere Web Client.

Once you log in to the vSphere Web Client, the first thing you should notice is the new **Networking & Security** icon in the Inventories view as shown in Figure 3-12. And if this is not the first thing you notice, I might have to question your desire to become an NSX Ninja.

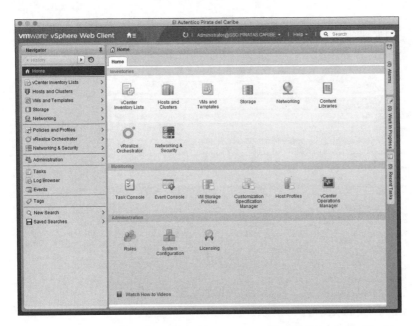

Figure 3-12   vSphere Web Client home page with NSX Manager plugin

Also notice the Licensing icon in Figure 3-12. NSX Manager comes with a 60-day all-you-can-eat evaluation mode, just like most other VMware products. You need to get a license from VMware to continue using NSX after the 60 days, and the license is added under **Licenses > Assets > Solutions**. The license comes with two options: license per ESXi host socket or license per virtual machine using NSX services. Either one of the options unlocks for the licensed asset (ESXi host or virtual machine) all features NSX has to offer.

Clicking on **Networking & Security** takes you to the Networking & Security access page as shown in Figure 3-13. This is where you execute all configuration changes for NSX and view NSX Manager logs. As we go through the book, we reference this page multiple times.

Since this is our first time together in the Networking & Security access page, let's take a quick walk describing the different fields you see and the options available to you as outlined in Table 3-2. I do not go into great detail here because we revisit most of these areas in later chapters as we add NSX components, such as logical switches, and make configuration changes to the NSX domain.

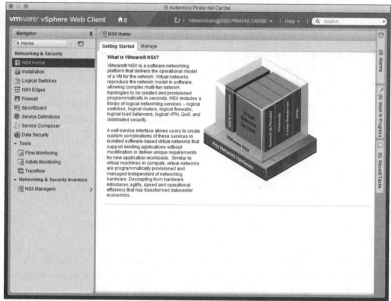

Figure 3-13 Networking & Security access portal

Table 3-2 Network and Security Access Portal

Network and Security Field	Available Actions
NSX Home	This is the landing page for the Network & Security view. Here we can add a tag to audit logs for operations performed on the NSX Manager by the user that is logged in.
Installation	This field is our next stop, as we cover how to make an NSX Manager a primary in a cross vCenter NSX deployment. In addition, one can deploy NSX Controllers in this field; prepare and configure the ESXi hosts for NSX; define the cluster diameter of logical switches with transport zones; select the range of VXLAN Network IDs, VNI, and IP Multicast groups to be used by logical switches; and deploy network and security services provided by VMware and VMware-approved technology partners.
Logical Switches	In this field we can create, edit, and manage logical switches.
NSX Edges	In this field, we can create, configure, and manage distributed logical routers and NSX Edges.
Firewall	In this field, we can add, edit, and delete Layer 2, Layer 3, and Layer 4 distributed firewall policies. From this field we can also save and restore distributed firewall configurations.

Network and Security Field	Available Actions
SpoofGuard	In this field, we can enable IP and MAC Spoof Guard protection for virtual machines to ensure the virtual machine only uses the IP and MAC addresses assigned to it.
Service Definitions	In this field, we can add, edit, and remove network and security services provided by VMware and VMware-approved technology partners.
Service Composer	In this field, we can create, edit, and remove groups, called security groups, of virtual machines that can then have security policies applied. Security policies can contain distributed firewall policies and/or network and security services provided by VMware and VMware-approved technology partners.
Data Security	In this field, we can run scans to monitor compliance with regulations and standards.
Flow Monitoring	In this field, we can configure the capturing of traffic flow metadata. We can use this information to view interesting data flows, such as top talkers, and execute an action on the data flow, such as blocking it.
Activity Monitoring	In this field, we can enable, edit, and view detailed reports on virtual machines' applications and traffic.
Traceflow	In this field, you can do some troubleshooting by having NSX inject traffic by sourcing it from a virtual machine.
NSX Managers	In this field, we can view logs, events, and tasks of the NSX Manager(s). We can also add virtual machines to the exclusion list from enforcement in of the distributed firewall rules, create security tags, add Active Directory and LDAP domains, edit Role Based Access Control for NSX Manager, and update object sets and pools.

Cross vCenter NSX

As of NSX 6.2, there is a feature called cross vCenter NSX. With cross vCenter NSX it is possible to have two or more NSX Managers, up to eight (8), and each one associated with its own vCenter, centrally managed, and exchanging management plane information. With cross vCenter NSX, one of the NSX Managers is manually elected as the primary, while the rest of the NSX Managers are manually configured as secondary. Cross vCenter NSX allows you to extend some features of NSX among multiple environments managed by separate vCenters while maintaining a single point of management, namely the primary NSX Manager.

Some use cases where cross vCenter NSX may be beneficial:

- Multi-vCenter cloud deployments

- To support applications that have a business need to be deployed across multiple vCenters

- To support virtualization products that require multiple vCenters, such as virtual desktop environments like Horizon View

- To scale up your virtual environment beyond the limits of a single vCenter

- To provide for dynamic disaster recovery scenarios

Table 3-3 shows the list of NSX features supported in cross vCenter NSX. We cover each feature in detail throughout the book. Do take note that all NSX features supported in cross vCenter NSX are prepended with the word "universal."

Table 3-3   Cross vCenter NSX Features

NSX Feature	Cross vCenter NSX Support
Universal VXLAN Network IDs (VNI)	Yes.
Universal transport zone	Yes.
Universal logical switch	Yes.
Universal logical (distributed) router	Yes, but does not support Layer 2 bridging.
Universal Firewall Rules	Yes, but only for the DFW rules when using rules with IPs or MACs for source/destination. Universal Firewall Rules can include universal IP sets, universal MAC sets, and universal security groups.
NSX Edge	No (an NSX Edge is not distributed and can only be supported in a single Data Center at a time).
Universal IP address groups (IP sets)	Yes.
Universal MAC address groups (MAC sets)	Yes.
Universal security groups	Yes, but only for *included objects* and only if the objects reference universal IP sets, universal MAC sets, or another universal security group. Neither *dynamic membership* nor *excluded objects* are supported.
Universal services	Yes.
Security groups	Yes.
IP pools	No.

In this chapter we learned how to deploy NSX Manager 6.2 and how to associate it with a vCenter running 6.0 or higher. At this moment our NSX Manager is configured in standalone mode, meaning it is not aware of the existence of any other NSX Managers. To make our NSX Manager aware of other NSX Managers, so that the NSX features listed as Yes in Table 3-3 may be used across multiple vCenters, you need to assign the NSX Manager either the Primary role or, if an existing NSX Manager already has the Primary role, the Secondary role.

The responsibilities of the Primary NSX Manager include

- The assignment of the Secondary role to other NSX Managers

- The configuration and deployment of all NSX services provided to virtual machines of its associated vCenter

- The configuration of all NSX services in virtual machines in vCenters associated with Secondary NSX Managers

- The configuration and deployment of all universal NSX services (all marked Yes in Table 3-3) provided to all virtual machines in all vCenters

- The universal controller cluster (All secondary NSX Manager controller clusters need to be removed.)

Chapter 4 covers controller clusters in greater detail. All cross vCenter NSX feature configurations are done via the Primary NSX Manager, which replicates them to all secondary NSX Managers. This replication is done via the NSX Manager's NSX universal synchronization service. The secondary NSX Managers cannot make changes to cross vCenter NSX features; however, NSX features that are local to a vCenter continue to be done by the NSX Manager paired with that vCenter.

To assign an NSX Manager the Primary role to support cross vCenter NSX, go to the Network and Security view in the vSphere Web Client. From the Installation field, select the Management tab. Select an NSX Manager, click the Actions icon, and select Assign Primary Role.

After you have assigned the Primary role to an NSX Manager, you can assign the Secondary role to other NSX Managers. Figure 3-14 shows how to assign the Secondary role from the Primary NSX Manager, which is NSXMGR-A with an IP of 10.154.8.32. Notice that NSX Manager NSXMGR-B, with an IP of 10.154.8.33, is currently labeled as Standalone.

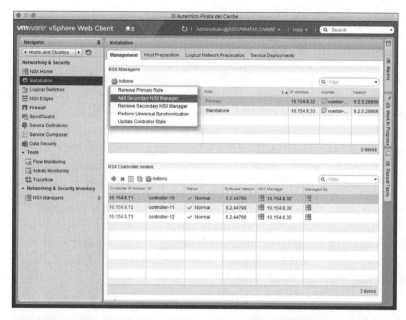

Figure 3-14   Add NSX Manager cross vCenter NSX Secondary role

Figure 3-15 shows the pop-up window where you select the NSX Manager to assign the Secondary role. We are selecting NSX Manager NSXMGR-B, with an IP of 10.154.8.33.

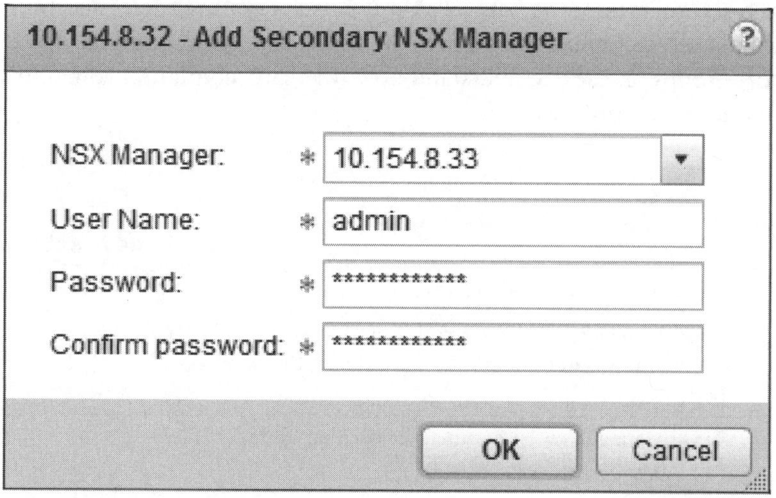

10.154.8.32 - Add Secondary NSX Manager   ?

NSX Manager:	*	10.154.8.33	▼
User Name:	*	admin	
Password:	*	************	
Confirm password:	*	************	

OK   Cancel

Figure 3-15   Select Secondary NSX Manager

In the event that the Primary NSX Manager becomes unavailable, any Secondary NSX Manager can be manually promoted to Primary. In such an event, a new NSX universal controller needs to be deployed by the new Primary NSX Manager.

In the event that a Primary NSX Manager's role is changed from Primary to Stand-alone, the NSX Manager acts in a Transit role. While in a Transit role, the NSX Manager retains existing cross vCenter NSX features, such as a universal logical switch, but the NSX Manager does not allow changes to those features nor would it accept new cross vCenter NSX features. The NSX Manager allows for those existing features to be deleted (by the new Primary NSX Manager). VMware recommends that a Transit role be used temporarily while the Primary role assignment is changed.

One final point is somewhat related to cross vCenter NSX. NSX 6.2 introduced the capability to do local egress routing. NSX goes about it by assigning each NSX Manager a unique locale ID. By default, the local ID is the NSX Manager's UUID. If needed, the local ID can be changed on a per cluster, ESXi host, or DLR basis. We cover local ID in more detail in Chapter 7.

Exam Preparation Tasks

Review All the Key Topics

Review the most important topics from inside the chapter, noted with the Key Topic icon in the outer margin of the page. Table 3-4 lists these key topics and the page numbers where each is found. Know the main differences between vSSes and vDSes and the port groups on each. Understand how to create, configure, edit, and delete these components and policies.

Table 3-4 Key Topics for Chapter 3

Key Topic Element	Description	Page Number
Figure 3-2	NSX components and vCenter	66
Paragraph	NSX Manager, NSX Controllers and the distributed router control VM are not in the data path.	68
Paragraph	NSX Manager's CLI commands were expanded in NSX 6.2	71
Figure 3-7	NSX Manager Appliance summary view	72
Paragraph	NSX communication is 1-1 with vCenter.	73
Paragraph	Cross vCenter NSX requires vCenter 6.0	73

Key Topic Element	Description	Page Number
Figure 3-9	NSX Manager home page	75
Figure 3-10	Integrating vCenter with NSX Manager	76
Figure 3-11	vCenter successful integration with NSX Manager	77
Paragraph	NSX license is added in the vSphere Web Client under Licenses > Assets > Solutions	78
Figure 3-13	Networking and Security access portal	79
Table 3-2	Network and Security Access Portal	79
Table 3-3	Cross vCenter NSX Features	81
Paragraph	During a Primary NSX Manager failure, any Secondary NSX Manager can become Primary	84

Complete Tables and Lists from Memory

Download and print a copy of Appendix C, "Memory Tables" (found on the book's website), or at least the section for this chapter, and complete the tables and lists from memory. Appendix D, "Memory Tables Answer Key," also on the website, includes the completed tables and lists so you can check your work.

Define Key Terms

Define the following key terms from this chapter, and check your answers in the Glossary:

network planes, management plane, control plane, data plane, virtual network, software defined data center, logical switch, distributed logical router, distributed firewall, NSX Edge, NSX Controller, logical router control VM, cross vCenter NSX, Primary NSX Manager, Secondary NSX Manager, Transit NSX Manager, Standalone NSX Manager, locale ID

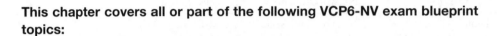

This chapter covers all or part of the following VCP6-NV exam blueprint topics:

- **Objective 4.2**—Deploy VMware NSX Components

- **Objective 4.4**—Expand Transport Zone to Include New Cluster(s)

- **Objective 5.2**—Configure VXLAN

- **Objective 6.2**—Configure and Manage Logical Virtual Private Networks (VPN)

- **Objective 8.2**—Determine Cross-vCenter Requirements and Configurations

- **Objective 10.3**—Troubleshoot Common NSX Component Issues

- **Objective 10.4**—Troubleshoot Common Connectivity Issues

CHAPTER 4

VXLAN, NSX Controllers, and NSX Preparation

Deploying NSX Manager and attaching it to vCenter are the first steps in allowing you to deploy your software defined network. Your goal is to have logical switches, distributed logical routers, and create and enforce security policies with the distributed firewall and service composer.

Before you can reach your goal, you need to deploy our NSX Controllers and tell NSX Manager which ESXi hosts will be part of the NSX domain. The steps to tell NSX Manager which ESXi hosts will be part of the NSX Domain are

- Install NSX modules.

- Configure VXLAN networking in each ESXi host.

- Create VNI pools.

- Create transport zones.

This chapter covers all the steps needed to prepare your NSX domain. The chapter begins with a proper introduction of what VXLAN is.

Do I Know This Already?

The "Do I Know This Already?" quiz allows you to assess whether you should read this entire chapter or simply jump to the "Exam Preparation Tasks" section for review. If you are in doubt, read the entire chapter. Table 4-1 outlines the major headings in this chapter and the corresponding "Do I Know This Already?" quiz questions. You can find the answers in Appendix A, "Answers to the 'Do I Know This Already?' Quizzes."

Table 4-1   Headings and Questions

Foundation Topic Section	Questions Covered in This Section
VXLAN	1–2
NSX Controllers	3–4
IP Pools	5
Host Preparation	6–7

Foundation Topic Section	Questions Covered in This Section
Host Configuration	8-9
VNI Pools, Multicast Pools, and Transport Zones	10

1. What is the source Layer 4 port number of a VXLAN frame?

   a. It is statically configured to TCP 8472.

   b. It is statically configured to UDP 8472.

   c. It is randomly generated by the VTEP.

   d. It is derived from the encapsulated frame.

2. At least how many bytes does the VXLAN encapsulation add to the encapsulated frame?

   a. 50

   b. 100

   c. 1500

   d. 9000

3. How many NSX universal controllers are required to be deployed in a production NSX environment?

   a. 1

   b. 2

   c. 3

   d. 4

4. What NSX entity is responsible for slicing the distributed logical router?

   a. The NSX Manager

   b. The distributed router control virtual machine

   c. The API provider NSX Controller Master

   d. The Layer 3 NSX Controller Master

5. What are two use cases of IP pools by NSX Manager? (Choose two.)

   a. To assign IPs to virtual machines in the virtual network.

   b. To assign the default gateway for VTEPs.

   c. To assign IPs to NSX Manager.

   d. To assign IPs to NSX Controllers.

6. Which of the following is an action that takes place during host preparation?

   a. The NSX Manager tells vCenter to add the selected hosts in the NSX host clusters.

   b. The NSX Manager installs NSX modules on the ESXi hosts.

   c. vCenter adds the VXLAN VMkernel port to the ESXi hosts.

   d. The NSX Controller Master uploads the NSX configuration data to the ESXi hosts.

7. Which NSX feature does not require logical networking preparation to be completed before it can be used?

   a. VXLAN

   b. Logical switches

   c. Distributed firewall

   d. Distributed logical routers

8. How many vDS switches does NSX Manager support in a single host cluster?

   a. 1

   b. 2

   c. 32

   d. 128

9. During host configuration you select a VMKNic teaming policy of enhanced LACP. How many VTEPs does NSX Manager create per ESXi host?

   a. 1

   b. 2

   c. As many dvUplinks as are configured on the vDS

   d. As many VMNICs as are installed on the ESXi hosts

10. How many universal transport zones are supported in a cross vCenter NSX domain?

   a. 1

   b. 1 per NSX Manager in the cross vCenter NSX domain

   c. Up to the number of VNIs in the segment ID pool

   d. 1 per NSX universal controller

Foundation Topics

VXLAN Introduction

Multitier applications have long been designed to use separate Ethernet broadcast domains or virtual local area networks (VLANs) to separate tiers within the application. In a vSphere environment, the number of multitier applications can be quite large, which eats up the number of available VLANs and makes it challenging to scale the virtual environment. For example, if a client has 100 four-tier applications, the client may need 400 separate Ethernet broadcast domains or VLANs to support these applications. Now multiply that by 10 clients. You are basically hitting the limit on how many Ethernet broadcast domains you can support using VLANs. As the virtual machines (VMs) for these applications are distributed among multiple vSphere clusters or even different data centers, the Ethernet broadcast domains must be spanned across the physical network, necessitating the configuration of Spanning Tree Protocol to prevent Ethernet loops.

Virtual Extensible LAN (VXLAN) addresses the Layer 2 scaling challenges in today's data centers by natively allowing for the transparent spanning of millions of distinct Ethernet broadcast domains over any IP physical network or IP transport, reducing VLAN sprawl and thus eliminating the need to enable Ethernet loop-preventing solutions such as Spanning Tree.

VXLAN

VXLAN is an open standard supported by many of the key data center technology companies, such as VMware. VXLAN is a Layer 2 encapsulation technology that substitutes the usage of VLAN numbers to label Ethernet broadcast domains with VXLAN numbers. A traditional Ethernet switch can support up to 2^{12} (4096) Ethernet broadcast domains or VLAN numbers. VXLAN supports 2^{24} Ethernet broadcast domains or VXLAN numbers. That is 16,777,216 Ethernet broadcast domains. A VXLAN number ID is referred to as VNI. There is a one-to-one relationship between an Ethernet broadcast domain and a VNI. A single Ethernet broadcast domain can't have more than one VNI. Two distinct Ethernet broadcast domains can't have the same VNI.

Figure 4-1 shows a traditional design with two ESXi hosts in different racks, each one with a powered on VM. If both VMs need to be in the same Ethernet broadcast domain, the broadcast domain must be spanned, or extended, across all the Ethernet switches shown in the diagram. This makes it necessary for either the Spanning Tree Protocol to be configured in all the Ethernet switches or a more expensive loop-preventing solution such as Transparent Interconnection of Lots of Links

(TRILL) to be deployed. With VXLAN deployed, the ESXi hosts can encapsulate the VM traffic in a VXLAN frame and send it over the physical network, which can be IP-based rather than Ethernet-based, thus removing the need to configure Spanning Tree or deploy solutions such as TRILL.

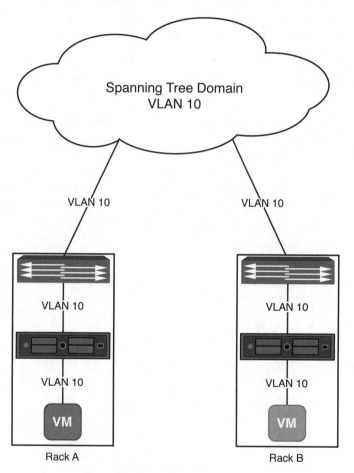

Figure 4-1 Spanning broadcast domain across multiple ESXi racks

Traditionally, any network technology that encapsulates traffic the way VXLAN does is called a *tunnel*. A tunnel hides the original frame's network information from the IP physical network. A good example of a tunnel is Genetic Routing Encapsulation (GRE), which hides Layer 3 and Layer 4 information from IP network devices, although GRE could be set up to also hide Layer 2 information. VXLAN tunnels hide Layer 2, Layer 3, and Layer 4 information. It is possible to deploy a new IP network topology by just using tunnels, without having to do major reconfiguration of the IP physical network. Such a network topology is called an *overlay*, whereas the

IP physical network that switches and routes the tunnels that make up the overlay is called the *underlay*.

Just as GRE requires two devices to create and terminate the tunnel, VXLAN requires two devices to create and terminate VXLAN tunnels. A device that can create or terminate the VXLAN tunnel is called the VXLAN Tunnel Endpoint (VTEP). NSX enables ESXi hosts to have VTEPs. A VTEP performs these two roles:

- Receive Layer 2 traffic from a source, such as a VM, in an Ethernet broadcast domain, encapsulating it within a VXLAN frame and sending it to the destination VTEP.

- Receive the VXLAN frame, stripping the encapsulation to reveal the encapsulated Ethernet frame, and forwarding the frame toward the destination included in the encapsulated Ethernet frame.

Figure 4-2 shows an Ethernet frame from a VM encapsulated in a VXLAN frame. The source VTEP of the VXLAN frame is a VMkernel port in the ESXi host. You can see the encapsulated Ethernet frame, or original frame, and the new header, thus creating the VXLAN overlay.

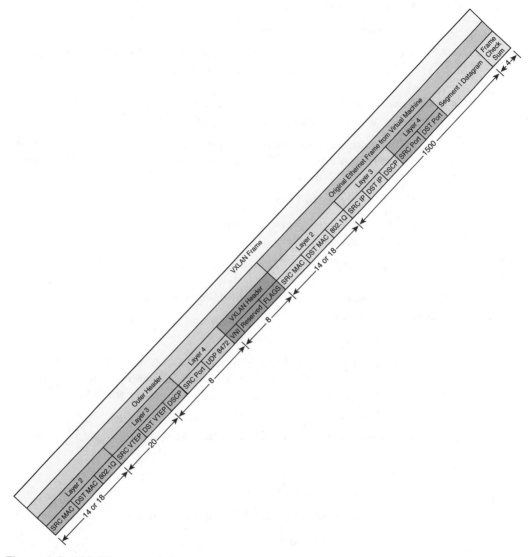

Figure 4-2   VXLAN encapsulation

The VXLAN frame contains the following components:

■ New Layer 2 header distinct from the encapsulated Layer 2 header. This header has new source and destination MAC addresses and a new 802.1Q field.

- This header is 14 bytes long if not using 802.1Q.

- If using 802.1Q, this header is 18 bytes long.

- Class of Service (CoS) markings copied from the original frame's 802.1Q field in the Layer 2 header, if any.

- New Layer 3 header distinct from the encapsulated Layer 3 header. This header has new source and destination IP addresses, including

  - The source and destination IPs are VTEPs. In some cases the destination IP could be a multicast group (we expand further on this during Chapter 5, "NSX Switches").

  - This header is 20 bytes long, with no extensions.

  - DSCP markings, if any, are copied from the encapsulated DSCP files in the Layer 3 header.

  - The *do not fragment (DF) bit* is set to 1.

- New Layer 4 header distinct from the encapsulated Layer 4 header. This header is always UDP.

  - This header is be 8 bytes long.

  - NSX VTEPs use a destination port of 8472. As of April 2013, the standard VXLAN UDP port is 4789. NSX supports changing the UDP port number via the NSX APIs. We cover the NSX APIs in Chapter 18, "NSX Automation."

  - The source port is derived from the encapsulated Layer 4 header.

- New VXLAN header.

  - This header is 8 bytes long.

  - 3 bytes are dedicated for VNI labeling of the tunnel.

  - 4 bytes are reserved for future use.

  - 1 byte is dedicated for flags.

To aggregate a few things stated in the preceding content about VXLAN: Any QoS markings, such as DSCP and CoS from the VM Ethernet frame being encapsulated, are copied to the VXLAN frame, and the destination UDP port of the VXLAN frame is derived from the header information from the encapsulated frame. For this to work, VXLAN has to support virtual guest VLAN Tagging (VGT). Without VGT support, the VM's guest OS couldn't do QoS markings. If the encapsulated frame does not have any QoS markings, none would be copied to the VXLAN frame; however, there is nothing stopping you from adding QoS markings directly to the VXLAN frame.

Then there is the part where the VXLAN frame traverses the physical network, called the *VXLAN underlay* or simply *underlay*. The underlay uses VLANs. It is almost certain that the VXLAN underlay will place the VXLAN frames in their own Ethernet broadcast domain, thus requiring its own VLAN. The VLAN used by the underlay for VXLAN frames is referred to as the *VXLAN VLAN*. If the ESXi host with the source VTEP is connected to a physical switch via a trunk port, the ESXi host could be configured to add a VLAN tag, 802.1Q, to the VXLAN frame or send the VXLAN frame without a VLAN tab, in which case the physical switch's trunk needs to be configured with a native VLAN.

 All this means that VXLAN encapsulation adds 50+ bytes to the original frame from the VM. The 50+ byes come from the following addition:

Original Layer 2 (minus Frame Check Sum) + VXLAN Header + Outer Layer 4 Header + Outer Layer 3 Header

Without Original Frame 802.1Q field: 14 + 8 + 8 + 20 = 50

With Original Frame 802.1Q field: 18 + 8 + 8 + 20 = 54

VMware recommends that the underlay for VXLAN support jumbo frames with an MTU of at least 1600 bytes to support VMs sending frames with the standard 1500 bytes MTU. This includes any routers that are part of the underlay; otherwise, the routers will discard the VXLAN frames when they realize they can't fragment the VXLAN frames with more than 1500 bytes payload. ESXi hosts with VTEPs also configure the VXLAN tunnel with the Do Not Fragment bit, DF, in the IP header of the VXLAN overlay to 1.

Figure 4-3 shows two VMs on the same Ethernet broadcast domain communicating with each other. The two VMs are connected to the same VNI, and the two ESXi hosts have the VTEPs. This diagram does not show the nuances of how the VTEPs know about each other's existence or how they determine where to forward the VXLAN frame. Chapter 5 covers these details in more depth.

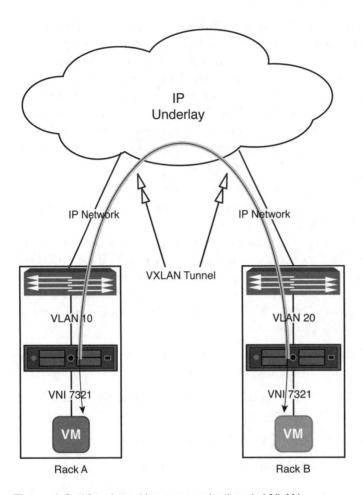

Figure 4-3 Virtual machine communication via VXLAN

NSX Controllers

The NSX Controllers are responsible for most of the control plane. The NSX Controllers handle the Layer 2 control plane for the logical switches, and together with the distributed logical router control virtual machine, the NSX Controllers handle the Layer 3 control plane. We review the role of the Layer 3 control plane and the distributed logical router control virtual machine in Chapter 7, "Logical Router."

For Layer 2, the NSX Controllers have the principal copy of three tables per logical switch, which are used to facilitate control plane decisions by the ESXi host. The three tables are

- **VTEP table**: Principal table that lists all VTEPs that have at least one VM connected to the logical switch. There is one VTEP table per logical switch.

- **MAC table**: Principal table containing the MAC addresses for VMs connected to logical switches as well as any physical end system in the same broadcast domain as the logical switch.

- **ARP table**: Principal table containing the ARP entries for VMs connected to logical switches as well as any physical end system in the same broadcast domain as the logical switch.

For Layer 3, the NSX Controllers have the routing table for each distributed logical router as well as the list of all hosts running a copy of each distributed logical router.

 NSX Controllers do not play any role in security, such as the distributed firewall, nor do they provide control plane services to the NSX Edge Service Gateway.

Deploying NSX Controllers

The NSX Controllers are virtual appliances deployed by the NSX Manager. The NSX Controllers must be deployed in the same vCenter associated with NSX Manager. In our examples from the figures, that would be vCenter-A if the NSX Controller is from NSXMGR-A. At least one NSX Controller must be deployed before logical switches and distributed logical routers can be deployed in an NSX Manager with a Standalone role.

Deploying NSX Controllers might be the most infuriating thing about setting up an NSX environment. I restate some of this in context a little later, but in short if NSX Manager can't establish communication with the NSX Controller after it is deployed, it has the NSX Controller appliance deleted. The process of deploying the NSX Controller can take a few minutes or more, depending on the available resources in the ESXi host where you deploy it and the datastore. If the NSX Controller deployment fails for whatever reason, NSX Manager doesn't attempt to deploy a new one. You can view the NSX Manager's log to find the reason to why the deployment failed and then try again. But you won't be doing much networking with NSX until you get at least one NSX Controller deployed.

Let's now cover the steps to deploying the NSX Controllers, but I wanted to point out this *little* annoyance first. A single NSX Controller is all that is needed to deploy logical switches and distributed logical routers; however for redundancy and failover capability, VMware supports only production environments with three NSX Controllers per standalone NSX Manager. The NSX Controllers can be deployed in separate ESXi clusters as long as

- Each NSX Controller has IP connectivity with NSX Manager, over TCP port 443.

- Each NSX Controller has IP connectivity with each other, over TCP port 443.

- Each NSX Controller has IP connectivity with the management VMkernel port of ESXi hosts that will be part of the NSX domain over TCP port 1234.

The following steps guide you in how to deploy NSX Controllers via the vSphere Web Client. You can also deploy NSX Controllers using the NSX APIs.

You must be an NSX administrator or enterprise administrator to be allowed to deploy NSX Controllers. We cover Role Based Access Control (RBAC), in Chapter 17, "Additional NSX Features."

Step 1. From the Networking and Security home page, select the **Installation** field.

Step 2. Select the **Management** tab.

Step 3. In the NSX Controller Nodes section click the green + icon, as shown in Figure 4-4.

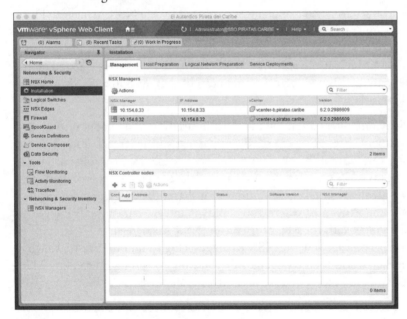

Figure 4-4 Add NSX Controller

Step 4. In the NSX Controller Wizard, select the NSX Manager that would deploy the NSX Controller.

The vSphere Web Client supports multiple vCenters, and thus multiple NSX Managers.

Step 5. Select the data center on which you are adding the NSX Controller.

Step 6.   Select the datastore where the NSX Controller will be deployed.

Step 7.   Select the ESXi cluster or resource pool where the NSX Controller will be deployed.

Step 8.   Optionally, select the ESXi host and folder where the NSX Controller will be deployed. If the ESXi cluster selected in step 5 is configured with DRS with automatic virtual machine placement, you can skip the host selection.

Step 9.   Select the standard portgroup or vDS portgroup where the NSX Controller's management interface will be connected. All communication from the NSX Controller to NSX Manager, other NSX Controllers, and the ESXi hosts will take place over this connection.

Step 10.   Select the pool of IPs from which the NSX Controller will be assigned an IP by the NSX Manager.

   If no IP pool exists, you have the option to create one now. We review the creation of an IP pool later in this chapter.

Step 11.   If this is your first NSX Controller, you need to provide a CLI password, as shown in Figure 4-5. You do not need to provide a password for subsequent NSX Controllers as the NSX Manager automatically assigns them all the same password from the first deployed NSX Controller. The default username of the CLI prompt is **admin**.

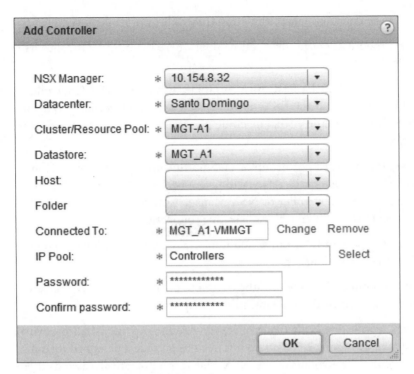

Figure 4-5 Adding first NSX Controller

When NSX Controllers get deployed, they automatically form a cluster among themselves. The first NSX Controller needs to be deployed and have joined the NSX Controller cluster by itself before the other NSX Controllers can be deployed. If you try to deploy a second NSX Controller before the first one is deployed, you get an error message.

When NSX Manager receives the request to deploy an NSX Controller from vCenter, who got it from the vSphere Web Client, or when NSX Manager receives the request via the NSX APIs, the following workflow takes place:

Step 1. NSX Manager gives the NSX Controller off to vCenter to deploy, per your configurations during the Add NSX Controller Wizard. This includes

- The data center, datastore, and cluster/resource pool to place the NSX Controller

- The ovf import specifications, which includes the IP from the IP pool, the private and public certificates for communication back to NSX Manager, and the cluster IP, which is the IP of the first NSX Controller

- A request to place the NSX Controller in the Automatic Startup of the ESXi host

Step 2.   vCenter deploys the NSX Controller, powers it on, and then tells NSX Manager the Controllers are powered on.

Step 3.   NSX Manager makes contact with the NSX Controller.

If NSX Manager cannot establish an IP connection to the NSX Controller to complete its configuration, the NSX Manager has vCenter power off the NSX Controller and delete it.

Verifying NSX Controllers

You can verify the status of the NSX Controller installation by selecting the Installation view from the Networking and Security page, as shown in Figure 4-6.

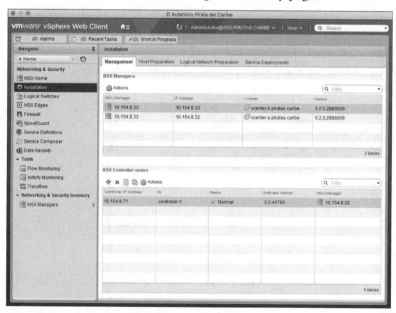

Figure 4-6   An NSX Controller successfully deployed

In this view you can verify the following:

- **Controller IP Address**: The IP address of the NSX Controller. This is one of the IP addresses from the IP pool. Clicking on the controller IP address brings up information about the ESXi host and datastore the NSX Controller is in, as shown in Figure 4-7.

- **ID**: The ID of the NSX Controller. This ID is assigned by the NSX Manager that is communicating with the NSX Controller and has no impact on the role or function of the NSX Controller.

- **Status**: This is the status of the NSX Controller. The statuses we care about are Deploying and Normal.

  - Deploying is self-explanatory.

  - Disconnected means the NSX Manager lost connectivity to the NSX Controller.

  - Normal means the NSX Controller is powered up and NSX Manager has normal operation communication with it.

- **Software Version**: The version of NSX software running in the NSX Controller. The version number is independent of the NSX Manager's version.

- **NSX Manager**: The NSX Manager that is communicating with this NSX Controller. Yes, this is here because a single vSphere Web Client supports multiple vCenters and thus Multiple NSX Managers. If one of the NSX Managers is participating in cross vCenter NSX, a sixth column becomes visible:

- **Managed By**: The IP of the Primary NSX Manager that deployed the NSX Controller.

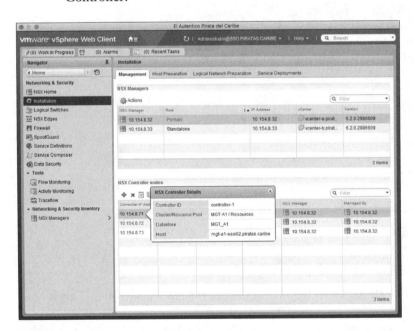

Figure 4-7   NSX Controller details

If you assign a role of Primary to an NSX Manager, the NSX Manager's three NSX Controllers become NSX universal controllers. NSX universal controllers can communicate with Secondary NSX Managers in the same cross vCenter NSX domain as well as Secondary NSX Manager's participating entities such as ESXi hosts. Before you add Secondary NSX Managers, their existing NSX Controllers, if any, must be deleted.

You can also verify the deployment of the NSX Controllers by viewing the NSX Controller virtual machine in the Host and Clusters or VM and Templates view. The NSX Controller is deployed using the name **NSX_Controller_** followed by the NSX Controller's UUID. Figure 4-8 shows the first NSX Controller in the Host and Clusters view. Notice in Figure 4-8 the number of vCPUs, memory, memory reservation, and HDD configured in the NSX Controller.

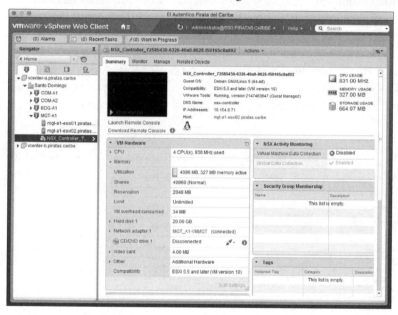

Figure 4-8   NSX Controller's virtual machine Summary view

Each NSX Controller gets deployed with these settings:

- 4 vCPUs
- 4 GB vRAM, with 2 GB reservation
- 20 GB HDD
- 1 vNIC
- VM hardware version 10

VMware does not support changing the hardware settings of the NSX Controllers.

If the NSX Manager is participating in a Secondary role in cross vCenter NSX, the NSX Manager will not have any NSX Controllers of its own. Instead the Secondary NSX Managers create a logical connection to the existing NSX universal controllers from the Primary NSX Manager in the same cross vCenter NSX domain.

Creating an NSX Controller Cluster

When more than one NSX Controller is deployed, the NSX Controllers automatically form a cluster. They know how to find each other because NSX Manager makes them aware of each other's presence. To verify that the NSX Controller has joined the cluster successfully, connect to the NSX Controllers via SSH or console using the username of **admin** and the password you configured during the first NSX Controller deployment. Once logged in the NSX Controller, issue the CLI command **show control-cluster status** to view the NSX Controller's cluster status. You need to do this for each NSX Controller to verify its cluster status. Figure 4-9 shows the output of the command for an NSX Controller that has joined the cluster successfully.

TIP You can use the Tab key to autocomplete CLI commands in NSX Manager and the NSX Controllers.

```
                                          El Autentico Pirata del Caribe
                                     Controller-71.piratas.caribe - PuTTY

nsx-controller # show control-cluster status
Type               Status                                   Since
----------------------------------------------------------------------
Join status:       Join complete                            10/21 04:29:19
Majority status:   Connected to cluster majority            10/21 04:58:16
Restart status:    This controller can be safely restarted  10/21 04:58:05
Cluster ID:        b3f7d956-e177-43b1-aeb8-e5ae8532e67e
Node UUID:         b3f7d956-e177-43b1-aeb8-e5ae8532e67e

Role               Configured status    Active status
----------------------------------------------------------------------
api_provider       enabled              activated
persistence_server enabled              activated
switch_manager     enabled              activated
logical_manager    enabled              activated
directory_server   enabled              activated
nsx-controller #
```

Figure 4-9 Output of **show control-cluster status**

Figure 4-9 depicts the following cluster messages:

- **Join status**: Join complete. This message indicates this NSX Controller has joined the cluster.

- **Majority status**: Connected to cluster majority. This message indicates that this NSX Controller can see the majority of NSX Controllers (counting itself). If this NSX Controller were not connected to the cluster majority, it would remove itself from participation in the control plane until it can see the majority of NSX Controllers again.

- **Restart status**: This controller can be safely restarted.

- **Cluster ID**: {UUID}. This is the Universal Unique ID of the cluster.

- **Node UUID**: {UUID}. This is the Universal Unique ID of this NSX Controller.

The clustering algorithm used by the NSX Controllers depends on each NSX Controller having IP communication with a majority of the NSX Controllers, counting itself. If the NSX Controller does not belong to the majority, or quorum, it removes itself from control plane participation. To avoid a split-brain situation where no NSX Controller is connected to the cluster majority and potentially each one removing itself from control plane participation, VMware requires that three of the NSX Controllers be deployed in production environments.

Figure 4-10 shows the output of the command **show control-cluster startup-nodes**, which shows the NSX Controllers that are known to be cluster members. All NSX Controllers should provide the same output. You can also issue the NSX Manager basic mode command **show controller list all** to list all the NSX Controllers the NSX Manager is communicating with plus their running status.

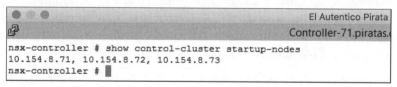

Figure 4-10 Output of **show control-cluster startup-nodes**

Additional CLI commands that could be used in the NSX Controllers to verify cluster functionally and availability are as follows:

- **show control-cluster roles**: Displays which NSX Controller is the master for different roles. We cover roles in the next section.

- **show control-cluster connections**: Displays the port number for the different roles and the number of established connections.

- **show control-cluster management-address**: Displays the IP used by the NSX Controller for management.

We review additional CLI commands in NSX Manager and NSX Controllers related to logical switches and distributed logical routers in Chapter 5 and Chapter 7.

NSX Controller Master and Recovery

When deploying multiple NSX Controllers, the control plane responsibilities for Layer 2 and Layer 3 are shared among all controllers. To determine which portions each NSX Controller handles, the NSX Controllers cluster elects an API provider, Layer 2 and Layer 3 NSX Controller Master. The masters are selected after the cluster is formed. The API provider master receives internal NSX API calls from NSX Manager. The Layer 2 NSX Controller Master assigns Layer 2 control plane responsibility on a per logical switch basis to each NSX Controller in the cluster, including the master. The Layer 3 NSX Controller Master assigns the Layer 3 forwarding table, on a per distributed logical router basis, to each NSX Controller in the cluster, including the master.

The process of assigning logical switches to different NSX Controllers and distributed logical routers to different NSX Controllers is called *slicing*. By doing slicing, the NSX Controller Master for Layer 2 and Layer 3 distributes the load of managing the control plane for logical switches and distributed routers among all the NSX Controllers. No two NSX Controllers share the Layer 2 control plane for a logical switch nor share the Layer 3 control plane for a distributed logical router. Slicing also makes the NSX Layer 2 and Layer 3 control planes more robust and tolerant of NSX Controller failures.

Once the master has assigned Layer 2 and Layer 3 control plane responsibilities, it tells all NSX Controllers about it so all NSX Controllers know what each NSX Controller is responsible for. This information is also used by the NSX Controllers in case the NSX Controller Master becomes unresponsive or fails.

If your NSX environment has only a single distributed logical router and three NSX Controllers, only one of the NSX Controllers would be responsible for the distributed logical router while the other two would serve as backups. No two NSX Controllers are responsible for the Layer 2 control plane of the same logical switch. No two NSX Controllers are responsible for the Layer 3 forwarding table of the same logical router.

When an NSX Controller goes down or becomes unresponsive, the data plane continues to operate; however, the Layer 2 NSX Controller Master splits among the surviving NSX Controllers Layer 2 control plane responsibilities for all the impacted logical switches. The Layer 3 NSX Controller Master splits among all the surviving NSX Controllers Layer 3 control plane responsibilities for all the affected distributed logical routers.

What if the NSX Controller that fails was the master? In this case, the surviving NSX Controllers elect a new master, and the new master then proceeds to recover the control plane of the affected logical switches and/or distributed logical routers. How does the new master determine which logical switches and/or distributed logical routers were affected and need to have their control plane responsibilities reassigned? The new master uses the assignment information distributed to the cluster by the old master.

For Layer 2 control plane, the newly responsible NSX Controller queries the hosts in the transport zone so it can repopulate the logical switch's control plane information. We learn about transport zones later in this chapter. For Layer 3, the newly responsible NSX Controller queries the logical router control virtual machine. We learn about the logical router control virtual machine in Chapter 7.

IP Pools

IP pools are the only means to provide an IP address to the NSX Controllers. IP pools may also be used to provide an IP address to the ESXi hosts during NSX host preparations. We review NSX host preparation later in this chapter in the section "Host Preparation." IP pools are created by an NSX administrator and are managed by NSX Manager. Each NSX Manager manages its own set of IP pools. NSX Manager selects an IP from the IP pool whenever it needs one, such as when deploying an NSX Controller. If the entity using the IP from the IP pool is removed or deleted, NSX Manager places the IP back into the pool. The IPs in the IP pool should be unique in the entire IP network (both physical and virtual).

There are two ways to start the creation of an IP pool. The first method we mentioned during the deployment of the NSX Controllers. This option to create an IP pool is also available during NSX host preparation, which we discuss later in this chapter.

The second method involves the following steps:

Step 1.   Select the **NSX Managers** field in the Networking and Security page.

Step 2.   Select the NSX Manager you want to create an IP pool in.

Step 3.   Select the **Manage** tab.

Step 4.   Select the **Grouping Objects** button.

Step 5.   Select **IP Pools**.

Step 6.   Click the green + icon, as shown in Figure 4-11.

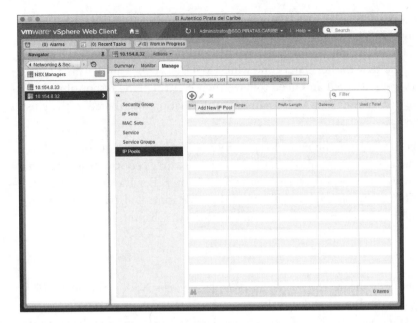

Figure 4-11   Create an IP pool

Regardless of how you choose to create an IP pool, the same IP Pool Wizard comes up, as shown in Figure 4-12.

Add Static IP Pool

| Name: | * | Controllers |
| Gateway: | * | 10.154.8.1 |

A gateway can be any IPv4 or IPv6 address.

Prefix Length:	*	24
Primary DNS:		10.154.8.20
Secondary DNS:		
DNS Suffix:		piratas.caribe
Static IP Pool:	*	10.154.8.71-10.154.8.73

for example 192.168.1.2-192.168.1.100 or abcd:87:87::10-abcd:87:87::20

OK   Cancel

Figure 4-12   IP Pool Wizard

In the IP Pool Wizard, populate the following information:

Step 1.   Give the IP pool a unique name.

Step 2.   Enter the default gateway for this IP pool. This entry cannot be changed once the IP pool is created.

Step 3.   Enter the subnet prefix for the IP pool. For example, enter 24 for a mask for 255.255.255.0.

Step 4.   Optionally, enter the IP of the primary and secondary DNS servers.

Step 5.   Optionally, enter a DNS suffix.

Step 6.   Enter the range of IPs that will be part of this IP pool.

Once an IP pool is created, you can modify or delete it. To make changes to an IP pool, follow these steps:

Step 1.   Return to Object Groupings for the NSX Manager that owns the IP pool.

Step 2.   Select **IP Pools**.

Step 3.   Select the IP pool you want to modify.

Step 4.   Click the **Edit IP Pools** icon.

Step 5.   You can change almost all fields desired, including adding IPs to the pool, except the name and the default gateway fields.

The IP pool's IP range can't be shrunk if at least one IP has already been assigned. An IP pool can't be deleted if at least one IP has been already assigned.

Host Preparation

Now that you deployed your NSX Controllers, it's time to focus on the next steps that must take place before you can start deploying your virtual network and deploying security services. The NSX Controllers can also be deployed *after* host preparation.

The next step is to install the NSX vSphere Infrastructure Bundles (VIBs) in the ESXi hosts that will be in the NSX domain. The VIBs give the ESXi hosts the capability to participate in NSX's data plane and in kernel security. We do this by selecting the Host Preparation tab from the Installation view in the Networking and Security page, as shown in Figure 4-13. An alternative would be to use vSphere ESXi Image Builder to create an image with the NSX VIBs installed.

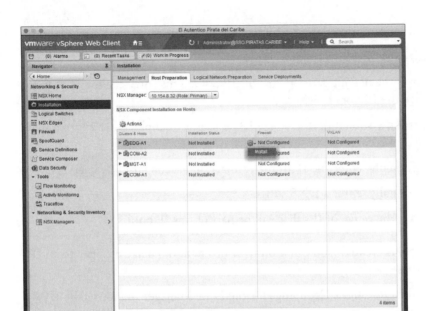

Figure 4-13   Host Preparation tab

In the Host Preparation tab you see a list of all the ESXi host clusters configured in vCenter. Under the Installation Status column, hover toward the right until the mouse is over the cog, click it and select **Install**. That's it. NSX Manager pushes the VIBs to each ESXi host that is in the cluster. Successfully adding the VIBs is non-disruptive, and there is no need to place the ESXi host in maintenance. Yes, I wrote "successfully" because if the VIB installation fails you might need to reboot the ESXi host(s) to complete it, as shown in Figure 4-14. The good thing is that NSX Manager tries to reboot the ESXi host for you, first putting in Maintenance mode. The moral of this: Don't execute any type of infrastructure changes or upgrades outside of a maintenance window. You would also need to reboot the ESXi host if you wanted to remove the NSX VIBs.

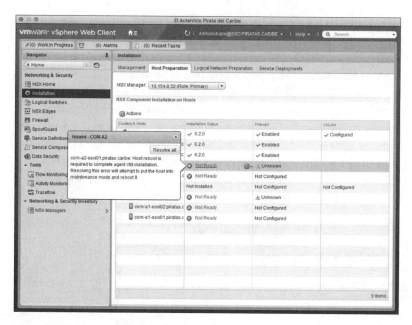

Figure 4-14 Incomplete NSX VIB installation

So what superpowers exactly are these VIBs giving the ESXi hosts? The modules and the over-and-above human capabilities they give the ESXi hosts are as follows:

- **The VXLAN module**: Enables the ESXi host to have logical switches. We discuss logical switching in Chapter 5.

- **The Switch Security (SwSec) module**: It is the logical switch's assistant. It is a dvFilter that sits in Slot 1 of the IOChain and helps with Layer 2 broadcast suppression.

- **The Routing module**: Enables the ESXi host to run distributed logical routers. We review distributed logical routers in Chapter 7.

- **The distributed firewall**: Enables the ESXi host to do Layer 2, Layer 3, and Layer 4 security in kernel. It also allows the ESXi host to leverage, out of network, additional security services. We start the conversation about the distributed firewall and security in Chapter 15, "Distributed Logical Firewall."

Any other superpowers? Well, maybe this can be considered as a superpower: If you add an ESXi host to a cluster that has already been prepared, the ESXi host gets the NSX VIBs automatically. How about that for cool?! And before I forget, installing the VIBs takes minimal time. Even in my nested-ESXi-hosts running lab with scant available CPU, memory, and an NFS share that is slower at delivering I/O than a delivery pigeon, the VIBs install quickly.

Figure 4-15 shows the ESXi host clusters that have been prepared with version 6.2.0 of the NSX VIBs by NSMGR-A, 10.154.8.32. Have a look at the two columns to the right, the Firewall and VXLAN columns. The Firewall module has its own column because it can be installed independently from the other modules. The VIB that has the Firewall module is called VSFWD. If the Firewall status reads Enabled, with the green check mark, you could go over to the Firewall view of Networking and Security, where the distributed firewall policies get created and applied, or the Service Composer view of Networking and Security, where service chaining is configured, to start creating and applying security rules for VMs. The distributed firewall VIB for NSX 6.0 can be installed with ESXi hosts running version 5.1 or higher. For NSX 6.1 and higher, the ESXi hosts must run 5.5 or higher.

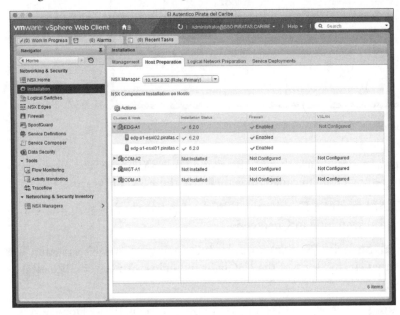

Figure 4-15   Host Preparation tab after NSX modules have been installed

The VXLAN column confirms the installation of the VXLAN VIB. The VXLAN VIB has the VXLAN module, the Security module, and the Routing module. If the column reads **Not Configured** with a hyperlink, the VXLAN VIB is installed. The VXLAN VIB can be installed with ESXi hosts running version 5.1 or higher; however, with version 5.1 ESXi hosts logical switches can only be deployed in Multicast Replication Mode. We cover Replication Mode in Chapter 5. For NSX 6.1 and higher, the ESXi hosts must run 5.5 or higher. The Routing module only works in ESXi hosts running vSphere 5.5 or higher. Table 4-2 shows the vSphere and vCenter version supported by each module.

Table 4-2   vSphere Versions Supported by the NSX Modules

NSX Modules	vSphere Version
Security	5.1 or later
VXLAN	5.1 (only for Multicast Replication Mode) and later
Routing	5.5 or later

Host Configuration

If you want to deploy logical switches, you must complete the Logical Network Preparation tab in the Installation view. In this section you set up an NSX domain with the variables needed to create VXLAN overlays. Three sections need to be configured. If you skip any of them, you are not going to be deploying logical switches.

First, you need to tell NSX Manager how to configure the ESXi hosts. Oddly enough, you don't start the logical network configuration from the Logical Network Preparation tab. Rather, click the **Configure** hyperlink in the VXLAN column in the Host Preparation tab to open the Configure VXLAN Networking Wizard. Optionally, hover toward the right and click on the cog to see a menu list and choose **Configure VXLAN**, as shown in Figure 4-16.

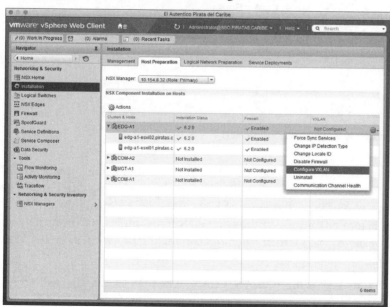

Figure 4-16   VXLAN host configuration

Figure 4-17 shows the Configure VXLAN Networking window. Here we can configure the following:

- The vDS where the new VXLAN VMkernel portgroup will be created.

- The IP ESXi hosts will use as their VTEP. A new VMkernel port gets created for this, typically referred to as the VXLAN VMkernel port, and it is this VMkernel port that is the VTEP. Since the ESXi host owns the VXLAN VMkernel port, it is common practice to refer to the ESXi host as the VTEP itself. Moving forward, from time to time I refer to both the ESXi hosts and the VXLAN VMkernel ports as VTEPs.

- The number of VXLAN VMkernel ports, per ESXi hosts, that will be configured. Each VXLAN VMkernel port will have a different IP.

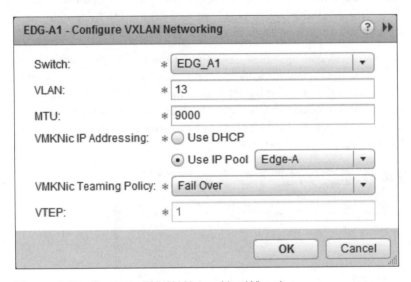

Figure 4-17   Configure VXLAN Networking Wizard

All ESXi hosts, per host cluster, must be in the same vDS that will be used by NSX for host configuration. NSX can work with different clusters having different vDSes. This has zero impact on the performance of VMs in the NSX domain. If running a vSphere version before 6.0, not using the same vDS across multiple clusters may impact the capability of vMotion virtual machines connecting to logical switches. We touch on this topic in Chapter 5.

The VLAN in Figure 4-17 is the VXLAN VLAN. The vDS switch selected in Figure 4-17 will be used by NSX Manager to create a portgroup for the VXLAN VMkernel port and portgroups to back the logical switches, which we cover in Chapter 5. All these portgroups will be configured by NSX Manager with the VXLAN VLAN. If the MTU configured is larger than the MTU already configured in the vDS, the vDS's MTU will be updated. The vDS that gets assigned to the cluster for VXLAN may also continue to be used for other non-NSX connectivity, such as a portgroup for vMotion.

You can assign an IP address to the VXLAN VMkernel port by using DHCP or an IP pool. In both cases, the VXLAN VMkernel port would be getting a default gateway. This would typically present a problem for the ESXi host since it already has a default gateway, most likely pointing out of the management VMkernel port. Luckily for NSX, vSphere has supported multiple TCP/IP stacks since version 5.1. In other words, the ESXi host can now have multiple default gateways. The original default gateway, oddly enough referred to as *default*, would still point out of the management VMkernel port, or wherever you originally had it configured for. The new default gateway, which you probably correctly guessed is referred to as VXLAN, would point out of the VXLAN VMkernel port. The VXLAN TCP/IP stack default gateway and the VXLAN VMkernel port will only be used for the creation and termination of VXLAN overlays. Figure 4-18 shows the VMkernel ports of an ESXi host, with only the VXLAN VMkernel port using the VXLAN TCP/IP stack.

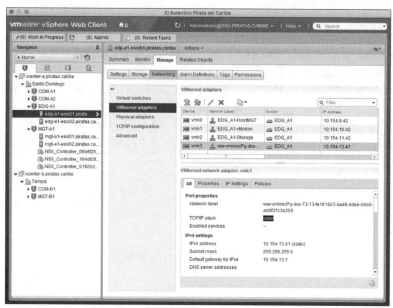

Figure 4-18   VXLAN VMkernel port with VXLAN TCP/IP stack

One final thing you can configure here is the VMKNic Teaming Policy, a name I'm not too fond of. Why couldn't they name it VXLAN Load Share Policy? After all, this is how the vDS load shares egress traffic from the VXLAN VMkernel port. Anyhow, the selection you make here has great implications for the behavior of your VXLAN overlays. For one, the policy must match the configuration of the physical switches to which the vDS uplinks connect, which means the vDS must also be configured to match the selected policy, such as enhanced LACP.

These are the VMKNic Teaming Policy options available:

- Fail over
- Static EtherChannel
- Enhanced LACP
- Load Balance – SRCID
- Load Balance – SRCMAC

Go back and have a look at Figure 4-17. Do you see the VTEP field at the bottom? It says 1, meaning 1 VXLAN VMkernel port is created for each ESXi host in the cluster being configured. Where did the 1 come from? NSX Manager put it there. Notice the text box for the 1 is grayed out, which means you can't edit it. And how did NSX Manager know to put a 1 in there? Go back to the VMKNic Teaming Policy selection. If you choose anything other than Load Balance – SRCID or Load Balance – SRCMAC, NSX Manager puts a 1 in the VTEP text box.

If, on the other hand, you choose VMKNic Teaming Policy of Load Balance – SRCID or Load Balance – SRCMAC, NSX Manager creates multiple VXLAN VMkernel ports, one per dvUplink in the vDS. Now that the ESXi hosts have multiple VXLAN VMkernel ports, load sharing can be achieved on a per VM basis by pinning each VM to a different VXLAN VMkernel port and mapping each VXLAN VMkernel port to a single dvUplink in the vDS. Figure 4-19 shows the configured ESXi hosts with multiple VXLAN VMkernel ports.

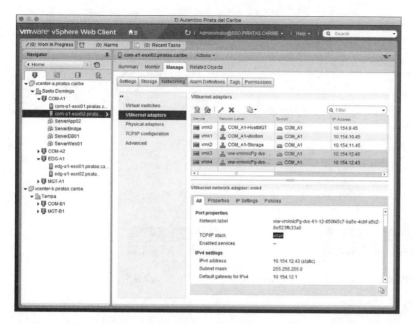

Figure 4-19   ESXi hosts with multiple VTEPs

Figure 4-20 shows the logical/physical view of two ESXi hosts, each with two dvUp-links, two VMs, and two VTEPs. The VMs are connected to logical switches.

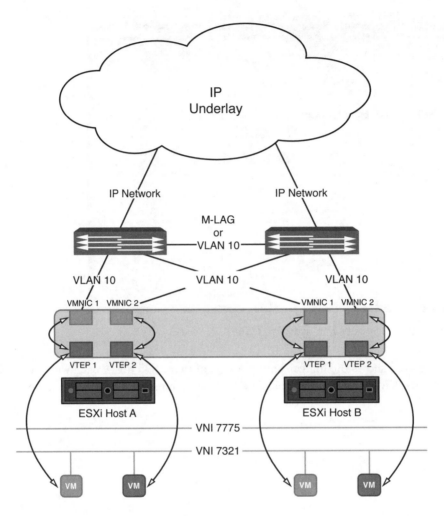

Figure 4-20 Logical/physical view of ESXi hosts with two VTEPs

Table 4-3 shows the VMKNic Teaming Policy options, the multi-VTEP support, how they match to the vDS Teaming modes, and the minimum vDS version number that supports the teaming policy.

Table 4-3 VMKNic Teaming Policies

Key Topic Element	Multi-VTEP Support	vDS Teaming Mode	vDS Version
Fail Over	No	Failover	5.1 or later
Static EtherChannel	No	Ether Channel	5.1 or later
Enhanced LACP	No	LACPv2	5.5 and later

Key Topic Element	Multi-VTEP Support	vDS Teaming Mode	vDS Version
Load Balance - SRCID	Yes	Source Port	5.5 and later
Load Balance - SRCMAC	Yes	Source MAC (MAC Hash)	5.5 and later

Now why would NSX Manager allow the option of multiple VTEPs in the same ESXi host? It allows the option because there is no other good way to load share, yes *load share*, egress traffic sourced from an ESXi host if the load sharing hash is using the source interface (SRCID) or the source MAC (SRCMAC). I won't spend too long explaining why NSX Manager achieves the load sharing the way it does. I would just say, think of how the physical network would react if the source MAC in egress frames from the ESXi host were seen in more than one discrete dvUplink from the same ESXi host.

After you finish the Configure VXLAN Networking Wizard, you can go over to the Logical Network Preparation tab to verify the configuration. Figure 4-21 shows the VXLAN Transport section listing the ESXi hosts that have been configured and the details of their configuration.

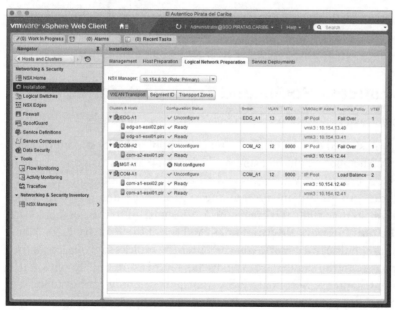

Figure 4-21   ESXi host clusters that have been configured for VXLAN

In the Network view of vCenter, you can verify that the portgroup was created for connecting the VXLAN VMkernel port. Figure 4-22 shows the VXLAN VLAN for the EDG-A1 host cluster, 13, is configured in the portgroup. Notice that there are other portgroups in the same vDS. If you were to look at the vDS configuration, you would see the MTU is set to at least the size you configured in Configure VX-LAN networking.

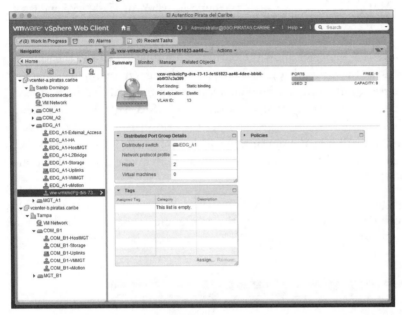

Figure 4-22   VXLAN vDS

VNI Pools, Multicast Pools, and Transport Zones

You need to undertake two more preparations for the NSX networks.

The first thing you should do is provide the range or pool of VNIs and multicast groups that NSX Manager would be using for its local use as well as do the same for cross vCenter NSX use. Local VNI pools and universal VNI pools shouldn't overlap. Local multicast groups and universal multicast groups shouldn't overlap either. The VNI pool can start at 5000. To create the VNI pools, go to the Segment ID section of the Logical Network Preparation tab and select the Primary NSX Manager. If you require multicast support, you can enter the multicast group pools for NSX Manager to use in the same place. We discuss multicast in the "Replication Mode" section of Chapter 5. Secondary NSX Managers can only configure local VNI and multicast group pools.

The second thing you should do is create global transport zones, at least one per NSX Manager, and a universal transport zone. When a logical switch is created, NSX Manager needs to know which ESXi hosts in the NSX domain have to be informed about the logical switch. The global transport zone is a group of ESXi host clusters under the same NSX domain that would be told about the creation of logical switches. Global transport zone only includes ESXi host clusters local to a vCenter. The universal transport zone is a group of ESXi host clusters under the same cross vCenter NSX domain that would be told about the creation of universal logical switches. Universal transport zones may include ESXi host clusters in all vCenters in the same cross vCenter NSX domain. The logical switch's global transport zone assignment and a universal logical switch's universal transport zone assignment are done during the creation of the switches.

NOTE   For the rest of the book, when I refer to *transport zone*, my comment applies to both the global transport zone and the universal transport zone.

A transport zone can contain as many clusters as you want. An ESXi host cluster can be in as many transport zones as you want, and it can belong to both types of transport zones at the same time. And yes, you can have as many global transport zones as your heart desires, although you typically don't deploy more than one or two per NSX Manager. However, you can only have a single universal transport zone. More importantly, both types of transport zones can have ESXi host clusters each with a different vDS selected during Configure VXLAN networking. Again, transport zones matter only for the purpose of letting the NSX Manager know which ESXi hosts should be told about a particular logical switch or universal logical switch.

To create a transport zone, head over to the Logical Network Preparation tab, select the NSX Manager that will own the transport zone, and go to the Transport Zones section. There, click the green + sign. There you can assign the transport zone a name, select its Replication Mode, and choose the ESXi host clusters that will be part of the transport zone. If the NSX Manager is the Primary NSX Manager, you have a check box to turn this transport zone into a universal transport zone, as shown in Figure 4-23.

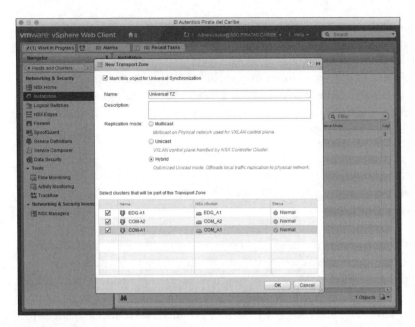

Figure 4-23   Creating a transport zone

As mentioned, Chapter 5 discusses what Replication Mode is. For now, you should know that if you select **Multicast** or **Hybrid** you need to create a multicast group pool in the Segment ID section mentioned previously. Finally, after a transport zone is created, you can't change the transport zone type. However, you can modify it by adding or removing ESXi host clusters from the NSX Manager that owns the association to the vCenter that owns those clusters. If an NSX switch (a logical switch or a universal logical switch) has already been created before the ESXi host cluster is added to the transport zone, NSX Manager automatically updates the newly added ESXi hosts in the ESXi host cluster with the NSX switch information.

To add an ESXi host cluster in a transport zone, return to the Transport Zone section of the Logical Network Preparation tab and select the NSX Manager that prepared the ESXi host cluster that will be added. Select the Transport Zone and click the Connect Clusters icon. Select the ESXi host clusters you want to add and click **OK**.

To remove an ESXi host cluster from a transport zone, select the transport zone in the Transport Zones section and select the Disconnect Clusters icon. Select the ESXi host clusters you want to remove and click **OK**. For the operation to succeed, all VMs (powered on or not) in the ESXi host you want to remove must be disconnected from all logical switches that belong to the transport zone. We cover how to disconnect a VM from a logical switch in Chapter 5.

A transport zone that has any logical switches can't be deleted. The logical switches must be deleted first. We cover how to delete logical switches in Chapter 5. To delete a transport zone, select the transport zone, then select **Actions**, **All NSX User Interface Plugin Actions**, and then select **Remove**.

One more note on this section. It should be clear by now that NSX Manager *loves* ESXi host clusters. If you add an ESXi host to an already prepared and configured ESXi host cluster, NSX Manager would make sure that the ESXi host gets the NSX VIBs, the VXLAN VMkernel ports get created with the right IP and subnets, and make the new ESXi host aware of any logical switches, and so forth. On the reverse, if you remove an ESXi host from an already prepared and configured ESXi host cluster, the ESXi host would lose its VXLAN VMkernel ports and IPs, and lose knowledge of any logical switches.

That wraps up all the prep work that needs to be done to get your NSX network and security going. The next chapter begins the coverage of the process of actually building stuff that you can put virtual machines on.

Exam Preparation Tasks

Review All the Key Topics

Review the most important topics from inside the chapter, noted with the Key Topic icon in the outer margin of the page. Table 4-4 lists these key topics and the page numbers where each is found.

Table 4-4 Key Topics for Chapter 4

Key Topic Element	Description	Page Number
Paragraph	Define what VXLAN is and the scaling capabilities native to the protocol.	90
List	VXLAN frame inherits Layer 2 and Layer 3 QoS from the encapsulated frame. The source UDP port is derived from the encapsulated frame.	93
Paragraph	VXLAN requires jumbo frame support from the underlay.	95
Paragraph	The NSX Controllers maintain the principle copies of the VTEP, MAC, and ARP tables.	96
Paragraph	NSX Controllers have no role in Network Security	97
Paragraph	The user must have the correct administrator account to deploy NSX Controllers.	98
Paragraph	Changing the NSX Controllers's hardware settings is not supported by VMware.	103
Paragraph	Secondary NSX Managers do not deploy NSX Controllers	104
Paragraph	VMware requires three NSX Controllers in a production deployment of NSX.	105
Paragraph	The NSX Controller taking over for a failed one queries the ESXi hosts in the VTEP table.	105
Table 4-2	The versions of vSphere supported by the NSX modules.	113
Paragraph	All members of the ESXi host cluster must belong to the same vDS for NSX host preparation.	114
Paragraph	NSX supports multiple VTEPs per ESXi host.	116
Paragraph	Each NSX Manager in the cross vCenter NSX domain is responsible for adding clusters to the universal transport zone.	122
Paragraph	NSX Manager only interacts with ESXi hosts that are members of clusters.	123

Complete Tables and Lists from Memory

Download and print a copy of Appendix C, "Memory Tables" (found on the book's website), or at least the section for this chapter, and complete the tables and lists from memory. Appendix D, "Memory Tables Answer Key," also on the website, includes the completed tables and lists so you can check your work.

Define Key Terms

Define the following key terms from this chapter, and check your answers in the Glossary:

VXLAN, VTEP, VNI, NSX Controller Master, VXLAN module, Routing module, Distributed Firewall module, transport zone, slicing

This chapter covers all or part of the following VCP6-NV exam blueprint topics:

- **Objective 5.1**—Create and Administer Logical Switches

- **Objective 5.2**—Configure VXLAN

- **Objective 8.1**—Differentiate Single and Cross-vCenter NSX Deployments

- **Objective 8.2**—Determine Cross-vCenter Requirements and Configurations

CHAPTER 5

NSX Switches

Your team is in charge of the vSphere environment at your company. Your company has experienced substantial growth over the last two quarters, and forecasts show the growth will continue at the same rate over the next four quarters. You have been tasked to prepare the IT infrastructure to allow for the quick expansion of existing Ethernet broadcast domains to support the virtual machines (VMs) that will be deployed in support of your company's phenomenal growth. Making frequent changes to the physical networks is not a viable alternative. So what options do you have? NSX switches.

NSX switches allow for the extension of Ethernet broadcast domains over any IP network without requiring any configuration changes to that network (beyond those discussed in Chapter 2, "Network and VMware vSphere Requirements for NSX," and Chapter 4, "VXLAN, NSX Controllers, and NSX Preparation"). This chapter goes deeper into the two types of NSX switches, the logical switch and the universal logical switch, and what all the fuss about them is. Hint: The fuss is warranted.

Do I Know This Already?

The "Do I Know This Already?" quiz allows you to assess whether you should read this entire chapter or simply jump to the "Exam Preparation Tasks" section for review. If you are in doubt, read the entire chapter. Table 5-1 outlines the major headings in this chapter and the corresponding "Do I Know This Already?" quiz questions. You can find the answers in Appendix A, "Answers to the 'Do I Know This Already?' Quizzes."

Table 5-1   Headings and Questions

Foundation Topic Section	Questions Covered in This Section
Logical Switches	1-2
VTEP Table	3
MAC Table	4
ARP Table	5
Unknown Unicast or ARP Request	6-7
Replication Mode	8-10

1. Which statement is true regarding logical switches?

   a. A global logical switch supports a single VXLAN network ID.

   b. A universal logical switch supports all the broadcast domains in a cross vCenter NSX domain.

   c. A universal logical switch supports up to 64 ESXi hosts.

   d. Global logical switches have their own VXLAN table.

2. How many logical switches may be deployed in an NSX domain?

   a. 1

   b. 4095

   c. 10,000

   d. 16,777,216

3. Which two entries are not present in the VTEP table? (Choose two.)

   a. The VTEP IP

   b. The VTEP subnet mask

   c. The VTEP MAC address

   d. The ESXi host management IP

4. How does a universal logical switch learn the MAC address assigned by the ESXi host to a connected vNIC of a virtual machine?

   a. Via MAC learning. The logical switch reads the source MAC address of frames sent by the virtual machine.

   b. From the NSX universal controller. The NSX Controller updates the logical switch with the MAC address of the virtual machine.

   c. From the vmx file. The logical switch reads the MAC address of the virtual machine by looking in the virtual machine's vmx file.

   d. From the Primary NSX Manager. NSX Manager obtains virtual machine MAC addresses from vCenter and then updates the logical switch.

5. Which entity populates the ARP table?

   a. The distributed firewall.

   b. The NSX Controller.

   c. The universal logical switch.

   d. The Security module.

6. What action does a logical switch take if it receives a non-ARP broadcast when configured with Hybrid Replication Mode?

   a. The logical switch sends a multicast to all ESXi hosts in the NSX domain.

   b. The logical switch sends a multicast to all ESXi hosts in the global transport zone.

    c. The logical switch sends a broadcast to all ESXi hosts in the same VTEP subnet.

    d. The logical switch sends a unicast to all proxy VTEPs.

7. What two actions does a universal logical switch take if it receives an unknown unicast when configured with Unicast Replication Mode? (Choose two.)

    a. The universal logical switch sends a multicast to all ESXi hosts in the NSX domain.

    b. The universal logical switch sends a MAC table query to the NSX universal controller responsible for the universal logical switch where the frame was received.

    c. The universal logical switch sends a multicast to all ESXi hosts in the universal transport zone.

    d. The universal logical switch sends a unicast to all ESXi hosts in the same VTEP subnet.

8. In what two locations is the Replication Mode configured for a logical switch? (Choose two.)

    a. In NSX Manager

    b. In the NSX Controller

    c. In the global transport zone

    d. In the logical switch

9. What is an advantage of Multicast Replication Mode?

    a. Each VTEP has a list of all VTEPs with powered on virtual machines.

    b. The underlay does not have to be configured with multicast.

    c. The source VTEP only sends one replication VXLAN frame.

    d. The NSX Controller communicates with ESXi hosts in the VTEP table via multicast.

10. What is a disadvantage of Unicast Replication Mode?

    a. If the MAC table is large, the source VTEP will drop the BUM.

    b. If the VTEP table is large, the source VTEP will have to send many replication VXLAN frames.

    c. If the VTEP table is large, the source VTEP will drop the BUM.

    d. If the MAC table is large, the source VTEP will only send the replication VXLAN frame if the underlay is configured for multicast.

Foundation Topics

Logical Switches

Simply stated, a global logical switch and a universal logical switch are virtual switches that are distributed and use VXLAN Network Identifiers (VNIs) instead of VLAN numbers to label Ethernet broadcast domains. The ESXi host running a virtual machine connected to a global logical switch or a universal logical switch has the source VXLAN Tunnel End Point (VTEP) for any Layer 2 traffic from the virtual machine with a destination MAC address residing in a different VTEP. Both the global logical switch and the universal logical switch support a single Ethernet broadcast domain, which means they both support only a single VNI. Because of the one-to-one relation between the logical switch and the assigned VNI, the names *logical switch* and *VNI* are often used interchangeably.

You might have noticed from this first paragraph that the global logical switch and the universal logical switch seem to have the same feature. That is because they are almost identical with respect to what they are and what they support. The only difference between a global logical switch and the universal logical switch is the transport zone. Global logical switches are the NSX switches belonging to a global transport zone. Universal logical switches are the NSX switches belonging to the universal transport zone. For the rest of this chapter, I simply refer to both of them as logical switches except where I need to make a point or clarify a feature.

Because the logical switch is distributed in nature, NSX Manager owns the management plane of the logical switch (and the Primary NSX Manager for the universal logical switch), while each ESXi host owns its own data plane for the logical switch. The NSX Controllers, or NSX universal controllers, handle most of the control plane for the logical switches. The ESXi hosts with VMs connected to a logical switch handle the control plane for those VMs.

The ESXi host's local copies of the MAC tables contain the MAC addresses of all locally running VMs, per logical switch. The MAC tables also have any remote MAC addresses from any active flows in the logical switch where one of its VMs is the destination. If the logical switch does not see activity from the remote MAC address for more than five minutes, the logical switch in the ESXi host flushes the MAC entry from the MAC table. In other words: The logical switch in the ESXi host does MAC learning for external sources.

So what is MAC learning? It is what physical switches have been doing for the last 30 years or so. For every ingress Ethernet frame from the overlay that is processed by the logical switch in an ESXi host, the logical switch reads the source MAC address. If the source MAC address is not in the logical switch's MAC table, the logical switch adds it to its MAC table. If the source MAC address is in the logical switch's MAC table but it arrived at the logical switch via a path different from what is in the MAC table, the logical switch updates the path in the MAC table. Table 5-2 shows the MAC table of ESXi host C4-H4 with a logical switch with VNI 7321.

Table 5-2   Logical Switch 7321's MAC Table in an ESXi Host C4-H4

VNI	Inner MAC	Outer MAC	Outer IP
7321	00:AB:BB:CC:CC:D1	00:73:21:09:0A:38	10.41.10.56
7321	00:EE:FF:AB:CD:C1	ff:ff:ff:ff:ff:ff	10.42.11.52
7321	00:73:21:BB:77:75	00:73:21:09:0A:33	10.42.10.51

The output of Table 5-2 was obtained from the NSX Manager privilege CLI command **show logical-switch host** [*host-id*] **vni 7321 mac**. The same output may be obtained directly from the ESXi host by using the command **esxcli network vswitch dvs vmware vxlan network mac list --vds-name=**[*vDS used by VXLAN*] **--vxlan-id=7321**. I reformatted the output into a table and added the VNI column (it is not part of the actual output) to make it easier to read. The Inner MAC column is the MAC address of the remote entity (the learned MAC address). The Outer MAC column is the MAC address of the destination MAC of the VXLAN frame created to forward traffic to the Inner MAC. The Outer IP is the destination IP of the VXLAN frame (the destination VTEP). If the Outer IP is in a different subnet from the source Outer IP (source VTEP), then the Inner MAC address is listed as all Fs. All Fs tells the source VTEP to use its VXLAN TCP/IP stack default gateway to reach the Outer IP.

The logical switch does not, by default, do MAC learning for traffic sourced directly from connected VMs. Instead, the logical switch learns the VM's MAC address from the vmx file of the VM. This default behavior can be changed in the logical switch.

Creating a Logical Switch

Logical switches are created via the NSX Manager that owns the transport zone where the logical switch will be added. Logical switches may be created via the vSphere Web Client or by using the NSX APIs. Either way, you must be an NSX enterprise or NSX administrator to create a logical switch.

Global logical switches must be assigned to a global transport zone at the time of creation. Universal logical switches must be assigned to the universal transport zone at the time of creation. A few paragraphs ago I stated that logical switches are a type of distributed switch. In reality, logical switches are represented, or backed, at the

ESXi host by a dvPortgroup in the vDS assigned to each NSX cluster during logical network preparation, covered in Chapter 4.

Being backed by a dvPortgroup has implications for the number of logical switches that can be deployed in the NSX domain and how big a Segment ID pool can be. Each vCenter can support a maximum of 10,000 dvPortgroups; therefore, the maximum number of logical switches that can be deployed in an NSX domain (global logical switches and universal logical switches combined) is also 10,000. It should be stressed that if vCenter was able to support 16,777,216 dvPortgroups, that's how many logical switches would be supported in the NSX domain or Cross vCenter NSX domain.

The steps to create a logical switch via the vSphere Web Client are as follows:

Step 1.   From the Networking and Security page, select **Logical Switches**.

Step 2.   Select the NSX Manager where you are creating the logical switch.

If creating a universal logical switch, select the Primary NSX Manager.

Step 3.   Click the green + icon and wait for the Logical Switch Wizard to open, as shown in Figure 5-1.

Step 4.   Assign a name to the logical switch. Two logical switches can't have the same name.

Step 5.   Select the Transport Zone for the logical switch.

Select the Global Transport Zone to make this a global logical switch.

Select the Universal Transport Zone for cross vCenter NSX to make this a universal logical switch.

Multiple global logical switches can be in the same global transport zone.

Multiple universal logical switches can be in the same universal transport zone.

Step 6.   Optionally, choose a Replication Mode if you want it to be different from the one configured in the transport zone. We talk more about Replication Mode later in this chapter.

Step 7.   Optionally, check the **Enable MAC Learning** box. This enables MAC learning for traffic coming from virtual machines.

You should only enable this feature if you will have VMs sourcing traffic using a MAC different from the one in the vmx file, such as Security Appliances (IPS/IDS), Guess OS MAC Cloning, and so on.

Step 8.   Click **OK**.

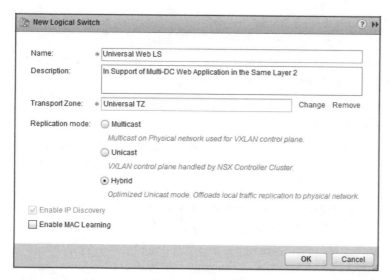

Figure 5-1   New Logical Switch Wizard

If you create the global logical switch via the vSphere Web Client, the vSphere Web Client passes along the request to vCenter, which forwards it to the corresponding NSX Manager. If you create the global logical switch via the NSX APIs, then NSX Manager gets the request directly. If creating a universal logical switch via the vSphere Web Client, the vSphere Web Client passes the request to the vCenter of the Primary NSX Manager, which then passes it along to the Primary NSX Manager.

Regardless of how NSX Manager gets the request, the following workflow takes place:

Step 1.   If creating a global logical switch, NSX Manager selects a VNI from the Segment ID pool created during Segment ID preparation, reviewed in Chapter 4.

If needed, NSX Manager selects a multicast group from the Multicast pool created during Segment ID preparation.

If this is a universal logical switch, the Primary NSX Manager selects a VNI from the Universal Segment ID pool and a multicast group from the Universal Multicast pool. These would be shared via NSX universal synchronization with the Secondary NSX Managers.

Step 2.   NSX Manager looks up the cluster membership of the transport zone where the logical switch is created to obtain the list of vDSes that will be supporting the logical switch.

These are the same vDSes you configured in the VXLAN transport configuration during logical network preparation in chapter 4.

Step 3.   NSX Manager requests its vCenter to create a dvPortgroup for each vDS obtained from the transport zone.

- NSX Manager provides the VNI and multicast group (if any) to vCenter as OpaqueNetworks.

- OpaqueNetwork is a managed object of the vDS that allows for non-vSphere network features (managed by a non-vSphere entity) to be included in a dvPortgroup.

- The dvPortgroup name format for a logical switch is *vxw-dvs-[vds MOID]-universalwire-#-sid-[logical switch VNI]-[logical switch name]*.

- For a universal logical switch, this step 3 is done by each NSX Manager in the cross vCenter NSX domain. The Primary NSX Manager only talks to its own vCenter.

Step 4.   vCenter creates the dvPortgroup(s) and pushes the new group information to all of its ESXi hosts that belong to the corresponding vDS, including the OpaqueNetwork parameters.

These dvPortgroups have the same VLAN as the VXLAN VLAN and the same VMKnic Teaming Policy configured during host preparation.

When the ESXi hosts receive the OpaqueNetwork VXLAN parameters (VNI, multicast), they automatically start using the VXLAN VIB to process traffic in these dvPortgroups.

Step 5.   If the Replication Mode is not multicast, the NSX Manager informs the NSX Controllers about the new logical switch.

This communication takes place with the NSX Controller API provider master, which then passes this information to the NSX Controller L2 master.

In there is a universal logical switch, only the Primary NSX Manager informs the universal NSX Controllers.

Step 6.   The NSX Controller L2 master does some slicing and selects one of the NSX Controllers to be responsible for the new logical switch.

This information is replicated among all NSX Controllers (three of them). Any of the NSX Controllers can respond to requests for this information.

Step 7. If the Replication Mode is not multicast, the ESXi hosts in the transport zone send a request to any of the NSX Controllers to find out the NSX Controller responsible for the logical switch.

For universal logical switches, all ESXi hosts in the universal transport zone send the request to the NSX universal controllers. Remember that only the Primary NSX Manager has any NSX Controllers in cross vCenter NSX.

In step 3, notice the name of the dvPortgroup backing the logical switch includes the vDS *MOID*. The managed object ID (MOID) is a unique identifier used by vCenter to track vSphere objects in its database. vCenter assigns each vDS its own MOID. If multiple vDSes are part of the transport zone, the dvPortgroups backing the logical switch each have a different name. vMotion is a vCenter feature and prior to vSphere 6.0 it required the source and destination dvPortgroups to have the same name. Thus prior to vSphere 6.0 vMotion wouldn't work for a VM connected to a logical switch if the destination ESXi host had the logical switch backed by a different vDS dvPortgroup. As of vSphere 6.0, vMotion supports migrations to different vdPortgroups names, including those dvPortgroups backing logical switches.

Verifying Logical Switches

Once the logical switch has been created, you see the new logical switch listed in the Logical Switches view of the Networking and Security page, as shown in Figure 5-2. In this view, you can see the logical switch name, the transport zone to which it belongs, the VNI that has been assigned, and if applicable the multicast group assigned to it. In the Scope column, you can verify whether the logical switch is a global logical switch or a universal logical switch.

You can also verify the dvPortgroups backing the logical switch by going to the vSphere Web Client home page, selecting the **Network** view and expanding each vDS that belongs in the transport zone. Each vDS has a dvPortgroup with the name format mentioned earlier in this chapter. Selecting any of these dvPortgroups shows them to belong to the same VLAN as the VXLAN VLAN, assigned to the vDS during logical network preparation. Figure 5-3 shows the dvPortgroup backing the universal logical switch with VNI 10000. Notice that the dvPortgroup is assigned to VLAN 12.

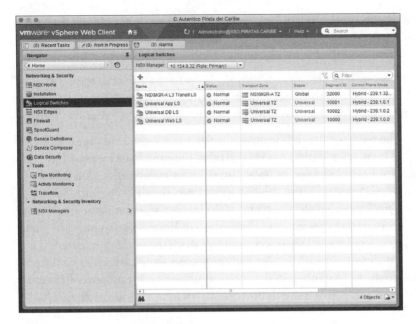

Figure 5-2 List of logical switches

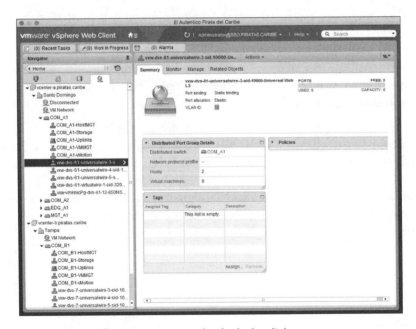

Figure 5-3 **dvPortgroup** supporting logical switch

Adding Virtual Machines to Logical Switches

Once a logical switch is created, you can migrate VMs to the logical switch. From the Logical Switches view follow these steps:

Step 1.   Select the NSX Manager where the VM is located.

Step 2.   Select the logical switch where you are connecting the VM.

Step 3.   Select the VM icon and wait for the Virtual Machine Migration Wizard to open.

Step 4.   From the VM list, find the VM that you want to migrate and check the box next to it.

Step 5.   Click **Next**.

Step 6.   For each virtual machine you are migrating, select the vNIC you want to migrate to the logical switch.

Step 7.   Click **Next**.

Step 8.   Review your selections and click **Finish**.

You can validate the VM has been migrated to the logical switch in one of two ways:

- From the vSphere Web Client's Virtual Machine and Templates view, select the VM and confirm it is connected to the dvPortgroup that supports the logical switch.

- In Logical Switches view, after selecting the NSX Managers where the VM is located, double-click the logical switch to reach the logical switch's home page and view the list of VMs connected to it, as shown in Figure 5-4.

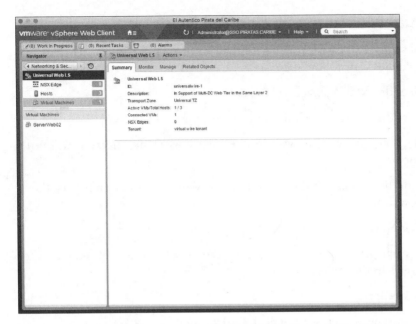

Figure 5-4   Verifying virtual machines connected to the logical switch

Logical Switch Tables

When a logical switch is created, and before the first VM is migrated to the logical switch, the following is true:

- The NSX Controller L2 master has assigned one of the NSX Controllers to be responsible for the logical switch.

- All NSX Controllers are informed about which NSX Controller was assigned to the logical switch.

- All ESXi hosts in the logical switch's transport zone have been informed, by the NSX Controllers, which NSX Controller is the one responsible for the logical switch.

The NSX Controllers become aware of the existence of the VNI only if the Replication Mode is not multicast. With Multicast Replication Mode, there is no NSX Controller assigned to the VNI and no communication exchange, about the VNI, between the NSX Controllers and the ESXi hosts in the transport zone.

The question to ask is: What exactly does it mean to be responsible for the logical switch? An NSX Controller being responsible for a VNI means the NSX Controller has the principal copy of these three tables for the logical switch:

- The VTEP table
- The MAC table
- The ARP table

The NSX Controller responsible for the logical switch also keeps a Connection table of every ESXi host that has at least one VM powered on and connected to the logical switch. The Connection table has the Management VMkernel port of the ESXi host, the TCP port of the connection, and a locally significant Connection-ID.

VTEP Table

For VMs that are powered on and connected to the logical switch, the VTEP table contains a list of the IP of all the VTEPs that have VMs. The VTEP IP was assigned to the VXLAN VMkernel ports during host configuration. The ESXi hosts in the transport zone update the VTEP table. The ESXi hosts populate the VTEP table for the logical switch when the first VM connects to the logical switch:

1. Powers up in the ESXi.
2. vMotions to the ESXi.

The ESXi host running the VM sends a request to the responsible NSX Controller to have the VTEP added to the VTEP table. Remember that all communication between the ESXi hosts and the NSX Controllers occurs over the Management VMkernel port on the ESXi host using the *NETCPA* agent over TCP port 1234.

An ESXi host's VTEPs are removed from the VTEP table upon request by the ESXi host or if the NSX Controller loses communications with the ESXi host. To be removed from the VTEP table, the host sends a request to the NSX Controller when the last VM connects to the logical switch:

1. Powers off.
2. vMotions from the ESXi host.

For its part, the NSX Controller sends a copy of the VTEP table to all ESXi hosts with VTEP entries in the table every time the VTEP table is updated, be it because a VTEP entry is added or a VTEP entry is removed.

The VTEP table has five fields, the first four of which are provided to the NSX Controller by the ESXi hosts:

- The VNI
- The VTEP IP

- The VTEP subnet
- The VTEP MAC address
- The Connection-ID (matching the Connection ID in the Connection table)

Example: Populating the VTEP Table

Let's do a packet walk on how the VTEP table gets populated, and I'm using the term *packet walk* lightly here since there are no data plane packets flowing around. This *packet walk* is true if the Replication Mode for the logical switch is configured to Unicast or Hybrid. We discuss this later in the "Replication Mode" section.

Figure 5-5 shows two ESXi hosts with a logical switch in VNI 7321, each with a VM connected to the logical switch. Each ESXi host has a single VTEP in the same VTEP subnet. Let's walk through the process of how the VTEP table gets populated.

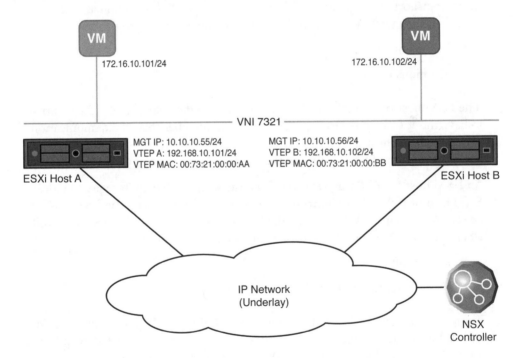

Figure 5-5   Base layout for VTEP table creation

Step 1.   Virtual Machine 1 in ESXi host A powers up.

Step 2.   ESXi host A sends a request, from its management VMkernel port over TCP 1234, to the NSX Controller to have its VTEP added to the VTEP table for VNI 7321. The request includes

- The VNI

- The VTEP IP

- The VTEP subnet

- The VTEP MAC address

Step 3.   The NSX Controller adds the entry to the VTEP table.

Step 4.   The NSX Controller sends a copy of the VTEP table to ESXi host A, as shown in Figure 5-6.

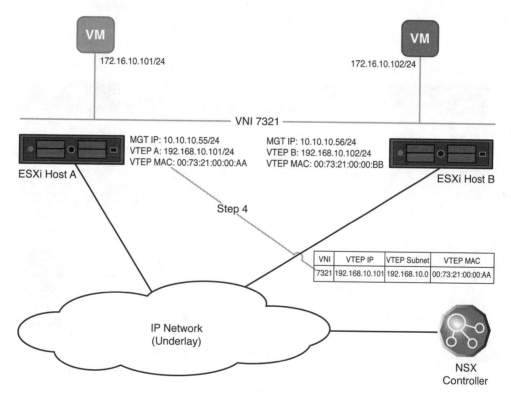

Figure 5-6   The NSX Controller sends the VTEP table to ESXi host A.

Step 5.   Virtual Machine 2 in ESXi host B powers up.

Step 6.   ESXi host B sends a request to the NSX Controller to have its VTEP added to the VTEP table for VNI 7321. The request includes

- The VNI

- The VTEP IP

- The VTEP subnet

- The VTEP MAC address

Step 7.   The NSX Controller adds the entry to the VTEP table.

Step 8.   The NSX Controller sends a copy of the VTEP table to both ESXi host
A and ESXi Host B, as shown in Figure 5-7.

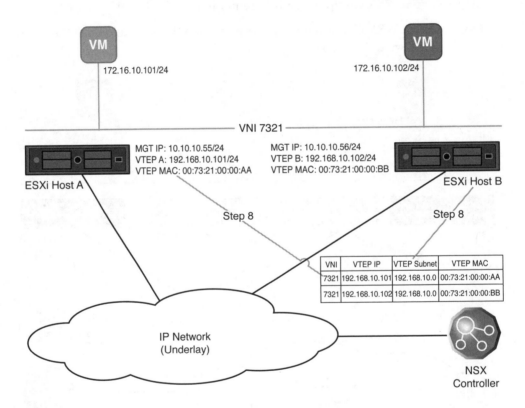

Figure 5-7   The NSX Controller sends an update to the VTEP table.

Example: Updating the VTEP Table

In this second packet walk, let's see what happens when the last VM in VNI 7321 in an ESXi host is powered down or vMotions. Figure 5-8 shows the state of our environment as we left it in our previous packet walk. In this example, the VM in ESXi host A powers off.

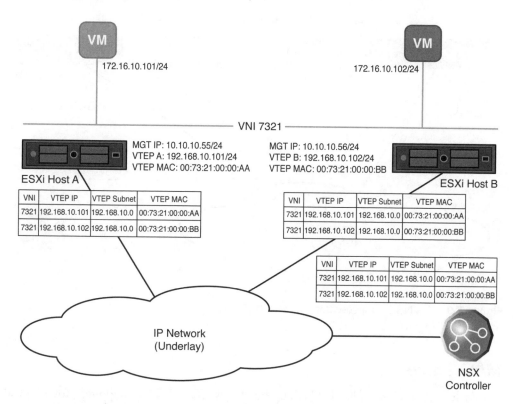

Figure 5-8   VTEP tables fully populated

Step 1.   The VM in ESXi host A powers off.

Step 2.   ESXi host A sends a request to the NSX Controller to be removed from the VTEP table for VNI 7321. At this point ESXi host A flushes its copy of the VTEP table.

Step 3.   The NSX Controller receives the request and removes ESXi host A's VTEP from the VTEP table.

Step 4.   The NSX Controller sends a copy of the VTEP table just to ESXi host B, as shown in Figure 5-9.

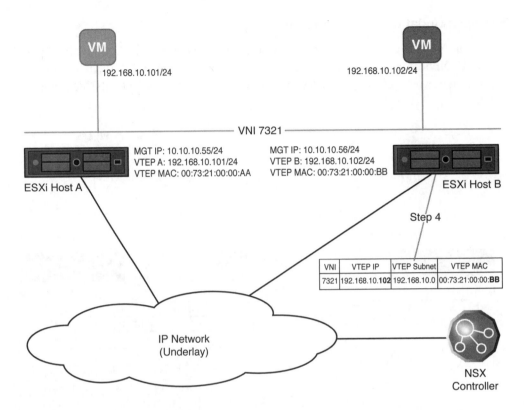

Figure 5-9   The NSX Controller updates the VTEP table

MAC Table

Earlier we saw a sample MAC table, showing MAC to VTEP mappings, for a logical switch in Table 5-2. Now we discuss how exactly the logical switch, and specifically the NSX Controller responsible for the VNI, populate the MAC tables.

There are three MAC tables to consider. One is the one from Table 5-2, which is locally owned by the logical switch per ESXi host. A second one is a MAC table created by the reading of vmx files (or doing MAC learning if you turn on the feature). Each ESXi host also locally owns its own copy of this second table. The third MAC table is kept by the NSX Controllers, and it maps MAC addresses to VTEPs, similar to the table in Table 5-2.

As mentioned earlier in the chapter, the logical switch uses a shortcut for learning the MAC address of powered on VMs by getting the MAC from the VM's vmx file. In reality, it is the vDS being used by the logical switch that learns the VM's MAC address from the vmx file and associates the MAC with a dvPort in the vDS. The logical switch taps on this information to make local (internal to the host) forwarding decisions. For VMs that use MAC addresses different from the ones in the vmx file, the logical switch could be configured to do traditional MAC learning as mentioned previously in the "Creating a Logical Switch" section.

The vDS MAC table leveraged by the logical switch is locally significant to the ESXi host where the virtual machine is running. Two ESXi hosts with the same VNI will not synchronize MAC tables.

Per ESXi host and per logical switch, the logical switch tells the NSX Controller about all MAC addresses in the MAC table created by the vDS (from reading vmx files). The NSX Controller in turn adds that MAC address to the MAC table it keeps for all ESXi hosts participating in the logical switch. There is an NSX Controller maintained MAC table per logical switch. Because all ESXi hosts tell the NSX Controller of all MAC addresses connected to the logical switch derived from the vmx file, or learned from a locally running virtual machine connected to the logical switch, the NSX Controllers have a full picture of every single MAC address in the NSX domain.

The NSX Controller does not push a copy of the MAC table to the ESXi hosts. Instead, the ESXi hosts, per logical switch, pull information from the NSX Controller's MAC table.

Whenever an ESXi host no longer has a MAC entry in its local MAC table for the logical switch, it lets the NSX Controller know so it can also flush the MAC entry from its MAC table. For example, when a virtual machine connected to a logical switch is powered off, the vDS removes that VM's MAC entry from its local MAC table, the logical switch informs the NSX Controller that it no longer has the MAC address, and the NSX Controller removes the MAC entry from its MAC table.

In Figure 5-10, two ESXi hosts with a logical switch in VNI 7321 have a powered on VM connected to VNI 7321. No communication has taken place in the previous five minutes between the VMs. Figure 5-10 shows three MAC tables for VNI 7321, one for each ESXi host (provided by the vDS) and the MAC table in the NSX Controller. The VNI MAC table of each ESXi host only contains the MAC entry for its VMs, whereas the MAC table at the NSX Controller has both MAC entries pointing to the VTEP where the MAC resides.

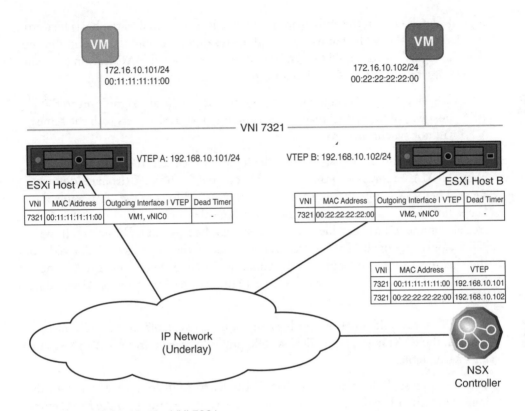

Figure 5-10   MAC tables for VNI 7321

The NSX Controller's MAC table does not have a dead timer. The NSX Controller depends on the ESXi hosts to keep it updated on the state changes of MAC addresses. The ESXi host does not keep a dead timer for MAC entries learned from the vmx file.

In case a VM connected to a logical switch vMotions, the source ESXi host notifies the NSX Controller that it no longer has the MAC entry in its MAC table. The NSX Controller then removes the MAC entry from its MAC table. At the completion of vMotion, the destination ESXi host does two things:

- Notifies the same NSX Controller, since it is the NSX Controller responsible for the logical switch, that it has a new MAC address. The NSX Controller updates its MAC table to include the MAC address of the VM with the destination ESXi host as the destination VTEP.

This is a function of NSX. Following what we have learned thus far, the destination ESXi host tells the NSX Controller of newly added local MAC entries to its MAC table.

- Sends a Reverse ARP, RARP, over the logical switch to let all other VTEPs know about the MAC address.

  This is a function of vMotion. The destination ESXi host sends an ARP request, on behalf of the VM, over the Ethernet broadcast domains the VMs connect.

Remember that vMotion is a feature of vCenter and as such NSX does not factor in the decision if vMotion can take place or not. That said, there is an advantage of doing vMotion in a logical switch over doing vMotion in a standard or dvPortgroup. With the logical switch, we no longer have to worry about ensuring that the vMotion source and destination ESXi hosts have access to the same VLAN, over the underlay, to which the VM is connected.

If the logical switch receives traffic with a destination MAC address that is not in its MAC table, the ESXi host sends a request for the entry to the NSX Controller responsible for the VNI. If the NSX Controller has the MAC address in its MAC table, it sends a response back to the ESXi host. The ESXi host adds the entry to its MAC table (refer to Table 5-2) with a dead timer of about 200 seconds. We discuss in the "Replication Mode" section of this chapter what happens when the NSX Controller does not have the MAC entry or does not reply.

ARP Table

Quick summary of what ARP is and is used for: Whenever an operating system (OS) wants to communicate via IP with another entity in the same Ethernet broadcast domain, it needs to match the destination IP address to a MAC address. The ARP table is where the OS looks for the IP-MAC mapping. An IP can only have a MAC address associated with it in the ARP table. If the entry the OS is looking for is missing from the ARP table, the OS sends out an ARP request.

ARP requests have a destination address of *FFFF.FFFF.FFFF*, better known as a Layer 2 broadcast, or just broadcast. Broadcasts can be detrimental to any environment because they are received by every system with a connection in the same broadcast domain. One of the most common and regular Ethernet broadcast domains is an ARP request.

To provide some level of broadcast suppression, ESXi hosts maintain an ARP table, per ESXi host. The NSX Controller maintains a second ARP table per logical switch. Each ESXi host, per logical switch, populates the local ARP table by doing snooping on ARP replies and DHCP acknowledgements. If the ESXi host updates its ARP table for one of its directly connected VMs, it sends a copy of the entry to the NSX Controller. Two ESXi hosts with the same VNI will not synchronize ARP tables.

Little secret: The logical switch doesn't actually keep an ARP table, as a logical switch is a Layer 2 entity and ARP tables are not really part of Layer 2 themselves. Instead, there is a fourth module, the Switch Security module (discussed briefly in Chapter 4), which maintains the ARP tables in the ESXi host. The logical switch and the Security module are really good friends and work exceptionally well together.

The ARP table has three fields:

- VNI
- MAC Address
- IP Address

By having a VNI field, the ARP table provides support for duplicate IP subnets in different logical switches. Or in other words, NSX supports multitenancy. Figure 5-11 shows the ARP tables for two ESXi hosts with powered on VMs in VNI 7321. The VMs have not communicated with each other at this point. The Switch Security module of each ESXi host has provided the NSX Controller an update, called an *IP report*, for the ARP table.

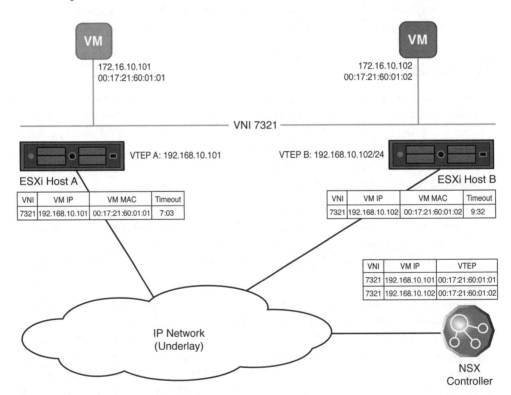

Figure 5-11   ARP tables for VNI 7321

Every time a VM sends an ARP request, it is processed by the Switch Security module to check the ARP table for a corresponding entry. If a match is found, the Switch Security module sends an ARP reply back to the requester and does not broadcast the ARP request. If a match is not found, the Switch Security module sends a request for the entry to the NSX Controller responsible for the VNI. We discuss in the "Replication Mode" section of this chapter what happens when the NSX Controller does not have the ARP entry or does not reply.

Logical Switch Table Verification

You can confirm that the NSX Controllers have their tables populated by connecting to the NSX Controllers via SSH or console. The administrator username for the NSX Controllers is *admin*, and the password is whatever you configured when you deployed the first NSX Controller.

All NSX Controllers know which NSX Controller is responsible for a particular VNI. From any NSX Manager privilege CLI prompt, enter the command **show logical-switch controller master vni** *X* **brief** to see the NSX Controller responsible for the logical switch with VNI of X, as shown in Figure 5-12 for VNI 10001. VNI 10001 is the universal logical switch *Universal App LS* shown in Figure 5-2. From the NSX Controller CLI, which is case sensitive, the same output would be obtained with the command **show control-cluster logical-switches vni** *X*. In Figure 5-12, we connected to NSXMGR-A. The command output shows the responsible NSX Controller for VNI 10001 is 10.154.8.71. Note that the connections say 0. To see the actual number of connections, you need to type the *ControllerID* instead of *master* in the command. The *ControllerID* is obtained with the command **show controller list all**.

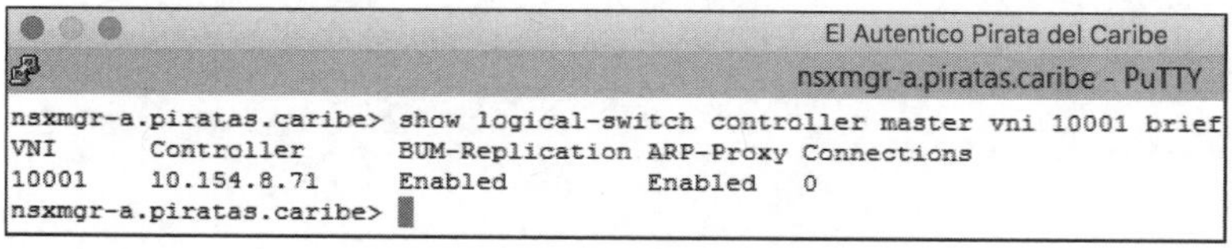

```
                                    El Autentico Pirata del Caribe
                                    nsxmgr-a.piratas.caribe - PuTTY
nsxmgr-a.piratas.caribe> show logical-switch controller master vni 10001 brief
VNI       Controller     BUM-Replication ARP-Proxy Connections
10001     10.154.8.71    Enabled         Enabled   0
nsxmgr-a.piratas.caribe>
```

Figure 5-12 NSX Controller responsible for VNI 10001

To view the principal tables in the NSX Controller using the NSX Controller CLI, we need to SSH or console in to the responsible NSX Controller. Once we are connected, we can execute our first command to confirm which ESXi hosts have powered up VMs in the VNI. The command is **show control-cluster logical-switches connection-table** *X*, where *X* is the VNI number. So we don't have to bounce around NSX Controllers to view multiple VNIs, we can execute the CLI commands from any NSX Manager. The command to view the Connection table is

show logical-switch controller master vni X **connection**. Figure 5-13 shows the output of the command for VNI 10001. The IPs you see are the IPs of the Management VMkernel port of each ESXi host. Host-IP 10.154.9.44 is the IP of an ESXi host in the Santo Domingo Data Center. Host-IP 10.154.9.49 is the IP of an ESXi host in the Tampa Data Center. Both hosts are in the VTEP table of the logical switch. The ID number is the locally significant, to the NSX Controller responsible for VNI 10001, Connection ID.

```
                                          El Autentico Pirata del Caribe
                                        nsxmgr-a.piratas.caribe - PuTTY
nsxmgr-a.piratas.caribe> show logical-switch controller master vni 10001 connection
Host-IP        Port  ID
10.154.9.44    59224 576
10.154.9.49    38162 578
masterControllerIp=10.154.8.71
nsxmgr-a.piratas.caribe>
```

Figure 5-13   Connection table for VNI 10001

The next table we want to look at is the VTEP table. The NSX Manager command to see the VTEP table is **show logical-switch controller master vni** X **vtep**, where X is the VNI number. The equivalent NSX Controller command is **show control-cluster logical-switches vtep-table** X. Figure 5-14 shows the output of the NSX Manager command for VNI 10001. All the IPs and MACs we see are from the VXLAN VMkernel ports of the host from Figure 5-13. These VTEPs have at least one pinned VM powered on and connected to logical switch 10001.

```
                                          El Autentico Pirata del Caribe
                                        nsxmgr-a.piratas.caribe - PuTTY
nsxmgr-a.piratas.caribe> show logical-switch controller master vni 10001 vtep
VNI    IP             Segment         MAC                  Connection-ID
10001  10.154.12.41   10.154.12.0     00:50:56:6b:2f:77    576
10001  10.154.14.40   10.154.14.0     00:50:56:63:ad:36    578
masterControllerIp=10.154.8.71
nsxmgr-a.piratas.caribe>
```

Figure 5-14   VTEP table for VNI 10001

For the MAC and ARP tables, you can execute these NSX Manager commands (with the equivalent NSX Controller commands in parentheses), shown in Figure 5-15 for VNI 10001:

```
show logical-switch controller master vni X mac (show control-cluster
   logical-switches mac-table X)
show logical-switch controller master vni X arp (show control-cluster
   logical-switches arp-table X)
```

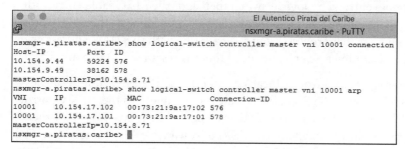

```
                                          El Autentico Pirata del Caribe
                                          nsxmgr-a.piratas.caribe - PuTTY
nsxmgr-a.piratas.caribe> show logical-switch controller master vni 10001 mac
VNI        MAC              VTEP-IP           Connection-ID
10001    00:73:21:9a:17:02 10.154.12.41      576
10001    00:73:21:9a:17:01 10.154.14.40      578
masterControllerIp=10.154.8.71
nsxmgr-a.piratas.caribe> show logical-switch controller master vni 10001 arp
VNI        IP              MAC               Connection-ID
10001    10.154.17.102    00:73:21:9a:17:02 576
10001    10.154.17.101    00:73:21:9a:17:01 578
masterControllerIp=10.154.8.71
nsxmgr-a.piratas.caribe> █
```

Figure 5-15 MAC and ARP tables for VNI 10001

Now, about that ID number we saw in the Connection table! The ID number, the Connection ID, is assigned by the NSX Controller to match entries from other tables back to the management IP of the host. For example, if you want to know which ESXi host provided an ARP entry in the ARP table, simply match the Connection ID in the ARP entry with the connection ID in the ID number in the Connection table, as shown in Figure 5-16. The figure shows that the ESXi host with a Connection ID of 576 provided the ARP entry for IP 10.154.17.102. Cross-referencing the Connection ID in the Connection table tells us the ESXi host's management IP is 10.154.9.45.

```
                                          El Autentico Pirata del Caribe
                                          nsxmgr-a.piratas.caribe - PuTTY
nsxmgr-a.piratas.caribe> show logical-switch controller master vni 10001 connection
Host-IP        Port   ID
10.154.9.44    59224  576
10.154.9.49    38162  578
masterControllerIp=10.154.8.71
nsxmgr-a.piratas.caribe> show logical-switch controller master vni 10001 arp
VNI        IP              MAC               Connection-ID
10001    10.154.17.102    00:73:21:9a:17:02 576
10001    10.154.17.101    00:73:21:9a:17:01 578
masterControllerIp=10.154.8.71
nsxmgr-a.piratas.caribe> █
```

Figure 5-16 Using Connection ID to find out the ESXi host that provided an ARP table entry

There are three additional commands that can be handy for troubleshooting that pull VNI information from the ESXi host. Figure 5-17 shows a list of the command options to pull information from the hosts local to the NSX Manager. To get the host-id, type the command **show cluster** *cluster-id*, where *cluster-id* is the cluster where the host belongs.

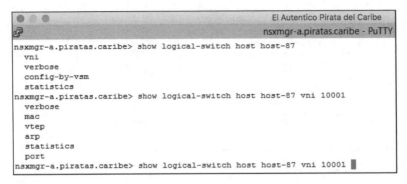

Figure 5-17   NSX Manager CLI commands for VNI host information

Unknown Unicast or ARP Request

If a logical switch receives a frame from a VM with a destination MAC address that is not present in the local MAC table, the logical switch sends a query to the NSX Controller responsible for the VNI, using the ESXi host's Management VMkernel port. The NSX Controller then replies back to the logical switch in the ESXi host with the MAC table entry. The logical switch then adds the MAC table entry with a dead timer of about 200 seconds and forwards the VM's frame to the destination VTEP. If the logical switch processes any return traffic with the MAC address as the source before the dead timer expires, the dead timer is reset back to five minutes.

If an ARP request is received from a local VM and the ARP entry is not in the Security module's ARP table, the Security module sends a query to the NSX Controller using the ESXi host's Management VMkernel port. The NSX Controller then replies back to the Security module in the ESXi host with the ARP table entry. The Switch Security module adds the ARP entry to the ARP table and sends an ARP reply back to the VM that sent the ARP request.

The NSX Controller ARP table entries do not have a timeout. The NSX Controller depends on the ESXi hosts to keep it updated on the state changes of ARP entries.

Replication Mode

Every time a logical switch receives a frame from a locally attached VM for which it does not have a MAC entry in its table or it is an ARP request for which the Security module does not have an entry in its ARP table, a request for the entry is sent to the NSX Controller responsible for the VNI. But what happens when any of these is true for the logical switch?

■ Receives broadcasts from locally connected VMs that are not an ARP request.

- Receives multicasts from locally connected VMs that are not in the IGMP Snooping table. (IGMP Snooping is supported by the vDS in vSphere 6.0.)

- The NSX Controller does not have the unknown unicast MAC address in its MAC table.

- The NSX Controller does not have the ARP entry in its ARP table for the ARP request.

- The NSX Controller is down or unavailable.

If any of these cases happen, the logical switch goes into Replication Mode. Replication Mode provides a mechanism to ensure that every host with a VM connected to the VNI receives a copy of the original frame. Remember that a logical switch has only a single VNI and vice versa, and that each ESXi host keeps its own local copy of the MAC and ARP tables per logical switch/VNI.

Think of Replication Mode as what a physical Ethernet switch does when it receives a Broadcast, Unknown unicast, or Multicast (BUM). When receiving a BUM, the physical Ethernet switch would either flood the frame (if it is an unknown unicast) or broadcast the frame (if it is a broadcast or multicast that is not in the IGMP Snooping table). In either case, every other physical Ethernet switch configured in the same broadcast domain as the BUM receives the BUM frame.

When dealing with physical Ethernet switches, it is simple to ensure that every other physical Ethernet switch receives a copy of the BUM: Simply replicate the BUM out of each interface of the physical Ethernet switch (except the interface the BUM arrived in) that is in the same Ethernet broadcast domain. But with logical switches we don't have interfaces but rather tunnels, VXLAN overlays, which create a design challenge (or opportunity if you are the endless optimist):

Of all the other VTEPs in the NSX domain, which ones have VMs in the same VNI as the BUM, and thus need a copy of the frame?

The answer to the question can be found in the VTEP table. Take a minute to go back to earlier in the chapter and review the fields included in the VTEP table and what the NSX Controller does when it updates the VTEP table. I'll wait.

Now that you are back, it should be clear that the VTEP table provides an accurate list of every VTEP that has at least one VM in the VNI. Because the NSX Controller responsible for the logical switch sends updated copies of the VTEP table to each ESXi host with a VTEP in the table, all VTEPs can execute Replication Mode even if the NSX Controller responsible for the logical switch is down.

For completeness, there is an alternative to solving the design challenge mentioned above that does not depend on the VTEP table, or leveraging the NSX Controller for that matter. That option involves using Multicast Replication Mode, and we review it in the next section.

There are three ways, or modes, in which the source ESXi host can replicate the frame so that all ESXi hosts with VMs in the same VNI get a copy. The three modes are

- Multicast (This option does not leverage the VTEP table.)

- Unicast

- Hybrid

The Replication Mode the logical switch will use is selected when you create the transport zone. Alternatively, you can overwrite the Replication Mode, per logical switch, when you create the logical switch.

Multicast Replication Mode

I mentioned earlier that VXLAN is an open standard supported by the big data center companies, such as VMware. The VXLAN standard does not include the role of a centralized controller, such as the NSX Controller. Therefore to solve the design challenge mentioned earlier, the VXLAN standard's solution is to associate each VNI, or logical switch, with a multicast group address. Because there is no NSX Controller to query when there is BUM, each logical switch would default to replicating each and every BUM but encapsulating the BUM in a VXLAN frame with a destination IP address of the multicast group for the VNI. That last sentence was a mouthful; so let me rephrase it this way:

> If the logical switch doesn't have it in the MAC table or the vDS IGMP Snooping table, multicast it.

All VTEPs that receive the multicast VXLAN frame decapsulate the frame and send a copy of the BUM to each powered on VM connected to the logical switch. In the case the BUM is an unknown unicast, the VM that owns the destination MAC address of the BUM replies back to the VM that sent the BUM. When the logical switch in the ESXi host where the BUM originated from processes the response frame, it learns the MAC address of the VM that owns the unknown unicast MAC (and it will no longer be unknown). We review this process further in Chapter 6, "Logical Switch Packet Walks."

For any logical switch configured with Multicast Replication Mode, the NSX Controller will *not* keep a VTEP table, a MAC table, or an ARP table.

During Segment ID configuration, where you provided NSX Manager with the pool of VNIs to use for logical switches, there is an option to enable multicast addressing. You need to select this option and provide the pool of multicast addresses if you plan to use Multicast Replication Mode.

If the pool of multicast groups is smaller than the pool of VNIs, then the NSX Manager maps multiple VNIs to the same multicast group address.

For Multicast Replication Mode to work, every VTEP that has at least one VM powered on has to join the multicast group so it can be a source and receiver for the multicast group. After the ESXi host is informed of the creation of a logical switch and the first VM in the logical switch powers up or vMotions to the ESXi host, the ESXi host sends an IGMP Join request, for the multicast group that was provided to it by NSX Manager, over the VXLAN VMkernel port, the VTEP. When the last VM in the VNI in the ESXi host powers off or vMotions from the ESXi host, the ESXi host sends an IGMP Leave request for the multicast group.

NSX VTEPs support IPv4 multicast. For Multicast Replication Mode to work, PIM (if VTEPs are in different subnets) and IGMP must be configured in the underlay.

One potential downside of using Multicast Replication Mode is that every single BUM is seen and processed by each ESXi host with powered on VMs in the VNI, and additional resources are consumed in the underlay to process all the multicast traffic. On the plus side, the source ESXi host sends only a single VXLAN frame for each BUM.

Unicast Replication Mode and Proxy VTEP

With Multicast Replication Mode, none of the VTEPs have a full list of all VTEPs that have powered on VMs in the logical switches. As mentioned earlier, the other alternative to the replication design challenge is to leverage the VTEP table to provide all VTEPs a full view of which VTEPs have running VMs in each VNI. With this full view of things, instead of multicasting whenever a frame needs to be replicated, the frame that needs to be replicated could be unicasted inside a VXLAN frame to each VTEP that is in the VTEP table for the VNI.

In Unicast Replication Mode, a frame will be replicated if any of the following is true for the logical switch:

- Receives broadcasts from locally connected VMs that are not an ARP request.

- Receives multicasts from locally connected VMs, and it is not in the IGMP Snooping table of the vDS.

- The NSX Controller does not have a unicast MAC address in its MAC table (unknown unicast).

- The NSX Controller does not have the ARP entry in its ARP table for the ARP request.

- The NSX Controller is down or unavailable.

One immediate advantage to Unicast Replication Mode is a reduction in the number of frames that need to be replicated since the NSX Controller has the principal tables for MAC and ARP. Another advantage to Unicast Replication Mode is that it makes it unnecessary to enable IGMP or PIM in the underlay.

A disadvantage to Unicast Replication Mode is that if the VTEP table is large, the source VTEP might have to send many VXLAN frames, one per VTEP in the VTEP table. To reduce the impact of this disadvantage, the ESXi hosts use something called the Proxy VTEP field. The role of Proxy VTEP is to receive the BUM-replicated VXLAN frame from the source VTEP. The Proxy VTEP then sends a unicast copy of the BUM-replicated VXLAN frame to all VTEPs in its VTEP subnet. The source VTEP is still responsible to unicast the BUM-replicated VXLAN frame to all VTEPs in its local VTEP subnet. The proxy VTEP is selected at random from the VTEP table by the source ESXi host. The source ESXi host selects a proxy VTEP per VTEP subnet in the VTEP table.

How does the proxy VTEP know that it needs to replicate the VXLAN frame it just received? It knows because it sees that in the VXLAN flags field, the Replication bit is set to 1. The source VTEP sets the Replication bit to 1 before sending the VX-LAN frame to the proxy VTEPs. Before the proxy VTEP replicates the VXLAN frame to the VTEPs in its VTEP segment, it resets the Replication bit back to 0.

Because the proxy VTEP is itself forwarding the replicated VXLAN frame via uni-cast, it is called a *unicast proxy VTEP (UTEP)*.

Hybrid Replication Mode

Yes, Hybrid Replication Mode is the happy union of Unicast Replication Mode and Multicast Replication Mode. Hybrid Replication Mode leverages the NSX Controller for the principal tables of VTEP, MAC, and ARP. In Hybrid Replication Mode, a frame will be replicated if any of the following is true for the logical switch:

- Receives broadcasts from locally connected VMs that are not an ARP request.

- Receives multicasts from locally connected VMs, and it is not in the IGMP Snooping table of the vDS.

- The NSX Controller does not have a unicast MAC address in its MAC table (unknown unicast).

- The NSX Controller does not have the ARP entry in its ARP table for the ARP request.

- The NSX Controller is down or unavailable.

With Unicast Replication Mode, you have the source VTEP and Proxy VTEPs sending unicast VXLAN frames to all VTEPs in their local VTEP subnets. With Hybrid Replication Mode, the source VTEP sends a single Multicast VXLAN frame to its local VTEP subnet while sending a single unicast VXLAN frame to the proxy VTEPs. The proxy VTEPs, upon receiving the unicast VXLAN frame with the Replication bit set to 1, then sends a single multicast VXLAN frame to their local VTEP subnet.

In Hybrid Replication Mode, the proxy VTEP is called *multicast proxy VTEP (MTEP)*.

An advantage of Hybrid Replication Mode is that it can greatly reduce the number of replicated VXLAN frames the source VTEP needs to send. A potential disadvantage for Hybrid Replication Mode is that IGMP Querier and IGMP Snooping should be configured in the underlay for the local VTEP broadcast domains. If IGMP Snooping is not configured, the underlay Ethernet switch treats all replicated multicast VXLAN frames as broadcast.

Just as in Multicast Replication Mode, a multicast group is required for each VNI in Hybrid Replication Mode. Each VTEP that has a powered on VM connected to the VNI sends an IGMP Join for the multicast group assigned to the VNI. PIM is not required in the underlay to support Multicast Replication Mode. To prevent the replicated multicast VXLAN replicated frame from crossing Layer 2 boundaries, the Time to Live (TTL) in the multicast VXLAN frame's IP header is set to 1.

Something that should be pointed out now, and I already mentioned for Multicast Replication Mode: All VTEPs receiving the replicated VXLAN frame decapsulate the frame and forward a copy of the BUM to all powered on virtual machines connected to the VNI. For any unknown unicast and ARP request not in the local ARP table, the source VTEP learns the MAC or ARP entry when the destination virtual machine responds. This is true for all three modes of replication. We see more of this in Chapter 6 when we discuss packet walks for logical switches.

Exam Preparation Tasks

Review All the Key Topics

Review the most important topics from inside the chapter, noted with the Key Topic icon in the outer margin of the page. Table 5-3 lists these key topics and the page numbers where each is found.

Table 5-3   Key Topics for Chapter 5

Key Topic Element	Description	Page Number
Paragraph	Each ESXi host keeps a local MAC table copy per logical switch.	130
Paragraph	The logical switch populates MAC addresses from the vmx file	131
Paragraph	The NSX domain and cross vCenter NSX domain can have a maximum of 10,000 logical switches.	132
Paragraph	A virtual machine in a logical switch can only vMotion if the source and destination ESXi hosts have the logical switch backed by the same dvPortgroup or if environment is running vSphere 6.0.	135
Paragraph	The NSX Controllers keep a fourth table, the Connection Table	139
Paragraph	Different ESXi hosts won't synchronize MAC tables.	145
Paragraph	ESXi hosts pull MAC Table information from the NSX Controllers	145
Paragraph	The NSX Controller does not keep a dead timer in its ARP tables.	146
Paragraph	The ARP table is maintained by the Security module.	148
Paragraph	The NSX Controller does not have a timeout in its ARP tables.	152
Paragraph	The logical switch inherits the Replication Mode from the transport zone or directly from its configuration, if different.	154
Paragraph	Multicast Replication Mode does not make use of the NSX Controllers.	154
Paragraph	The same multicast group is assigned to multiple VNIs if the pool is not big enough to assign each VNI its own multicast group.	155
Paragraph	NSX VTEPs make use of IPv4 multicast.	155

Complete Tables and Lists from Memory

Download and print a copy of Appendix C, "Memory Tables" (found on the book's website), or at least the section for this chapter, and complete the tables and lists from memory. Appendix D, "Memory Tables Answer Key," also on the website, includes the completed tables and lists so you can check your work.

Define Key Terms

Define the following key terms from this chapter, and check your answers in the Glossary:

logical switch, universal logical switch, VNI, VTEP, Switch Security module, MAC learning, VTEP table, ARP table, Replication Mode, proxy VTEP, UTEP, MTEP

This chapter covers all or part of the following VCP6-NV exam blueprint topics:

- **Objective 5.1**—Create and Administer Logical Switches

CHAPTER 6

Logical Switch Packet Walks

Chapter 5, "NSX Switches," discussed what a logical switch and universal logical switch are but didn't quite visualize how traffic is sent between virtual machines (VMs) in the same VNI. This chapter does packet walks for multiple scenarios of VMs in the same logical switch communicating with each other. This chapter also covers the different cases of what the logical switch and universal logical switch do when they receive a broadcast, unknown unicast, and multicast (BUM).

Do I Know This Already?

The "Do I Know This Already?" quiz allows you to assess whether you should read this entire chapter or simply jump to the "Exam Preparation Tasks" section for review. If you are in doubt, read the entire chapter. Table 6-1 outlines the major headings in this chapter and the corresponding "Do I Know This Already?" quiz questions. You can find the answers in Appendix A, "Answers to the 'Do I Know This Already?' Quizzes."

Table 6-1   Headings and Questions

Foundation Topic Section	Questions Covered in This Section
Logical Switch Packet Walk Example 1	1
Logical Switch Packet Walk Example 2	2-3
Logical Switch Packet Walk Example 3	4-5
Logical Switch Packet Walk Example 4	6-9
Logical Switch Packet Walk Example 5	10

Use the following information to answer the questions that follow. In Figure 6-1, Host A-1 and Host A-2 are part of the same cluster in Data Center A managed by vCenter-A and paired with NSX Manager-A. Host B-1 and Host B-2 are part of the same cluster in Data Center B managed by vCenter-B and paired with NSX Manager-B. NSX is configured for cross vCenter NSX. NSX Manager-A is the Primary NSX Manager and NSX Manager-B is a Secondary NSX Manager. VMA-1 and VMA-2 are running in Host A-1. VMA-3 is running in

Host A-2. VMB-1 and VMB-2 are running in Host B-1. VMB-3 is running in Host B-2. All VMs are connected to Universal Logical Switch 7321.

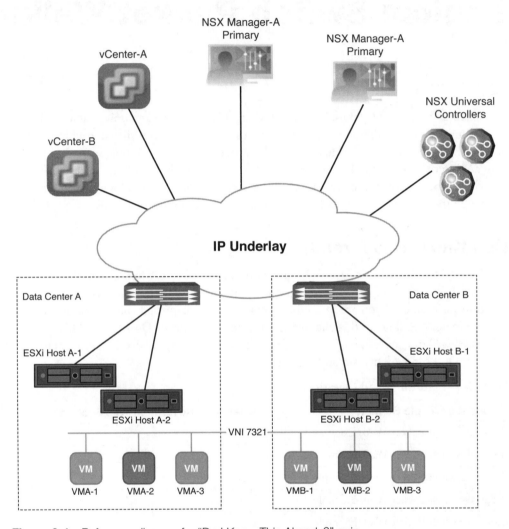

Figure 6-1 Reference diagram for "Do I Know This Already?" quiz

1. VMA-1 sends traffic to VMA-2. Based on the diagram, how does the logical switch in ESXi Host A-1 know to forward the frame to VMA-2?

   a. The logical switch in Host A-1 will have the MAC address for VMA-2 in its MAC table since it was provided by the NSX Universal Controller.

   b. The logical switch in Host A-1 will have the MAC address for VMA-2 in its MAC table because it copied it from the vmx file.

   c. The logical switch in Host A-1 will have the MAC address for VMA-2 in its MAC table because it was provided by the NSX Manager.

   d. The logical switch in Host A-1 will not know where to forward the frame and will therefore broadcast it.

2. VMA-1 sends traffic to VMA-2. The logical switch in ESXi Host A-1 does not have an entry for VMA-1's MAC address in the MAC table. Based on the diagram, what could be the reason for this?

   a. The NSX VXLAN module in Host A-1 is disabled.

   b. The NSX Universal Controller can't communicate with Host A-1.

   c. VMA-1's guest OS is forging its MAC address.

   d. VMA-1 is booting up.

3. The logical switch in Host B-2 learns a MAC address from one of its VMs. Based on the diagram, what action is then taken by the logical switch?

   a. The logical switch in Host B-2 adds the MAC address to its MAC table and informs the Switch Security module in Host B-2 so the ARP table can be updated.

   b. The logical switch in Host B-2 tells all the NSX Universal Controllers about the MAC address.

   c. If the resulting size of the logical switch in Host B-2's MAC table is bigger than the NSX Universal Controllers MAC table, Host B-1 becomes the keeper of the principal MAC table for VNI 7321.

   d. The logical switch in Host B-2 will learn the MAC address and send an update to the NSX Universal Controller responsible for the logical switch.

4. The Top of Rack (ToR) switch receives a VXLAN frame from Host B-1. The frame is transporting traffic from VMB-2 destined for VMA-3. Based on the diagram, what two actions does the ToR switch take? (Choose two.)

   a. The ToR learns the MAC address of Host B-1's VTEP.

   b. The ToR learns the MAC address of VMB-2.

   c. If the destination MAC address is the MAC of Host A-2's VTEP and the ToR does not know the MAC address of Host A-2 VTEP, it will broadcast the VXLAN frame.

   d. If the VXLAN frame's destination MAC address is a unicast and it is not the MAC address of Host A-2 VTEP, the switch will not send a copy of the frame to Host A-2 VTEP.

5. Based on the diagram, if all the VTEPs of the ESXi hosts in the Data Center B cluster are in the same VLAN, the same subnet, and connected to the same ToR, which statement is true?

   a. Spanning Tree must be configured in the ToR on all ports connected to the ESXi hosts.

   b. A default gateway must be configured for the VTEPs to communicate with each other.

   c. The ToR switch never learns the MAC address of the virtual machines.

   d. The VTEPs can't communicate with each other because they are in the same Ethernet broadcast domain.

6. Based on the diagram, if all the VTEPs of the ESXi hosts in Data Center A are in the same VTEP subnet, which Replication Mode causes the VTEPs to send the least amount of replication frames?

   a. Hybrid

   b. Unicast

   c. Broadcast

   d. Directional

7. Based on the diagram, if Host B-1 is the MTEP, what replication mode has been configured for the logical switch?

   a. Broadcast

   b. Multicast

   c. Unicast

   d. Hybrid

8. Based on the diagram, if no Host has selected an MTEP or UTEP for Universal Logical Switch 7321, what is the Replication Mode for logical switch 7321?

   a. Broadcast

   b. Multicast

   c. Unicast

   d. Hybrid

9. Logical switch 7321 in Host B-2 receives an ARP reply from VMB-2. Based on the diagram, what two actions will the logical switch take with regards to the frame? (Choose two.)

    a. It will broadcast the frame to VMA-3.

    b. It will unicast the frame to VMA-3.

    c. It will send the frame to the Switch Security module to add it to the ARP table.

    d. It will reset the dead timer to five minutes if VMB-2's MAC address is in its MAC table.

10. VMB-3 vMotions to Host B-1. Based on the diagram, what does Host B-2 do after the vMotion migration is completed?

    a. The Universal NSX Controller tells Host B-1 the MAC address of VMB-3.

    b. Host B-2 tells the NSX Universal Controller to remove it from the VTEP table.

    c. Host B-2 tells the NSX Universal Controller that Host B-1 has the MAC address of VMB-3.

    d. Host B-2 sends an RARP to all other hosts to let them know VMB-3 is now in Host B-1.

Foundation Topics

Logical Switches Packet Walks

This section reviews multiple packet walks involving communications between VMs connected to the same Ethernet broadcast domain. Each packet walk shows a different aspect of the process the logical switches follow to deliver a frame to its destination. All packet walks reference Figure 6-2 or a derivative thereof, with some figures including different step numbers relevant to the packet walk. Each packet walk uses Universal Logical Switch 7321 as the broadcast domain. The packet walk steps would be the same if you used a logical switch instead of a universal logical switch. Thus I interchange logical switch and universal logical switch through the packet walks as well as NSX Universal Controllers and NSX Controllers.

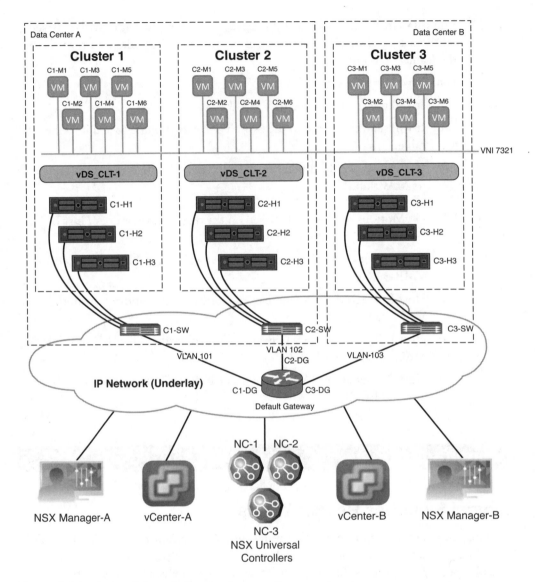

Figure 6-2 Logical switch packet walk reference diagram

Figure 6-2 has three sets of ESXi clusters, all configured to support NSX.

- vCenter-A is paired with NSX Manager-A, which is the Primary NSX Manager in the cross vCenter NSX domain.

- vCenter-B is paired with NSX Manager-B, which is a Secondary NSX Manager in the cross vCenter NSX domain.

- Both data centers share a common Layer 3 physical router (named Default Gateway in Figure 6-2).

- Cluster 1 and Cluster 2 are in Data Center A. Cluster 3 is in Data Center B.

- Each ESXi cluster has its own vDS, which is also used for the portgroups backing the logical switches.

- Each ESXi cluster has three ESXi hosts.

- Each ESXi host has two powered on virtual machines.

- There are three NSX Universal Controllers.

- Each ESXi host has IP connectivity via the Management VMkernel port to all NSX Universal Controllers, its corresponding NSX Manager, and vCenter.

- Each ESXi host has a single VTEP.

- Each ESXi host is shown with a single VMNIC to the physical network.
  - ESXi host Management, vMotion, IP storage, and VXLAN encapsulated traffic will traverse this interface.
  - ESXi host Management traffic will use VLAN 10.
  - vMotion traffic will use VLAN 20.
  - IP Storage traffic will use VLAN 30.
  - Cluster-1 VXLAN encapsulated traffic will use VLAN 101.
  - Cluster-2 VXLAN encapsulated traffic will use VLAN 102.
  - Cluster-3 VXLAN encapsulated traffic will use VLAN 103.

Table 6-2 shows where each VM is running, its IP address, and its MAC address. The naming convention used is Cluster#-Machine# and Cluster#-Host#.

Table 6-2 VM Information

VM Name	ESXi Host	VM IP Address	VM MAC Address
C1-M1	C1-H1	C1-M1-IP	C1-M1-MAC
C1-M2	C1-H1	C1-M2-IP	C1-M2-MAC
C1-M3	C1-H2	C1-M3-IP	C1-M3-MAC
C1-M4	C1-H2	C1-M4-IP	C1-M4-MAC
C1-M5	C1-H3	C1-M5-IP	C1-M5-MAC
C1-M6	C2-H1	C1-M6-IP	C1-M6-MAC

VM Name	ESXi Host	VM IP Address	VM MAC Address
C2-M1	C2-H1	C2-M1-IP	C2-M1-MAC
C2-M2	C2-H2	C2-M2-IP	C2-M2-MAC
C2-M3	C2-H2	C2-M3-IP	C2-M3-MAC
C2-M4	C2-H3	C2-M4-IP	C2-M4-MAC
C2-M5	C2-H1	C2-M5-IP	C2-M5-MAC
C2-M6	C3-H1	C2-M6-IP	C2-M6-MAC
C3-M1	C3-H2	C3-M1-IP	C3-M1-MAC
C3-M2	C3-H2	C3-M2-IP	C3-M2-MAC
C3-M3	C3-H3	C3-M3-IP	C3-M3-MAC
C3-M4	C3-H1	C3-M4-IP	C3-M4-MAC
C3-M5	C3-H1	C3-M5-IP	C3-M5-MAC
C3-M6	C3-H2	C3-M6-IP	C3-M6-MAC

Table 6-3 shows each ESXi host's management IP address, VTEP IP address, and VTEP MAC address.

Table 6-3 ESXi Host Information

ESXi Host	Cluster	VXLAN vDS	Host MGT IP	Host VTEP IP	Host VTEP MAC	VXLAN Default GW IP	Default GW MAC
C1-H1	Cluster 1	vDS_CLT-1	C1-H1-IP	C1-H1-VTEP	C1-H1-MAC	C1-DG	C1-DG-MAC
C1-H2	Cluster 1	vDS_CLT-1	C1-H2-IP	C1-H2-VTEP	C1-H2-MAC	C1-DG	C1-DG-MAC
C1-H3	Cluster 1	vDS_CLT-1	C1-H3-IP	C1-H3-VTEP	C1-H3-MAC	C1-DG	C1-DG-MAC
C2-H1	Cluster 2	vDS_CLT-2	C2-H1-IP	C2-H1-VTEP	C2-H1-MAC	C2-DG	C2-DG-MAC
C2-H2	Cluster 2	vDS_CLT-2	C2-H2-IP	C2-H2-VTEP	C2-H2-MAC	C2-DG	C2-DG-MAC
C2-H3	Cluster 2	vDS_CLT-2	C2-H3-IP	C2-H3-VTEP	C2-H3-MAC	C2-DG	C2-DG-MAC
C3-H1	Cluster 3	vDS_CLT-3	C3-H1-IP	C3-H1-VTEP	C3-H1-MAC	C3-DG	C3-DG-MAC
C3-H2	Cluster 3	vDS_CLT-3	C3-H2-IP	C3-H2-VTEP	C3-H2-MAC	C3-DG	C3-DG-MAC
C3-H3	Cluster 3	vDS_CLT-3	C3-H3-IP	C3-H3-VTEP	C3-H3-MAC	C3-DG	C3-DG-MAC

Logical Switch Packet Walk Example 1

In this packet walk, Virtual Machine C1-M1 sends a frame to Virtual Machine C1-M2. Assume the following to be true:

- All VMs have been powered on for some time.

- C1-M1 and C1-M2 are connected to Universal Logical Switch 7321.

- C1-M1 and C1-M2 are using the MAC addresses in their vmx files.

- Logical Switch 7321 is configured with MAC learning.

- NSX Universal Controller NC-2 is responsible for VNI 7321.

- C1-M1 knows the MAC address of C1-M2.

Step 1.   C1-M1 sends a frame with the source IP C1-M1-IP, destination IP of C1-M2-IP, Source MAC of C1-M1-MAC, and destination MAC of C1-M2-MAC, as shown in Figure 6-3.

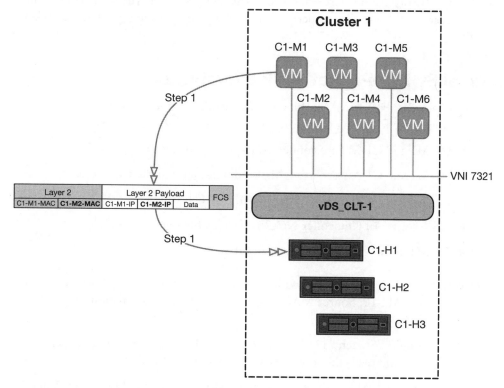

Figure 6-3   Frame from C1-M1 destined for C1-M2

Step 2.   Logical Switch 7321 in ESXi host C1-H1 receives the frame from C1-M1 and reads the source MAC address, C1-M1-MAC.

Step 3.   Because the source MAC address C1-M1-MAC is the same MAC address in the vmx file of C1-M1, it is already in the MAC table of logical switch 7321 in C1-H1 (courtesy of the vDS being used for VXLAN). The logical switch moves on to read the destination MAC address of the frame.

Step 4.   Because the destination MAC address C1-M2-MAC is the same MAC address that is in the vmx file of Virtual Machine C1-M2, then the MAC address is already in logical switch 7321 MAC table in C1-H1 (again, courtesy of the vDS...thank you vDS).

Step 5.   Logical switch 7321 in C1-H1 delivers the frame to C1-M2.

Now that was easy. This packet walk had an identical behavior to that of the vDS with a VLAN dvPortgroup, except for the MAC learning part. If MAC learning was not configured in the logical switch, the behavior would be identical to the vDS with a VLAN dvPortgroup where the source MAC address of the virtual machine's frame is not read. Let's raise the temperature a notch by doing a slightly different packet walk.

Logical Switch Packet Walk Example 2

In this packet walk, Virtual Machine C1-M1 sends a frame to Virtual Machine C1-M2. Assume the following to be true:

- C1-M1 and C1-M2 are connected to Universal Logical Switch 7321.

- C1-M1 and C1-M2 are using MAC addresses not in their vmx file.

- Logical Switch 7321 is configured with MAC learning.

- NSX Universal Controller NC-2 is responsible for VNI 7321.

- C1-M1 knows the MAC address of C1-M2.

Step 1.   C1-M1 sends a frame with the source IP of C1-M1-IP, destination IP of C1-M2-IP, Source MAC of C1-M1-MAC, and destination MAC of C1-M2-MAC.

Step 2.   Logical Switch 7321 in ESXi host C1-H1 receives the frame from C1-M1 and reads the source MAC address, C1-M1-MAC.

   a. If the MAC address is not in its MAC table, logical switch 7321 in C1-H1 will add it to its MAC table and tell the NSX Controller NC-2 if the Replication Mode for the logical switch is Unicast or Hybrid.

b. If the MAC address is in the MAC table of logical switch 7321 in C1-H1 but it shows as belonging to a different virtual machine in C1-H1, it will update its MAC table and *not* tell NC-2.

c. If the MAC address is in the MAC table of logical switch 7321 in C1-H1 but it shows as belonging to a different virtual machine in a VTEP different from C1-H1, it will update its MAC table and tell NC-2 if the Replication Mode for the logical switch is Unicast or Hybrid.

In each case a copy of the MAC address will also be given to the Switch Security module. If C1-M1 used an 802.1Q tab, the VLAN number will also be given to the Switch Security module; otherwise, the VLAN number given to the Switch Security module is 0.

Step 3. Logical switch 7321 in C1-H1 reads the destination MAC address C1-M2-MAC.

If the destination MAC address is not in the MAC table of logical switch 7321 in C1-H1, the logical switch will query NC-2 for the MAC address if the Replication Mode for the logical switch is Unicast or Hybrid. If C1-H1 does not receive a response from NC-2, NC-2 is down, or if the Replication Mode is Multicast, the logical switch will replicate the frame.

In this case, since the MAC C1-M2-MAC is local to C1-M2, it is expected that NC-2 will not have an entry for it.

Logical Switch Packet Walk Example 4 reviews Replication Modes in more detail.

Step 4. Following step 3, logical switch 7321 in C1-H1 forwards the frame to C1-M2.

Once C1-M2 replies back to C1-M1 using source MAC address C1-M2-MAC, logical switch 7321 in C1-H1 will learn it, as explained in step 2a.

How are you feeling? Or better yet, are you FEELING it? The temperature is rising with these packet walks. Next let's bring the heat up until it gets to Florida hot. The next packet walk follows a frame between virtual machines in different ESXi hosts.

Logical Switch Packet Walk Example 3

In this packet walk, Virtual Machine C1-M3 sends a frame to Virtual Machine C2-M4. Assume the following to be true:

- C1-M3 and C2-M4 are connected to Universal Logical Switch 7321.

- C1-M3 and C2-M4 are using the MAC addresses in their vmx files.

- Logical switch 7321 is configured with MAC learning.

- NSX Universal Controller NC-2 is responsible for VNI 7321.

- C1-M3 knows the MAC address of C2-M4.

- C1-M3 and C2-M4 have communicated with each other recently (around 200 seconds).

Step 1.   C1-M3 sends a frame with the source IP C1-M3-IP, destination IP of C2-M4-IP, Source MAC of C1-M3-MAC, and destination MAC of C2-M4-MAC.

Step 2.   Logical switch 7321 in ESXi host C1-H2 receives the frame from C1-M3 and reads the source MAC address, C1-M3-MAC.

The source MAC address C1-M3-MAC is the same MAC address in the vmx file of C1-M3; it is already known by logical switch 7321 in C1-H2.

Step 3.   Logical switch 7321 in C1-H2 reads the destination MAC address. The destination MAC address C2-M4-MAC is in the MAC table because it has recently seen traffic coming from C2-M4.

The MAC table of logical switch 7321 in C1-H2 has the following entries, as shown in Table 6-4.

Table 6-4   MAC Table of Logical Switch 7321 in C1-H2

VNI	Inner MAC	Outer MAC	Outer IP
7321	**C2-M4-MAC**	**FFFF.FFFF.FFFF**	**C2-H2-VTEP**

Step 4.   Logical switch 7321 passes the frame from C1-M3 to the VXLAN module to create a VXLAN encapsulation.

Step 5.   The VTEP in C1-H2 encapsulates the frame using the following information, as shown in Figure 6-4. Note that a new Frame Check Sum (FCS) replaces the FCS from C1-M3.

- **VNI**: 7321

- **Source UDP Port**: Derived from the frame sent by C1-M3

- **Destination UDP Port**: 8472 (the default port, this can be changed with an NSX API call)

- **Source IP**: C1-H2-VTEP

If C1-H2 had multiple VTEPs, the VXLAN module would have used the IP of the VXLAN VMkernel port (VTEP) to which C1-M3 was pinned.

- **Destination IP**: C2-H2-VTEP

- **Source MAC**: C1-H2-MAC

If C1-H2 had multiple VTEPs, the VXLAN module would have used the MAC of the VXLAN VMkernel port (VTEP) to which C1-M3 was pinned.

- **Destination MAC**: C1-DG-MAC

Remember from Chapter 5 that an Outer MAC of all Fs (refer to Table 6-4) means the destination MAC will be the MAC of the default gateway in the VXLAN TCP/IP Stack.

- **802.1Q VLAN**: 101

Not shown in the diagram are these two fields:

- **DSCP value**: Copied from frame sent by C1-M3, if honored or not overwritten by vDS

- **802.1Q CoS**: Copied from frame sent by C1-M3, if honored or not overwritten by vDS

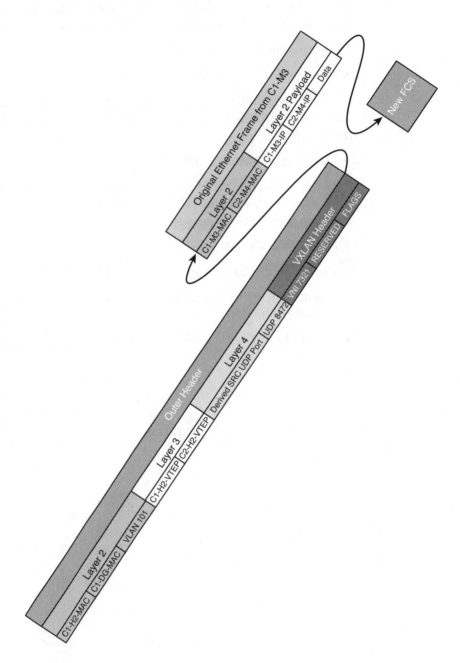

Figure 6-4   VXLAN frame from C1-H2

Step 6.   The underlay switch C1-SW receives the VXLAN frame, examines the VXLAN Layer 2 header, and forwards it to the default router over interface C1-DG.

C1-SW conducts regular Ethernet switch processing, such as MAC learning and CoS enforcement, on the VXLAN Layer 2 header.

Important: The interface from C1-H2 connecting to C1-SW is configured as a Trunk allowing VLAN 101.

Important: If the default gateway interfaces are not configured as Trunk, thus their switch ports are set up as access ports. Switch C1-SW removes the VLAN tag from the VXLAN frame before sending it to the default gateway.

Step 7.   The default gateway receives the frame over interface C1-DG, processes the VXLAN Layer 3 header, does CoS enforcement, and routes the packet over interface C2-DG.

If the default gateway is executing a firewall function, it may also inspect the VXLAN Layer 4 header.

The VXLAN Layer 2 header is changed by the default gateway to include these new values, as shown in Figure 6-5.

- **Source MAC**: C2-DG-MAC

- **Destination MAC**: C2-H2-MAC

NOTE   Every time a frame crosses Layer 2 boundaries (goes through a router), the FCS is dropped and a new one is created.

NOTE   The default gateway does not add a VLAN tag of 102 to the VXLAN frame since it is not a Trunk port. The switch C2-SW does that when it forwards the frame to C2-H2 via the Trunk port.

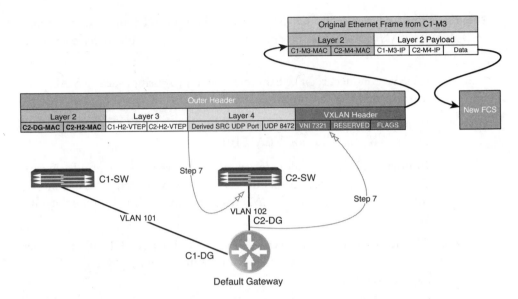

Figure 6-5   VXLAN frame after being processed by the default gateway

Step 8.   The overlay switch C2-SW receives the VXLAN frame from the default gateway, examines the VXLAN Layer 2 header, and forwards it to C2-H2.

   Important: C2-DG is connected to an access port in switch C2-SW in VLAN 102. All frames that arrive from interface C2-DG are placed in VLAN 102.

   Important: The interface C2-H2 connecting to C2-SW is configured as a Trunk allowing VLAN 102.

Step 9.   C2-H2 receives the frame over VXLAN VMkernel port MAC address, C2-H2-MAC.

   The VXLAN module in C2-H2 reads the VNI, 7321, in the VXLAN frame, decapsulates the VXLAN frame, and passes the frame from C1-M3 to logical switch 7321 in C2-H2 for processing.

Step 10.   Logical switch 7321 in C2-H2 reads the source MAC address, C1-M3-MAC.

   Logical switch 7321 in C2-H2 already has MAC address C1-M3-MAC in its MAC table because it has recently seen traffic coming from C1-M3.

Step 11.   Logical switch 7321 in C2-H2 then reads the destination MAC address, C2-M4-MAC, sees that it knows which virtual machine owns it, and passes the frame to Virtual Machine C2-M4.

> Logical switch 7321 in C2-H2 knows MAC address C2-M4-MAC because C2-M4-MAC is in the vmx file of C2-M4.

Well, if you can't take the heat, stay in the Northeast (or is it don't go in the kitchen?). And since you are reading this book, you must want to be a chef—an "NSX chef."

This packet walk demonstrates some of the advantages of logical switches (global logical switches and universal logical switches). First, it shows how the Ethernet broadcast domain to which the VMs are connected can be extended across an IP network. For all we know, Cluster-1 could be located in one end of Data Center A in Santo Domingo, Dominican Republic; Cluster-2 could be located at the other end of Data Center A; and Cluster-3 could be located in Data Center B in Tampa, Florida.

Second, there is no Spanning Tree, TRILL, or any other Layer 2 loop-avoiding technology in place. All traffic outside the clusters' local VTEP subnet goes over Layer 3, IP, which has built-in loop avoidance mechanisms. Yes, you could deploy all VTEPs to be in the same VTEP subnet, necessitating the VTEP VLAN to be extended among all the clusters; however, unless you already have an underlay that has Layer 2 loop-avoiding technology, you don't have to—nor should you, to be honest.

Third, and an important feature to be aware of as we decide which Top of Rack (ToR) switches to deploy: The underlay never learns the MAC addresses of any VMs. Neither C1-SW or C2-SW read the MAC addresses of C1-M3 or C1-M4. The same was true for the default gateway. The underlay only needs to learn the MAC addresses of the VMkernel ports (the VTEPs), in addition to the MAC address of the default gateway, as they are the source/destination of the VXLAN frame in this example. The number of MAC addresses the ToR or End of Row (EoR) needs to have in its MAC table dramatically decreases when using VXLAN.

Let's take this thing to the top by raising the heat once more. In the next packet walk we follow a BUM in the form of an ARP request from a VM connected to our Universal Logical Switch 7321.

Logical Switch Packet Walk Example 4

If you've been reading over these packet walks in one sitting, perhaps you should take a rest after this next packet walk to digest what we have discussed. Sip on a Piña Colada and come back to it later.

This packet walk explores what happens when an ARP request is sent. We take this packet walk all the way home, including the replication required for its delivery.

Virtual Machine C2-M5 wants to communicate with Virtual Machine C3-M3. Assume the following to be true:

- C2-M5 and C3-M3 are connected to Universal Logical Switch 7321.

- C2-M5 and C3-M3 are using the MAC addresses in their vmx files.

- Logical Switch 7321 is configured with MAC learning.

- NSX Universal Controller NC-2 is responsible for VNI 7321.

- C2-M5 knows the IP address of C3-M3 but not the MAC address.

Step 1. Virtual Machine C2-M5 sends an ARP request with the sender IP C2-M5-IP, target IP of C3-M3-IP, Source MAC of C2-M5-MAC, destination MAC of all Fs, Ethernet broadcast, and an Ethertype of 0X0806 (ARP Request), as shown in Figure 6-6.

Layer 2			ARP Request Header			FCS
C2-M5-MAC	FFFF.FFFF.FFFF	0X0806	C2-M5-IP	C2-M3-IP	ARP Fields	

Figure 6-6 ARP request from C2-M5

Step 2. The Switch Security module in ESXi host C2-H3 inspects the frame after realizing it is an ARP request and checks its ARP table for VNI 7321.

If the Switch Security module in C2-H3 has an entry for the ARP request in its ARP table, it will directly respond to C2-M5 and that would be the end of this packet walk. Instead, let's assume the Switch Security module does not have an entry in its ARP table for the ARP request.

Step 3. The Switch Security module C2-H3 sends a request to NSX Controller NC-2 for the ARP entry in the ARP table.

If NC-2 has an entry, it will reply back to the Switch Security module in C2-H3 with the entry. The Switch Security module in C2-H3 will add the entry to its ARP table, and directly respond to C2-M5. Again this would be the end of our packet walk. Instead, let's assume that either:

- NC-2 does not have an ARP entry for our ARP request and responds back to C2-H3 with FFFF.FFFF.FFFF, which translates in English to "I don't have an entry for IP C3-M3-IP."

- NC-2 is down or unresponsive.

- Replication Mode is set to Multicast.

Step 4.   The Switch Security module ESXi host C2-H3 hands the frame to the logical switch 7321.

Step 5.   Logical switch 7321 in ESXi host C2-H3 forwards a copy of the ARP request to all local virtual machines, except C2-M5.

Step 6.   Logical switch 7321 in C2-H3 hands the frame to the VXLAN module to replicate the ARP request.

Important: If not using Multicast Replication Mode, the VTEP consults its copy of the VTEP table to determine where to send the replicated frames. In our case, where all VMs are powered on, all ESXi hosts are in the VTEP table.

NOTE   We are skipping the underlay steps. They are almost identical to the steps in "Logical Switch Packet Walk Sample 3."

a.   If using Multicast Replication Mode, a single VXLAN frame is sent out by C2-H3 with a destination IP of the multicast group assigned to VNI 7321, as shown in Figure 6-7. In this example, all ESXi hosts will have joined the multicast group and thus receive the multicast frame.

b.   If using Unicast Replication Mode, ESXi host C2-H3 sends out unicast VXLAN frames, one each to C2-H1 and C2-H2 in the local VXLAN subnet, and one each to the proxy VTEPs C1-H1 and C3-H1, as shown in Figure 6-8. The proxy VTEPs are locally chosen by C2-H3 per remote VTEP subnet. We are going to assume that C2-H3 chose as proxy VTEPs C1-H1 and C3-H1.

The unicast to the proxy VTEPs will have its Replication bit set to 1. Figure 6-9 shows the VXLAN frames that are sent by C2-H3.

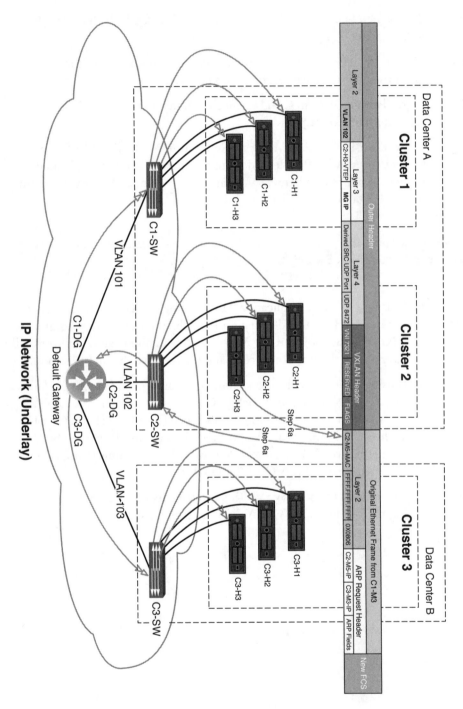

Figure 6-7   VXLAN multicast replication frame being sent by C2-H3

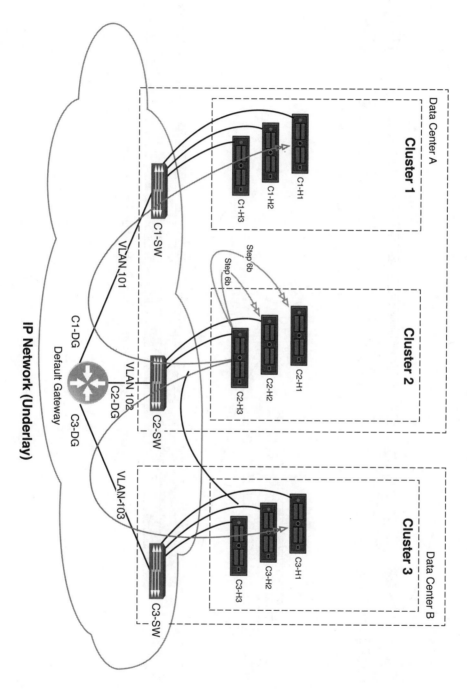

Figure 6-8   Path of VXLAN unicast replication frames sent by C2-H3

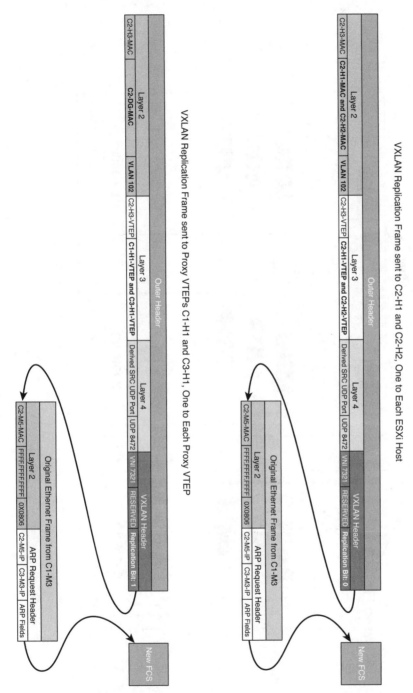

Figure 6-9 VXLAN replication frames sent by C2-H3 in Unicast Replication Mode

Because C1-H1 and C3-H1 are UTEPs, each one in turn sends unicast VXLAN frames to their local VTEPs, with the Replication bit set to 0.

C1-H1 sends the unicast VXLAN frame to C1-H2 and C1-H3. Figure 6-10 shows the two VXLAN frames that are sent by C1-H1.

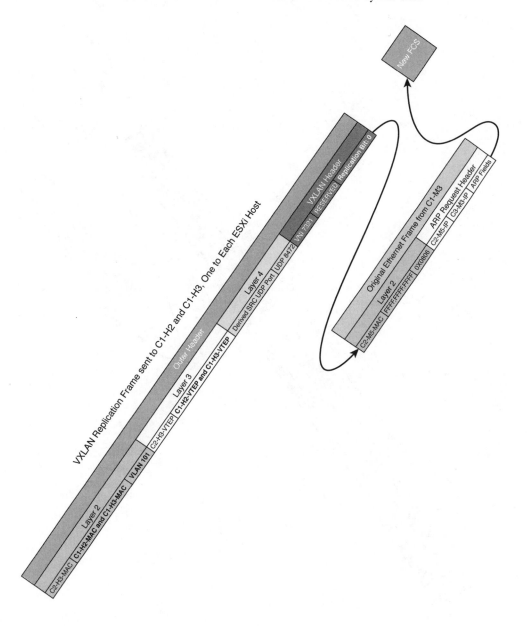

Figure 6-10   VXLAN replication frames sent by C1-H1 in Unicast Replication Mode

C3-H1 sends the unicast VXLAN frame to C3-H2 and C3-H3. Figure 6-11 shows the two VXLAN frames that are sent by C1-H1.

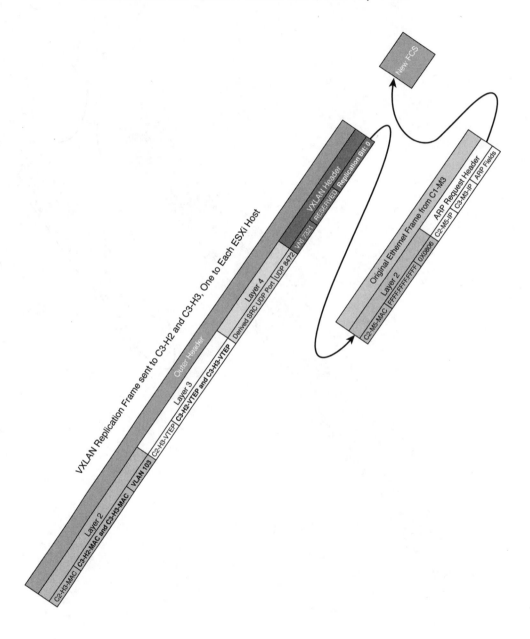

Figure 6-11   VXLAN replication frames sent by C3-H1 in Unicast Replication Mode

c. If using Hybrid Replication Mode, a single multicast VXLAN frame is sent out by C2-H3 with a destination IP of the multicast group assigned to VNI 7321 and the TTL set to 1, and two unicast VXLAN frames are sent out by C2-H3, one to each proxy VTEP C1-H1 and C3-H1, as shown in Figure 6-12.

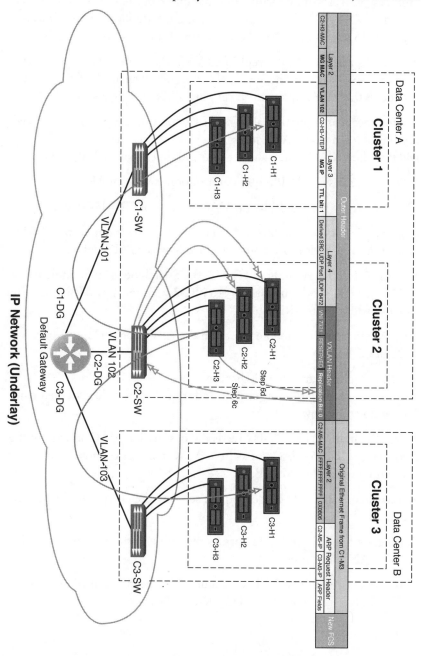

Figure 6-12   Path of VXLAN hybrid replication frames being sent by C2-H3

The unicast to the proxy VTEPs has its Replication bit set to 1, just like in Figure 6-10.

Because C1-H1 and C3-H1 are MTEPs, each one in turn sends a single multicast VXLAN frame with a destination IP of the multicast group assigned to VNI 7321, the TTL set to 1, and the Replication bit set to 0. Figure 6-13 shows the VXLAN replication frame sent by the MTEPs.

Step 7.   All VTEPs that receive the replicated VXLAN frame have to process it, read the VNI, 7321, in the VXLAN frame, decapsulate the frame, and broadcast the ARP request to all running VMs in logical switch 7321.

In the process of doing this, all logical switches with a VNI of 7321 in every ESXi host learn that MAC address C2-M5-MAC is on C1-H3-VTEP and add it to their MAC tables, and set the dead timer to about 200 seconds.

Step 8.   C3-M3 receives the ARP request and responds with an ARP reply.

The ARP reply has a destination MAC address of C2-M5-MAC.

Step 9.   The Switch Security module in C3-H2 inspects the frame from C3-M3, realizes it is an ARP reply, and adds the entry to its ARP table.

Step 10.   Because C3-M3 is running in C3-H2, the Switch Security module in 7321 in C3-H2 sends an IP report to NC-2 with the new ARP entry so it can also add it to its ARP table.

Step 11.   The Switch Security module passes on the ARP reply to logical switch 7321 in C3-H2.

I'm skipping the part where logical switch 7321 in C3-H2 does MAC learning by reading the source MAC address. You should have that part locked down by now.

Step 12.   Logical switch 7321 in C3-H2 reads the destination MAC address of the ARP reply, C2-M5-MAC, looks in its MAC table, and finds an entry for it pointing to C2-H3-VTEP.

Reread step 7 above if you don't quite see why the entry is in the MAC table.

Step 13.   Logical switch 7321 in C3-H2 passes the frame to the VXLAN module for VXLAN frame creation.

This would be a unicast VXLAN frame with a destination IP of C2-H3-VTEP and destination MAC of C3-DG-MAC.

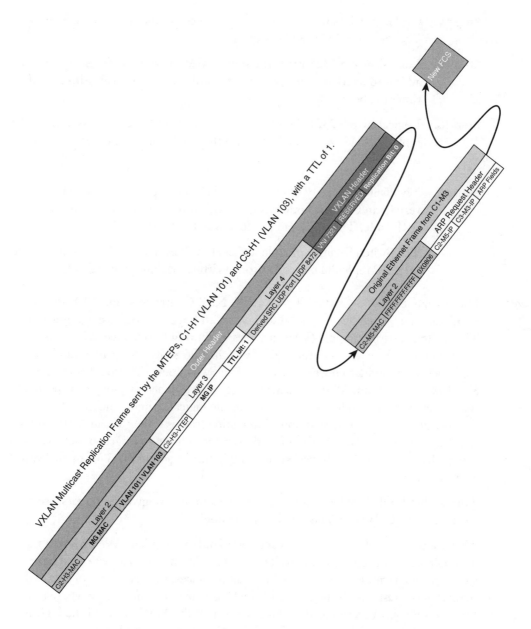

Figure 6-13   VXLAN multicast replication frames sent by the MTEPs

Step 14.   C2-H3 receives the VXLAN frame, processes the frame by reading the VNI number, 7321, and decapsulates it.

Step 15.   Logical switch 7321 reads the source MAC address of the ARP reply and adds it to its MAC table pointing towards C3-H2-VTEP, with a dead timer of about 200 seconds.

Step 16.   Logical switch 7321 then reads the destination MAC address of the ARP reply, C2-M5-MAC, looks it up in the ARP table, and forwards the frame to C2-M5.

Step 17.   The Switch Security module in C2-H3 intercepts the frame before it reaches in C2-M5, notices it is an ARP reply, and adds the entry to its ARP table. Then the frame is forwarded to C2-M5.

The Switch Security module in C2-H3 will *not* tell NC-2 about it because the ARP reply did not come from a virtual machine running in C2-H3.

I briefly mentioned in Chapter 4, "VXLAN, NSX Controllers, and NSX Preparation," that the Switch Security module helps with Layer 2 broadcast suppression. The Switch Security module (VMware likes to shorten it to SwSec dvFilter) sits between the VM's vNIC and the logical switch. The Switch Security module occupies a slot in the ESXi host's IOChain. The Switch Security module occupies Slot 1 of the IOChain. All traffic leaving (egress) the virtual machine is inspected by the Switch Security module before reaching the logical switch. The Switch Security module only inspects, or snoops, interesting frames if they are an ARP request, ARP reply, or DHCP offer. All interesting traffic coming to (ingress) the VM also is snooped, after leaving the logical switch and before reaching the VM, by the Switch Security module.

This is what I call Caribbean hot. Let me take a minute to give my fingers a rest, have that Piña Colada, and take a dive in the pool.

This last packet walk was action packed (pun kind of intended). We reviewed the different modes of replication as well as all the different options that could be taken when an ARP request is sent by a VM. In all instances, the originator of the +ARP request gets a response if the owner of the IP is reachable. In the case where replication is invoked, there was the added bonus that the MAC tables of the logical switches (of the ESXi hosts in the VNI's VTEP table) were updated.

I'm feeling the juices flowing again now that my fingers are no longer sore. Let's do one more packet walk, this time having a virtual machine vMotion.

Logical Switch Packet Walk Example 5

In the next and last packet walk, C2-M5 will vMotion to ESXi host C2-H1, as shown in Figure 6-14. I've removed all other VMs to clean up the diagram a bit. Before reading on, take a few moments to review the roles of the VTEP table, MAC table, and ARP table. We touch on each of those as we do the next packet walk.

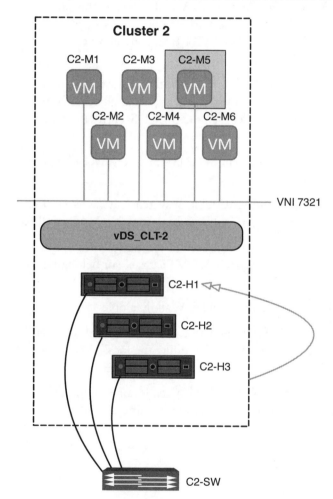

Figure 6-14   Virtual Machine C2-M5 vMotions

Step 1.   The vSphere administrator, or DRS, initiates a vMotion for Virtual Machine C2-M5.

Important: This is where the Switch Security module plays a role of informing the vMotion destination host, C2-H1, about the MAC addresses that C2-M5 has.

Step 2.   When vMotion is completed, ESXi host C2-H3 updates the NSX Controller that it no longer has the MAC address of C2-M5-MAC, as shown in Figure 6-15.

If C2-M5 was the last powered on VM in logical switch 7321 in host C2-H3, C2-H3 will also send the NSX Controller a request to remove its VTEP, C2-H3-VTEP, from the 7321's VTEP table. At this point, the NSX Controller would update the VTEP table, removing C2-H3-VTEP, and send a copy of the updated VTEP table to all other hosts that have a VTEP in the VTEP table.

Step 3.   ESXi host C2-H1 updates the NSX Controller that it has the MAC address C2-M5-MAC, as shown in Figure 6-16, as well as all other MAC addresses associated with C2-M5 (which the Switch Security module in C2-H3 told C2-H1 about).

Step 4.   Host C2-H1 sends a RARP on behalf of C2-M5, for all MAC addresses associated with C2-M5.

The RARP is used to update the MAC table of switches. It has as a source the MAC to be updated in the MAC table and a destination MAC of all Fs.

Step 5.   Following the Replication Mode configured in the logical switch, the RARP is replicated to all ESXi hosts in the VTEP table or belonging to the multicast group for VNI 7321.

Review step 6 in the Logical Switch Packet Walk Example 4.

Step 6.   All ESXi hosts receiving the RARP add an entry in their local MAC table for VNI 7321 for MAC C2-M5-MAC, including the local MAC table on host C2-H3, the vMotion source host.

The MAC entry is added in VNI 7321's MAC tables of each logical switch in the ESXi host, with a dead timer of five minutes.

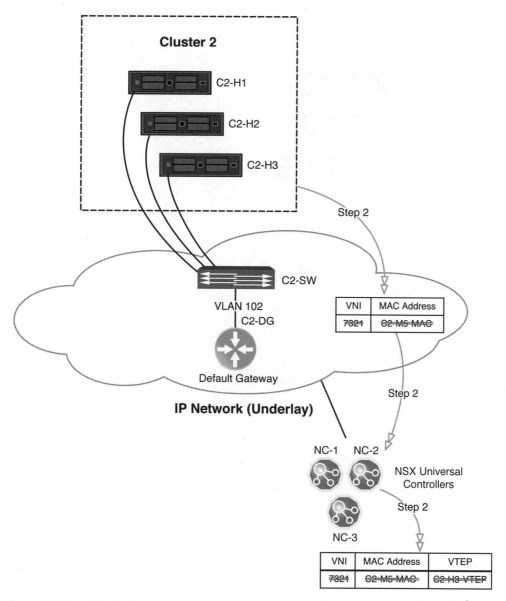

Figure 6-15 The NSX Controller removes the MAC entry for C2-M5-MAC from the MAC table.

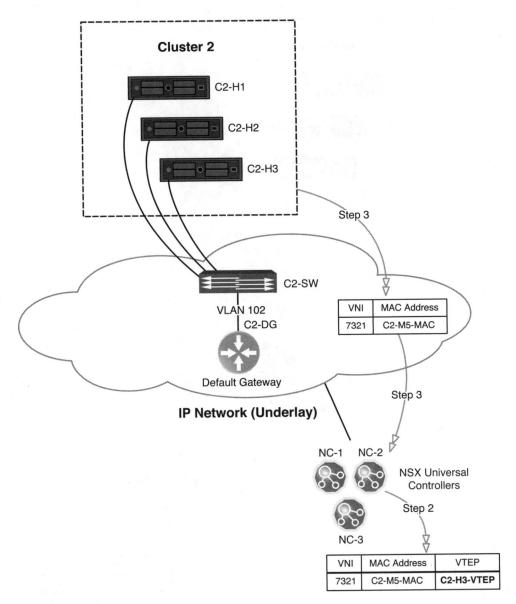

Figure 6-16   The NSX Controller adds in the MAC table the MAC entry for C2-M5-MAC pointing to C2-H1 VTEP.

Exam Preparation Tasks

Review All the Key Topics

Review the most important topics from inside the chapter, noted with the Key Topic icon in the outer margin of the page. Table 6-5 lists these key topics and the page numbers where each is found.

Table 6-5 Key Topics for Chapter 6

Key Topic Element	Description	Page Number
Paragraph	Underlay switches do not learn the MAC address of virtual machines whose frames are encapsulated in a VXLAN frame.	177
Paragraph	The Switch Security module populates its ARP table by snooping on ARP frames and DHCP Ack frames.	188

Define Key Terms

Define the following key terms from this chapter, and check your answers in the Glossary:

logical switch, universal logical switch, cross vCenter NSX, VNI, VTEP, Switch Security module, MAC learning, VTEP table, ARP table, Replication Mode, proxy VTEP, UTEP, MTEP

This chapter covers all or part of the following VCP6-NV exam blueprint topics:

- **Objective 5.4**—Configure and Manage Logical Routers
- **Objective 8.1**—Differentiate single and Cross-vCenter NSX deployments
- **Objective 8.2**—Determine Cross-vCenter Requirements and Configurations
- **Objective 10.3**—Troubleshoot Common NSX Component Issues

CHAPTER 7

Logical Router

We learned how NSX provides ways in which two virtual machines (VMs) can be in the same Ethernet broadcast domain regardless of the location of the ESXi hosts (where the VMs are running). In today's data center, most of the traffic between VMs does not take place in the same broadcast domain, where the VMs are in the same subnet, but rather between VMs in different broadcast domains or subnets.

The traditional model of having an entity acting as the default gateway eliminates some of the benefits of using logical switches. Think about it: Without NSX all traffic that leaves a broadcast domain would have to be pinned back to the default gateway, wherever it is physically located. In this chapter, you learn about NSX's logical routers. You learn how the logical routers can be leveraged to handle east-west traffic between VMs in different subnets.

Do I Know This Already?

The "Do I Know This Already?" quiz allows you to assess whether you should read this entire chapter or simply jump to the "Exam Preparation Tasks" section for review. If you are in doubt, read the entire chapter. Table 7-1 outlines the major headings in this chapter and the corresponding "Do I Know This Already?" quiz questions. You can find the answers in Appendix A, "Answers to the 'Do I Know This Already?' Quizzes."

Table 7-1 Headings and Questions

Foundation Topic Section	Questions Covered in This Section
NSX Logical Router	1-5
Logical Router Control VM	6-9
Logical Router Verification	10

1. In which plane does the logical router reside?

   a. Management plane

   b. Forwarding plane

   c. Data plane

   d. Control plane

2. How many distributed logical router instances are supported by an ESXi host?

   a. 100

   b. 1,000

   c. 1,200

   d. 2,400

3. How many universal logical router instances are supported in an NSX domain?

   a. 100

   b. 1,000

   c. 1,200

   d. 2,400

4. Which of the following interfaces is not supported by a universal logical router?

   a. Uplink VXLAN LIF

   b. Internal VXLAN LIF

   c. Uplink VLAN LIF

   d. vdrPort

5. Which two types of interfaces can be configured on a logical router? (Choose two.)

   a. Internal

   b. External

   c. Downlink

   d. Uplink

6. How many logical router control VMs are supported by the universal logical router?

    a. 1

    b. 2

    c. 4

    d. 8

7. In which plane does the distributed logical control VM reside?

    a. Management plane

    b. Forwarding plane

    c. Data plane

    d. Control plane

8. How much memory does the control VM have?

    a. 512 MB

    b. 1 GB

    c. 2 GB

    d. 4 GB

9. A universal logical router is deployed in a cross-vCenter NSX domain with three vCenter servers. How many universal logical router control VMs could be deployed in this scenario?

    a. 1 control VM, to be deployed to any of the three vCenter servers

    b. 3 control VMs, to be deployed one to each vCenter server

    c. 2 control VMs in Edge HA mode, to be deployed to the vCenter server paired with the Primary NSX Manager

    d. 2 control VMs in Edge HA mode, to be deployed to at least two of the three vCenter servers

10. Which entity does not have a copy of the logical router's routing table?

    a. ESXi host

    b. NSX Manager

    c. NSX Controller

    d. Control VM

Foundation Topics

NSX Logical Router

The NSX logical router, or just logical router for short, is a router whose data plane runs in the ESXi host kernel. We installed the logical router module in the ESXi host during host preparation in Chapter 4, "VXLAN, NSX Controllers, and NSX Preparation;" it is part of the VXLAN VIB. What makes the logical router different from your traditional router is that it is 1) distributed and 2) has a separate entity handling the control plane.

The logical router has a data plane running in the kernel of each ESXi host that has a copy of it. If two ESXi hosts are running a copy of the same logical router instance, it is still considered one router. The copies are almost identical to each other. We talk a bit about the exceptions to being identical later in this chapter. The logical router is similar to how two ESXi hosts have different data planes for the same logical switch or vDS.

Figure 7-1 shows a logical router instance with two connections to logical switches 7321 and 7322. There are two ESXi hosts, each with a powered on VM connected to each logical switch. The logical router instance copies in each ESXi host are similar.

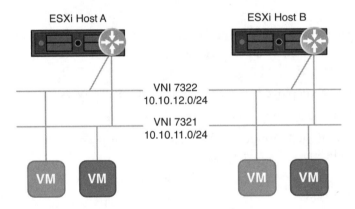

Figure 7-1   Distributed logical router instance

A single ESXi host can run 100 different logical router instances. Each logical router instance in the ESXi host is totally and completely independent and separate from all other logical router instances running in the same ESXi host. The closest analogy that comes to mind is a physical router with multiple Virtual Routing and Forwarding (VRF) tables. Each VRF table is independent of the other. An NSX domain can have a total of 1,200 different logical router instances running. Each logical router can also have 1,000 logical interfaces (LIFs).

Each logical router is assigned, by the NSX Controller Layer 3 master, to an NSX Controller to manage its control plane. The NSX Controller responsible for the logical router instance keeps a copy of the master routing table for the logical router. The NSX Controller pushes a copy of the routing table to each ESXi host running an instance of the logical router. All copies of the logical router in each ESXi host with the same Locale ID have the same routing table. We cover Locale IDs later in this chapter in the section "Locale ID." If there is a change in the routing table, the responsible NSX Controller pushes the updated routing table to the corresponding ESXi hosts running the logical router.

A logical router's LIF can connect to a logical switch or dvPortgroup. A logical router's LIF can't connect to a standard portgroup. Recall from Chapter 5, "NSX Switches," a logical switch is represented by a dvPortgroup. Thus a logical router LIF can connect to a VXLAN backed dvPortgroup (logical switch) or a VLAN backed dvPortgroup.

Every ESXi host in the transport zone of the logical switch an LIF connects to gets a copy of the logical router instance. In the case of an LIF connecting to a VLAN backed dvPortgroup, but has no LIFs connected to a logical switch, all ESXi hosts that belong to the same vDS where the dvPortgroup is get a copy of the logical router instance.

Figure 7-2 shows three ESXi hosts, four logical switches in the same transport zone, and two logical router instances. The four powered-on VMs connect to the four logical switches, one VM per logical switch. Regardless of the placement of the VMs, the NSX Controller places copies of both logical router instances on all three ESXi hosts.

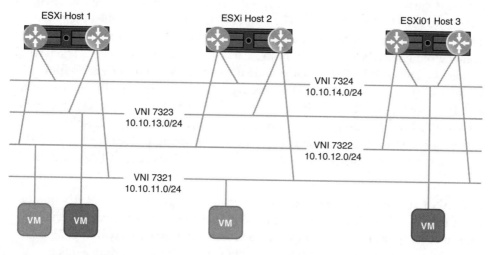

Figure 7-2 Distributed logical router instance placement

The logical router can have two types of LIFs:

- **Internal LIF**: Intended for connections to logical switches that have virtual machines. We refer to these Layer 2 segments with an Internal LIF as *internal segments*. No Layer 3 control plane traffic, such as OSPF hellos, should ever be seen in the internal segment.

- **Uplink LIF**: Intended to connect to logical switches that have other routing entities connected to them, such as the NSX Edge Services Gateway, as well as entities participating in Layer 3 control plane traffic, such as the logical router control VM. We discuss the logical router control VM later in this chapter. A logical router can have up to eight Uplink LIFs. We refer to these Layer 2 segments with an Uplink LIF as *uplink segments*. No non-appliance virtual machine should be connecting to an uplink segment.

When connecting an LIF to a logical switch, the LIF is also referred to as a *VXLAN LIF*. When connecting an LIF to a VLAN backed dvPortgroup, the LIF is also referred to as a *VLAN LIF*. Both the Internal and Uplink LIFs can be connected to a VLAN backed dvPortgroup instead of logical switches. The benefits of having a VLAN Internal LIF are between minimal to none, and it is generally not a good idea as it constrains the egress points for Layer 3 traffic and would require all clusters in the same transport zone to use the same vDS. The VLAN Uplink LIF could be used so the logical router can do routing directly with the physical network. We review this design further in Chapter 11, "Layer 3 Connectivity Between Virtual and Physical Networks."

Each copy of the logical router instance in the ESXi hosts gets at least two MAC addresses. One is called the vMAC, and it is the same MAC in all logical router copies. The vMAC is 02:50:56:56:44:52. The other MAC addresses are called the pMAC, assigned one per dvUplink based on the Teaming Policy selected during host preparation. Each pMAC is different in each copy of the logical router. The pMAC is generated by each ESXi host independently and has VMware's Organization Unique ID (OUI) of 00:50:56. When the logical router sends an ARP request from an LIF or when it sends an ARP reply for an IP of one of its LIFs, it responds with the vMAC. Also, for egress traffic from any of its VXLAN LIFs, it uses the vMAC as the source MAC address. For all other traffic, including traffic over VLAN LIFs, it uses the corresponding pMAC. Chapter 11 covers pMAC over VLAN LIFs in more detail.

A VLAN LIF can only connect to a dvPortgroup configured with a VLAN number, other than 0 and 4095, and is present in all ESXi hosts that have a copy of the logical router instance. In other words, all ESXi hosts that have a copy of the logical router instance must be part of the same vDS where the dvPortgroup exists.

Not only do all copies of the logical router instance use the same vMAC of 02:50:56:56:44:52, but *ALL* logical router instances do as well. This is one reason why two LIFs, from the same logical router or from different logical routers, can't be connected to the same logical switch.

There are two types of logical routers. A logical router can only connect to global logical switches or universal logical switches, but not both at the same time. If a logical router connects to global logical switches it is called a *distributed logical router*. If a logical router connects to a universal logical switch it is called a *universal logical router (ULR)*. A ULR does not support VLAN LIFs, only VXLAN LIFs. The Primary NSX Manager in the Cross vCenter NSX domain is the only one that can deploy the ULR. At time of deployment you must select which type of logical router you are deploying.

Assume you have a VM connected to a logical switch, a logical router with an internal LIF in the same logical switch, and the VM has a default gateway of the LIF's IP. When the VM sends an ARP request for its default gateway's MAC, the logical router in the same ESXi host where the VM is running sends back an ARP reply with the vMAC.

In this case, when the virtual machine vMotions, the MAC address of the VMs' default gateway will be the same at the destination host because it is the vMAC. The same is true if the VM is connected to a universal logical switch with a ULR for its default gateway.

The pMAC is the one of three differences that can be found in the copies of the logical router instances in each ESXi host. The other differences occur when using Locale IDs, in the case of universal logical routers, and when doing Layer 2 Bridging, in the case of distributed logical routers. We review Layer 2 Bridging in Chapter 10, "Layer 2 Extensions." Everything else in the logical router instance's copies is identical.

It is not possible to connect a logical router to logical switches in different transport zones, as there might be a cluster in one transport zone that is not a member of the other transport zone. Thus, it wouldn't be possible to have the same identical copy of the logical router in all of the ESXi hosts in both transport zones.

Logical Router Control VM

For each logical router instance created, at least one virtual appliance called the Logical Router Control Virtual Machine, or Control VM for short, is deployed... if you want—more on this shortly. The Control VM's job is to handle the dynamic component of the logical router's control plane by making routing neighbor adjacencies and creating the forwarding database, or routing table, for dynamic entries.

A Control VM does not perform control plane functions for more than one logical router instance; however, in the case of the ULR, you may deploy multiple independent Control VMs, one per NSX Manager in the Cross vCenter domain.

After the Control VM puts together the dynamic routing table, a copy of it needs to be given to each ESXi host that is running a copy of the logical router instance. The only entity that actually knows of all the ESXi hosts that are running the copy of the logical router is the NSX Controller responsible for the logical router instance. Thus the Control VM forwards the dynamic routing table to the NSX Controller, which would merge it with its copy of the static routing table to create the master routing table. A copy of the master routing table is forwarded by the NSX Controller to the ESXi hosts that are running a copy of the logical router instance. Future dynamic routing table updates follow the same communication path.

So I teased you by saying that you can choose whether to deploy a Control VM. The Control VM is a modified NSX Edge appliance that consumes compute and storage resources in an ESXi host somewhere. Chapter 9, "NSX Edge Services Gateway," begins coverage of the NSX Edge. The Control VM has 1 vCPU, 512 MB of RAM, and 500 MB of thin-provisioned storage. If you are not interested in having the logical router do any dynamic routing, you don't need the Control VM. However, once you deploy a logical router without a Control VM, you can't go back and add the Control VM later. It is a "take it or leave it" kind of deal. If you choose to deploy a Control VM, the Control VM won't do much, if anything, until you configure a dynamic routing protocol.

Do you recall the Uplink LIF? That's the segment where all the routing control plane would be taking place, such as forming OSPF adjacencies. The logical router instance itself is a data plane entity and therefore can't do any dynamic control plane, such as running BGP. To participate in the routing control plane process the Control VM automatically has one of its interfaces connected to the uplink segment of the Uplink LIF. When I say the Control VM would connect itself, I mean the NSX Manager selects one of the available Control VM interfaces to connect to the uplink segment and asks vCenter to make the connection. The Control VM should never have one of its interfaces connected to an internal segment, with one optional exception: You may connect the Control VM's High Availability (HA) interface to an internal segment. Prior to NSX 6.2, the High Availability interface was called the Management interface.

Why, you ask, does the Control VM need to have one of its interfaces connected to the uplink segment? Because the Control VM needs a Layer 2 path to exchange control plane routing information with whichever device it needs to communicate with. For example, if you configure OSPF in the Uplink LIF, the Control VM needs to exchange Layer 2 OSPF LSAs over the uplink segment.

The Control VM, being that it is a virtual machine, has 10 interfaces, one of which must be reserved for the HA interface. The HA interface is used to get SSH access to the Control VM as well as for syslog. By accessing the Control VM via SSH or via the VM console in the vSphere Web Client, you can get CLI access to view the Control VM's interfaces as well as the IPs of logical router interfaces, the routing table, and routing process neighbors. You can also perform control plane debugging from the CLI. You cannot make configuration changes for the logical router from the Control VM CLI.

Any routing peers the Control VM has will not be aware that the logical router and the Control VM are two different entities. We review how dynamic routing is achieved in Chapter 12, "Routing Protocols."

Figure 7-3 shows a logical view of the Control VM with an interface connected to an uplink segment, where an NSX Edge Services Gateway is connected, and the HA interface connected to a management segment.

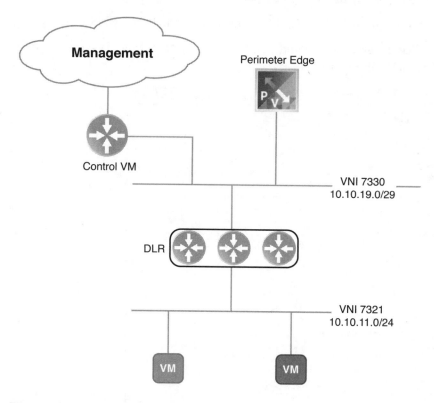

Figure 7-3   Logical router Control VM

Creating and Deploying the Logical Router

The logical router is created by the NSX Manager, either by use of the vSphere Web Client or via the NSX APIs.

Before you deploy the logical router, you must have the following:

- The role of enterprise administrator or NSX administrator.

- The NSX Controller cluster must be up and available.

- A VNI pool must have been created.

To deploy the logical router using the vSphere Web Client, follow these steps:

Step 1.   From the NSX Home page select NSX Edges.

Step 2.   In the NSX Manager drop-down menu, select the NSX Manager that will be deploying the logical router.

   If you want to deploy a ULR, you must select the Primary NSX Manager.

Step 3.   Click the green + icon and wait for the New NSX Edge Wizard to open, as shown in Figure 7-4.

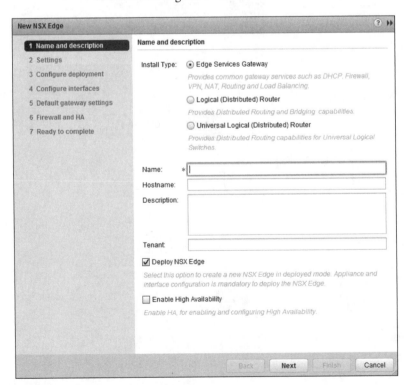

Figure 7-4   New NSX Edge Wizard

Step 4. In the Name and Description step, fill out these values:

    a. Install Type: Select whether to deploy an NSX Edge, a DLR, or a ULR. We select **Universal Logical (Distributed) Router**.

        You will notice in step 6, the *New NSX Edge wizard*, *Firewall* and *HA* disappears.

        You will also notice the box **Enable Local Egress**. This feature allows the ULR to send egress traffic to NSX Edges that are in the same location as the copy of the ULR sending the egress traffic. We learn about this feature later in this chapter when we learn about Locale ID.

    b. Enter a name for the logical router.

        This name will be used by vCenter to name the Control VM.

    c. Optionally enter the hostname, a description, and a tenant name.

        The Tenant field is used for management and naming of the logical routers. This field has no impact on the performance or functionality of the logical router.

    d. Check the **Deploy NSX Edge** box if you want to deploy the Control VM.

        If deploying an NSX Edge, this option allows you to configure the NSX Edge without actually deploying the appliance. This is handy for staging. If deploying a logical router, this option allows you to deploy the Control VM. Once the logical router is deployed, you can't add the Control VM later.

    e. Check the **Enable High Availability** box if you want to enable Edge HA.

        This option deploys two NSX Edges or Control VMs, one in Active and one in Standby mode. Chapter 9 covers the NSX Edge HA feature in more detail.

    f. After you have completed this step, it should look like Figure 7-5. Click **Next** to continue.

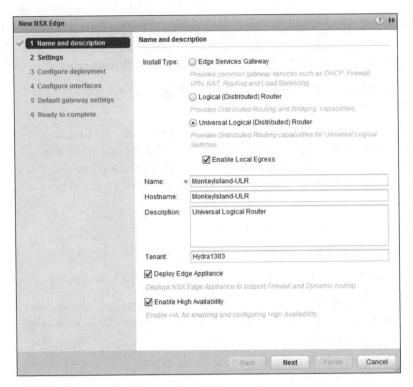

Figure 7-5   Name and Description field

Step 5.   In the Settings step, enter the administrator's username and password, and click **Next**.

   a.   This credential is used when logging in, via SSH or the console, to the Control VM. The password must be 12 characters long containing:

   At least one uppercase letter

   At least one lowercase letter

   At least one number

   At least one special character, such as ! or $

   b.   You can enable SSH access to the Control VM here.

   If you enable SSH access, the Control VM adds an internal Firewall rule allowing the SSH access.

Step 6.   In the Configure Deployment step, choose among the following options:

   a.   Datacenter: Select the data center where the Control VM will be deployed.

The data center options are for the vCenter paired with the NSX Manager from step 2.

b. NSX Edge Appliances: Select the resource pool or cluster and datastore where to deploy the Control VM. This is an optional field.

If configuring the logical router with NSX Edge HA, as mentioned in step 4e above, you can select where the second Control VM will be deployed.

c. After you complete this step, it should look similar to Figure 7-6. Click **Next** to continue.

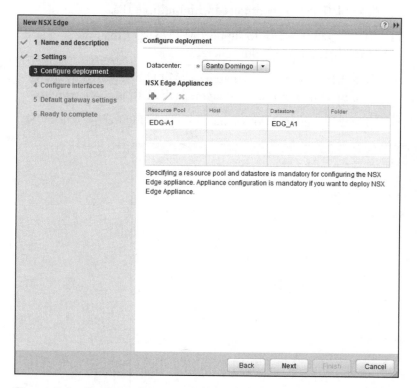

Figure 7-6   Configure Deployment field

Step 7.   In the Configure Interfaces step, you do two things. First, tell NSX Manager where to connect the Control VM's HA interface. Second, tell NSX Manager the LIFs the logical router instance will have. You can always add, edit, and remove LIFs after the wizard is completed.

a. HA Interface Configuration: Select the dvPortgroup or logical switch the Control VM's HA interface will connect to.

b. Configure Interfaces of this NSX Edge: These are the LIFs for the logical router. You can add up to 1,000 LIFs.

    i.   Clicking on the green + icon opens the Add Interface Wizard.

        Give the LIF a name and assign it as an Internal or Uplink LIF.

        Select the logical switch the ULR's LIF will connect to. If this was for a DLR, you would have a choice to connect the LIF to a VLAN backed dvPortgroup.

    ii.   Add the IP address for each LIF.

        Each LIF can be configured with multiple IPs.

    iii.   If you want the LIF to support MTU larger than the standard 1500 bytes, you can do so here.

        The LIF MTU should match the MTU being used by the virtual machines in the same segment the LIF is connecting to.

    iv.   The LIF configurations should look as in Figure 7-7. Click **OK**.

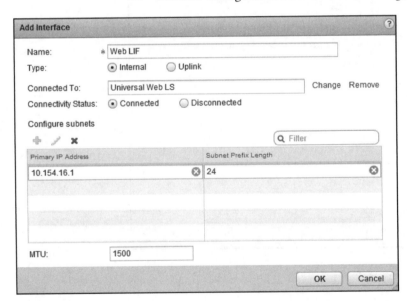

Figure 7-7   LIF configuration

c. After you complete step 7, the configuration should look similar to Figure 7-8. Click **Next** to continue.

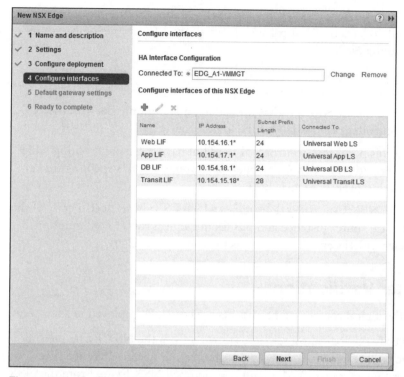

Figure 7-8   Configure Interfaces field

Step 8.   The Default Gateway Settings field allows you to enter the default gateway for the logical router and the outgoing LIF. This is optional and you can add a default gateway after deployment.

Step 9.   In Ready to Complete, review your settings. You may go back to make any desired changes. Once you are satisfied click **Finish**.

After you click **Finish**, the following happens in the background:

a.   The vSphere Web Client hands off the configuration to vCenter, which then passes it to NSX Manager.

b.   NSX Manager reviews the configuration for any errors.

If NSX Manager finds any errors, an error message is displayed to the user in the vSphere Web Client.

c.   If all checks out, NSX Manager hands the Control VM OVF to vCenter with instructions to deploy it per the configurations.

Remember that NSX Manager has an OVF for every type of NSX appliance that needs to be deployed.

d.   Once the Control VM is powered on, vCenter notifies NSX Manager.

e. NSX Manager accesses the Control VM, finishes the configuration, and updates the Control VM about all the LIFs in the logical router and the NSX Controllers.

f. NSX Manager updates the NSX Controller with any relevant information, such as default gateway.

g. Once the Control VM has booted up, it communicates with the NSX Controller responsible for the logical router.

At this point the Control VM does not have a dynamic routing table to provide the NSX Controller since you have not yet configured a routing process such as BGP.

h. The NSX Controller determines which ESXi hosts need a copy of the logical router instance and pushes the logical router configuration, such as LIFs and IPs, as well as the routing table.

Logical Router Verification

You can verify the logical router instance has been successfully deployed in a few ways.

One way is to verify the logical router status directly from the NSX Edges view in the NSX Home page. Figure 7-9 shows the logical router instance has been created. Remember that a Control VM is simply a modified NSX Edge. From the NSX Edges view you can see both the logical router information and the NSX Edges.

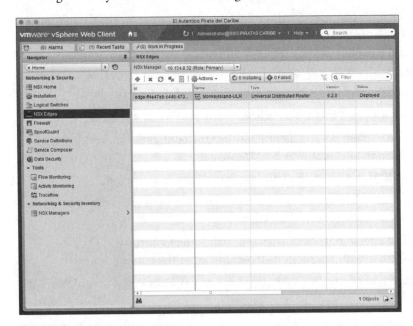

Figure 7-9   NSX Edges view

The following fields can be inspected from this view:

- **Id**: An NSX Manager provided tracking ID. It always starts with the word *edge* followed by a dash "-," and a number. The ID is unique to each logical router and NSX Edge. For a DLR, the number starts at 1 and goes up. For a URL, the number is a UUID provided by NSX Manager.

- **Name**: The name of the logical router assigned during installation. In vCenter, the Control VM's name of a ULR will be the ID followed by this name.

- **Type**: The type of router. In Figure 7-9 it states that this is a ULR. The other options for Type are NSX Edge and logical router (for a DLR).

- **Version**: This version matches the version of the NSX Manager.

- **Status**: The logical router can be Busy, Deployed, or Undeployed. If it states Undeployed it means the logical router configurations are saved in NSX Manager, but the actual Control VM has not been deployed by vCenter.

- **Tenant (to the right but not shown in Figure 7-9)**: This lists the name of the tenant you provided during configuration.

- **Interfaces (to the right but not shown in Figure 7-9)**: The number of interfaces configured in the logical router.

- **Size (to the right but not shown in Figure 7-9)**: The size of the Control VM. We review what the different size options are in Chapter 9.

Double-clicking the logical router, from the Primary NSX Manager, opens the logical router Home view for the selected NSX Manager. Here you can verify additional configuration and some operation state of the logical router. Figure 7-10 shows the **Manage > Settings > Configuration** page. In this page, you can get a quick summary of the settings configured in the logical router and the number of Control VMs deployed by this NSX Manager and where they have been deployed. If the Control VM has not been deployed, you can deploy it here.

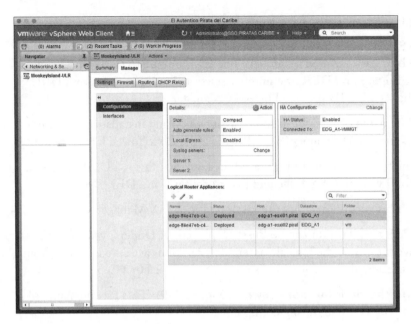

Figure 7-10 Logical router Configuration page

The ULR is visible from all NSX Managers in the same cross vCenter NSX domain. Earlier in the chapter, I mentioned that the ULR could have multiple Control VMs operating independently of each other. To add additional Control VMs, up to 8 total, go to the ULR Home page view from the Secondary NSX Manager you want to own the Control VM and add it from the **Manage > Settings > Configuration** page.

From the Interfaces page, as shown in Figure 7-11, you can see the LIFs, their IPs, the switch to which they connect, and their status. From here you can add new LIFs, edit the configuration of an existing LIF, disconnect it, or connect it. Only the Primary NSX Manager can make any changes to LIFs. The Secondary NSX Managers only have read-only access to the LIFs.

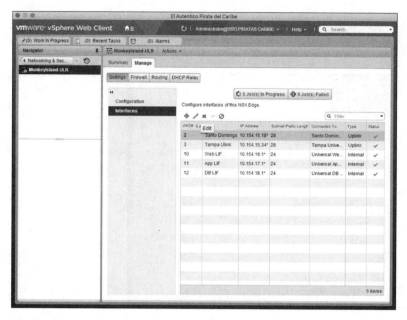

Figure 7-11   Editing LIFs

Another option to verify the status of the Control VM is to go to the Host and Clusters or VM and Templates views in the vCenter associated with the NSX Manager that deployed it and look for the Control VM. The name of the Control VM for a logical router matches the name you assigned it during installation followed by a number (0 or 1). The name of the Control VM for the ULR is the ULR ID followed by a number (0 or 1) followed by the ULR name. The number 0 means this is the first Control VM. If you have enabled Edge HA for the Control VM, the second Control VM has the same name as the first but with the number 1. Figure 7-12 shows the summary page of a Control VM after being deployed. In the figure you can see the following:

- The number of vCPUs assigned to the Control VM, which is 1.

- The amount of vRAM given to the Control VM, 512 MB.

- The size of the HDD given to the Control VM, 500 MB.

- The host where the Control VM is deployed.

Figure 7-12   Distributed logical router Control VMs deployed in ESXi hosts

In Figure 7-12, notice Network adapter 4 is connected to the uplink segment Universal Transit LS. This is where the uplink segment the ULR's Uplink LIF Universal Transit is connected.

While in the Control VM Summary page, you can click **Launch Remote Console** to get CLI access to the Control VM. Optionally, if you have allowed SSH access to the Control VM, you can SSH to the Control VM to get the same CLI access. From the CLI you can execute commands to verify the configuration of the logical router. For example, as shown in Figure 7-13, you can execute the command **show interface**. The output shows all the Control VM interfaces, including the IP information per interface. Take a look at the first interface, *Interface VDR*, where **VDR** stands for *Viva Dominican Republic* (or is it *virtual distributed router*? I can't seem to recall which one it is). That interface is the placeholder for the logical router interfaces, listing all the IPs configured in the logical router LIFs. You can also see the Control VM's management interface, vNic_0. It includes the IP of the HA interface and the IP for the HA heartbeat since we have configured Edge HA. Remember that we expand on the HA heartbeat in Chapter 9. One more thing before we delve into Figure 7-13. Do you recognize the hostname of the Control VM? It is the hostname we gave it during the Name and Description step.

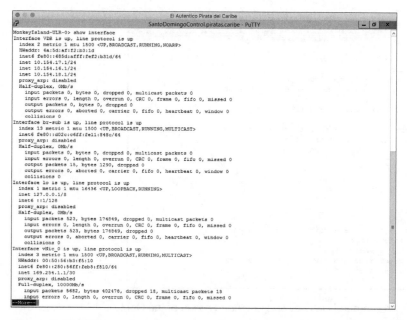

```
El Autentico Pirata del Caribe
SantoDomingoControl.piratas.caribe - PuTTY                    _ □ X
MonkeyIsland-ULR-0> show interface
Interface VDR is up, line protocol is up
 index 2 metric 1 mtu 1500 <UP,BROADCAST,RUNNING,NOARP>
 HWaddr: 6a:5d:af:f2:b3:1d
 inet6 fe80::685d:afff:fef2:b31d/64
 inet 10.154.17.1/24
 inet 10.154.16.1/24
 inet 10.154.18.1/24
 proxy_arp: disabled
 Half-duplex, 0Mb/s
   input packets 0, bytes 0, dropped 0, multicast packets 0
   input errors 0, length 0, overrun 0, CRC 0, frame 0, fifo 0, missed 0
   output packets 0, bytes 0, dropped 0
   output errors 0, aborted 0, carrier 0, fifo 0, heartbeat 0, window 0
   collisions 0
Interface br-sub is up, line protocol is up
 index 13 metric 1 mtu 1500 <UP,BROADCAST,RUNNING,MULTICAST>
 inet6 fe80::d02c:c6ff:fe11:848c/64
 proxy_arp: disabled
 Half-duplex, 0Mb/s
   input packets 0, bytes 0, dropped 0, multicast packets 0
   input errors 0, length 0, overrun 0, CRC 0, frame 0, fifo 0, missed 0
   output packets 15, bytes 1290, dropped 0
   output errors 0, aborted 0, carrier 0, fifo 0, heartbeat 0, window 0
   collisions 0
Interface lo is up, line protocol is up
 index 1 metric 1 mtu 16436 <UP,LOOPBACK,RUNNING>
 inet 127.0.0.1/8
 inet6 ::1/128
 proxy_arp: disabled
 Half-duplex, 0Mb/s
   input packets 523, bytes 174849, dropped 0, multicast packets 0
   input errors 0, length 0, overrun 0, CRC 0, frame 0, fifo 0, missed 0
   output packets 523, bytes 174849, dropped 0
   output errors 0, aborted 0, carrier 0, fifo 0, heartbeat 0, window 0
   collisions 0
Interface vNic_0 is up, line protocol is up
 index 3 metric 1 mtu 1500 <UP,BROADCAST,RUNNING,MULTICAST>
 HWaddr: 00:50:56:b3:f5:10
 inet6 fe80::250:56ff:feb3:f510/64
 inet 169.254.1.1/30
 proxy_arp: disabled
 Full-duplex, 10000Mb/s
   input packets 5682, bytes 402478, dropped 18, multicast packets 13
   input errors 0, length 0, overrun 0, CRC 0, frame 0, fifo 0, missed 0
--More--
```

Figure 7-13   Trimmed output from the command **show interface** in the Control VM CLI

As a reminder, configuration changes can only be made via NSX Manager. You can't make any configuration changes to the Control VM or the logical router instance from the CLI. Most commands are strictly for viewing current status, such as configuration and debugging. Figure 7-14 shows the available commands for the Control VM in *user mode and privileged mode*. As it is shown, there are no commands to make configuration changes.

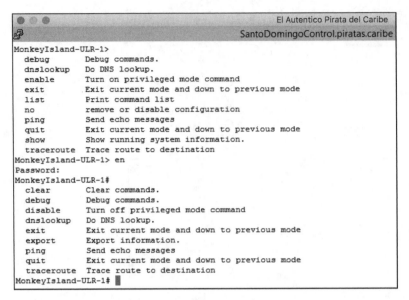

```
                                          El Autentico Pirata del Caribe
                                   SantoDomingoControl.piratas.caribe
MonkeyIsland-ULR-1>
  debug      Debug commands.
  dnslookup  Do DNS lookup.
  enable     Turn on privileged mode command
  exit       Exit current mode and down to previous mode
  list       Print command list
  no         remove or disable configuration
  ping       Send echo messages
  quit       Exit current mode and down to previous mode
  show       Show running system information.
  traceroute Trace route to destination
MonkeyIsland-ULR-1> en
Password:
MonkeyIsland-ULR-1#
  clear      Clear commands.
  debug      Debug commands.
  disable    Turn off privileged mode command
  dnslookup  Do DNS lookup.
  exit       Exit current mode and down to previous mode
  export     Export information.
  ping       Send echo messages
  quit       Exit current mode and down to previous mode
  traceroute Trace route to destination
MonkeyIsland-ULR-1#
```

Figure 7-14   Available commands in user and privileged mode of the Control VM

Connectivity Testing

Let's test our connectivity by doing some pings across some VMs. Figure 7-15 shows a logical diagram of our environment, which includes the ESXi hosts where each VM is running. The logical router has an LIF in each logical switch, and it is the default gateway for each VM. The default gateway of each segment is the 10.10.X.1 IP.

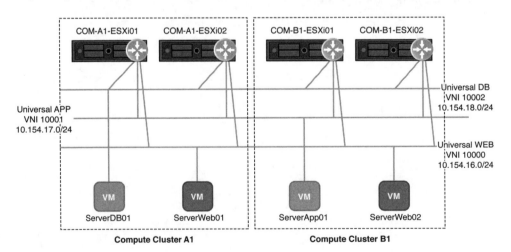

Figure 7-15   Logical view of virtual network with logical router

If our ULR is configured correctly, ServerDB01 should be able to ping its default gateway, 10.154.16.1, and ping any other virtual machine from the WebApp, such as ServerApp01. Figure 7-16 shows the results of the pings.

```
●  ●  ●                            El Autentico Pirata del Caribe
                                   ServerWeb01.piratas.caribe - PuTTY
ServerWeb01:~ # ping -c 3 10.154.16.1
PING 10.154.16.1 (10.154.16.1) 56(84) bytes of data.
64 bytes from 10.154.16.1: icmp_seq=1 ttl=64 time=0.246 ms
64 bytes from 10.154.16.1: icmp_seq=2 ttl=64 time=0.332 ms
64 bytes from 10.154.16.1: icmp_seq=3 ttl=64 time=0.361 ms

--- 10.154.16.1 ping statistics ---
3 packets transmitted, 3 received, 0% packet loss, time 1998ms
rtt min/avg/max/mdev = 0.246/0.313/0.361/0.048 ms
ServerWeb01:~ # ping -c 3 10.154.17.101
PING 10.154.17.101 (10.154.17.101) 56(84) bytes of data.
64 bytes from 10.154.17.101: icmp_seq=1 ttl=63 time=8.86 ms
64 bytes from 10.154.17.101: icmp_seq=2 ttl=63 time=2.88 ms
64 bytes from 10.154.17.101: icmp_seq=3 ttl=63 time=1.27 ms

--- 10.154.17.101 ping statistics ---
3 packets transmitted, 3 received, 0% packet loss, time 2000ms
rtt min/avg/max/mdev = 1.274/4.341/8.869/3.268 ms
ServerWeb01:~ # 
```

Figure 7-16 Pings from ServerDB01

If we take a look at the MonkeyIsland-ULR Control VM, we can execute the command **show IP route** to see the routing table. As shown in Figure 7-17, the routing table only includes directly connected subnets and the default gateway we added during deployment of the logical router. In Chapter 12 we introduce routing protocols and see our routing table grow to include additional subnets.

```
●  ●  ●                            El Autentico Pirata del Caribe
                                   SantoDomingoControl.piratas.caribe - PuTTY
MonkeyIsland-ULR-1> show ip route connected

Codes: O - OSPF derived, i - IS-IS derived, B - BGP derived,
C - connected, S - static, L1 - IS-IS level-1, L2 - IS-IS level-2,
IA - OSPF inter area, E1 - OSPF external type 1, E2 - OSPF external type 2,
N1 - OSPF NSSA external type 1, N2 - OSPF NSSA external type 2


C      10.154.15.16/28     [0/0]        via 10.154.15.19
C      10.154.15.48/28     [0/0]        via 10.154.15.50
C      10.154.16.0/24      [0/0]        via 10.154.16.1
C      10.154.17.0/24      [0/0]        via 10.154.17.1
C      10.154.18.0/24      [0/0]        via 10.154.18.1
C      169.254.1.0/30      [0/0]        via 169.254.1.2
MonkeyIsland-ULR-1> 
```

Figure 7-17 Routing table in the Control VM

If we go to the NSX Manager, we can determine which NSX Controller is responsible for our MonkeyIsland-ULR logical router, as shown in Figure 7-18. Figure 7-18 shows the output of the command **show logical-router controller master dlr all**

brief (the NSX Controller equivalent command is **show control-cluster logical-routers instance all**). The fields shown are as follows:

- **LR-Id**: Each logical router has a unique LR-ID.

- **LR-Name**: NSX Manager assigns the logical router name. If the logical router was assigned a tenant, the tenant is part of the name. Otherwise, the word *default* is used.

- **Universal**: If this is a URL or not.

- **Service-Controller**: The NSX Controller responsible for the logical router.

- **Egress-Locale**: If this logical router is doing local egress. All DLRs do local egress.

- **In-Sync**: If the logical router is synchronized among the NSX Controller and the ESXi hosts.

- **Sync-Category**: The category of the synchronization state.

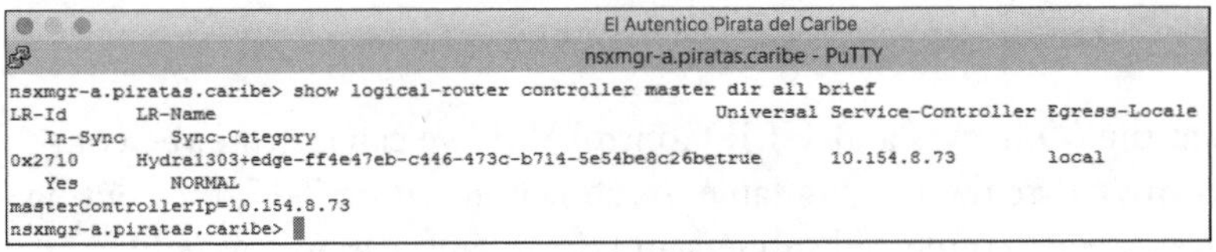

```
●  ●  ●                        El Autentico Pirata del Caribe
                              nsxmgr-a.piratas.caribe - PuTTY
nsxmgr-a.piratas.caribe> show logical-router controller master dlr all brief
LR-Id    LR-Name                                   Universal Service-Controller Egress-Locale
  In-Sync    Sync-Category
0x2710     Hydra1303+edge-ff4e47eb-c446-473c-b714-5e54be8c26betrue     10.154.8.73          local
   Yes         NORMAL
masterControllerIp=10.154.8.73
nsxmgr-a.piratas.caribe>
```

Figure 7-18   Output of **show logical-router controller master dlr all brief** command

To see all the ESXi hosts that have a copy of the ULR, and their host-id, use the NSX Manager CLI command **show logical-router list dlr dlr-id host**. The equivalent NSX Controller command is **show control-cluster logical-router connections router-id**. Figure 7-19 shows the output of the command **show logical-router list dlr 0x2710 host**.

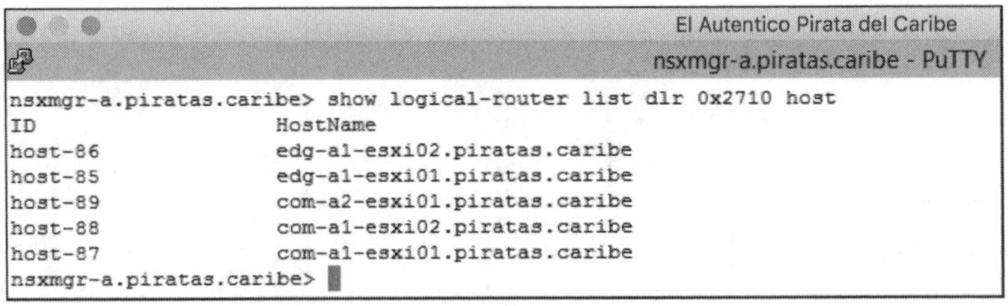

```
●  ●  ●                                 El Autentico Pirata del Caribe
                                      nsxmgr-a.piratas.caribe - PuTTY
nsxmgr-a.piratas.caribe> show logical-router list dlr 0x2710 host
ID                      HostName
host-86                 edg-a1-esxi02.piratas.caribe
host-85                 edg-a1-esxi01.piratas.caribe
host-89                 com-a2-esxi01.piratas.caribe
host-88                 com-a1-esxi02.piratas.caribe
host-87                 com-a1-esxi01.piratas.caribe
nsxmgr-a.piratas.caribe>
```

Figure 7-19   Output of **show logical-router list dlr dlr-id host** command

If we execute the command **show logical-router host *host-id* connection**, we can see some information regarding the ESXi host's copies of the logical routers (the

ESXi host CLI equivalent command is **net-vdr -C -l**). In Figure 7-20, we can see the output of the command using host-id **host-89**. The fields displayed by the command are as follows:

- **Host Locale Id**: The Locale ID assigned to this ESXi host. More on Locale ID later in this chapter.

- **DvsName**: The vDS used during host preparation.

- **VdrPort**: The type of interface in the vDS used by the logical routers. All LIFs are assigned to a special interface in the vDS called vdrPort.

- **NumLifs**: The number of VXLAN LIFs in this ESXi host.

- **VdrMAC**: The vMAC.

- **Teaming Policy**: The teaming policy selected during host preparation

- **Uplink**: The uplinks, from the teaming policy, that are being used by NSX, the interface number, the pMAC assigned to each uplink, and if the uplink is participating in the teaming.

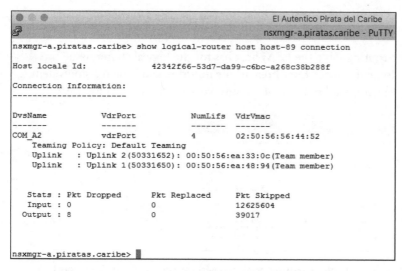

Figure 7-20   Output of **show logical-router host host-id connection** Command

Yes, I said logical routers in plural. You should notice that there are only two pMACs in Figure 7-20, which tells us that all copies of logical routers running in the same ESXi hosts use the same pMACs. This is another reason you can't connect two LIFs from different logical routers in the same logical switch.

You can use the command **show logical-router host host-id dlr dlr-id /brief |
verbose/** to see the status of the ULR in the ESXi host. The verbose version of this
command is equivalent to the ESXi host CLI command **net-vdr –I –l dlr-id**. To get
the brief version of the command, add **--brief**. Figure 7-21 shows the output of the
command **show logical-router host host-89 dlr 0x2710 verbose**.

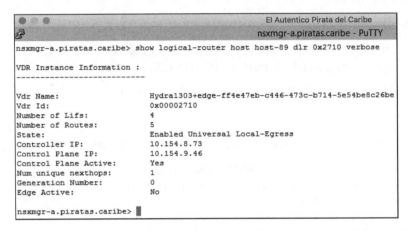

```
El Autentico Pirata del Caribe
nsxmgr-a.piratas.caribe - PuTTY

nsxmgr-a.piratas.caribe> show logical-router host host-89 dlr 0x2710 verbose

VDR Instance Information :
-----------------------------

Vdr Name:                    Hydra1303+edge-ff4e47eb-c446-473c-b714-5e54be8c26be
Vdr Id:                      0x00002710
Number of Lifs:              4
Number of Routes:            5
State:                       Enabled Universal Local-Egress
Controller IP:               10.154.8.73
Control Plane IP:            10.154.9.46
Control Plane Active:        Yes
Num unique nexthops:         1
Generation Number:           0
Edge Active:                 No

nsxmgr-a.piratas.caribe>
```

Figure 7-21   Output of **show logical-router host host-id dlr dlr-id verbose** Command

Finally, to see the routing table the ESXi host has for the logical router, issue the
command **show logical-router host host-id dlr dlr-id route**, which is equivalent to
the ESXi host CLI command **net-vdr -l --route vdr-id**, as shown in Figure 7-22.

```
El Autentico Pirata del Caribe
nsxmgr-a.piratas.caribe - PuTTY

nsxmgr-a.piratas.caribe> show logical-router host host-89 dlr 0x2710 route

VDR Hydra1303+edge-ff4e47eb-c446-473c-b714-5e54be8c26be Route Table
Legend: [U: Up], [G: Gateway], [C: Connected], [I: Interface]
Legend: [H: Host], [F: Soft Flush] [!: Reject] [E: ECMP]

Destination    GenMask          Gateway        Flags  Ref Origin  UpTime  Interface
-----------    -------          -------         -----  --- ------  ------  ---------
0.0.0.0        0.0.0.0          10.154.15.17   UG     1   AUTO    15512   271000000003
10.154.15.16   255.255.255.240  0.0.0.0        UCI    1   MANUAL  15516   271000000003
10.154.16.0    255.255.255.0    0.0.0.0        UCI    1   MANUAL  15516   27100000000a
10.154.17.0    255.255.255.0    0.0.0.0        UCI    1   MANUAL  15516   27100000000b
10.154.18.0    255.255.255.0    0.0.0.0        UCI    1   MANUAL  15486   27100000000c
nsxmgr-a.piratas.caribe>
```

Figure 7-22   Output of **show logical-router host host-id dlr dlr-id route** Command

Locale ID

The universal logical router has one special feature not available to the distributed logical router. Before I explain the feature, have a look at Figure 7-23, which shows a ULR in two data centers. Virtual machine ServerWeb01 is in Data Center Santo Domingo, and ServerWeb02 is in Data Center Tampa.

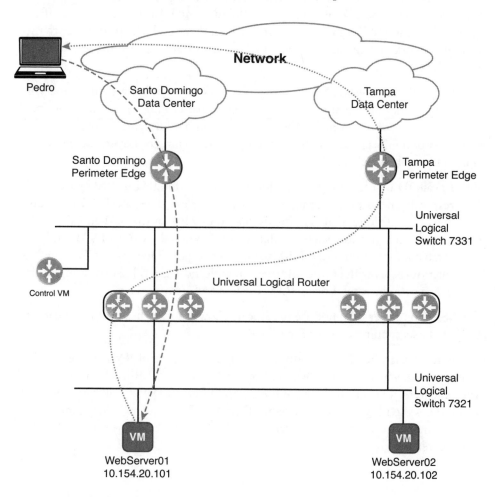

Figure 7-23   Multi-data center routing

Both the NSX Edge in Data Center Santo Domingo and the NSX Edge in Data Center Tampa are advertising the subnet of ServerWeb01 and ServerWeb02 to the physical world while advertising a default route to the ULR. A user in the city of Santo Domingo sends a web page request to ServerWeb01, which is routed via the Santo Domingo NSX Edge. The response from ServerWeb01 is received by the local copy of the ULR in Data Center Santo Domingo, which sees two default routes, one to each NSX Edge. About half the time the ULR forwards the traffic to the NSX Edge in the Tampa Data Center, which then sends the traffic over to the physical network in Tampa. If the user had requested the page from ServerWeb02, the reverse would be true.

This is an example of *network tromboning*. Network tromboning is defined as asymmetrical network traffic that does not use the best path to the destination, causing traffic to flow over nonoptimal paths. Network tromboning typically occurs when subnet location information is obfuscated by the stretching of Layer 2, such as when we use universal logical switches.

With Locale ID we can provide some locality information that is used by the ULR for egress traffic decisions, thus allowing for local egress. The Locale ID is a number in hex, 128 bits long, that is mutually shared by the Control VM and all ULR copies in the same location, such as a data center. When the Control VM sends routing table information to the NSX Controller responsible for the ULR, the NSX Controller only shares the route information with those ESXi hosts running copies of the ULR with the same Locale ID as the Control VM.

The NSX Controller does not use the Locale ID when it pushes routing updates to the ESXi hosts running copies of the DLR.

Do you recall that the ULR supports having multiple Control VMs? Have a look at Figure 7-24, which now has two Control VMs and the ULR has been configured for local egress. The Control VM in the Santo Domingo Data Center has the same Locale ID as the ESXi hosts in the Santo Domingo Data Center. The Control VM in the Tampa Data Center has the same Locale ID as the ESXi host in the Tampa Data Center.

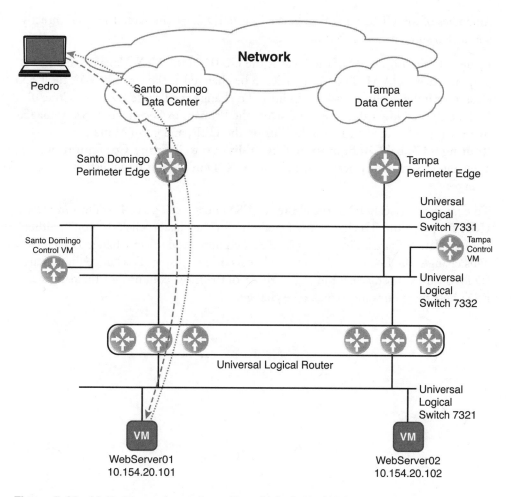

Figure 7-24 Multi-data center routing with multiple Control VMs

The Control VM in Santo Domingo only exchanges routing information with the NSX Edge in Santo Domingo. The Control VM in Tampa only exchanges routing information with the NSX Edge in Tampa. Now when ServerWeb01 responds to the user, the ULR in Santo Domingo only knows of the routes advertised by the NSX Edge in Santo Domingo, thus it forwards all traffic to the NSX Edge in Santo Domingo.

All copies of the ULR, regardless of the Locale ID, have the same LIFs and directly connected subnets in the routing table.

By default, the Locale ID of the ULR is the UUID of the NSX Manager that deploys the Control VM. The Locale ID can be changed at the Control VM, the ESXi cluster, or individually at each ESXi host. To change the Locale ID at the Control VM, go to the NSX Edges view and select the Primary or Secondary NSX Manager that owns the Control VM, double-click on the ULR, and go to **Manage > Routing > Global Configuration**. Click **Edit** next to **Routing Configuration**, enter the 128-bit Hex Locale ID, and click **OK**. Don't forget to publish the changes.

To change the Locale ID at the cluster or ESXi host level, go to **Installation view > Host Preparation**. To change the Locale ID for the cluster, click the cog in either the Installation Status, Firewall, or VXLAN columns and select Change Locale ID. This changes the Locale ID for all ESXi hosts in the cluster. To change the Locale ID for an ESXi host, select the cog in either of the three columns for the particular ESXi host that you want to make the change.

Exam Preparation Tasks

Review All the Key Topics

Review the most important topics from inside the chapter, noted with the Key Topic icon in the outer margin of the page. Table 7-2 lists these key topics and the page numbers where each is found.

Table 7-2   Key Topics for Chapter 7

Key Topic Element	Description	Page Number
Paragraph	Each ESXi host can have 100 different logical router instances.	198
Paragraph	LIFs can connect to VXLAN and VLAN dvPortgroups.	199
Paragraph	The universal logical router can have up to eight Control VMs.	200
Paragraph	The same vMAC is used by all logical routers	201
Paragraph	The routing neighbor of the logical router does not know it is communicating with the Control VM.	203
Paragraph	The universal logical router can have up to eight Control VMs.	212
Paragraph	The NSX Controllers do not use the Locale ID with the DLR	222
Paragraph	All copies of the ULR have the same LIFs and directly connected subsets	224

Define Key Terms

Define the following key terms from this chapter, and check your answers in the Glossary:

DLR, ULR, LIF, Internal LIF, Uplink LIF, VXLAN LIF, VLAN LIF, vMAC, pMAC, Locale ID

This chapter covers all or part of the following VCP6-NV exam blueprint topics:

- **Objective 5.4**—Configure and Manage Logical Routers

CHAPTER 8

Logical Router Packet Walks

Now that we know what a logical router is and how to deploy it, let's see it in action by doing some packet walks. The packet walks are going to be for east-west traffic for virtual machines in different subnets, while in the same host and different hosts. We also have a packet walk where we see what happens when a virtual machine vMotions during an active flow.

Do I Know This Already?

The "Do I Know This Already?" quiz allows you to assess whether you should read this entire chapter or simply jump to the "Exam Preparation Tasks" section for review. If you are in doubt, read the entire chapter. Table 8-1 outlines the major headings in this chapter and the corresponding "Do I Know This Already?" quiz questions. You can find the answers in Appendix A, "Answers to the 'Do I Know This Already?' Quizzes."

Table 8-1 Headings and Questions

Foundation Topic Section	Questions Covered in This Section
Logical Router Packet Walk Example 1	1-5
Logical Router Packet Walk Example 2	6-9
Logical Router Packet Walk Example 3	10

In Figure 8-1, COM-A1-ESXi01 and COM-A1-ESXi02 are part of Compute Cluster A1. Hosts COM-B1-ESXi01 and COM-B1-ESXi02 are part of Compute Cluster B1. Virtual machines SERVERWEB01 and SERVERDB01 are running in hosts in Compute Cluster A1. Virtual machines SERVERWEB02 and SERVERAPP01 are running in hosts in Compute Cluster B1. All virtual machines are connected to logical switches as depicted in the diagram. A universal logical router, named Monkey Island, is configured to have LIFs in all three logical switches and is the default gateway for each segment.

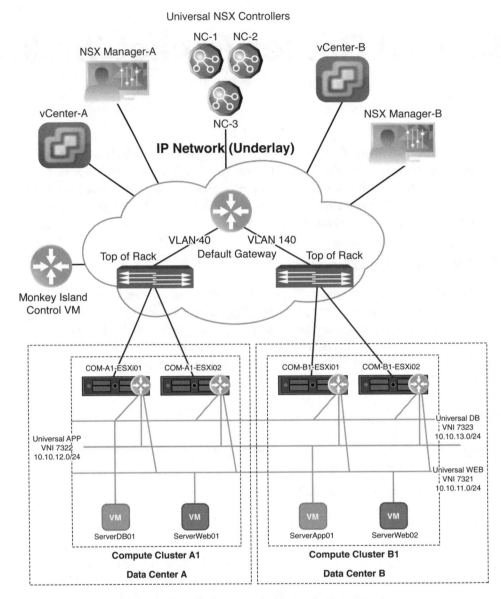

Figure 8-1   Reference diagram for "Do I Know This Already" quiz

Use Figure 8-1 to answer the following questions.

   1. Virtual machine SERVERWEB01, running on ESXi host COM-A1-ESXi01,
      is powered off and SERVERWEB02 takes over the handling of web traffic.
      SERVERWEB02 is running in ESXi host COM-B1-ESXi02. SERVERDB01
      is running in ESXi host COM-A1-ESXi01.

Based on the diagram, which statement describes the action that will be taken with the Monkey Island logical router?

   a. The logical router Monkey Island moves the LIF connected to the WEB logical switch in ESXi host COM-A1-ESXi01 to the WEB logical switch in ESXi host COM-B1-ESXi02.

   b. ESXi host COM-A1-ESXi01 loses its copy of the Monkey Island logical router.

   c. ESXi host COM-B1-ESXi02 gains a copy of the Monkey Island logical router with LIFs connected to only the WEB and DB logical switches.

   d. ESXi host COM-A1-ESXi01 and COM-B1-ESXi02 have the same copy of the Monkey Island logical router.

2. Virtual machines SERVERWEB02 and SERVERDB01 are both powered on and are running on the same ESXi host. SERVERWEB02 sends a packet to SERVERDB01.

Based on the diagram, what is the destination MAC address of the frame sent by SERVERWEB02?

   a. It is a broadcast, FFFF.FFFF.FFFF.

   b. The MAC address of SERVERDB01.

   c. The vMAC address of the LIF connected to the WEB logical switch.

   d. The pMAC address of the LIF connected to the WEB logical switch.

3. Virtual machines SERVERWEB02 and SERVERDB01 are both powered on and running on the same ESXi host. SERVERWEB02 sends a packet to SERVERDB01.

Based on the diagram, what is the destination MAC address of the first frame sent by Monkey Island using the LIF connected to the DB logical switch?

   a. It is a broadcast, FFFF.FFFF.FFFF.

   b. The MAC address of SERVERDB01.

   c. The vMAC address of the LIF connected to the DB logical switch.

   d. The pMAC address of the LIF connected to the DB logical switch.

4. Virtual machines SERVERWEB02 and SERVERDB01 are both powered on and running on the same ESXi host. SERVERWEB02 sends a packet to SERVERDB01. SERVERDB01 has not sent any frames of its own.

Based on the diagram, what is the destination MAC address of the first frame sent by SERVERDB01 as a result of the packet just received from SERVERWEB02?

    a. It is a broadcast, FFFF.FFFF.FFFF.

    b. The MAC address of SERVERWEB02.

    c. The vMAC address of the LIF connected to the DB logical switch.

    d. The pMAC address of the LIF connected to the DB logical switch.

5. Virtual machine SERVERAPP01 is running on ESXi host COM-B1-ESXi02. VMware Tools is not installed. SERVERAPP01 sends an ARP reply back to the Monkey Island logical router over logical switch APP.

Based on the diagram, what does the Switch Security module do with the ARP reply frame?

    a. The Switch Security module snoops the ARP reply and hands the frame to the Monkey Island logical router copy running on ESXi host COM-B1-ESXi02.

    b. The Switch Security module snoops the ARP reply and sends an IP report to the Primary NSX Manager.

    c. The Switch Security module snoops the ARP reply and sends an IP report to the Universal NSX Controller Layer 2 Master.

    d. The Switch Security module snoops the ARP reply and sends an IP report to the Universal NSX Controller responsible for logical switch APP.

6. Virtual machines SERVERWEB01 and SERVERAPP01 are both powered on.

Based on the diagram, how many LIFs will be configured on the Monkey Island logical router copy running on the same ESXi host where SERVER-APP01 is running?

    a. 1

    b. 2

    c. 3

    d. 4

7. Virtual machines SERVERWEB01 and SERVERAPP01 are just powered on. SERVERWEB01 sends a packet to SERVERAPP01.

Based on the diagram, which copy of the Monkey Island logical router sends the ARP request to SERVERAPP01?

    a. The copy on the ESXi host where SERVERAPP01 is running, using the LIF connected to the APP logical switch.

    b. The copy on the ESXi host where SERVERAPP01 is running, using the LIF connected to the WEB logical switch.

    c. The copy on the ESXi host where SERVERWEB01 is running, using the LIF connected to the APP logical switch.

    d. The copy on the ESXi host where SERVERWEB01 is running, using the LIF connected to the WEB logical switch.

8. Virtual machine SERVERDB01 receives a frame from SERVERAPP01 in Compute Cluster B1.

Based on the diagram, when SERVERDB01 sends a response packet, which logical switch's VNI is included in the VXLAN frame back to Compute Cluster A1?

    a. The APP logical switch.

    b. The DB logical switch.

    c. No VNI is included.

    d. The WEB logical switch.

9. The Monkey Island logical router receives an ingress packet from the LIF connected to the APP logical switch. There are no security breaches and all virtual machines are operating as designed.

Based on the diagram, which statement is true regarding the ingress packet?

    a. The packet indicates that SERVERWEB01 or SERVERWEB02 is communicating with SERVERAPP01.

    b. The packet originated from either SERVERWEB01 or SERVERDB01.

    c. The packet is not destined for SERVERAPP01.

    d. The packet was received by the copy of the Monkey Island logical router running on ESXi host COM-B1-ESXi02.

10. Virtual machine SERVERWEB02 undergoes a vMotion migration while having an active conversation with SERVERAPP01.

Based on the diagram, what is the impact to the conversation with SERVERAPP01?

    a. The destination ESXi host sends the NSX Controller an ARP query for SERVERAPP01's IP.

    b. SERVERAPP01 has to send a new ARP request for SERVERWEB02's MAC.

    c. The Monkey Island logical router on the source ESXi host forwards its ARP tables to the destination ESXi host.

    d. The Switch Security module's ARP entry for SERVERWEB02 on the source ESXi host is sent to the destination ESXi host's Switch Security module.

Foundation Topics

Logical Router Packet Walks

In this section we review some packet walks involving east-west communications among virtual machines connected to different subnets. Each packet walk shows a different aspect of the process the logical router follows to route packets. All packet walks reference a derivative of Figure 8-2, with some figures including different step numbers relevant to the packet walk.

Figure 8-2 has two ESXi clusters, in the same universal transport zone, all configured to support NSX.

Reminder: A distributed logical router and a universal logical router are functionally identical in the data plane. The steps in these packet walks would be the same if we were using a distributed logical router.

- Two data centers.

- Two vCenters, one per data center.

- Two NSX Managers, one per vCenter.

- Two ESXi host clusters, one per vCenter, with two ESXi hosts in each.

- Each ESXi host cluster has its own vDS with a single dvUplink, which is also used for the portgroups backing the logical switches.

- There are three universal NSX Controllers.

- Each ESXi host has IP connectivity via the Management VMkernel port to all NSX Controllers, their corresponding NSX Manager, and vCenter.

- Each ESXi host is shown with a single VMNIC to the physical network.

- ESXi host management, vMotion, IP storage, and VXLAN encapsulated traffic traverses this interface.

- ESXi host management traffic uses VLAN 10 in Santo Domingo Data Center and VLAN 110 in Tampa Data Center.

- vMotion traffic uses VLAN 20 in Santo Domingo Data Center and VLAN 120 in Tampa Data Center.

- IP storage traffic uses VLAN 30 in Santo Domingo Data Center and VLAN 130 in Tampa Data Center.

- Cluster A1 uses VLAN 40 for VXLAN traffic encapsulation.

- Cluster B1 uses VLAN 140 for VXLAN traffic encapsulation.

- Web logical switch uses VNI 7321.

- App logical switch uses VNI 7322.
- DB logical switch uses VNI 7323.
- The Monkey Island logical router is the default gateway for the Web, App, and DB subnets.

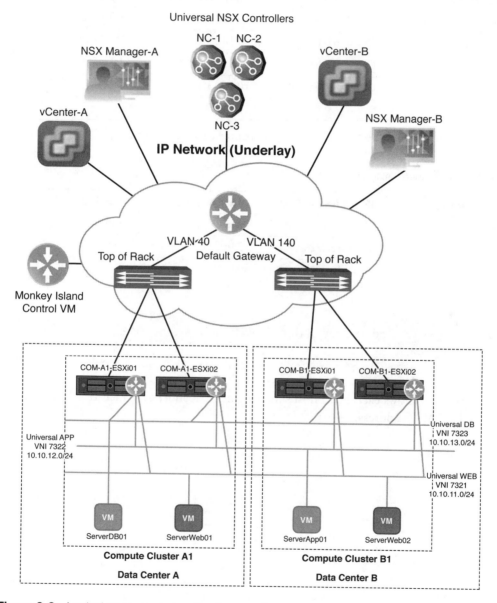

Figure 8-2   Logical router packet walk reference diagram

Table 8-2 shows where each virtual machine is running, its IP address, and its MAC address.

Table 8-2 Virtual Machines' information

VM Name	ESXi Host	VM IP Address	VM MAC Address
SERVERWEB01	COM-A1-ESXi01	10.10.11.101	W01-MAC
SERVERWEB02	COM-B1-ESXi02	10.10.11.102	W02-MAC
SERVERAPP01	COM-B1-ESXi01	10.10.12.101	A01-MAC
SERVERDB01	COM-B1-ESXi01	10.10.13.101	D01-MAC

Table 8-3 shows the LIFs of the logical router Monkey Island.

Table 8-3 Monkey Island's LIFs

LIF Name	IP Address/Mask	MAC Address	LIF Type
WEB	10.10.11.1/24	vMAC	Internal
APP	10.10.12.1/24	vMAC	Internal
DB	10.10.13.1/24	vMAC	Internal

NOTE The MAC address for all three LIFs is the same, the vMAC 02:50:56:56:44:52.

Table 8-4 shows each ESXi host's management IP address, VTEP IP address, and VTEP MAC address.

Table 8-4   ESXi Host Information

ESXi Host	Cluster	VXLAN vDS	Host MGT IP	Host VTEP IP	pMAC	Host VTEP MAC	VXLAN Default GW IP	Default GW MAC
COM-A1-ESXi01	Compute Cluster A1	COM-A_ vDS	10.10.10.55	10.10.40.55	CA11-pMAC	CA11-MAC	CA1-DG	CA1-DG-MAC
COM-A1-ESXi02	Compute Cluster A1	COM-A_ vDS	10.10.10.56	10.10.40.56	CA12-pMAC	CA12-MAC	CA1-DG	CA1-DG-MAC
COM-B1-ESXi01	Compute Cluster B1	COM-B_ vDS	10.10.110.55	10.10.140.55	CB11-pMAC	CB11-MAC	CB1-DG	CB1-DG-MAC
COM-B1-ESXi02	Compute Cluster B1	COM-B_ vDS	10.10.110.56	10.10.140.56	CB12-pMAC	CB12-MAC	CB1-DG	CB1-DG-MAC

NOTE   The VXLAN vDS has a single dvUplink, thus each ESXi host has a single pMAC.

Logical Router Packet Walk Example 1

In this packet walk, virtual machine SERVERWEB01 sends a packet to virtual machine SERVERDB01, which then responds back to SERVERWEB01. Assume the following to be true:

- SERVERWEB01 and SERVERDB01 have just powered on and have not sent any traffic.

- SERVERWEB01 and SERVERDB01 are running on ESXi host COM-A1-ESXi01.

- SERVERWEB01 and SERVERDB01 have a default gateway of .1 in their respective subnets.

- Monkey Island is the default gateway for SERVERWEB01 and SERVERDB01.

- SERVERWEB01 knows the IP of SERVERDB01.

Figure 8-3 shows the logical view of the scenario for Logical Router Packet Walk Example 1.

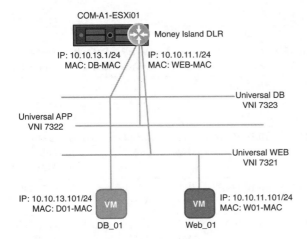

Figure 8-3 Logical Router Packet Walk Example 1

Step 1. SERVERWEB01 notices the IP of SERVERDB01 is in a different subnet from its own and sends an ARP request for its default gateway's MAC address.

That is Monkey Island's LIF in the web logical switch.

Step 2. As it is a broadcast, the ARP request is received by Monkey Island's WEB LIF in VNI 7321 in COM-A1-ESXi01.

SERVERWEB01's Switch Security module knows this ARP request is for the logical router thus the ARP request is not forwarded to all other VTEPs in the VTEP table. (I told you the Switch Security module plays nice with the logical switch…and the logical router, too.)

Step 3. Monkey Island in COM-A1-ESXi01 sends back a unicast to SERVER-WEB01 with the ARP reply, with a source MAC of vMAC.

Step 4. SERVERWEB01 receives the ARP reply and uses the information to create the packet to send to SERVERDB01.

- **Source IP:** 10.10.11.101

- **Destination IP:** 10.10.13.101

- **Source MAC:** W01-MAC

- **Destination MAC:** vMAC

Step 5. Monkey Island receives the frame in the WEB LIF in COM-A1-ESXi01 and discards the Layer 2 header after confirming that the destination MAC address is the WEB LIF's.

Step 6.   Monkey Island, in COM-A1-ESXi01, then reads the destination IP and searches for the most specific match in the routing table.

The most specific route in the routing table matches the subnet in the DB LIF. This is commonly referred to as "directly connected" or "directly attached."

Step 7.   Monkey Island then looks in its local ARP table for an entry for IP 10.10.13.101.

By "local" ARP table I mean the logical router's ARP table in ESXi host COM-A1-ESXi01.

Step 8.   Not finding an entry, Monkey Island sends out an ARP request for IP 10.10.13.101.

Remember that SERVERDB01 has sent no traffic and therefore Monkey Island couldn't have an ARP entry for it yet.

The ARP request is sent over the DB LIF in COM-A1-ESXi01.

Important: As of NSX 6.2, the source MAC for the ARP request is the vMAC (before it used to be the pMAC).

Step 9.   SERVERDB01 receives the ARP request and sends back a unicast ARP reply to Monkey Island's DB LIF in COM-A1-ESXi01.

The Switch Security module in SERVERDB01 snoops the ARP reply and sends an IP report to the universal NSX Controller responsible for the DB logical switch.

Step 10.   Monkey Island receives the ARP reply and uses the information to forward the packet to SERVERDB01.

The packet is forwarded over the DB LIF.

- **Source IP**: 10.10.11.101
- **Destination IP**: 10.10.13.101
- **Source MAC**: vMAC
- **Destination MAC**: D01-MAC

Logical routers use the vMAC as the source of all packets sent over LIFs.

Step 11.   SERVERDB01 receives the frame and processes it.

NOTE   Steps 12 through 14 only take place if the OS in SERVERDB01 does not add an ARP entry when it receives, and replies, to an ARP request. Most major OSes do not do this.

Step 12.   SERVERDB01 wants to reply back to SERVERWEB01, notices that it is in a separate subnet, and sends an ARP request for its default gateway's MAC address.

SERVERDB01 sends back an ARP reply to Monkey Island in Step 9, *but* it does not add DB LIF's IP/MAC to the ARP table.

This is normal ARP operation of major operating systems to only add a new ARP entry to their ARP table only upon receiving an ARP reply to an ARP request they sent.

Step 13.   Monkey Island receives the ARP request over the DB LIF in COM-A1-ESXi01.

Step 14.   Monkey Island sends an ARP reply back to SERVERDB01.

Step 15.   SERVERDB01 uses the ARP reply info to send the packet to SERVER-WEB01.

- **Source IP**: 10.10.13.101

- **Destination IP**: 10.10.11.101

- **Source MAC**: D01-MAC

- **Destination MAC**: vMAC

Step 16.   Monkey Island receives the frame in the DB LIF in COM-A1-ESXi01 and discards the Layer 2 header after confirming that the destination MAC address is the DB LIF's.

Step 17.   Monkey Island, in COM-A1-ESXi01, then reads the destination IP and searches for the most specific match in the routing table.

The most specific route in the routing table is directly connected to the WEB LIF.

Step 18.   Monkey Island then looks in its local ARP table for an entry for IP 10.10.11.101.

Step 19.   Not finding an entry, Monkey Island sends out an ARP request for IP 10.10.11.101 over the WEB LIF.

This is for the same reason as in Step 12.

Important: As mentioned in Chapter 7, "Logical Router," the logical router's LIFs are a special vDS port called vdrPort. The vdrPort does not have the Switch Security module, and thus does not enjoy the benefits of ARP suppression.

Step 20.   SERVERWEB01 receives the ARP request and sends back a unicast ARP reply to Monkey Island's WEB LIF in COM-A1-ESXi01.

Step 21.   Monkey Island receives the ARP reply and uses the information to forward the packet to SERVERWEB01.

The packet is forwarded over the WEB LIF.

- **Source IP**: 10.10.13.101
- **Destination IP**: 10.10.11.101
- **Source MAC**: vMAC
- **Destination MAC**: W01-MAC

Step 22.   SERVERWEB01 receives the frame and processes it.

Step 23.   Subsequent traffic from SERVERWEB01 toward SERVERDB01 does not require ARP requests.

As long as the ARP entries don't age out in SERVERWEB01, SERVERDB01 nor in the local ARP table copies of the logical router where the virtual machines are running. The virtual machines, the copies of the logical router, and the Switch Security module will not age out the ARP entries if they continue to see traffic sourced from the corresponding IPs before the aged-out timer expires, which is 180 seconds (3 minutes). Remember that if Switch Security module ages out an ARP entry, it sends an IP report to the NSX Controller.

You should know what I'm going to say: That was easy! This is your normal routing process taking place between two end systems that have the same entity as their default gateway. In the next example we do another packet walk between two virtual machines with the same router, Monkey Island, as their default gateway but running in different hosts.

Logical Router Packet Walk Example 2

In this packet walk, virtual machine SERVERWEB01 sends a packet to virtual machine SERVERAPP01, which then responds back to SERVERWEB01. Assume the following to be true:

- SERVERAPP01 has just powered on and has not sent any traffic.
- SERVERWEB01 is running on ESXi host COM-A1-ESXi01.
- SERVERAPP01 is running on ESXi host COM-B1-ESXi01.
- SERVERWEB01 and SERVERAPP01 have a default gateway of .1 in their respective subnets.
- Monkey Island is the default gateway for SERVERWEB01 and SERVER-APP01.
- SERVERWEB01 knows the IP of SERVERAPP01.

Figure 8-4 shows the logical view of the scenario for Logical Router Packet Walk Example 2.

Step 1.   SERVERWEB01 notices the IP of SERVERAPP01 is in a different subnet from its own and sends a packet to SERVERAPP01 using the default gateway ARP entry in its ARP table.

The ARP table entry was created in Logical Router Packet Walk Example 1.

- **Source IP**: 10.10.11.101
- **Destination IP**: 10.10.12.101
- **Source MAC**: W01-MAC
- **Destination MAC**: vMAC

Step 2.   Monkey Island receives the frame in the WEB LIF in COM-A1-ESXi01 and discards the Layer 2 header after confirming that the destination MAC address is the WEB LIF's.

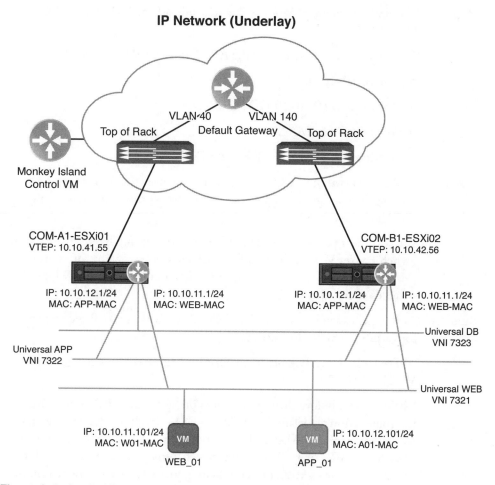

Figure 8-4   Logical Packet Walk Example 2

Step 3.   Monkey Island, in COM-A1-ESXi01, then reads the destination IP, searches for the most specific match in the routing table, and concludes it is directly connected in the APP LIF.

Step 3 is critical to understanding the functionality of the distributed logical router. The copy of Monkey Island running in COM-A1-ESXi01 does not care in which host SERVERAPP01 is actually located. All that matters is that the IP for SERVERAPP01 is in the subnet directly attached to Monkey Island's APP LIF.

Step 4.   Monkey Island then looks in its local ARP table for an entry for IP 10.10.12.101.

Step 5. Not finding an entry, Monkey Island sends out an ARP request for IP 10.10.12.101.

The ARP request is sent over the APP LIF in COM-A1-ESXi01.

- **Source IP:** 10.10.12.1
- **Destination IP:** 10.10.12.101
- **Source MAC:** vMAC
- **Destination MAC:** FFFF.FFFF.FFFF

Step 6. APP logical switch in COM-A1-ESXi01 receives the ARP request and executes its configured Replication Mode to get the frame sent to all ESXi hosts that need it.

We covered a packet walk for Replication Modes in Chapter 6, "Logical Switch Packet Walks." Take a few moments to review the different types (Multicast, Unicast, and Hybrid) of Replication Modes used by logical switches to forward BUMs.

Step 7. APP logical switch in COM-B1-ESXi02 receives the ARP request and forwards it to SERVERAPP01.

APP logical switch will *not* learn MAC address vMAC as coming from VTEP 10.10.40.55.

Little Secret: Before the logical switch processes the ARP request, the logical router Monkey Island in COM-B1-ESXi02 will see the ARP request with a source of the vMAC. Make a note of the ESXi host that sent it, and await for an ARP reply. The logical switch also coordinates with the logical router so it knows vMAC does not belong to a VM. That's one reason the logical switch never advertises the LIF MAC to the NSX Controller.

Step 8. SERVERAPP01 receives the ARP request and sends back a unicast ARP reply to Monkey Island's APP LIF.

- **Source IP**: 10.10.12.101
- **Destination IP**: 10.10.12.1
- **Source MAC**: A01-MAC
- **Destination MAC**: vMAC

Step 9. The APP logical switch in COM-B1-ESXi01 sees the ARP reply being sent to the vMAC, and gives it to the local copy of Monkey Island. Using the cached information from step 7, the local copy of Monkey Island in COM-B1-ESXi01 shares the ARP reply, via OOB communications, with the copy of Monkey Island in COM-A1-ESXi01.

Step 10. Monkey Island in COM-A1-ESXi01 receives the ARP update and uses the information to forward the packet to SERVERAPP01 over the APP LIF.

The packet is forwarded over the APP LIF.

- **Source IP**: 10.10.11.101
- **Destination IP**: 10.10.12.101
- **Source MAC**: vMAC
- **Destination MAC**: A01-MAC

NOTE   Before NSX 6.2, every non-ARP packet sent by a logical switch that would not stay local to the ESXi host used the pMAC as the source MAC address. The pMAC chosen depended on the dvUplink the packet would egress. As of NSX 6.2, all packets sent over a VXLAN LIF use the vMAC as the source MAC.

Step 11. SERVERAPP01 receives the frame and processes it.

Step 12. SERVERAPP01 wants to reply back to SERVERWEB01, notices that it is in a separate subnet, and sends an ARP request for its default gateway's MAC address.

Review step 12 in Logical Router Packet Walk Example 1 if you are not sure as to why the ARP request is needed.

Step 13. Monkey Island receives the ARP request over the APP LIF in COM-B1-ESXi02.

Step 14. Monkey Island sends back an ARP reply to SERVERAPP01.

Step 15. SERVERAPP01 uses the ARP reply info to send the packet to SERVERWEB01.

- **Source IP:** 10.10.12.101
- **Destination IP:** 10.10.11.101
- **Source MAC:** A01-MAC
- **Destination MAC:** vMAC

Step 16. Monkey Island in COM-B1-ESXi02 receives the frame in the APP LIF and discards the Layer 2 header after confirming that the destination MAC address is the APP LIF's.

Step 17. Monkey Island, in COM-B1-ESXi02, then reads the destination IP and searches for the most specific match in the routing table.

The most specific route in the routing table is directly connected to the WEB LIF.

Step 18.   Monkey Island then looks in its local ARP table for an entry for IP 10.10.11.101.

Step 19.   Not finding an entry, Monkey Island sends out an ARP request for IP 10.10.11.101.

The ARP request is sent over the WEB LIF in COM-B1-ESXi02.

- **Source IP**: 10.10.11.1
- **Destination IP**: 10.10.11.101
- **Source MAC**: vMAC
- **Destination MAC**: FFFF.FFFF.FFFF

Step 20.   Web logical switch in COM-B1-ESXi02 receives the ARP request and follows Replication Mode to get the frame sent to all ESXI hosts that need it.

Step 21.   WEB logical switch in COM-A1-ESXi01 receives the ARP request and forwards it to SERVERWEB01.

Monkey Island in COM-A1-ESXi01 notices the ARP request was sent from Monkey Island's copy in COM-B1-ESXi02.

Step 22.   SERVERWEB01 receives the ARP request and sends back a unicast ARP reply to Monkey Island's WEB LIF in COM-A1-ESXi01.

- **Source IP**: 10.10.11.101
- **Destination IP**: 10.10.11.1
- **Source MAC**: W01-MAC
- **Destination MAC**: vMAC

Step 23.   The WEB logical switch in COM-A1-ESXi01 sees the ARP reply being sent to the vMAC and gives it to the local copy of Monkey Island. Via OOB communications, the ARP entry is provided to the copy of Monkey Island in COM-B1-ESXi02.

Step 24.   Monkey Island in COM-B1-ESXi02 receives the ARP update over its WEB LIF, and uses the information to forward the packet to SERVERWEB01.

The packet is forwarded over the WEB LIF.

- **Source IP**: 10.10.12.101
- **Destination IP**: 10.10.11.101
- **Source MAC**: vMAC
- **Destination MAC**: W01-MAC

Step 25.   SERVERWEB01 receives the frame and processes it.

Step 26.   Subsequent traffic from SERVERWEB01 toward SERVERAPP01 does not require ARP requests.

As long as the ARP entries don't age out in SERVERWEB01, SERVER-APP01 nor in the local ARP table copies of the logical router.

There are a few points that we need to get from this packet walk. The first one is about routers and directly connected subnets. *All* routers need to find a match in the routing table matching a directly connected subnet so they can put a Layer 2 header in the packet before forwarding it. The logical router follows the same principle. In the case of Ethernet interfaces, once the router has forwarded the packet to the Ethernet switch, inside an Ethernet frame, it is the Ethernet switch's job to decide the best way to get the frame to the owner of the destination MAC address.

 Second, the logical router copy is sent to each ESXi host in the transport zone of the logical switches the LIFs connect to. Each logical router copy in the ESXi hosts has the same LIFs. If this were not the case, the logical router wouldn't be able to reach all the VMs in the logical switches. For instance, if the copy of Monkey Island in COM-A1-ESXi01 did not have an APP LIF, there would be no way for traffic from SERVERWEB01 to reach SERVERAPP01.

 Third, routing packets from VMs is always performed by the copy of the logical router in the ESXi host where the source VM is. In other words, the logical router's routing is asymmetrical. This asymmetry is not a problem because all logical router copies are making decisions using the (mostly) same routing table.

Fourth, the logical router has little interest in what VXLAN or a VNI are, nor does it care much about them. The job of the logical router is to take ingress traffic, make a routing decision, and forward the packet. The logical switches are the only ones that deal with VXLAN directly. Because the local copy of the logical router performs routing, it means that any VXLAN overlays supporting a flow between two VMs will also be asymmetrical, with the logical switch where the destination VM resides handling the VXLAN encapsulation.

This example covers about every major point there is to know about the logical router. From the logical router perspective, traffic will ingress over one LIF and egress over another LIF. That's its job and not much more. The part that can lead to confusion in understanding the functionality of the logical router is realizing that the local logical router copy makes the data plane decision using its local copy of its routing table, which it received from the NSX Controller responsible for the logical router. Although each logical router copy has the same routing table (almost always, more on that when we talk about local egress in Chapter 11, "Layer 3 Connectivity Between Virtual and Physical Networks"), each logical router copy is mostly unaware of the existence of the other logical router copies. We cover a bit more on logical router copies becoming aware of each other in Chapter 11 as well.

Let's do one more packet walk, this time to understand what happens when a VM vMotions. We covered what transpires at Layer 2 during vMotion in Chapter 6. We build on that example to see what happens at Layer 3 when the logical router is the default gateway.

Logical Router Packet Walk Example 3

In this packet walk, virtual machine SERVERWEB01 has an active bidirectional traffic flow with virtual machine SERVERAPP01. Assume the following to be true:

- SERVERWEB01 is running on ESXi host COM-A1-ESXi01.

- SERVERAPP01 is running on ESXi host COM-B1-ESXi01.

- SERVERWEB01 and SERVERAPP01 have a default gateway of .1 in their respective subnets.

- Monkey Island is the default gateway for SERVERWEB01 and SERVER-APP01.

- Monkey Island's WEB LIF is an Internal LIF.

- SERVERWEB01 knows the IP of SERVERAPP01.

Figure 8-5 shows the logical view of the scenario for Logical Router Packet Walk Example 3.

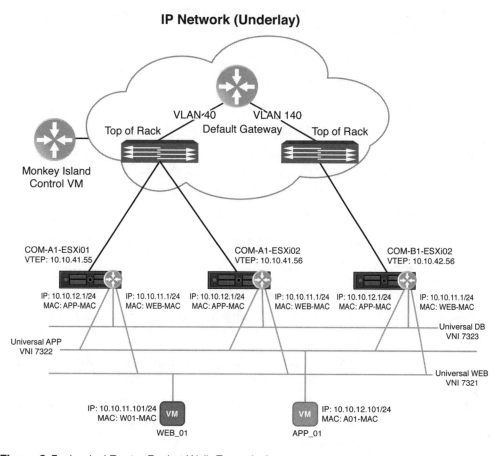

Figure 8-5 Logical Router Packet Walk Example 3

Step 1. DRS or a user initiates vMotion for SERVERWEB01 toward COM-A1-ESXi02.

Step 2. The moment vMotion completes, ESXi host COM-A1-ESXi02 sends an RARP over the WEB logical switch with SERVERWEB01's MAC address.

Remember that after vMotion completes, COM-A1-ESXi01 sends an "I don't have MAC address W01-MAC" update to the NSX Controller responsible for the WEB logical switch, while COM-A1-ESXi02 sends an "I have MAC address W01-MAC" to the same NSX Controller. This was covered in Chapter 6. Also, the Switch Security module in COM-A1-ESXi02 receives the ARP entry associated with the vMotioned VM, SERVERWEB01.

Step 3.   Immediately after vMotion completes, SERVERWEB01 sends a packet to SERVERAPP01.

- **Source IP:** 10.10.11.101
- **Destination IP:** 10.10.12.101
- **Source MAC:** W01-MAC
- **Destination MAC:** vMAC

Step 4.   The copy of Monkey Island in COM-A1-ESXi02 performs routing, determines the destination IP to be directly connected to APP LIF, and sends an ARP request over the APP LIF for 10.10.12.101.

- **Source IP:** 10.10.12.1
- **Destination IP:** 10.10.12.101
- **Source MAC:** vMAC
- **Destination MAC:** FFFF.FFFF.FFFF

Step 5.   SERVERAPP01 receives the ARP request and sends a unicast ARP reply to Monkey Island.

SERVERAPP01 has an ARP entry for the vMAC in its ARP table with an IP of 10.10.12.1, thus it makes no changes to its ARP table.

Step 6.   Monkey Island in COM-A1-ESXi02 receives the ARP update and uses the information to forward the packet to SERVERAPP01.

- **Source IP:** 10.10.11.101
- **Destination IP:** 10.10.12.101
- **Source MAC:** vMAC
- **Destination MAC:** A01-MAC

Step 7.   SERVERAPP01 receives the packet from SERVERWEB01 and replies back to SERVERWEB01.

- **Source IP:** 10.10.12.101
- **Destination IP:** 10.10.11.101
- **Source MAC:** A01-MAC
- **Destination MAC:** vMAC

Step 8.   The frame from SERVERAPP01 is received by the copy of Monkey Island in COM-B1-ESXi01, which does routing and concludes the destination IP is directly connected to WEB LIF.

Step 9.   With the information in the ARP table, Monkey Island in COM-B1-ESXi01 forwards the packet out of WEB LIF.

- **Source IP**: 10.10.12.101

- **Destination IP**: 10.10.11.101

- **Source MAC**: vMAC

- **Destination MAC**: W01-MAC

vMotions had no impact in the copy of Monkey Island in COM-B1-ESXi01. Thus there should be an ARP entry for SERVERWEB01 in the ARP table.

Step 10.   WEB logical switch in COM-B1-ESXi01 forwards the frame to VTEP 10.10.41.56, COM-A1-ESXi02.

WEB logical switch in COM-B1-ESXi01 would have been updated of the new location of MAC address W01-MAC as part of the vMotion process. This was covered in Chapter 6.

Step 11.   SERVERWEB01 receives the frame.

During vMotion, the only impact to any active flows is that the local logical router copy in the vMotion destination host, COM-A1-ESXi02, has to send an ARP request. The vMotioned virtual machine's default gateway MAC address is the same because it is the vMAC, 02:50:56:56:44:52.

This was our last logical router packet walk scenario for east-west traffic between VMs. In previous chapters we covered how logical switches can be used to allow and scale VMs to share an Ethernet broadcast domain even when the ESXi hosts where they are running are separated by Layer 3 boundaries. Now we are seeing how we can extend east-west traffic for VMs in different subnets, transparently to the underlay, and while also running in ESXi hosts separated by Layer 3 boundaries.

Our next step in our exam preparation journey is to discuss ways in which NSX can provide a mechanism to allow VMs to share an Ethernet broadcast domain when deploying VXLAN across a Layer 3 boundary is not an option, and to allow VMs to share an Ethernet broadcast domain with physical workloads. However, before we do this, we need to formally introduce the NSX Edge, which is the topic of the next chapter.

Exam Preparation Tasks

Review All the Key Topics

Review the most important topics from inside the chapter, noted with the Key Topic icon in the outer margin of the page. Table 8-5 lists these key topics and the page numbers where each is found.

Table 8-5   Key Topics for Chapter 8

Key Topic Element	Description	Page Number
Paragraph	The logical router makes routing decisions without consideration as to where a virtual machine is actually running.	241
Paragraph	Each ESXi host with the copy of the logical router instance has the same LIFs.	245
Paragraph	The logical router copy that is local to the source virtual machine performs the routing.	245
Steps	The logical router copy in the vMotion destination host has to recreate part of the ARP table to support the flows from the vMotioned VM.	247

Define Key Terms

Define the following key terms from this chapter, and check your answers in the Glossary:

LIF, Internal LIF, VXLAN LIF, VLAN LIF, vMAC, pMAC

This chapter covers all or part of the following VCP6-NV exam blueprint topics:

- **Objective 5.4**—Configure and Manage Logical Routers

- **Objective 6.4**—Configure and Manage Edge Services High Availability

CHAPTER 9

NSX Edge Services Gateway

Up to this point in the book we have covered how NSX can perform distributed routing and switching in the ESXi host kernel. Networking involves more than just routing and switching, however. We have yet to cover how NSX handles other network functions and services, such as IPsec VPNs and appliance-based Load Balancing. These services are not distributed in NSX.

The NSX Edge is the entity that provides the functions and services beyond those offered by the logical router. Like the logical router, a large number of NSX Edges can be deployed, each one with the ability to run different services or functions independent of the other NSX Edges.

Do I Know This Already?

The "Do I Know This Already?" quiz allows you to assess whether you should read this entire chapter or simply jump to the "Exam Preparation Tasks" section for review. If you are in doubt, read the entire chapter. Table 9-1 outlines the major headings in this chapter and the corresponding "Do I Know This Already?" quiz questions. You can find the answers in Appendix A, "Answers to the 'Do I Know This Already?' Quizzes."

Table 9-1 Headings and Questions

Foundation Topic Section	Questions Covered in This Section
NSX Edge	1-5
NSX Edge Size	6
Edge HA	7
Creating and Deploying an NSX Edge	8-10

1. Which entity handles the control plane of the NSX Edge?

   a. The NSX Manager

   b. The NSX Controller

   c. The NSX Edge

   d. The ESXi hosts prepared for NSX

2. What is a Standalone Edge?

   a. An NSX Edge that is not deployed in HA mode

   b. An NSX Edge deployed without an NSX Manager

   c. An NSX Edge with only static routes

   d. An NSX Edge that has lost routing adjacencies with its neighbors

3. Why is no information exchanged between the NSX Edge and the NSX Controllers?

   a. Because the NSX Edge device does not communicate across the control plane

   b. Because the NSX Manager communicates across the management plane

   c. Because the NSX Manager does not communicate across the control plane

   d. Because the NSX Edge owns its own control plane

4. Which of the following services does the NSX Edge not offer?

   a. IPSec VPN

   b. Layer 2 Firewall

   c. Network Address Translation

   d. DHCP

5. What is the maximum number of NSX Edges that can be deployed in an NSX domain?

   a. 1,000

   b. 2,000

   c. 10,000

   d. 15,000

6. How much disk space is required if an Edge gets deployed as a Quad-Large?

   a. 512 MB

   b. 1 GB

    c. 4G

    d. 4.5 GB

7. An NSX Edge is deployed in Edge HA mode. The Edge is configured for Layer 2 VPN over its uplink interface. What would happen if the primary Edge goes down?

    a. After the HA dead timer expires, one of the Standby Edges becomes the Active Edge and reestablishes the Layer 2 VPN.

    b. After the HA dead timer expires, the Standby Edge becomes the Active Edge. Layer 2 VPN tunnels are not reestablished.

    c. After the HA dead timer expires, NSX Manager deploys a new Edge with the same configuration as the Active Edge.

    d. After the HA dead timer expires, the Standby Edge becomes the primary and resumes the Layer 2 VPN with minimal impact.

8. How is the NSX Edge configured?

    a. By connecting to the console of the NSX Edge and entering the **configuration terminal** command

    b. By connecting to the NSX Edge via SSH and entering the **configuration terminal** command

    c. By connecting to the vSphere Client and choosing NSX Edges from the Networking and Security home page

    d. By sending NSX API commands directly to the NSX Edge device

9. Where does the NSX Edge get deployed?

    a. The NSX Edge is deployed on the ESXi host that is running the Control VM.

    b. The NSX Edge is deployed to the same vSphere cluster where the NSX Controllers reside.

    c. The NSX Edge gets deployed in a resource pool chosen by the NSX administrator.

    d. The NSX Edge gets deployed to the Management Cluster.

10. How many subinterfaces can be configured on an NSX Edge?

    a. 1

    b. 10

    c. 200

    d. 1,000

Foundation Topics

NSX Edge

The NSX Edge Services Gateway is an appliance, or virtual machine (VM). It comes as an Open Virtualization Format (OVF) utility that gets deployed by NSX Manager in the vCenter paired with that NSX Manager. It can also be deployed independently of the NSX Manager, in a mode called *Standalone NSX Edge*, to provide Layer 2 VPN support. The term *NSX Edge Services Gateway* is the long form of saying *NSX Edge*, or the *Edge*. You also find it referred to by the service that it is providing, for example, the *NSX Edge Load Balancer*. Throughout the chapter, and the rest of the book, we use the terms *NSX Edge* or *Edge* interchangeably.

The NSX Edge is as close as you can get to virtualizing a physical router with centralized management. If you know what a router is, you more or less already know what an NSX Edge is. The NSX Edge is not distributed nor does it run in kernel. NSX Manager handles the NSX Edge management plane while the NSX Edge handles the control and data planes. As such, the Edge never communicates with the NSX Controllers. The NSX Edge may be deployed without doing any of the host preparation or logical network preparation covered in Chapter 4, "VXLAN, NSX Controllers, and NSX Preparation."

While you may access the command-line interface (CLI) of a router via Secure Shell (SSH) or console to configure it, you would use the vSphere Web Client or the NSX APIs to configure the NSX Edge. From the vSphere Web Client, any configuration you enter is passed on to NSX Manager. NSX Manager would validate the configurations before it uses them to configure the NSX Edge. A similar process occurs if using the NSX APIs instead of the vSphere Web Client. The NSX Edge's CLI may be accessed by SSH or console; however, you have no ability to make configuration changes from the CLI.

The Standalone NSX Edge is deployed via an ovf obtained from VMware. In the case of the Standalone NSX Edge, initial configuration is done during the deployment of the Edge and, as of NSX 6.2, additional Layer 2 VPN configuration is allowed once it is deployed. Layer 2 VPN is covered in Chapter 10, "Layer 2 Extensions."

Figure 9-1 shows a logical network view of an Edge doing routing between the virtual and physical network. An Edge that is placed at the border of the virtual and physical networks and does routing between the two networks is referred to as the *Perimeter Edge*. The VLAN that the Perimeter Edge connects to for physical network reachability is referred to as the *Edge VLAN*.

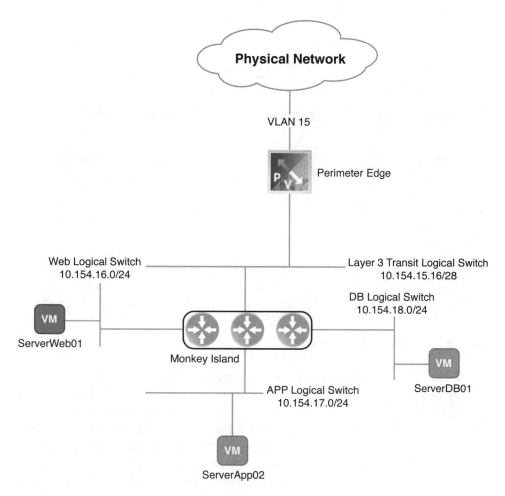

Figure 9-1   Logical network view of a Perimeter Edge

Figure 9-2 shows the network shown in Figure 9-1 with the ESXi hosts included and the Perimeter Edge running in the Edge Cluster. Notice in the diagram that only the Edge Cluster has access to the Edge VLAN.

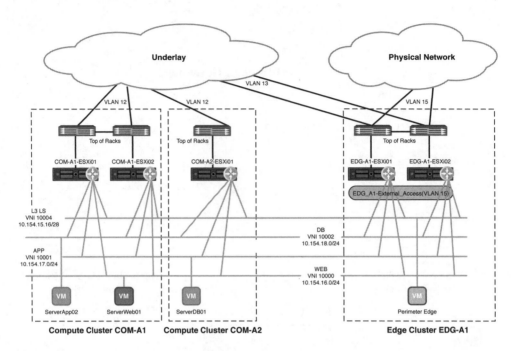

Figure 9-2   Perimeter Edge in Edge Cluster

As wonderful as the logical router may be, it provides only two primary services: routing and Layer 2 Bridging, which is covered in greater detail in Chapter 10. The NSX Edge provides services that complement and/or supplement the services provided by the logical router. A single NSX Edge can be configured with one or more of these services. For example, you can have an NSX Edge configured solely for the purpose of doing routing while a second NSX Edge can be deployed to perform Network Address Translation (NAT) and firewall functions. The services the NSX Edge can provide are as follows:

- Routing
- NAT
- Load balancing
- Stateful firewall (Layer 3 and 4)
- IPsec VPN
- SSL VPN
- Layer 2 VPN
- DHCP
- DNS relay

NSX Manager supports up to 2,000 NSX Edges, each being a separate and independent entity. Each NSX Edge deployed counts against the maximum number of VMs that can be registered with vCenter. vCenter supports 10,000 powered up VMs and 15,000 total VMs.

NSX Edge Size

Did I mention that the NSX Edge is a VM? A question that should come to mind is: How much CPU, memory, and storage should the NSX Edge have? NSX Manager allows for four configuration options for the deployment of the VM as listed in Table 9-2.

Table 9-2 NSX Edge Virtual Machine Sizes

Size Option	vCPU	vMemory	Disk
Compact	1	512 MB	512 MB
Large	2	1 GB	512 MB
Quad-Large	4	1 GB	512 MB
X-Large	6	8 GB (4G SWAP file)	4.5 GB

If after you have deployed an NSX Edge you decide that you need to change its size (up or down), you can do it. Start by selecting your Edge from the NSX Edges view, choosing **Actions**, and selecting **Change Appliance Size**. In the Change Appliance Size window that pops up, select the size you want, as shown in Figure 9-3.

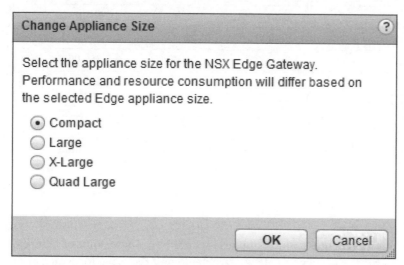

Figure 9-3 Converting the size of an NSX Edge

Selecting the size of the NSX Edge has an impact on the capacity that the NSX Edge may have based on the service you have configured in the age. The smaller the Edge is, the smaller the capacity it has.

Table 9-3 shows the maximum limits in the NSX domain for some NSX Edge's services and features.

Table 9-3   NSX Edge Service and Feature Limits per NSX Domain

Service or Feature	Limit
NAT rules	20,000
Load balance virtual servers	6,000
Load balance pool members	60,000
DHCP pools	20,000
DHCP static bindings	200,000
IPSec tunnels	128,000
Firewall rules	20,000
Static routes	100,000

Table 9-4 shows the routing limits, per some of the Edge sizes.

Table 9-4   NSX Edge Service and Feature Limits per Edge Size

Service or Feature	Compact	Large	X-Large
OSPF routes	20,000	50,000	100,000
BGP routes	20,000	50,000	250,000
OSPF adjacencies	10	20	40
BGP neighbors	10	20	50
Route redistribution: To OSPF	2,000	5,000	20,000
Route redistribution: To BGP	Unlimited	Unlimited	Unlimited

Edge HA

The NSX Edge is a single entity, which implies it could be a single point of failure. If that is a concern for the particular role you are deploying the Edge for, you can deploy the NSX Edge in Edge HA mode. When deploying the Edge in HA (not to be confused with DRS HA), two Edges are deployed each with the identical configurations and powered on. Oh, and that second Edge counts against the 2,000 NSX Edge limit for NSX Manager.

In Edge HA, NSX Manager designates one of the two Edges as the Active Edge while the other Edge is Standby. The two Edges communicate and send keepalives over the HA interface. The Active Edge also sends sync data and tables based on the service that is running. If the Active Edge is unresponsive by the time the dead timer expires, the Standby takes over the role of the Active Edge. Whenever the original Active Edge is operational again it takes the Standby role. The dead timer default is 15 seconds and can be changed to as little as 6 seconds.

When deploying Edges in HA, place them in a cluster with DRS. NSX Manager has an anti-affinity rule created, a Separate Virtual Machines DRS rule, so the two Edges in the HA pair do not run in the same ESXi host. VMware does not support user changes to this anti-affinity rule. NSX Manager also creates an Automatic Startup rule in the ESXi host where an NSX Edge is deployed, including one for the Logical Router Control VM.

Table 9-5 shows the impact to some Edge services when the Standby Edge takes over from the unresponsive Active Edge.

Table 9-5   Impact per Service of Standby Edge Becoming Active Edge

Service or Feature	Support	Active Edge Failure Impact
Firewall	Yes	Stateful failover. Connection entries are synced to the Standby Edge.
NAT	Yes	Stateful failover. Connection entries are synced to the Standby Edge.
Load balancer	Yes	At Layer 7, Sticky tables, health, and backend pool servers are synced. Standby performs back-end health check before becoming Active.
IPSec VPN	Yes	Tunnels need to be reestablished when Standby becomes Active.
SSL VPN	Yes	Tunnels need to be reestablished when Standby becomes Active.
Layer 2 VPN	No	Edge HA does not support this feature.
DHCP	Yes	DHCP allocation table state is synced.
Dynamic routing	Yes	Routing table is synced.

Creating and Deploying an NSX Edge

We have some experience deploying an NSX Edge. We sort of deployed one in Chapter 7, "Logical Router," when we deployed the logical router. The Control VM, as mentioned in Chapter 7, is a modified Edge, and the process of deploying an Edge is similar to what we already saw with the logical router.

To configure and deploy an NSX Edge using the vSphere Web Client, log in as an enterprise administrator or NSX administrator and follow these steps:

Step 1. From the Networking and Security page select **NSX Edges**.

Step 2. Click the green + icon and wait for the New NSX Edge Wizard to open.

Step 3. In the Name and Description step, fill out these values:

 a. Install Type: Select Edge Services Gateway.

 b. Enter a name for the NSX Edge.

 This name is used by vCenter to name the Edge virtual machine.

 c. Optionally enter the hostname, a description, and a tenant name.

 The Tenant field is used for management and naming of the Edge(s). This field has no impact on the performance or functionality of the Edge(s).

 d. If you want to deploy the NSX Edge now, check the **Deploy NSX Edge**. If you don't select this option, NSX Manager saves the configuration but does not deploy the NSX Edge. This is the equivalent of staging the Edge. You can deploy the NSX Edge later from the NSX Edge's home page.

 e. Check the box if you want to Enable High Availability.

Step 4. Click **Next** to continue.

Step 5. In the Settings step, enter the administrator's username and password, and click **Next**.

 a. This credential is used when logging in, via SSH or the console, to the NSX Edge. The password must be 12 characters long containing:

 - At least one uppercase letter

 - At least one lowercase letter

 - At least one number

 - At least one special character, such as ! or $

b. You can enable SSH access to the Edge here. If you enable SSH access, the NSX Edge adds a firewall rule allowing the SSH access.

c. You can enable the Firewall Auto Rule Generation here. If you do, the NSX Edge creates firewall rules to allow the control plane traffic for the services you configured in the NSX Edge. For example, if this field is checked and you configure OSPF, a firewall rule is added to allow the NSX Edge to receive and send OSPF LSAs.

d. Finally in this step, you can change the Logging level for this NSX Edge.

Step 6. In the Configure Deployment step, choose among the following options:

- **Datacenter**: Select the vCenter's data center where the NSX Edge will be deployed. This is the same vCenter associated with NSX Manager.

- **Appliance Size**: Select the configuration size you want for the NSX Edge. The options are Compact, Large, Quad-Large, and X-Large.

- **NSX Edge Appliances**: Select the resource pool or cluster and datastore where to deploy the NSX Edge. This is an optional field if you didn't choose to Deploy NSX Edge in step 3d.

If configuring the NSX Edge with NSX Edge HA, as mentioned in step 3e, you can select where the second NSX Edge will be deployed.

After you complete this step, it should look similar to Figure 9-4. Click **Next** to continue.

Figure 9-4 shows an Edge that has HA. The warning message at the bottom of Figure 9-4 can be ignored if the cluster is configured with DRS.

NOTE   I deployed a Compact NSX Edge for the screenshots, not an X-Large.

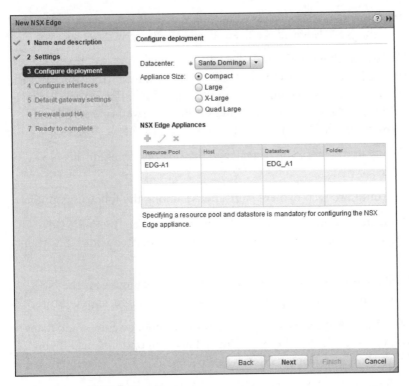

Figure 9-4   Configure Deployment field

Step 7.   In the Configure Interfaces step, you assign an IP to the interfaces of the NSX Edge and connect them to VLAN portgroups, standard or distributed, or VXLAN portgroups.

The NSX Edge can have up to 10 vmxnet3 vNICs, or Ethernet interfaces.

During NSX deployment configuration, each interface can be either Internal or Uplink.

There is a third interface option called Trunk, which is not available during the deployment of the NSX Edge. We cover the creation of a Trunk interface in Chapter 10.

The interface type has significance for firewall rules that look at the direction of the traffic as well as some routing configurations. For example OSPF and IS-IS can only be configured in Uplink interfaces. The interface type may be changed after the Edge is deployed. Chapter 14, "NSX Edge Network Services and Security," reviews NSX Edge Firewall rule direction in more detail, while Chapter 12, "Routing Protocols," covers routing.

Figure 9-5 shows how Configure Interfaces should look. Click **Next** to continue.

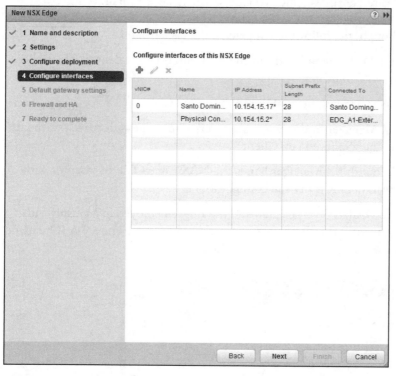

Figure 9-5 Configure Interfaces field

Step 8.   If you want to configure a default gateway for the NSX Edge, check the box and select the outgoing interface for the default route and the IP of the default gateway. Click **Next** to continue.

Step 9.   In Firewall and HA you can make these selections:

a. Choose what the default Firewall rule will be for the NSX Edge.

The NSX Edge has a default Firewall rule policy, the last entry in the Firewall rules, of deny all traffic. You can change it to allow all traffic.

Optionally, you can select whether to enable logging for this rule.

b. Choose the interface to use for the HA heartbeat between the two NSX Edges.

You can set the dead timer for HA.

The /30 subnet of the IPs each Edge will use for heartbeat.

If left blank, NSX Manager assigns IPs from the 169.254.1.X/30 subnet.

Step 10. In Ready to Complete, review your settings. You may go back to make any desired changes. Once you are satisfied, click **Finish**.

After you click **Finish**, the following happens in the background:

1. The vSphere Web Client hands off the configuration to vCenter, which then passes it to NSX Manager.

2. NSX Manager reviews the configuration for any errors.

   If NSX Manager finds any errors, an error message is displayed to the user in the vSphere Web Client.

3. If all checks out, NSX Manager hands the NSX Edge OVF to vCenter with instructions to deploy it per the configurations.

   If Edge HA has been selected and the Edges deployed in a cluster with DRS, an anti-affinity rule gets created, as shown in Figure 9-6. The name of the new Edge is SantoDomingoEdge.

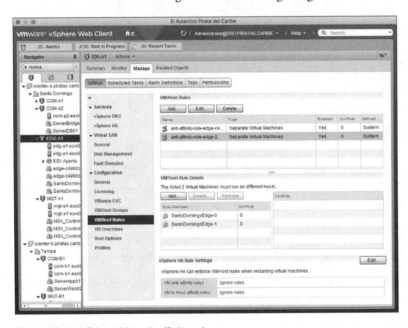

Figure 9-6 Edge HA anti-affinity rule

4. Once the NSX Edge(s) are powered on, vCenter notifies NSX Manager.

5. NSX Manager accesses the NSX Edge(s) and finishes the configuration.

Undeployed NSX Edge

If we have chosen in step 3d to not deploy the NSX Edge and in Step 6d to not select a resource pool or cluster to deploy the NSX Edge(s), the status would read **Undeployed** as shown in Figure 9-7 for the Edge named TampaEdge. Undeployed means the NSX Manager has saved the Edge configuration you provided and is ready to deploy an Edge with the configuration wherever you choose. In other words, this is a way to stage an Edge without production impact.

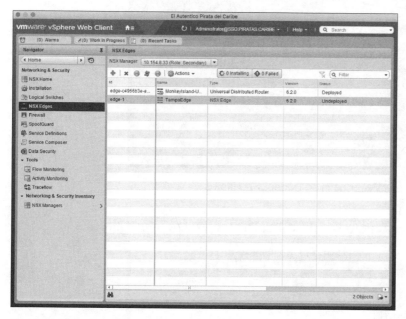

Figure 9-7   Undeployed NSX Edge

To deploy an Undeployed Edge, we first have to tell NSX Manager the resource pool or ESXi cluster in which to deploy the Edge and then deploy the NSX Edge.

Step 1.   Go to NSX Edges view and double-click the Undeployed Edge.

Step 2.   Select **Manage > Configuration** and look for NSX Edge Appliances.

Step 3.   Click the green + icon, enter the resource pool, or cluster information, and click **OK**. The configuration should look similar to Figure 9-8.

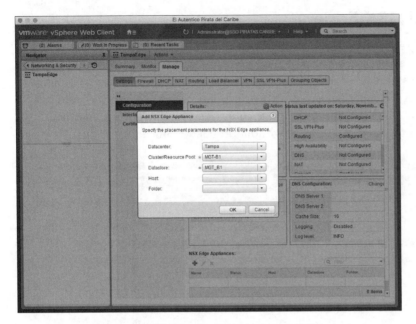

Figure 9-8   Adding an NSX Edge in an Undeployed status

Step 4.   Select **Actions** and then click **Deploy**, as shown in Figure 9-9.

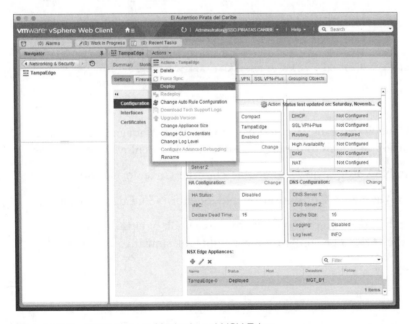

Figure 9-9   Deploying an Undeployed NSX Edge

Monitoring and Verifying the NSX Edge

You can monitor the deployment of the NSX Edge from the *NSX Edges* view in the Networking and Security page, as shown in Figure 9-10. In Figure 9-10 you can see the column Status reads Busy for our new NSX Edge. The NSX Edge is fully deployed once the status changes to Deployed.

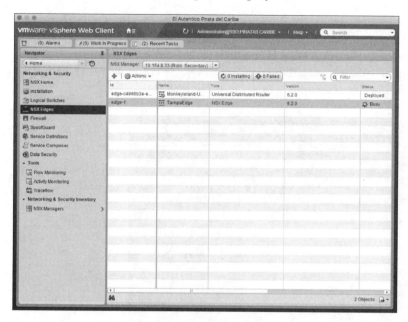

Figure 9-10   Monitoring NSX Edge deployment

The verification process for the NSX Edges is also similar to that of the Control VM. The first option we have is from the NSX Edges view in the Networking and Security page. The Status of the NSX Edge should say Deployed.

We already covered in Chapter 7 the fields that can be seen from this view, but here they are again for your review:

- **ID**: An NSX Manager provided tracking ID. It always starts with the word *edge* followed by a dash (-) and a number. The ID is unique to each logical router and NSX Edge. The number starts at 1 and goes up.

- **Name**: The name of the NSX Edge configured during installation. This is also the name of the NSX Edge in vCenter.

- **Type**: States that this is a distributed logical router. The other option for Type is NSX Edge.

- **Version**: This version matches the version of the NSX Manager.

- **Status**: The NSX Edge can be Busy, Deployed, or Undeployed.

- **Tenant**: This lists the name of the tenant you provided during configuration.

- **Interfaces**: The number of interfaces configured in the logical router.

- **Size**: The size of the NSX Edge.

Returning to the Home page of the NSX Edge (by double-clicking the NSX Edge), we can see a summary of the services configured in the NSX Edge and make some changes. For example, we can disable HA, which would cause the Standby NSX Edge to be powered off and deleted from vCenter. Or, we could decrease the Edge HA Dead Timer down to 6 seconds, as shown in Figure 9-11.

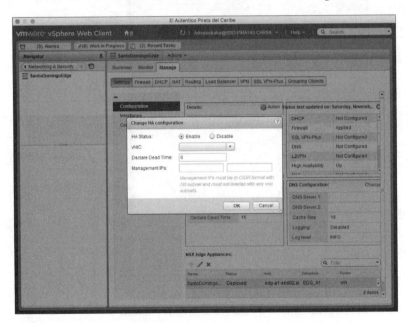

Figure 9-11   Making changes to the Edge HA configuration

Another option is to connect to Host and Clusters or VM and Templates views in vCenter and look for the NSX Edge. The name of the NSX Edge matches the name you assigned it during installation, which was SantoDomingoEdge. You will notice the NSX Edge name has a - followed by the number 0, SantoDomingoEdge-0. Because we enabled Edge HA for our Edge, the second NSX Edge has the name SantoDomingoEdge-1. Figure 9-12 shows the Summary page of Edge SantoDomingoEdge-0.

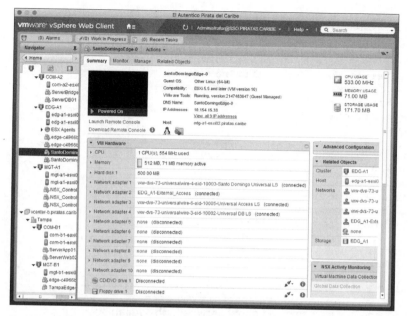

Figure 9-12   NSX Edge SantoDomingoEdge-0

While in the NSX Edge summary page you can click **Launch Remote Console** to get CLI access to the Edge. Since we enabled SSH during configuration, we could get CLI access via SSH into the Edge, using the IP of any of its interfaces. From the CLI you can execute commands to verify the configuration and operation of the NSX Edge. For example, as shown in Figure 9-13, after getting CLI access via SSH over the internal interface, 10.10.19.1, the command **show service high availability** was entered. The output shows the beginnings of the Edge HA configuration for Edge SantoDomingoEdge.

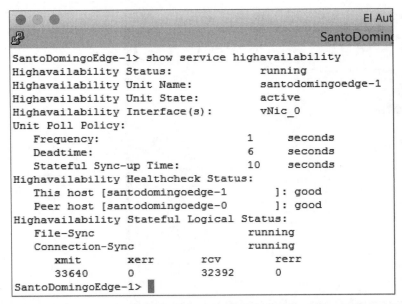

El Aut

SantoDomin

```
SantoDomingoEdge-1> show service highavailability
Highavailability Status:              running
Highavailability Unit Name:           santodomingoedge-1
Highavailability Unit State:          active
Highavailability Interface(s):        vNic_0
Unit Poll Policy:
    Frequency:                        1      seconds
    Deadtime:                         6      seconds
    Stateful Sync-up Time:            10     seconds
Highavailability Healthcheck Status:
    This host [santodomingoedge-1        ]: good
    Peer host [santodomingoedge-0        ]: good
Highavailability Stateful Logical Status:
    File-Sync                         running
    Connection-Sync                   running
       xmit       xerr      rcv        rerr
       33640      0         32392      0
SantoDomingoEdge-1>
```

Figure 9-13 Trimmed output of the command **show service high availability**

Just like in the Control VM, you can't make any configuration changes to the Edge
from the CLI. Most commands are strictly for viewing current status, such as configuration and debugging. Figure 9-14 shows the available commands for the Edge
in user mode and privileged mode. As it is shown, there are no commands to make
configuration changes.

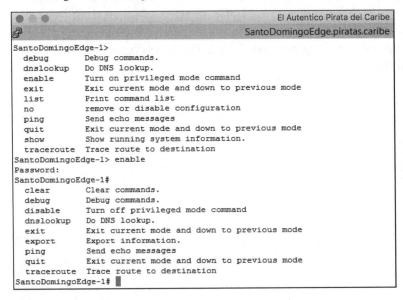

El Autentico Pirata del Caribe

SantoDomingoEdge.piratas.caribe

```
SantoDomingoEdge-1>
    debug       Debug commands.
    dnslookup   Do DNS lookup.
    enable      Turn on privileged mode command
    exit        Exit current mode and down to previous mode
    list        Print command list
    no          remove or disable configuration
    ping        Send echo messages
    quit        Exit current mode and down to previous mode
    show        Show running system information.
    traceroute  Trace route to destination
SantoDomingoEdge-1> enable
Password:
SantoDomingoEdge-1#
    clear       Clear commands.
    debug       Debug commands.
    disable     Turn off privileged mode command
    dnslookup   Do DNS lookup.
    exit        Exit current mode and down to previous mode
    export      Export information.
    ping        Send echo messages
    quit        Exit current mode and down to previous mode
    traceroute  Trace route to destination
SantoDomingoEdge-1#
```

Figure 9-14 Available commands in user mode and privileged mode of the NSX Edge

Exam Preparation Tasks

Review All the Key Topics

Review the most important topics from inside the chapter, noted with the Key Topic icon in the outer margin of the page. Table 9-6 lists these key topics and the page numbers where each is found.

Table 9-6 Key Topics for Chapter 9

Key Topic Element	Description	Page Number
Paragraph	The NSX Edge management plane is the responsibility of the NSX Manager.	256
Paragraph	The Standalone NSX Edge comes in an OVF.	256
Paragraph	An NSX domain can have up to 2,000 NSX Edges.	259
Paragraph	NSX Manager creates an anti-affinity rule to prevent the two Edges from running in the same ESXi host.	261
Paragraph	An enterprise administrator and an NSX administrator account is needed to deploy an Edge.	262
Step	The NSX Edge interface type is used for direction-based Firewall rules.	264

Complete Tables and Lists from Memory

Download and print a copy of Appendix C, "Memory Tables" (found on the book's website), or at least the section for this chapter, and complete the tables and lists from memory. Appendix D, "Memory Tables Answer Key," also on the website, includes the completed tables and lists so you can check your work.

Define Key Terms

Define the following key terms from this chapter, and check your answers in the Glossary:

Perimeter Edge, Edge VLAN, NAT, Undeployed Edge, Edge HA

This chapter covers all or part of the following VCP6-NV exam blueprint topics:

- **Objective 5.3**—Configure and Manage Layer 2 Bridging
- **Objective 6.2**—Configure and Manage Logical Virtual Private Networks (VPN)

CHAPTER 10

Layer 2 Extensions

Many applications have a network requirement of Layer 2 connectivity among tiers of the application. This requirement is easily met by extending a VLAN to the application tiers, but only if the tiers are within close physical proximity. You don't need NSX to extend the VLANs in this situation. If the tiers are not within close physical proximity, it can be a challenge to extend the Ethernet broadcast domain. The problem can be more daunting if the application is partially virtualized.

NSX provides three ways to extend Ethernet broadcast domains to different tiers of an application. The first method is by using logical switches, which we covered in Chapter 5, "NSX Switches." The other two methods are Layer 2 VPNs with the NSX Edge and Layer 2 Bridging with the distributed logical router (DLR). This chapter covers these two other methods and how to configure them.

Do I Know This Already?

The "Do I Know This Already?" quiz allows you to assess whether you should read this entire chapter or simply jump to the "Exam Preparation Tasks" section for review. If you are in doubt, read the entire chapter. Table 10-1 outlines the major headings in this chapter and the corresponding "Do I Know This Already?" quiz questions. You can find the answers in Appendix A, "Answers to the 'Do I Know This Already?' Quizzes."

Table 10-1 Headings and Questions

Foundation Topic Section	Questions Covered in This Section
Layer 2 VPN	1-4
Configuring Layer 2 VPN	5-6
Layer 2 Bridging	7-8
Configuring Layer 2 Bridging	9
Hardware VTEP	10

1. How many concurrent Layer 2 VPN tunnels does a distributed logical router support?

   a. 0

   b. 1

   c. 10

   d. 16

2. What is the default port number used by NSX for Layer 2 VPN?

   a. TCP 22

   b. TCP 443

   c. UDP 500

   d. TCP 1723

3. Which two encryption algorithms are not supported in Layer 2 VPN? (Choose two.)

   a. DES–CBC3

   b. AES-128

   c. 3DES

   d. AES-192

4. Two NSX Edges form a Layer 2 VPN. Which encryption algorithm is used?

   a. The encryption algorithm set on the first NSX Edge device that is configured

   b. The encryption algorithm set on the Layer 2 VPN Server

   c. The strongest encryption algorithm configured between the two NSX Edges as determined during tunnel negotiation

   d. The weakest encryption algorithm configured between the two NSX Edges as determined during tunnel negotiation

5. How many interfaces are needed on an NSX Edge to configure a Layer 2 VPN?

   a. One Uplink interface

   b. Two Uplink interfaces

   c. One Uplink interface and one Internal interface

   d. One Internal interface

6. An NSX administrator has two available IPs, 10.154.17.10 and 10.154.17.11. The IPs are for use with the interfaces connecting to segments that will be extended via two NSX Edges using a Layer 2 VPN.

   How must the IP addresses be configured on the interface of each NSX Edge?

   a. The Layer 2 VPN Server must have the first IP in the range, 10.154.17.10.

   b. Both NSX Edges must use the same IP.

   c. Each NSX Edge can use either IP, but not the same IP.

   d. The Layer 2 VPN Server is given both IPs and assigns them to the NSX Edges during tunnel negotiation.

7. Layer 2 Bridging supports which types of Ethernet extensions?

   a. VXLAN-VXLAN

   b. Layer 2 VPN

   c. VLAN-VLAN

   d. VLAN-VXLAN

8. What is the role of the Bridge Instance?

   a. To coordinate the bridging among all the logical switches in the transport zone

   b. To bridge between a logical switch and a VLAN

   c. To provide a logical connection between two clusters in different transport zones

   d. To back up the Layer 2 NSX Controller

9. Which of the following is not a requirement to configure Layer 2 Bridging?

   a. A distributed logical router

   b. An NSX Edge

   c. A logical switch linked to the Control VM

   d. A VLAN portgroup

10. In NSX 6.2, which NSX entity communicates with the hardware VTEP?

    a. NSX Manager

    b. NSX Controller

    c. NSX Edge

    d. Logical Router Control VM

Foundation Topics

Layer 2 VPN

The term *Layer 2 VPN* refers to mechanisms that can extend a Layer 2 domain, typically Ethernet, over an untrusted medium. The extension is normally done over a tunnel. Layer 2 VPNs have the capability of providing data security by using an encryption algorithm such as Data Encryption Standard (DES). Some sample uses of a Layer 2 VPN are as follows:

- Extend a Layer 2 between a remote office and the main office.
- Extend a Layer 2 between virtual machines in different data centers.
- Extend a Layer 2 between a private and a public cloud.

The NSX Edge supports Layer 2 VPN over Secure Sockets Layer (SSL), port TCP 443. If the NSX Edge is extending a VLAN, the VLAN must be configured in a distributed portgroup. Figure 10-1 shows a logical view of multiple pairs of NSX Edges creating a Layer 2 VPN between VXLANs, VLANs, and a VXLAN and a VLAN. If connecting to VLANs via Layer 2 VPN, the VLAN numbers can be different.

The NSX Edge can also be used to extend a VLAN between a private cloud and vCloud Hybrid Services, vCloud Air, as shown in Figure 10-2.

The NSX Edge supports Layer 2 VPN in a point-to-point deployment, and it must be with another NSX Edge in a server-client relationship. It does not matter which of the two Edges is the server as long as the other one is configured as the client. The NSX Edge can be used to extend a VLAN or VXLAN between two data centers even if the NSX Edges are managed by different NSX Managers or one of the Edges is a Standalone Edge.

If the NSX Edges are deployed in ESXi hosts with processors that support Advance Encryption Standard New Instructions (AES-NI), the NSX Edge can send up to 2 Gbps through the Layer 2 VPN tunnel. Of course, if the bandwidth in the path between the two Edges is less than 2 Gbps, the throughput would be less.

Table 10-2 shows the encryption algorithms supported by the NSX Edge for Layer 2 VPN. The Layer 2 VPN Server dictates the encryption algorithm upon tunnel negotiations with the Layer 2 VPN Client.

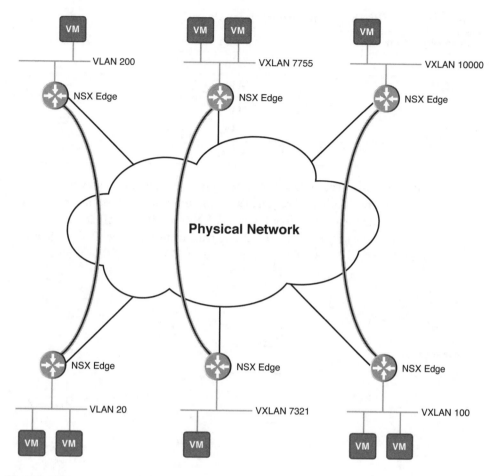

Figure 10-1   Layer 2 VPN between data centers

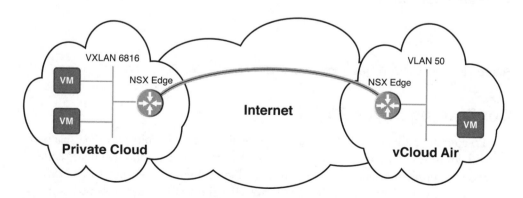

Figure 10-2   Layer 2 VPN between a private and public cloud

Table 10-2 Layer 2 VPN Supported Encryption Algorithms

Encryption Algorithm	Hash
AES-128	SHA
AES128-GCM	SHA256
AES-256	SHA
DES-CBC3	SHA
NULL	MD5

An NSX Edge can only support being either a client or a server at one time, but not both, and requires a Trunk interface with subinterfaces. A pair of Edges can only do a Layer 2 VPN for 200 pairs of Ethernet domains, as shown in Figure 10-3. The path from the Layer 2 VPN Server and the Layer 2 VPN Client must have an MTU of 1600 or higher.

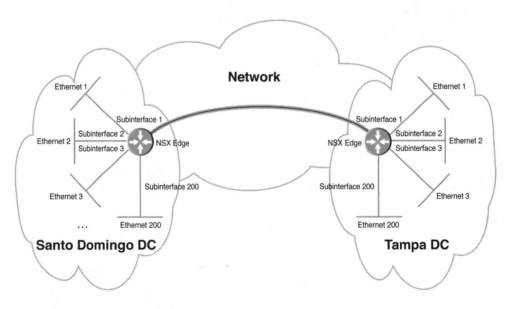

Figure 10-3   Two NSX Edges doing Layer 2 VPN for up to 200 Ethernet domain pairs

Configuring Layer 2 VPN

To configure a Layer 2 VPN, you must already have two deployed Edges, each one with an Internal interface connected to the Layer 2 segment that will be extended and an Uplink interface to be the tunnel endpoint. Figure 10-4 shows two NSX Edges, L2VPN-S and L2VPN-T, and two virtual machines, ServerApp01 and ServerApp02, in their respective data centers, Santo Domingo and Tampa.

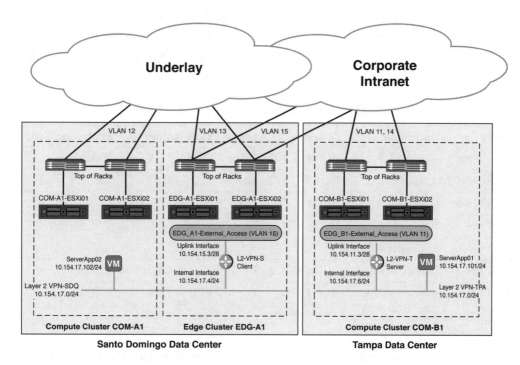

Figure 10-4   Layer 2 VPN Edges and virtual machines

We spend this section configuring a Layer 2 VPN between the two Edges in Figure 10-3. We assign L2VPN-T as the Layer 2 VPN Server and L2VPN-S as the Layer 2 VPN client. Figure 10-5 shows the logical diagram of how our Layer 2 VPN will look once we have completed our configuration.

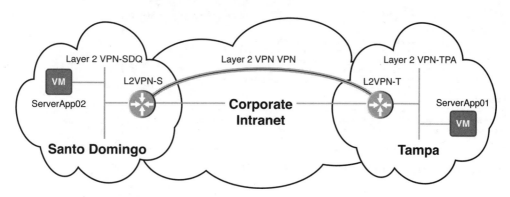

Figure 10-5   Layer 2 VPN logical view

Table 10-3 shows the IP configuration and Layer 2 connectivity for the NSX Edges and the virtual machines. Virtual Machine ServerApp01 is connected to logical switch Layer 2 VPN – TPA, and Virtual Machine ServerApp02 is connected to logical switch Layer 2 VPN – SDQ.

Table 10-3   NSX Edges and Virtual Machines IP and Layer 2 Connectivity

Entity	Interface	IP Address	Layer 2 Connection	Portgroup Type
ServerApp01	vNIC0	10.154.17.101	Layer 2 VPN – TPA	VXLAN
ServerApp02	vNIC0	10.154.17.102	Layer 2 VPN – SDQ	VXLAN
L2-VPN-S	External-SDQ	10.154.15.3	EDG_A1-External Access	VLAN
L2-VPN-S	Internal-SDQ (Subinterface)	10.154.17.4	Layer 2 VPN – SDQ	VXLAN
L2-VPN-T	External-TPA	10.154.11.3	COM_B1-External Access	VLAN
L2-VPN-T	Internal-TPA (Subinterface)	10.154.17.6	Layer 2 VPN – TPA	VXLAN

In Table 10-3 you should notice that both Edges have different IPs in the Layer 2 segment that will be extended. This is a VMware requirement for Layer 2 VPN.

One thing that is implied but still worth mentioning: Edge L2VPN-S's interface External-SDQ must have network reachability to Edge L2VPN-T's interface External-TPA. Figure 10-6 shows a ping from L2-VPN-T's External-TPA interface to L2-VPN-S's External-SDQ interface.

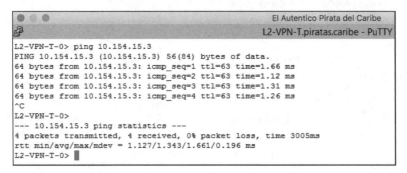

Figure 10-6   Pings from L2-VPN-T toward L2-VPN-S

Figure 10-7 shows the result of a ping from Virtual Machine ServerApp01 toward ServerApp02. The ping fails since we have not configured the Layer 2 VPN yet.

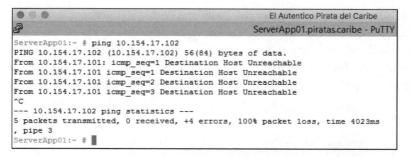

```
●  ●  ●                                    El Autentico Pirata del Caribe
                                    ServerApp01.piratas.caribe - PuTTY
ServerApp01:~ # ping 10.154.17.102
PING 10.154.17.102 (10.154.17.102) 56(84) bytes of data.
From 10.154.17.101: icmp_seq=1 Destination Host Unreachable
From 10.154.17.101 icmp_seq=1 Destination Host Unreachable
From 10.154.17.101 icmp_seq=2 Destination Host Unreachable
From 10.154.17.101 icmp_seq=3 Destination Host Unreachable
^C
--- 10.154.17.102 ping statistics ---
5 packets transmitted, 0 received, +4 errors, 100% packet loss, time 4023ms
, pipe 3
ServerApp01:~ # █
```

Figure 10-7   Failed pings from ServerApp01 toward ServerApp02

We are ready to start configuring a Layer 2 VPN. It does not matter which Edge we configure first, but it is not a bad idea to start with the server, so we start with the configuration of L2-VPN-T—the Layer 2 VPN Server.

Step 1.   From the NSX Edges view, double-click the L2-VPN-T Edge.

Step 2.   Go to **Manage > VPN** and select the **L2 VPN** view.

Step 3.   Select the dial next to Server and click **Change**.

Step 4.   In Server Details enter the following configuration:

    a. Listener IP: 10.154.11.3

    This is the IP over which the Layer 2 VPN tunnels will travel, and it must belong to an Uplink interface. The incoming request from the Layer 2 VPN client to form a Layer 2 VPN needs to arrive over this interface.

    b. Listener Port: 443.

    The SSL port number is 443. Unless you have reasons to change it, leave the default. If you do change the port number, you must also change it at the Layer 2 VPN Client.

    c. Encryption Algorithm: Select one of the options available:

- AES128-SHA
- AES128-GCM-SHA256
- AES256-SHA
- DEC-CBC3-SHA
- NULL-MD5

Step 5. If the Edge has any certificates they will be listed in the Server Certificate table, and you can select one for the Layer 2 VPN. If the Edge does not have any certificates or you don't want to use them, check the box **Use System Generated Certificate** (we cover how to add certificates to the Edge in Chapter 14, "NSX Edge Network Services and Security").

Step 6. Your configuration should look similar to Figure 10-8. Click **OK**.

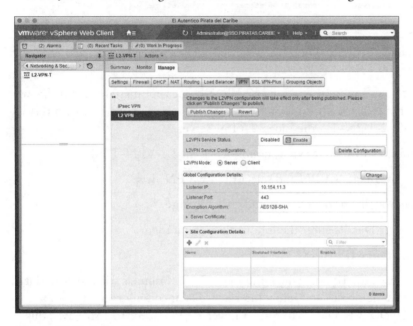

Figure 10-8 Layer 2 VPN server settings

Step 7. In Site Configuration Details, click the green add icon and enter the following configuration:

- **Enable Peer Site**: Check the box if you want to allow this Peer Site to establish an L2 VPN connection with this L2 VPN Server.

- **Name**: Santo Domingo.

- **Description**: Data Center in the Caribbean.

- **User Id**: Any username you want. It must match the username configured at the Layer 2 VPN Client.

- **Password**: Enter any password and retype in the next field.

- **Stretched Interfaces**: Click the Select Sub Interfaces link to add all subinterfaces you want to stretch to this L2 VPN peer site. We will be adding the Internal – TPA subinterface.

This is where the Tunnel ID of the subinterface comes into play. When the L2 VPN Client for this Peer site we are configuring connects to this L2 VPN Server, the Tunnel ID is used to match the subinterfaces on both sides that belong to the same Layer 2 domain.

- **Egress Optimization Gateway Address**: List all IPs for which this L2 VPN Server responds to ARP requests.

  This is a long way to say default gateway, but in the form of a Virtual IP (VIP). Traffic received by the VIP is routed by this Edge and not sent over the L2 VPN tunnel. This VIP should match on the L2 VPN Client side.

- **Enable Upstretched Networks**: Check the box and list any subnets that will not be sent over the L2 VPN tunnel.

Step 8.   Your configuration should look like the one in Figure 10-9. Click **OK** if you are satisfied with the configuration.

Add Peer Site	?

☑ Enable Peer Site

Name:	* Santo Domingo
Description:	Data Center in the Caribbean
User Id:	* Enriquillo
Password:	* ************
Confirm Password:	* ************
Stretched Interfaces:	* Internal-TPA

Select Sub Interfaces

| Egress Optimization Gateway Address: | 10.154.17.6 |

Example: Comma separated list of IP address
Ex:191.1.1.1,192.1.1.1

☐ Enable Unstretched Networks

Unstretched Networks:

Example: Comma separated list of networks
Ex:192.168.10.0/24,192.168.20.0/24

OK   Cancel

Figure 10-9   Layer 2 VPN user details and certificate

Step 9.   Click the **Enabled box**, click **Publish Changes**, and you are done, as shown in Figure 10-10. This Edge is now listening for a client request from the peer sites to start a Layer 2 VPN.

The Enabled box turns to Disable.

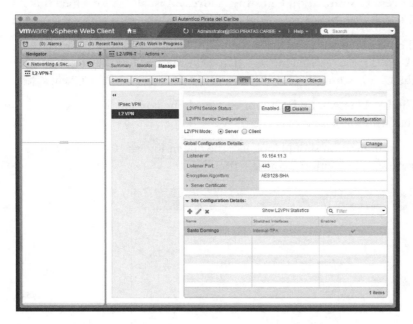

Figure 10-10   Layer 2 VPN Server

Let's configure the next Edge—L2-VPN-S—the one that acts as the Layer 2 VPN Client.

Step 1.   Return to the NSX Edges view and double-click the **L2-VPN-S Edge**.

Step 2.   Go to **Manage > VPN** and select the **L2 VPN** view.

Step 3.   Select the dial next to Client and click **Change**.

Step 4.   In the Client Details tab, enter the following configuration:

    a. Server Address: 10.154.11.3. This is the IP of the Layer 2 VPN Server.

    b. Server Port: 443. Unless you have configured a different SSL port number at the Layer 2 VPN Server, leave this at the default value of 443.

    c. Stretched Interfaces: Click the **Select Sub Interfaces** link to add all subinterfaces you want to stretch to this L2 VPN peer site. We will add the Internal – SDQ subinterface.

    d. Egress Optimization Gateway Address: List all IPs for which this L2 VPN Client will respond to ARP requests.

      e. **Enable Upstretched Networks**: Check the box and list any subnets that will not be sent over the L2 VPN tunnel.

Step 5. In User Details enter the following configuration:

      a. **User ID**: Any username you want. It must match the username configured at the Layer 2 VPN Server.

      b. **Password**: Enter the password configured in the Layer 2 VPN Server and retype it.

The configuration should look similar to Figure 10-11.

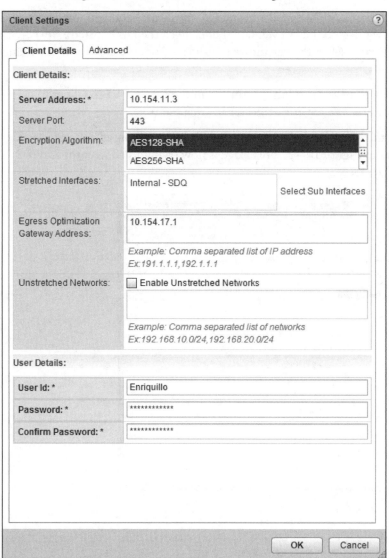

Figure 10-11   Layer 2 VPN Client details

Step 6. In the Advanced tab's Proxy Settings enter the following configuration if you want to use a proxy:

   a. **Enable Secure Proxy**: Check the box to enable the proxy.

   b. **Address**: The address of the proxy server.

   c. **Port**: The port number for the proxy server.

   d. **User Name and Password**: The credentials to have the Layer 2 VPN Client authenticate with the proxy server.

Step 7. If the Layer 2 VPN Server has any CA certificates and you want to have the Layer 2 VPN Client validate them, check the box **Validate Server Certificate**, select the certificate to validate from the certificate table, and click **OK**.

You would have to add the certificate in the Layer 2 VPN Client to use this feature. We cover certificates in Chapter 14.

Step 8. Click the box **Enabled** and then click **Publish Changes**. Things should look as in Figure 10-12. This Edge is now trying to contact the Layer 2 VPN Server.

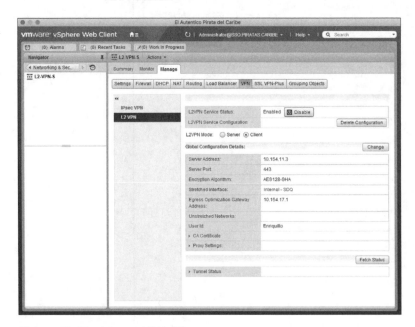

Figure 10-12   Layer 2 VPN Client

Verifying Layer 2 VPN

The best way to verify that your Layer 2 VPN is working is to send traffic, like a ping, across the tunnel. Figure 10-13 shows the ping test from Virtual Machine ServerApp01 toward ServerApp02. The ping is successful this time, meaning our tunnel is working.

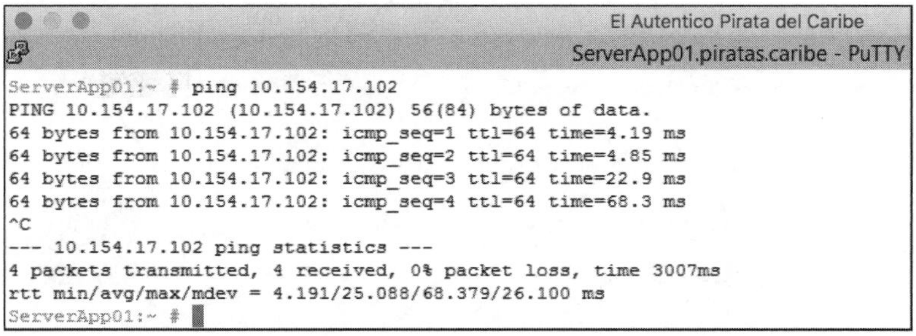

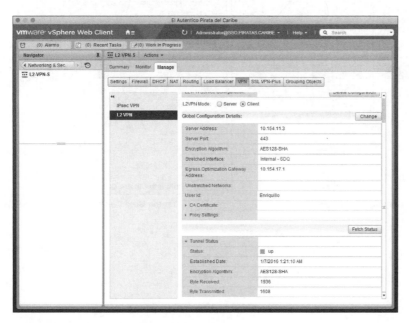

El Autentico Pirata del Caribe
ServerApp01.piratas.caribe - PuTTY
ServerApp01:~ # ping 10.154.17.102
PING 10.154.17.102 (10.154.17.102) 56(84) bytes of data.
64 bytes from 10.154.17.102: icmp_seq=1 ttl=64 time=4.19 ms
64 bytes from 10.154.17.102: icmp_seq=2 ttl=64 time=4.85 ms
64 bytes from 10.154.17.102: icmp_seq=3 ttl=64 time=22.9 ms
64 bytes from 10.154.17.102: icmp_seq=4 ttl=64 time=68.3 ms
^C
--- 10.154.17.102 ping statistics ---
4 packets transmitted, 4 received, 0% packet loss, time 3007ms
rtt min/avg/max/mdev = 4.191/25.088/68.379/26.100 ms
ServerApp01:~ #

Figure 10-13 Successful pings from ServerApp01 toward ServerApp02

Another way to verify the tunnel status is to check the tunnel status in both the client and server sides. Figure 10-14 shows the tunnel status client sides. To show the status, click the **Fetch Status** button.

El Autentico Pirata del Caribe
vmware vSphere Web Client
Navigator
L2-VPN-S
Summary
Monitor
Manage
Settings
Firewall
DHCP
NAT
Routing
Load Balancer
VPN
SSL VPN-Plus
Grouping Objects
IPsec VPN
L2 VPN
L2VPN Mode: Server Client
Global Configuration Details:
Change
Server Address: 10.154.11.3
Server Port: 443
Encryption Algorithm: AES128-SHA
Stretched Interface: Internal - SDQ
Egress Optimization Gateway Address: 10.154.17.1
Unstretched Networks:
User Id: Enriquillo
CA Certificate:
Proxy Settings:
Fetch Status
Tunnel Status
Status: up
Established Date: 1/7/2016 1:21:10 AM
Encryption Algorithm: AES128-SHA
Byte Received: 1936
Byte Transmitted: 1608

Figure 10-14 Layer 2 VPN Client side status

Layer 2 VPN Packet Walk

Figure 10-15 shows Figure 10-3 with the management plane entities and NSX Controllers added. We use Figure 10-15 to do a packet walk of the first ping sent from Virtual Machine ServerApp02 to ServerApp01.

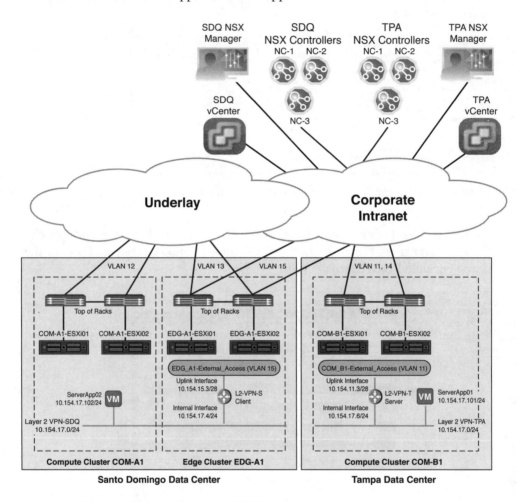

Figure 10-15   Layer 2 VPN with multiple ESXi hosts

We make the following assumptions for this packet walk:

- Each data center has its own vCenter and NSX Manager.

- Virtual Machine ServerApp01 is running in COM-B1-ESXi02.

- Virtual Machine ServerApp02 is running in COM-A1-ESXi02.

- NSX Edge L2-VPN-S is running in EDG-A1-ESXi02.

- NSX Edge L2-VPN-T is running in COM-B1ESXi01.

- ServerApp01 does not have an ARP entry for ServerApp02.

- ServerApp02 does not have an ARP entry for ServerApp01.

- Replication Mode for all logical switches is Hybrid or Unicast.

- The NSX Controllers do not have an ARP entry for ServerApp01 or Server-App02.

Step 1.   ServerApp02 wants to send a ping to ServerApp01 but does not have an ARP entry for it.

Step 2.   ServerApp02 sends an ARP request.

Step 3.   Logical switch Layer 2 VPN – SDQ receives the request and processes it.

We covered in Chapter 6, "Logical Switch Packet Walks," how ARP requests are handled by logical switches.

Step 4.   Logical switch Layer 2 VPN – SDQ replicates the ARP request, as shown in Figure 10-16.

The number of VXLAN tunnels created depends on the Replication Mode configured.

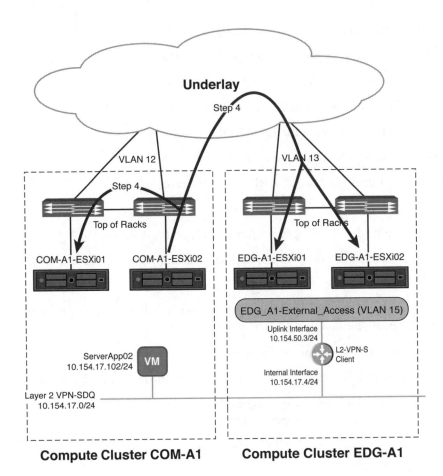

Figure 10-16 ARP request being replicated

Step 5. The ARP request is received by Edge L2-VPN-S' Internal interface, Internal-SDQ.

The local copy of Layer 2 VPN – SDQ in ESXi host EDG-A1-ESXi02 learns the MAC address of ServerApp02.

Step 6. L2-VPN-S takes the ARP request, puts it in a Layer 2 VPN tunnel, and sends it to Edge L2-VPN-T.

The tunnel goes out of the Uplink interface External-SDQ, toward the physical network.

Step 7. Edge L2-VPN-T receives the tunnel traffic, over its Uplink Interface External-TPA, validates it, and decapsulates it.

Step 8. Edge L2-VPN-T takes the ARP request and sends it to logical switch Layer 2 VPN – TPA.

The traffic is sent out over the Internal interface, Internal-TPA.

Step 9. Logical switch Layer 2 VPN – TPA learns the MAC address of Server-App02 and tells the NSX Controller.

If this had been a distributed portgroup instead of a logical switch, no MAC learning would've taken place.

Step 10. Logical switch Layer 2 VPN – TPA receives the ARP request and processes it.

Step 11. Logical switch Layer 2 VPN – TPA replicates the ARP request, as shown in Figure 10-17.

The replication happens over VXLAN overlays.

Step 12. ServerApp01 receives the ARP request and processes it.

The local copy of Layer 2 VPN – TPA in ESXi host COM-A1-ESXi02 learns the MAC address of ServerApp02.

Step 13. ServerApp01 sends a unicast ARP reply to ServerApp02.

Step 14. Logical switch Layer 2 VPN – TPA receives the ARP reply, processes it, and sends it over to COM-B1ESXi01 over a unicast VXLAN overlay.

The logical switch learned the MAC address of ServerApp02 in step 12.

We covered how ARP replies are handled in Chapter 6.

Step 15. Logical switch Layer 2 VPN – TPA in COM-B1ESXi01 receives the ARP reply, processes it, and sends it to Edge L2-VPN-T's interface Internal-TPA.

   a. The logical switch learns ServerApp01's MAC address.

   b. The logical switch learned ServerApp02's MAC address in step 10.

Step 16. Edge L2-VPN-T receives the ARP reply, puts it in a Layer 2 VPN tunnel, and sends it to Edge L2-VPN-S.

The tunnel goes out of the Uplink interface External-TPA, toward the physical network.

Step 17. Edge L2-VPN-S receives the tunnel traffic over its Uplink Interface External-SDQ, validates it, and decapsulates it.

Step 18. Edge L2-VPN-S takes the ARP reply and sends it to logical switch Layer 2 VPN – SDQ.

The traffic is sent out over the Internal interface, Internal-SDQ.

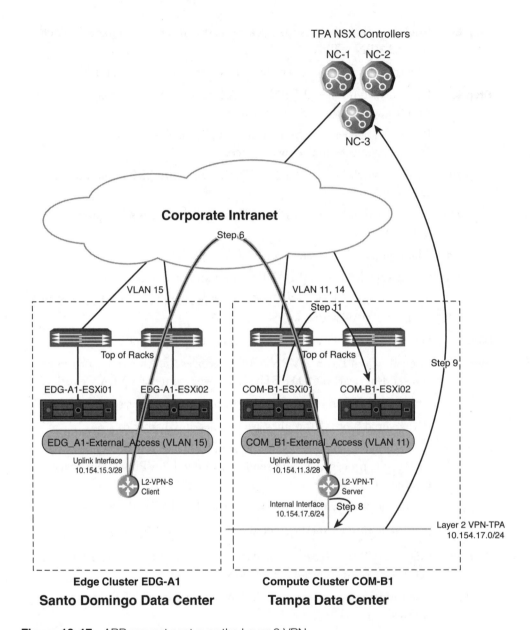

Figure 10-17   ARP request sent over the Layer 2 VPN

Step 19.   Logical switch Layer 2 VPN – SDQ learns the MAC address of Server-App01 and tells the NSX Controller.

Step 20.   Logical switch Layer 2 VPN – SDQ receives the ARP reply and processes it.

Step 21. Logical switch Layer 2 VPN – SDQ forwards the ARP request in a VX-LAN overlay unicast to COM-B1-ESXi02.

Step 22. ServerApp02 receives the ARP reply, adds the entry to its ARP table, and sends the first ping to L2-T-MV2, as shown in Figure 10-18.

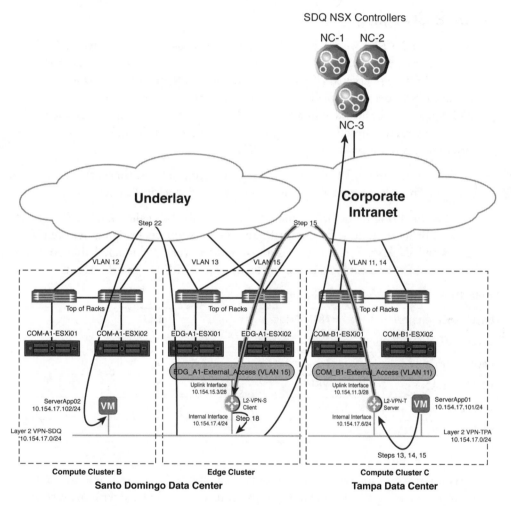

Figure 10-18 ARP reply

Step 23. ServerApp01 receives the ping, but it doesn't have an ARP entry in its ARP table for ServerApp02, so it sends out an ARP request for Server-App02's MAC.

Steps 1 thru 22 are repeated without the MAC learning by the logical switches.

This is a simple packet walk that has a lot of details (and many more that were left out because they were already covered in other chapters). As we continue our studying for the VCP6-NV exam you should expect some concepts to be a bit more involved as they will leverage a lot of the previous topics that we have already learned.

Layer 2 Bridging

With Layer 2 VPNs we can extend Ethernet broadcast domains, whether VXLAN, VLANs, or both, over untrusted mediums. We can also extend the broadcast domain by bridging between virtual workloads, VXLAN, and physical workloads, VLAN. NSX does not provide an option to bridge between a virtual workload in a VXLAN and a physical workload in a VLAN. NSX does not support connecting a physical workload directly to a VXLAN (only VMs can be in an NSX VNI); therefore there is no option to bridge two VXLANs.

If a VM resides in the VLAN that is being bridged, that VM shares the same broadcast domain with the virtual workloads in the bridged logical switch.

In NSX, the bridging of virtual and physical workloads is called *Layer 2 Bridging*. Layer 2 Bridging is done by the DLR, and it only supports bridging between VXLANs and VLANs. The ULR does not support Layer 2 Bridging. Table 10-4 shows the type of Layer 2 extensions supported by the NSX Edge and the DLR.

Table 10-4   Layer 2 Extension Support

Layer 2 Extension	NSX Edge	DLR
Layer 2 VPN	Yes	No
Layer 2 Bridging	No	Yes
VLAN-VLAN	Yes	No
VXLAN-VLAN	Yes	Yes
VXLAN-VXLAN	Yes	No

A typical use case for Layer 2 Bridging is for a mostly virtualized application. For example, an application has some or most of its tiers virtualized with the rest of the tiers continuing to run bare metal. The application has Layer 2 dependencies between some of the virtualized tiers and the physical tiers. Another use case is for physical to virtual migrations where the client does not want to change the IP of the application.

Layer 2 Bridging is done by selecting a logical switch and a distributed portgroup and telling a DLR to connect to each. These connections are LIFs but with connections to dvPorts in the vDS called *sinkports*. Remember that sinkports are special vDS ports that get a copy of all BUMs in the VLAN. Now, I know what you may be thinking "why is a router doing bridging?" It turns out that routers have been used as an inexpensive and quick way to do bridging for a long time. With the DLR, NSX is just honoring that tradition ☺.

You may connect a second LIF to the logical switch used for bridging and assign it an IP. This allows the DLR to be the default gateway for workloads connected to the logical switch or VLAN being bridged. Alternatively, workloads connecting to bridged segments may use an NSX Edge or a physical router as their default gateway. If the bridged LIF is not configured with an IP, the traffic in the bridge segment is kept completely isolated by the DLR doing Layer 2 Bridging from its other LIFs.

The function of Layer 2 Bridging is done in kernel, but it is not distributed. One of the ESXi hosts that has the DLR is selected to do all the bridging. That ESXi host is referred to as the *Bridge Instance*. The Bridge Instance is the only ESXi host that has the sinkport connections doing the bridging. None of the other ESXi hosts have the sinkport connections. This is the second setting (the pMAC being the first) where the copies of the DLR instances are not identical in each ESXi host. The Bridge Instance still does MAC learning and updates the NSX Controller responsible for the DLR. All MAC addresses learned by the Bridge Instance have a timer of 300 seconds, after which the entry is removed from the MAC table.

Figure 10-19 shows a DLR doing bridging between a VM in logical switch Santo Domingo Layer 2 Bridge and a physical server in VLAN 20.

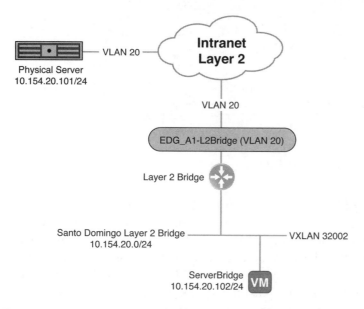

Figure 10-19   Layer 2 Bridging

The NSX Controller responsible for the DLR elects the ESXi host that will be the Bridge Instance. The selection is straightforward: Wherever the DLR Control VM is running, that ESXi host becomes the Bridge Instance. Thus you have control of which ESXi host becomes the Bridge Instance by choosing where the DLR Control VM runs. The NSX Controller provides a copy of the MAC table to the new Bridge Instance.

A single DLR can have multiple bridges as long as it always involves different pairs of VXLAN-VLAN LIFs; however, a DLR always has a single Bridge Instance. Multiple DLRs can be configured to do Layer 2 Bridging in different VXLAN-VLAN pairs. If you require having multiple Bridge Instances, you must deploy multiple DLRs to do Layer 2 Bridging. Figure 10-20 shows a single DLR doing Layer 2 Bridging for two different VXLAN-VLAN pairs. Traffic from one bridge pair is not seen by the other unless it is routed.

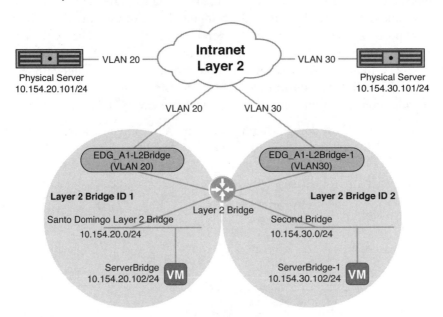

Figure 10-20 DLR doing multiple Layer 2 Bridging

In the event that the ESXi host that is the Bridge Instance fails, a new Bridge Instance is selected. The selection follows the placement of the DLR Control VM, with the new ESXi host that runs the DLR Control VM becoming the new Bridge Instance. This implies that the VLAN that is being bridged must be presented to all ESXi hosts in the cluster(s) that might run the DLR Control VM. To be more specific, the same distributed portgroup that the VLAN LIF connects to *must* be present in all ESXi hosts that might run the Control VM.

All ESXi hosts in the cluster(s) where the Control VM might run must be part of the same vDS because they all need access to the same portgroup with the VLAN being bridged. Although you can configure the same VLAN in different portgroups in different distributed switches, vCenter does not support the same portgroup to exist in more than one vDS. Figure 10-21 shows a configuration with the Control VM restricted to the edge cluster and the DLR doing Layer 2 Bridging between the logical switch Santo Domingo Layer 2 Bridge and portgroup EDG_A1_L2Bridge.

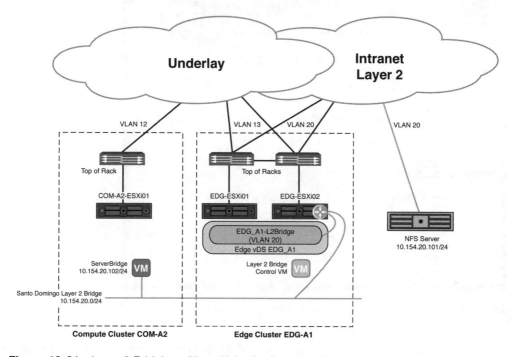

Figure 10-21 Layer 2 Bridging with multiple distributed switches

 The logical switch being bridged must belong to a transport zone that includes the Bridge Instance and all the ESXi hosts in the cluster where the DLR Control VM is.

Configuring Layer 2 Bridging

Configuring Layer 2 Bridging is straightforward. First let's go over the prerequisites:

- A logical switch in a transport zone that includes the cluster(s) where the Control VM may run

- A DLR

- A VLAN portgroup in a vDS that has as members all the ESXi hosts from the cluster(s) where the Control VM may run

Figure 10-22 shows the logical switch Santo Domingo Layer 2 Bridge and a dvPort-group EDG_A1_L2Bridge in vDS EDG_A1. Virtual Machine ServerBridge, not shown in Figure 10-22, is connected to logical switch Virtual Workload. The IP of ServerBridge is 10.154.20.102. For the DLR, we use DLR Layer 2 Bridge, acting as the default gateway with an IP of 10.154.20.1. An NFS share, with an IP of 10.154.20.101, is the physical entity.

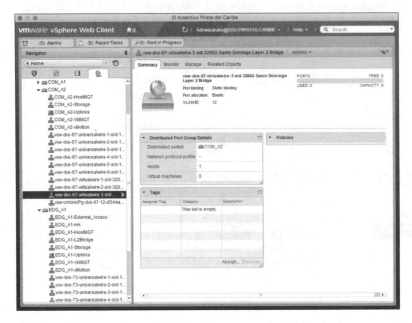

Figure 10-22   VXLAN and VLAN portgroups to be bridged

Before we start the configuration, let's validate that there is no connectivity between Virtual Machine ServerBridge and the physical NFS server. Figure 10-23 shows the failed pings.

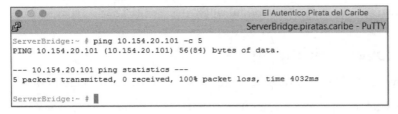

Figure 10-23   Failed pings from ServerBridge toward physical NFS server

Step 1.   From the NSX Edges view double-click the DLR Layer 2 Bridge.

Step 2.   Go to **Manage > Bridging**.

Step 3.   Click the green + icon.

Step 4.   In the Add Bridge Wizard, enter the following information:

a. **Name**: Assign the bridge a name.

b. **Logical Switches**: Select the logical switch where the virtual workload is connected.

c. **Distributed Virtual Port Group**: Select a portgroup that has the VLAN that will be bridged.

d. Your configuration should look similar to the one in Figure 10-24. Click **OK**.

Figure 10-24   Layer 2 Bridging configuration

Step 5.   Click **Publish**.

Verifying Layer 2 Bridging

Just as with Layer 2 VPN, the best test you can do to verify that the Layer 2 Bridge is operational is to send traffic between the two sides. Figure 10-25 shows a successful ping from ServerBridge to the physical NFS server.

```
                                          El Autentico Pirata del Caribe
                                     ServerBridge.piratas.caribe - PuTTY
ServerBridge:~ # ping 10.154.20.101 -c 5
PING 10.154.20.101 (10.154.20.101) 56(84) bytes of data.
64 bytes from 10.154.20.101: icmp_seq=1 ttl=64 time=1.62 ms
64 bytes from 10.154.20.101: icmp_seq=2 ttl=64 time=1.36 ms
64 bytes from 10.154.20.101: icmp_seq=3 ttl=64 time=1.53 ms
64 bytes from 10.154.20.101: icmp_seq=4 ttl=64 time=3.37 ms
64 bytes from 10.154.20.101: icmp_seq=5 ttl=64 time=1.60 ms

--- 10.154.20.101 ping statistics ---
5 packets transmitted, 5 received, 0% packet loss, time 4007ms
rtt min/avg/max/mdev = 1.361/1.900/3.375/0.744 ms
ServerBridge:~ #
```

Figure 10-25   Successful pings from ServerBridge toward physical NFS server

From the Bridge Instance we can run the command **net-vdr --bridge -l vdrName** to see the bridge configuration, as shown in Figure 10-26. The number 78798132 after the VDR name is the VDR ID.

```
                                        El Autentico Pirata del Caribe
                                    edg-a1-esxi01.piratas.caribe - PuTTY

[root@edg-a1-esxi01:~] net-vdr --bridge -l default+edge-4

VDR 'default+edge-4' bridge 'Layer 2 Bridging' config :

Bridge config:
Name:id              Layer 2 Bridging:1
Portset name:
DVS name:            EDG_A1
Ref count:           1
Number of networks: 2
Number of uplinks:  0

        Network 'vxlan-32002-type-bridging' config:
        Ref count:          2
        Network type:       2
        VLAN ID:            0
        VXLAN ID:           32002
        Ageing time:        300
        Fdb entry hold time:1
        FRP filter enable:  1

                Network port ID '0x3000009' config:
                Ref count:          1
                Port ID:            0x3000009
                VLAN ID:            4095
                IOChains installed: 0

        Network 'vlan-20-type-bridging' config:
        Ref count:          2
        Network type:       2
        VLAN ID:            20
        VXLAN ID:           0
        Ageing time:        300
        Fdb entry hold time:1
        FRP filter enable:  1

                Network port ID '0x3000009' config:
                Ref count:          1
                Port ID:            0x3000009
                VLAN ID:            4095
                IOChains installed: 0

[root@edg-a1-esxi01:~]
```

Figure 10-26   Output of command **net-vdr --bridge -l default+edge-4** in the Bridge Instance

In the Bridge Instance, we can also run the command **net-vdr --bridge --mac-address-table vdrName** to show the MAC table for the Layer 2 Bridge, as shown in Figure 10-27. The additional MAC addresses seen in the VLAN are a default gateway in the VLAN side and the MAC from which the Putty session was initiated.

```
                                    El Autentico Pirata del Caribe
                                  edg-a1-esxi01.piratas.caribe - PuTTY
[root@edg-a1-esxi01:~] net-vdr --bridge --mac-address-table default+edge-4

VDR 'default+edge-4' bridge 'Layer 2 Bridging' mac address tables :

total number of MAC addresses:    1
number of MAC addresses returned: 1
Destination Address  Address Type  VLAN ID  VXLAN ID  Destination Port  Age
-------------------  ------------  -------  --------  ----------------  ---
00:73:21:9a:20:02    Dynamic             0     32002          50331652  18

total number of MAC addresses:    3
number of MAC addresses returned: 3
Destination Address  Address Type  VLAN ID  VXLAN ID  Destination Port  Age
-------------------  ------------  -------  --------  ----------------  ---
00:27:f8:d5:9c:0e    Dynamic            20         0          50331652  109
00:73:21:9a:08:01    Dynamic            20         0          50331652  18
00:73:21:9a:20:01    Dynamic            20         0          50331652  10

[root@edg-a1-esxi01:~]
```

Figure 10-27 Output of command **net-vdr --bridge --mac-address-table default+edge-4** in the Bridge Instance

From the NSX Manger we can run the command **show logical-router controller master dlr vdr-id bridge bridge-id mac-address-table** (in the NSX Controller responsible for the DLR, we can run the related command **show control-cluster logical-routers bridge-mac** *logical-router-id bridge-id*) to see the MAC table provided by the Bridge Instance, as shown in Figure 10-28.

```
                                    El Autentico Pirata del Caribe
                                  nsxmgr-a.piratas.caribe - PuTTY
nsxmgr-a.piratas.caribe> show logical-router controller master dlr 0x7d00 bridge 1 mac-address-table
LR-Id    Bridge-Id  Mac                Vlan-Id Vxlan-Id Port-Id   Source
0x7d00   1          00:27:f8:d5:9c:0e  20      0        50331652  vlan
0x7d00   1          00:73:21:9a:08:01  20      0        50331652  vlan
0x7d00   1          00:73:21:9a:20:02  0       32002    50331652  vxlan
0x7d00   1          00:73:21:9a:20:01  20      0        50331652  vlan
masterControllerIp=10.154.8.71
nsxmgr-a.piratas.caribe>
```

Figure 10-28 Output of command **show logical-router controller master dlr 0x7d00 bridge 1 mac-address-table** in the NSX Controller

Layer 2 Bridging Packet Walk

Now on to a packet walk. Figure 10-29 shows two clusters, a VM and a physical NFS server. Each cluster has its own vDS, and the NFS server is in the same subnet (10.154.20.0/24) as the virtual machine (ServerBridge). We do a packet walk of the first ping ServerBridge sends to the physical NFS server. EDG-A1-ESXi02 is the Bridge Instance.

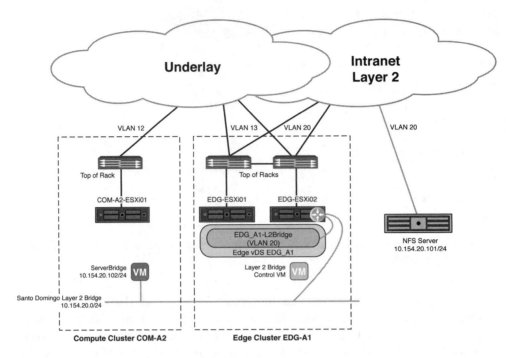

Figure 10-29   Layer 2 Bridge packet walk

Step 1.   Virtual machine ServerBridge wants to ping the NFS server but does not have an ARP entry for the NFS sever in its ARP table.

Step 2.   ServerBridge sends an ARP request.

Step 3.   The ARP request is received by logical switch Santo Domingo Layer 2 Bridge in ESXi host EDG-A1-ESXi02.

The ARP request was replicated.

Step 4.   Logical switch Santo Domingo Layer 2 Bridge in ESXi host EDG-A1-ESXi02, which is the Bridge Instance, broadcasts the frame locally, and a copy is received by the sinkport connected to the LIF of DLR Layer 2 Bridge.

Step 5.   Layer 2 Bridge learns the MAC address of ServerBridge and tells the NSX Controller.

Step 6.   Layer 2 Bridge forwards the ARP request out of the sinkport connected to the bridged VLAN LIF.

Step 7.   The frame is received by vDS EDG_A1's EDG_A1-L2Bridge dvPort-group in VLAN 20 in EDG-A1-ESXi02.

vDS EDG_A1 *does not* learn the MAC address of ServerBridge.

Step 8.   vDS EDG_A1 sends the frame out to the physical network, over VLAN 20, where every physical switch in the VLAN learns the MAC address of ServerBridge, as shown in Figure 10-30.

Bridged traffic is pinned to a single dvUplink in vDS EDG_A1.

The ARP request is a broadcast that will be processed by all switches in VLAN 20, including the local copy vDS EDG_A1 running in ESXi host EDG-A1-ESXi02.

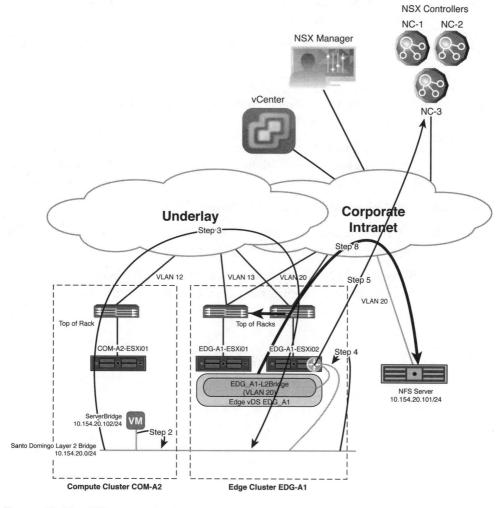

Figure 10-30   ARP request in physical network

Step 9.   The physical NFS server receives the ARP request and sends back a unicast ARP reply to ServerBridge.

Step 10.   The ARP reply is received by the dvUplink of vDS EDG_A1 in EDG-A1-ESXi02 to which the bridge traffic is pinned.

Step 11.   vDS EDG_vDS forwards the frame to all of its interfaces in VLAN 20, including the sinkport connected to the bridged VLAN LIF of DLR Layer 2 Bridge.

Step 12.   Layer 2 Bridge learns the MAC address of the physical NFS server and tells the NSX Controller.

Step 13.   Layer 2 Bridge sends the ARP reply out of the sinkport connected to the bridged VXLAN LIF.

Step 14.   Logical switch Santo Domingo Layer 2 Bridge in ESXi host EDG-A1-ESXi02 gets the ARP reply and learns the MAC address of the NFS server.

   The logical switch will not tell the NSX Controller about it. This is where the close working relationship between the logical switch and the DLR comes into play.

Step 15.   The ARP reply is forwarded to ServerBridge.

Step 16.   ServerBridge adds the ARP entry in its ARP table and sends a ping to the physical NFS server, as shown in Figure 10-31.

   If the physical NFS server sends an ARP request for ServerBridge before it can respond to the ping, the steps are similar to steps 1 through 15.

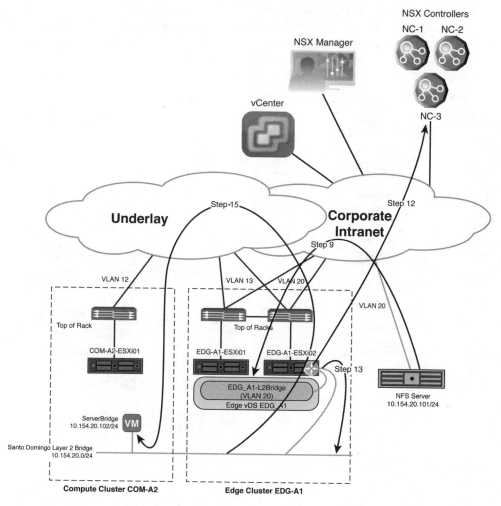

Figure 10-31   ARP reply

Packet walks could hardly get any simpler than this. A lot of the details were not included here, like the ARP replication, because we have covered them quite a bit. By now you should be familiar with what is happening at the logical switch.

Hardware VTEPs

The Layer 2 Bridge is a great way to extend the Layer 2 of your logical switches to VLANs so as to allow virtual and physical workloads that can only communicate via Layer 2 to do so. However, a Layer 2 Bridge has some scalability challenges that may be hard to overcome in some use cases. In Figure 10-32, you can see a sample deployment where multiple physical workloads need to share the same Layer 2 domains with a number of virtual workloads in logical switches. All traffic to/from the physical workloads would go over the same VMNIC in the Bridge Instance. It is easy to see how this may be a bottleneck.

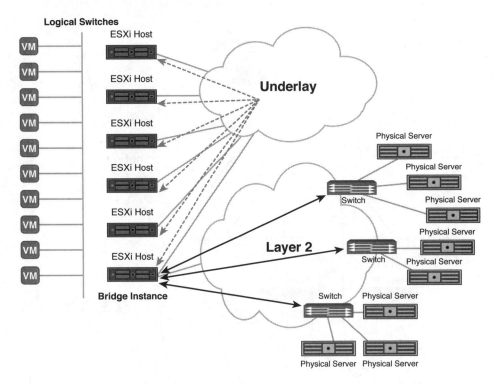

Figure 10-32 Use case of Layer 2 Bridge limitation

If instead of a Bridge Instance we could have a physical switch do the mapping of VXLAN to VLAN, we could have a deployment with increased available bandwidth and no single link acting as a bottleneck. A switch that can bridge VXLAN to VLAN traffic is called a hardware VTEP.

NSX supports deploying multiple hardware VTEPs to map a VXLAN to a VLAN. This is useful for cases where you have multiple physical workloads connecting to different switches; however, this comes with a *big* warning to avoid physical Layer 2 loops. Figure 10-33 shows multiple hardware VTEPs being used to extend VXLAN 7321 to VLANs.

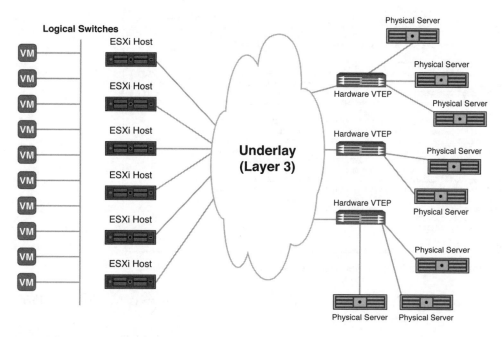

Figure 10-33   Multiple hardware VTEPs

Before NSX 6.2, the only option to add a hardware VTEP to the NSX environment was to have logical switches with Multicast Replication Mode. As of NSX 6.2, the hardware VTEPs can also be added to the NSX domain with both Unicast and Hybrid Replication Mode.

To add and verify a switch as a hardware VTEP to NSX, follow these steps. You must be an enterprise administrator or NSX administrator to add a hardware VTEP, the logical switch must already be created in NSX, and the VLAN must exist in the switch.

NOTE   The steps will reference a Brocade VDX 6740 as the hardware VTEP.

Step 1.   In the switch, connect to and activate the NSX Controller API master.

Step 2.   Copy the NSX Controller client certificate, as shown in Figure 10-34.

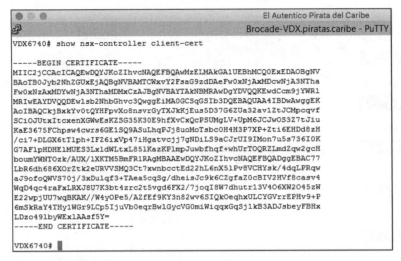

Figure 10-34   NSX Controller client certificate

Step 3.   In the Network and Security's Service Definition view, select the **Hard-ware Devices** tab.

Step 4.   Click the green plus sign to add the hardware VTEP.

Step 5.   In the **Add Hardware Bridge** pop-up window, assign the Hardware VTEP a name and paste the NSX Controller client certificate as shown in Figure 10-35. Then click **OK**.

Figure 10-35   Add hardware VTEP

Step 6.   Go back to the switch, type the command **show nsx-controller brief** to confirm the switch has a connection with all three NSX Controllers, as shown in Figure 10-36.

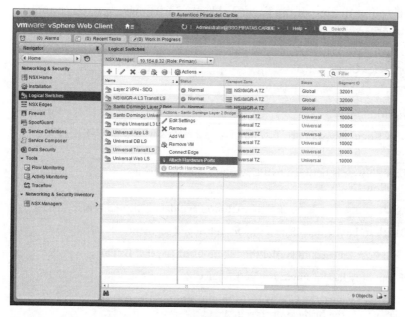

```
● ● ●                                    El Autentico Pirata del Caribe
                                         Brocade-VDX.piratas.caribe - PuTTY
VDX6740# show nsx-controller brief
Controller name      IP address       Port  Type  Connection state
================     =============    =====  ====  ======================
2V0-641              10.154.8.71      6640   SSL   Connected
2V0-641              10.154.8.73      6640   SSL   Connected
2V0-641              10.154.8.72      6640   SSL   Connected
VDX6740# ▮
```

Figure 10-36   Brocade VDX 6740 **show nsx-controller brief**

> **Step 7.**   From the Networking and Security's Logical Switches view, right-click
> the logical switch you want bridged to VLANs and select **Attach Hard-
> ware Ports,** as shown in Figure 10-37.

Figure 10-37   Attaching hardware VTEP to logical switch

> **Step 8.**   In the Attach Hardware Ports pop-up window, select the following values:
>
> > **a. Hardware Devices**: Select the Hardware VTEP from step 5.
> >
> > **b. Hardware Switch Ports**: Click the green plus sign to add VXLAN to
> > VLAN mapping.
> >
> > > **i. Switch**: Select the switch.
> > >
> > > **ii. Port**: Select a port in the switch to assign the VXLAN to.
> > >
> > > **iii.VLAN**: Enter the VLAN that will be bridged with the VXLAN
> > > and click **OK**.

Repeat step 8 to add more switches to this logical switch.

Step 9. Back in the switch, enter the command **show vlan #** to see the tunnels from the ESXi VTEPs.

Exam Preparation Tasks

Review All the Key Topics

Review the most important topics from inside the chapter, noted with the Key Topic icon in the outer margin of the page. Table 10-5 lists these key topics and the page numbers where each is found.

Table 10-5 Key Topics for Chapter 10

Key Topic Element	Description	Page Number
Paragraph	The NSX Edge only supports forming Layer 2 VPNs with other NSX Edges.	278
Paragraph	Layer 2 VPN works between two Edges in a Server-Client configuration.	280
Paragraph	Layer 2 VPN does not have an Ethernet loop avoidance mechanism.	296
Paragraph	The DLR can be the default gateway for a bridged segment.	297
Paragraph	The ESXi host executes in kernel the functions of Layer 2 Bridging.	297
Paragraph	A DLR can only have a single Bridge Instance.	298
Paragraph	The ESXi host where the Control VM might run must be part of the same vDS where the bridged portgroup resides.	299
Paragraph	The logical switch being bridged must belong to a transport zone that includes the Bridge Instance cluster.	299
Paragraph	Paragraph Bridged traffic is pinned to a dvUplink.	305
Paragraph	As of NSX 6.2, a hardware VTEP may be used with logical switches in any Replication Mode.	309

Complete Tables and Lists from Memory

Download and print a copy of Appendix C, "Memory Tables" (found on the book's website), or at least the section for this chapter, and complete the tables and lists from memory. Appendix D, "Memory Tables Answer Key," also on the website, includes the completed tables and lists so you can check your work.

Define Key Terms

Define the following key terms from this chapter, and check your answers in the Glossary:

Layer 2 VPN, AES-NI, Layer 2 Bridge, sinkport, Bridge Instance, hardware VTEP

This chapter covers all or part of the following VCP6-NV exam blueprint topics:

- **Objective 5.4**—Configure and Manage Logical Routers

CHAPTER 11

Layer 3 Connectivity Between Virtual and Physical Networks

We know how to extend Layer 2 communication between a virtual machine (VM) in a logical switch and a physical server, whether the server is in the same data center as the VM or not. Unfortunately (or fortunately if you are like me and not fond of extending Layer 2), VMs will be communicating with the physical side via IP, Layer 3. So what better time than now to discuss how to enable Layer 3 communication between a VM in a logical switch and a physical entity.

This is a short chapter to discuss how the Layer 3 connectivity is configured between the virtual and physical networks. NSX provides two options to configure Layer 3 between logical switches and VLANs. The first option is using a VLAN LIF in a logical router. The second option is to deploy an NSX Edge Gateway.

Do I Know This Already?

The "Do I Know This Already?" quiz allows you to assess whether you should read this entire chapter or simply jump to the "Exam Preparation Tasks" section for review. If you are in doubt, read the entire chapter. Table 11-1 outlines the major headings in this chapter and the corresponding "Do I Know This Already?" quiz questions. You can find the answers in Appendix A, "Answers to the 'Do I Know This Already?' Quizzes."

Table 11-1 Headings and Questions

Foundation Topic Section	Questions Covered in This Section
Logical Router VLAN LIF	1-3
Designated Instance	4-8
NSX Edge Gateway	9
Equal Cost Multipathing	10

1. Which two interfaces can be found on a DLR? (Choose two.)

   a. VXLAN LIF

   b. Logical switch interface

   c. VLAN logical interface

   d. VMNIC interface

2. Two vSphere clusters each have their own vDS assigned. Which NSX feature can't be configured or deployed in this scenario?

   a. Logical switches

   b. Distributed logical routers

   c. VXLAN

   d. VLAN LIF

3. Which statement is true regarding physical MAC addresses (pMACs) in an NSX deployment?

   a. Each ESXi host running an instance of the logical router has the same pMAC.

   b. Each ESXi host running an instance of the logical router has a unique pMAC.

   c. The MAC address of an NSX Edge's Uplink interface is a pMAC.

   d. The Top of Rack switch for the ESXi hosts has a pMAC in its MAC table for every ESXi host vMAC.

4. Which entity replies to an ARP request received over a VLAN LIF?

   a. The Designated Instance

   b. The Bridge Instance

   c. The ESXi host that first receives the ARP request

   d. The Logical Router Control VM

5. Which entity determines the ESXi host that will run the Designated Instance?

   a. The NSX Controller Master

   b. The NSX Controller responsible for the logical router

   c. The Logical Router Control VM

   d. The NSX Manager

6. If the Designated Instance is down, which ESXi host takes over?

   a. The ESXi host closest to the Designated Instance

   b. The ESXi host that has the lowest management IP

   c. An ESXi host randomly selected by the NSX Controller

   d. The ESXi host configured as the Bridge Instance

7. A logical router needs to send an ARP request over a VLAN LIF. Which ESXi host forwards the ARP request?

   a. The ESXi host running the logical router instance sending the ARP request

   b. The ESXi host that has the VLAN LIF

   c. The ESXi host that is the Designated Instance

   d. The ESXi host that has a VMkernel port with an IP in same subnet as the VLAN LIF

8. After a router table lookup, the logical router determines the next hop is out of the VLAN LIF. Which ESXi host sends egress traffic?

   a. The ESXi host that runs the Control VM

   b. The ESXi host that has the Designated Instance

   c. The ESXi host running the DLR instance that made the routing decision

   d. The Control VM

9. What is VMware's recommendation for providing Layer 3 connectivity between virtual and physical networks?

   a. Use a logical router with the VLAN LIF

   b. Use a logical router with an Uplink LIF

   c. Use a Perimeter Edge with an Uplink interface

   d. Extend the logical switch to the Top of Rack hardware VTEP

10. How many Equal Cost Multipath entries per destination does the NSX Edge support in its routing table?

    a. 2

    b. 4

    c. 8

    d. 16

Foundation Topics

Logical Router VLAN LIF

The logical router's LIFs may connect to VXLAN backed dvPortgroups (logical switches) or VLAN backed vPortgroups. Any logical router may have a direct Layer 3 connection to the physical world if the following condition is met: It is a distributed logical router and all ESXi hosts running the instance of the logical router have access to the same VLAN backed dvPortgroup. Remember from Chapter 7, "Logical Router," every ESXi host that is in the transport zones of the logical switches the VXLAN LIF connects to has a copy of the logical router. If any of the ESXi hosts in the transport zone did not have access to the VLAN backed dvPortgroup, there would be no way to configure the VLAN LIF for the logical router copy in that ESXi host.

I mentioned earlier in the book that the vMAC is the same across all ESXi hosts and the pMAC is different in each ESXi host, while the LIF IP remains the same in all ESXi hosts running the same copy of the logical router. The vMAC is seen by the physical switches when the logical router has VLAN LIFs. Nothing drives physical switches madder (other than knowing that a logical switch will replace them) than seeing the same MAC sourced from different interfaces. Let's do some packet walks to see what happens when the ESXi hosts running a copy of the same logical router send and respond to ARP requests over VLAN LIFs.

Figure 11-1 shows a logical router named Physical Access that has a VLAN LIF in dvPortgroup Physical-PG and the following configurations:

- Virtual machines L3-T-VM4 and L3-T-VM5 and logical router Physical Access are connected to the same logical switch.

- Virtual machines L3-T-VM4 and L3-T-VM5 have an ARP entry for their default gateway, which is the IP of logical router's Physical Access VXLAN LIF.

- Virtual machine L3-T-VM4 is running in ESXi host COM-B1-ESXi01.

- Virtual machine L3-T-VM5 is running in ESXi host COM-B1-ESXi02.

- dvPortgroup Physical-PG is in VLAN 55.

- Physical server L3-Server-P1 is connected to a physical switch in VLAN 55.

- Physical server L3-Server-P1's default gateway IP is the IP of the logical router's Physical Router VLAN LIF.

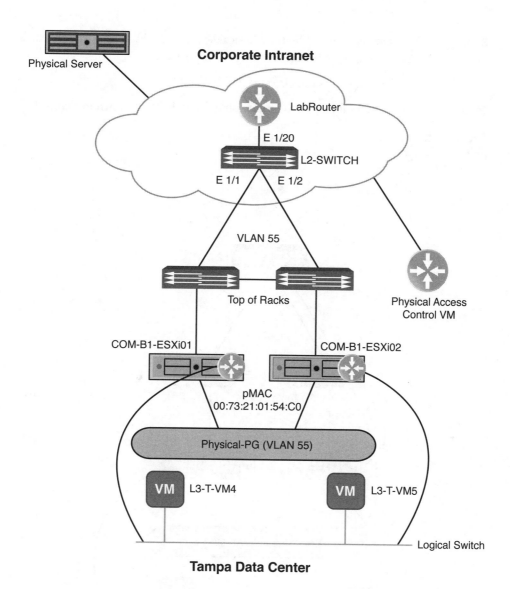

Figure 11-1   DLR with VLAN LIF

Step 1.   Virtual machine L3-T-VM4 sends traffic destined for L3-Server-P1.

The destination MAC is L3-T-VM4's default gateway, the vMAC.

Step 2.   Physical Access, in COM-B1-ESXi01, receives the frame, does a routing table lookup, and determines the egress interface to be the VLAN LIF.

Step 3.   Physical Access sends an ARP request out of VLAN LIF with a source MAC of the vMAC, 00:50:56:56:44:52.

Step 4.   The frame is received by the physical switch L2-SWITCH, which learns MAC 02:50:56:56:44:52 is coming from port 1/1.

L2-SWITCH adds the entry to its MAC table.

Step 5.   L2-SWITCH forwards the frame out of port 1/20, as shown in Figure 11-2.

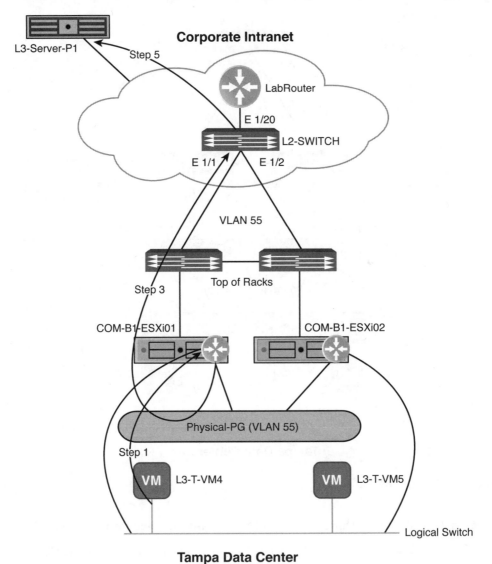

Figure 11-2   L2-SWITCH forwards the frame out of port 1/20.

Before I continue with this packet walk, let me remind you that L2-SWITCH learned MAC 02:50:56:56:44:52 can be found out of interface 1/1.

Step 6. Now virtual machine L3-T-VM5 sends traffic destined for L3-Server-P1, JUST after L3-T-VM4 had sent its packet.

The destination MAC is L3-T-VM5's default gateway, the vMAC.

Step 7. Physical Access, in COM-B1-ESXi02, receives the frame, does a routing table lookup, and determines the egress interface to be the VLAN LIF.

Step 8. Physical Access sends an ARP request out of VLAN LIF with a source MAC of the vMAC, 02:50:56:56:44:52.

This is the same MAC from step 3.

Step 9. The frame is received by L2-SWITCH, which learns MAC 02:50:56:56:44:52 is coming from port 1/2.

Do you see the problem? L2-SWITCH sees the same vMAC bouncing back and forth between ports 1/1 and 1/2. Switches have one port per MAC address so the second frame received in step 9 overrides the existing MAC entry for 02:50:56:56:44:52. Later when logical router Physical Access in COM-B1-ESXi01 sends another ARP request over the VLAN LIF, L2-SWITCH sees the vMAC come from 1/1 again. That's called a MAC flap, and it is *BAD*. MAC flaps can cause Layer 2 switches to start flooding frames. In this packet walk we just concluded, only L2-SWITCH experienced the MAC flap, but in practice, the MAC flap may be experienced by many of the physical switches in the same Layer 2 domain, including the Top of Rack switches.

Let's do another packet walk where we see what happens when an ARP request is sent for the IP of the VLAN LIF. Figure 11-3 is a replica of Figure 11-1.

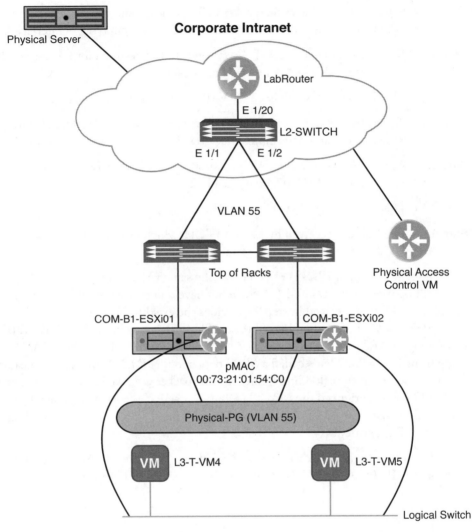

Figure 11-3   DLR with different pMACs

1. Physical server L3-Server-P1 wants to send traffic to L3-T-VM4 and sends an ARP request for its default gateway MAC.

2. The ARP request is received by L2-SWITCH, which broadcasts the ARP request out of ports 1/1 and 1/2, as shown in Figure 11-4.

3. Logical router Physical Access in ESXi host COM-B1-ESXi01 receives the ARP request and sends back an ARP reply with a source MAC of 02:50:56:56:44:52.

4. The L2-SWITCH sees the ARP reply and adds MAC 02:50:56:56:44:52 to its MAC table as located in port 1/1.

5. At about the same time step 3 is happening, logical router Physical Access in ESXi host COM-B1-ESXi02 also receives the ARP request and sends back a different ARP reply with a source MAC of 02:50:56:56:44:52.

6. The L2-SWITCH sees the ARP reply and updates its MAC table to show MAC 02:50:56:56:44:52 as located in port 1/2. Now we have a MAC flap situation again.

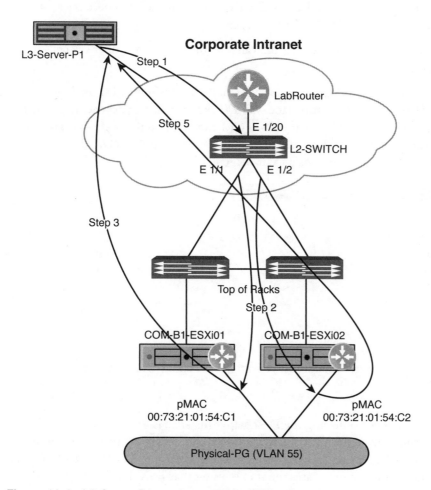

Figure 11-4 L3-Server-P1 receives multiple ARP replies.

The solution to avoiding MAC flaps with the vMAC over VLAN LIFs is to assign one of the ESXi hosts running a copy of the logical router as the Designated Instance.

Designated Instance

The Designated Instance is the ESXi host, randomly selected by the NSX Controller responsible for the logical router, that responds to ARP requests for the VLAN LIF IP and that sends out ARP requests over the VLAN LIF. No other ESXi host running a copy of the logical router sends an ARP request over the VLAN LIF nor responds to an ARP request for the IP of the VLAN LIF. By assigning the Designated Instance to send ARP requests over the VLAN LIF and to respond to ARP requests for the IP of the VLAN LIF, the vMAC will only be visible to physical switches over the port leading back to the Designated Instance. There is a single Designated Instance per VLAN LIF.

If the Designated Instance becomes unavailable, the NSX Controller selects a new Designated Instance.

Figure 11-5 shows the output of the NSX Manager CLI command **show logical-router host** *host-id* **dlr** *dlr-id* **interface** *vlan-LIF-interface-name* **verbose** (the same information may be obtained from the ESXi CLI command **net-vdr -L -n** *vlan-lif-name* **-I** *vdr-name*). The IP of the Designated Instance is shown in the *DI IP*: field. The *DI IP* is the IP of the Designated Instance management VMkernel port.

Figure 11-5   Output of **show logical-router host** *host-id* **dlr** *dlr-id* interface vlan-LIF-interface-name **verbose**

A direct consequence of having the Designated Instance is that all ingress traffic to the logical router over the VLAN LIF comes via the ESXi host that is the Designated Instance. All egress non-ARP request traffic leaves the VLAN LIF of the local logical router copy that originates the frame, using that ESXi host's pMAC as the source MAC address.

So how does a non-Designated Instance get its ARP entries for the VLAN LIF populated? By communicating with the Designated Instance and asking it for the ARP entry. If the Designated Instance does not have the ARP entry, the Designated

Instance then sends out an ARP request over the VLAN LIF and forwards the information from the ARP reply to the asking ESXi host.

Let's do one final packet walk in this section where we cover the actual steps that take place for a virtual machine communicating via IP with a physical entity with the logical router providing the Layer 3 connectivity to the physical network. Figure 11-6 shows the diagram we use for this packet walk. We assume the following:

- Virtual machine L3-T-VM5 has an ARP entry for its default gateway.

- ESXi host COM-B1-ESXi01 is the Designated Instance.

- L3-Server-P2's default gateway is the VLAN LIF's IP.

- L3-Server-P2 does not have an ARP entry for the VLAN LIF.

1. Virtual machine L3-T-VM5 sends a frame for L3-Server-P2 with a destination MAC of the vMAC.

2. Logical router Physical Access in COM-B1-ESXi02, the non-Designated Instance, gets the frame, does routing, and determines that the destination IP is directly connected in the VLAN LIF interface's subnet.

3. DLR Physical Access in COM-B1-ESXi02 sends a request to the Designated Instance, via DI IP, to send out an ARP request for L3-Server-P2's MAC address.

4. The Designated Instance sends the ARP request.

   The ARP request source MAC is the vMAC, 00:50:56:56:44:52.

5. L3-Server-P2 receives the ARP request and sends back an ARP reply, as shown in Figure 11-7.

   The destination MAC address is the vMAC.

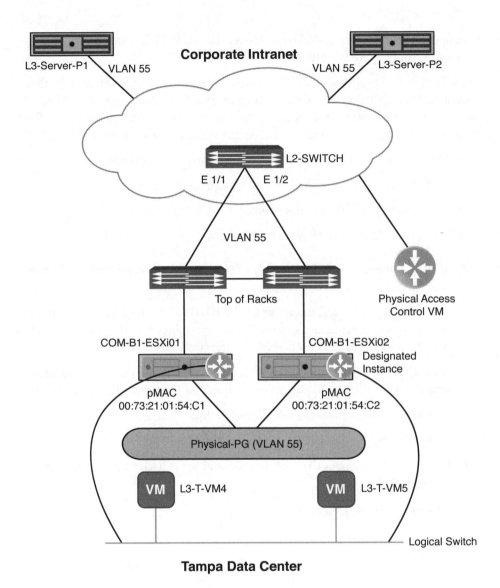

Figure 11-6   Packet walk for communication between L3-T-VM5 and L3-Server-P2

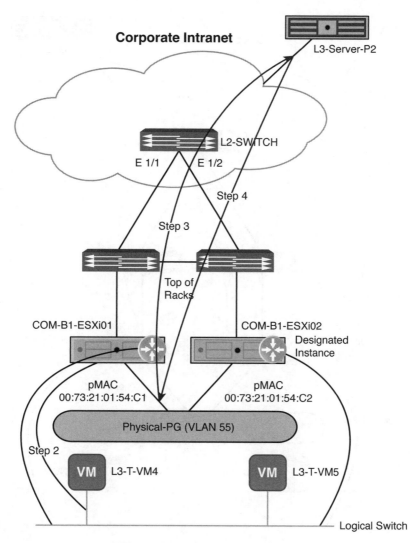

Figure 11-7 ARP request from Designated Instance

6. The Designated Instance forwards the ARP reply information to DLR Physical Access in COM-B1-ESXi02.

7. The DLR Physical Access in COM-B1-ESXi02 adds the entry in its ARP table and forwards the packet from L3-T-VM3.

   The source MAC address is COM-B1-ESXi02's pMAC, 00:73:21:01:54:C2.

8. L3-Server-P2 receives the packet from L3-T-VM4, as shown in Figure 11-8.

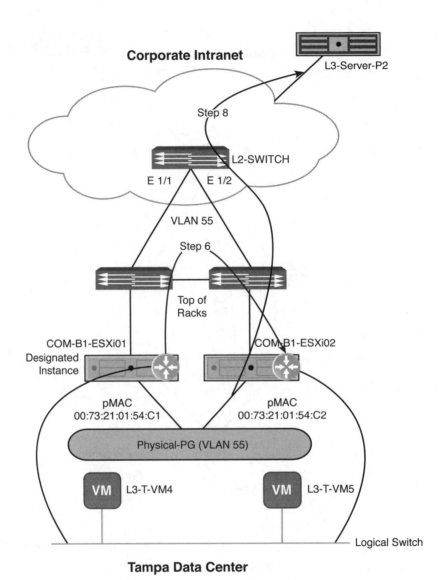

Figure 11-8   L3-Server-P2 receives the packet from L3-T-VM4.

9. L3-Server-P2 wants to reply to L3-T-VM4, but it does not have the MAC address of the VLAN LIF, so it sends out an ARP request.

10. Physical Access in COM-B1-ESXi02 receives the ARP request and ignores it because it is not the Designated Instance.

11. Physical Access in COM-B1-ESXi01 receives the ARP request and responds, because it is the Designated Instance, with an ARP reply with the vMAC.

12. L3-Server-P2 receives the ARP reply, adds the vMAC to the ARP table, and sends the packet to L3-T-VM4 inside a frame with a destination MAC address of 00:50:56:56:44:52.

13. The Designated Instance receives the frame, does routing, and forwards the packet out of the VXLAN LIF.

14. The logical switch delivers the frame to L3-T-VM4, as shown in Figure 11-9.

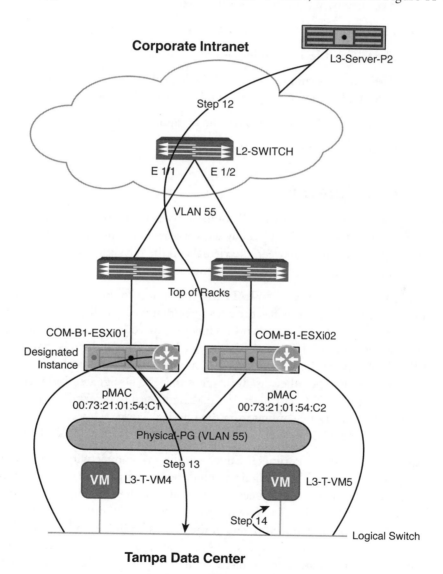

Figure 11-9   L3-Server-P2 receives the ARP reply from the Designated Instance

In our packet walks we assumed that the logical router was the default gateway for the physical servers communicating with the VMs. We could've changed the ARP packet exchanges in the packet walks to be between the logical router and physical routers instead of the physical server. The conclusions would've been the same.

To wrap up this section, and before we move on to talk about the NSX Edge Gateway, these are things to keep in mind if you decide to use the logical router for Layer 3 connectivity with the physical network:

- The logical router must be a distributed logical router.

- The VLAN LIF has a different pMAC in each ESXi host.

- All ESXi hosts running a copy of the logical router must be part of the same vDS that has the dvPortgroup the VLAN LIF connects to.

- All ingress traffic goes through the Designated Instance.

- Egress traffic goes out the local ESXi host.

NSX Edge Gateway

The second method to provide IP connectivity between the virtual and physical networks is via the NSX Edge Gateway with at least one Uplink interface. When providing IP connectivity between the virtual and the physical networks, the NSX Edge Gateway is usually referred to as a Perimeter Edge.

Using a logical router with a VLAN LIF to connect to the physical world using a Perimeter Edge gateway has the advantage that you get all ESXi hosts sending traffic directly to the physical world. However, there are potential disadvantages of using the VLAN LIF over the Perimeter Edge. One of them is that the VLAN LIF's VLAN might have to be stretched across multiple physical switches, thus necessitating STP. The other disadvantage is that the Designated Instance is randomly selected by the NSX Controller, thus making it hard to determine what the ingress point will be for traffic coming from the physical world. VMware recommends the use of a Perimeter Edge over using the logical router with a VLAN LIF.

Figure 11-10 shows a Perimeter Edge providing IP connectivity between the virtual and physical network. If the figure reminds you of figures you saw in Chapter 10, "Layer 2 Extensions," that is because this is almost the same figure. The process of enabling the NSX Edge Gateway to provide IP connectivity with the physical network is as simple as connecting one of the Edge's Uplinks to a VLAN dvPortgroup and... presto! Remember that this VLAN is called the Edge VLAN. The VLAN portgroup could be standard or distributed. The portgroup should be present on all the ESXi hosts where the Perimeter Edge may run, which is typically just the hosts in the Edge Cluster.

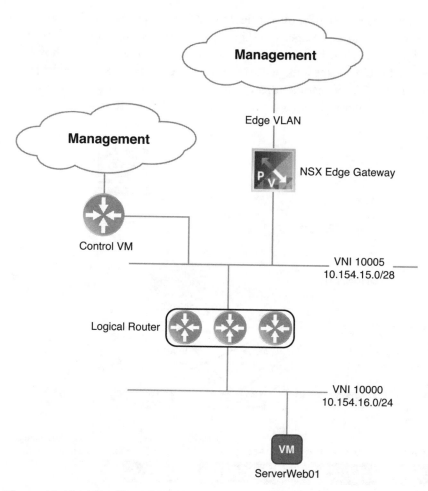

Figure 11-10   NSX Edge Gateway

When using a Perimeter Edge, all ingress and egress traffic goes through the ESXi host where the Edge is.

Table 11-2 shows the features and capabilities supported by the DLR and NSX Edge Gateway for IP connectivity to the physical network.

Table 11-2   Features and Capabilities

Feature or Capability	DLR	Perimeter Edge
Single Ingress ESXi host	Yes	Yes
Single Egress ESXi host	No	Yes
Multiple MAC addresses	Yes	No
Single vDS for all ESXi hosts	Yes	No

Let's do a quick packet walk to show traffic flowing between virtual and physical entities using a Perimeter Edge. We skip the ARP requests moving forward as those should be pretty clear by now (and that horse is dead). Figure 11-11 shows the network we use for the packet walk, with a user opening a web page in the virtual machine ServerWeb01. We assume the logical router Monkey Island, the Perimeter Edge Hook, and the physical router LabRouter all have full route visibility.

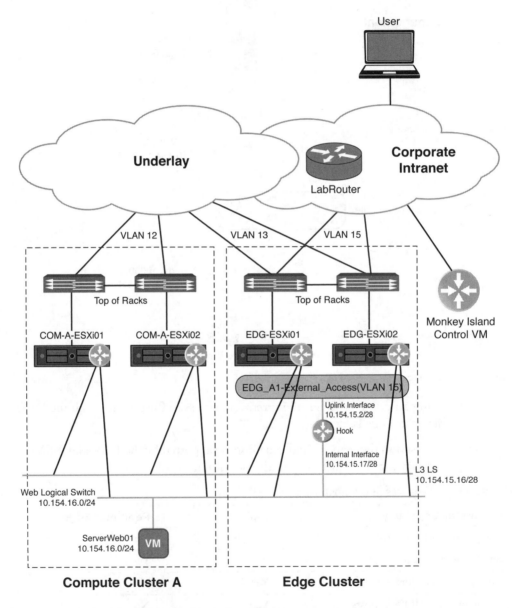

Figure 11-11   Perimeter Edge and logical router

1. The user sends a request to get a page from ServerWeb01.

2. The traffic arrives at LabRouter, which does a routing table lookup for ServerWeb01's IP.

3. LabRouter forwards the traffic to Hook's Uplink interface.

4. Hook receives the traffic, does a routing table lookup, and routes the traffic toward Monkey Island's Uplink interface through logical switch Layer 3 Transit.

5. Monkey Island receives the frame, does a routing table lookup, and concludes ServerWeb01 is directly connected over the Internal interface WEB.

   It should be clear that it is the logical router in the same host as the Perimeter Edge that receives the traffic.

6. Monkey Island sends the traffic to ServerWeb01 through logical switch WEB, as shown in Figure 11-12.

   a. Logical switch WEB takes care of delivering the frame to ServerWeb01, wherever it might be running.

7. ServerWeb01 sends the page to the user by sending a frame to its default gateway, Monkey Island.

8. Monkey Island receives the frame, does a routing table lookup, and concludes the next hop is Hook.

9. Monkey Island sends the traffic to Hook over logical switch Physical-Virtual Boundary.

   a. Logical switch Layer 3 Transit takes care of delivering the frame to Hook, wherever it might be running.

10. Hook receives the frame, does a routing table lookup, and determines the next hop is LabRouter.

11. Hook forwards the traffic to LabRouter, over the EDG_A1-External_Access Portgroup in VLAN 15.

12. LabRouter forwards the traffic to the user over the physical network, as shown in Figure 11-13.

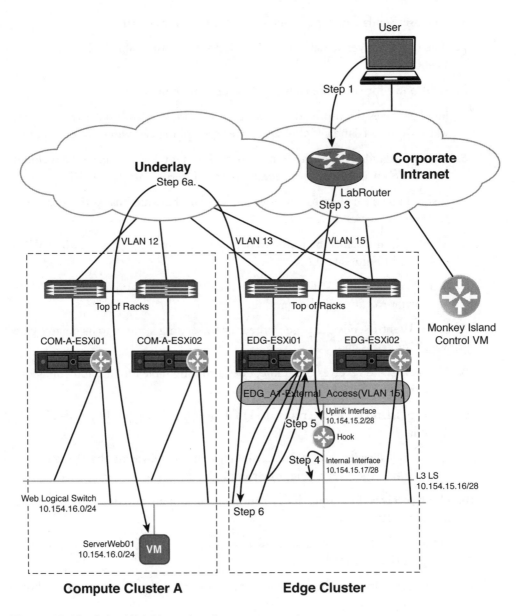

Figure 11-12   ServerWeb01 receives the page request.

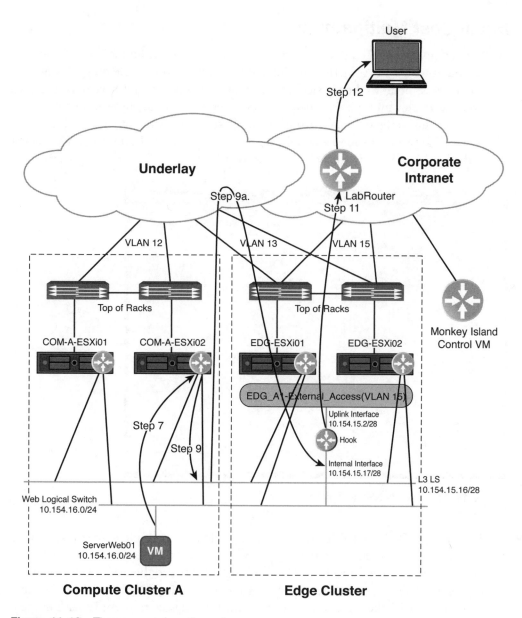

Figure 11-13   The user receives the web page.

Equal Cost Multipathing

You might have noticed that a Perimeter Edge has the same limitation as the logical router with a VLAN LIF of having a single ingress point while only allowing a single egress point to the physical world. However, this does not have to be the case. You may deploy multiple Perimeter Edges advertising to the physical routers the same subnets in the virtual environment while sharing a segment with the logical router. Figure 11-14 shows a sample implementation of two Perimeter Edges sitting at the border of the virtual and physical networks.

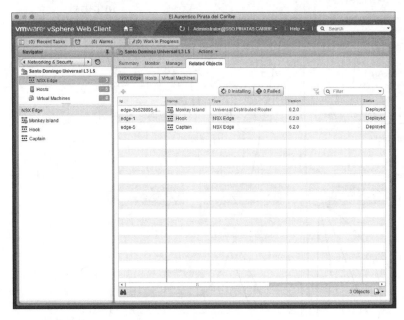

Figure 11-14 Multiple NSX Perimeter Edges

With a multi Perimeter Edge solution, you would have multiple ingress points from and multiple egress points to the physical world. For this solution to work, the logical router must have Equal Cost Multipathing (ECMP) configured. ECMP is the capability of a router to add in the routing table multiple paths, learned via the same method and with the same routing cost, to the same destination. An IP hash in the logical router determines, on a per packet basis, which of the available equal cost paths to take. The logical router can have in its routing table up to eight different paths to the same destination. The NSX Edge also supports ECMP with up to eight different paths to the same destination.

To enable ECMP in the logical router and the NSX Edge, double-click the logical router or NSX Edge from the **NSX Edges** view and go to **Manage > Routing > Global Configuration**. Click **Enable** next to ECMP and publish the changes.

In Figure 11-15, we have deployed two Perimeter Edges. Using Figure 11-15 as a reference point, let's do two packet walks, ignoring ARP requests, between two users in the physical world and a web server. We assume that all routers have all routes in their routing tables.

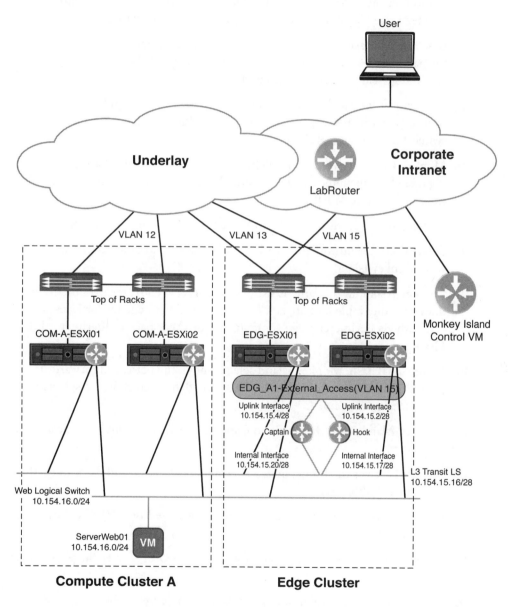

Figure 11-15   Multiple NSX Perimeter Edges

1. User_1 sends a request to get a page from ServerWeb01.

2. The traffic arrives at LabRouter, which does a routing table lookup for Server-Web01's IP.

3. LabRouter sees two equal cost paths for ServerWeb01's IP. One path via Perimeter Edge Captain, and the other path via Perimeter Edge Hook.

4. Based on the hashing algorithm configured in LabRouter, it selects one of the paths and forwards the packet to that Perimeter Edge. Let's assume that LabRouter selects Perimeter Edge Hook.

5. Perimeter Edge Hook receives the traffic, does a routing table lookup, and routes the traffic toward Monkey Island's Uplink interface through logical switch Physical-Virtual Boundary.

6. Monkey Island in the same ESXi host as Hook receives the frame, does a routing table lookup, and concludes ServerWeb01 is directly connected over the Internal interface WEB.

7. Monkey Island sends the traffic to ServerWeb01 through logical switch WEB.

8. ServerWeb01 sends the page to User_1 by sending a frame to its default gateway, Monkey Island.

9. Monkey Island, in the same ESXi host as ServerWeb01, receives the frame, does a routing table lookup, and finds two equal path entries for User_1's IP—one path via Perimeter Edge Captain and the other path via Perimeter Edge Hook.

10. Using an IP hash, Monkey Island selects one of the paths and forwards the packet to that Perimeter Edge. Let's assume that Monkey Island selects Perimeter Edge Captain.

11. Monkey Island sends the traffic to Captain over logical switch Physical-Virtual Boundary.

12. Captain receives the frame, does a routing table lookup, and determines the next hop is LabRouter.

13. Captain forwards the traffic to LabRouter, over the Edge_VLAN Portgroup in VLAN 50.

14. LabRouter receives the traffic and forwards it to User_1 over the physical network.

15. Now User_2 sends a request to get a page from ServerWeb01.

16. The traffic arrives at LabRouter, which does a routing table lookup for Server-Web01's IP.

17. LabRouter sees two equal cost paths for ServerWeb01's IP. It elects to forward the traffic to Perimeter Edge Hook again.

18. Perimeter Edge Hook receives the traffic, does a routing table lookup, and routes the traffic toward Monkey Island's Uplink interface through logical switch Physical-Virtual Boundary.

19. Monkey Island in the same ESXi host as Hook receives the frame, does a routing table lookup, and concludes ServerWeb01 is directly connected over the Internal interface WEB.

20. Monkey Island sends the traffic to ServerWeb01 through logical switch WEB.

21. ServerWeb01 sends the page to User_2 by sending a frame to its default gateway, Monkey Island.

22. Monkey Island, in the same ESXi host as ServerWeb01, receives the frame, does a routing table lookup, and again finds two equal path entries for User_2's IP—one path via Perimeter Edge Captain and the other path via Perimeter Edge Hook.

23. Using an IP hash, Monkey Island selects one of the paths and forwards the packet to that Perimeter Edge. This time the IP hash elects the path to Perimeter Edge Hook.

24. Monkey Island sends the traffic to Hook over logical switch Physical-Virtual Boundary.

25. Hook receives the frame, does a routing table lookup, and determines the next hop is LabRouter.

26. Hook forwards the traffic to LabRouter, over the Edge_VLAN Portgroup in VLAN 50.

27. LabRouter receives the traffic and forwards it to User_2 over the physical network.

You should probably note that the Perimeter Edge for the ingress traffic from the physical network is determined by the physical network. For the egress traffic, the local copy of the logical router where the source virtual machine resides determines the exit Perimeter Edge. From the logical router's point of view, each packet is routed based on the IP hash obtained from the source/destination IP of the packet.

Exam Preparation Tasks

Review All the Key Topics

Review the most important topics from inside the chapter, noted with the Key Topic icon in the outer margin of the page. Table 11-3 lists these key topics and the page numbers where each is found.

Table 11-3 Key Topics for Chapter 11

Key Topic Element	Description	Page Number
Paragraph	All logical router copies in the ESXi hosts send egress traffic over the VLAN LIF.	324
Paragraph	Considerations for doing Layer 3 between a logical router and the physical network	330
Paragraph	When using a Perimeter Edge, all ingress and egress traffic is hair-pinned	331
Paragraph	The logical router and the NSX Edge support up to eight ECMP routes per destination.	336

Complete Tables and Lists from Memory

Download and print a copy of Appendix C, "Memory Tables" (found on the book's website), or at least the section for this chapter, and complete the tables and lists from memory. Appendix D, "Memory Tables Answer Key," also on the website, includes the completed tables and lists so you can check your work.

Define Key Terms

Define the following key terms from this chapter, and check your answers in the Glossary:

VLAN LIF, pMAC, Designated Instance, Perimeter Edge, Equal Cost Multipath

This chapter covers all or part of the following VCP6-NV exam blueprint topics:

- **Objective 5.4**—Configure and Manage Logical Routers
- **Objective 9.5**—Administer Logging

CHAPTER 12

Routing Protocols

We have arrived at the chapter where we talk about how the NSX Edge and the logical router learn about routes for subnets not directly connected to them. There are many ways in physical networks for route information to be propagated. In the case of NSX, and its tendency to simplify the network, the features needed to advertise network reachability are less complex than what might be found in the physical network.

This chapter reviews the three routing protocols supported by NSX: OSPF, BGP, and IS-IS. The chapter also covers how to configure static routes and concludes with a configuration of route redistribution.

Do I Know This Already?

The "Do I Know This Already?" quiz allows you to assess whether you should read this entire chapter or simply jump to the "Exam Preparation Tasks" section for review. If you are in doubt, read the entire chapter. Table 12-1 outlines the major headings in this chapter and the corresponding "Do I Know This Already?" quiz questions. You can find the answers in Appendix A, "Answers to the 'Do I Know This Already?' Quizzes."

Table 12-1 Headings and Questions

Foundation Topic Section	Questions Covered in this Section
Routing	1-2
Static Routes	3
OSPF	4-6
BGP	7-8
IS-IS	9
Route Redistribution	10

1. Which routing protocol is not supported by a logical router?

   a. Static

   b. BGP

   c. IS-IS

   d. OSPFv2

2. Which routing protocol is not supported by an NSX Edge?

   a. OSPFv2

   b. BGP

   c. IS-IS

   d. OSPFv3

3. After configuring a static route, how long would the Control VM retain it before flushing it from the routing table?

   a. 10 minutes

   b. 24 hours

   c. 72 hours

   d. Permanently

4. Which OSPF authentication mechanism does the logical router not support?

   a. MD5

   b. SHA

   c. Cleartext

   d. None

5. Which OSPF area is not supported by the NSX Edge if configured as an ABR?

   a. Backbone area

   b. Normal area

   c. Stubby area

   d. Not So Stubby area

6. An NSX Edge is configured as an ABR. The Edge has a non-backbone interface link in the same segment as a logical router. Which Link State Advertisement Type is not received by the logical router from the NSX Edge?

   a. LSA Type 1

   b. LSA Type 2

   c. LSA Type 3

   d. LSA Type 7

7. A Perimeter Edge is being configured to run iBGP with a logical router. What BGP Neighbor IP address should be configured in the Perimeter Edge for the BGP Peers to come up?

   a. The IP of the Uplink interface in the Control VM.

   b. The forwarding IP configured in the logical router.

   c. The protocol IP configured in the Control VM.

   d. The management IP of the logical router.

8. Which of the following commands can be used to check the BGP route table?

   a. **show ip route bgp**

   b. **show ip bgp**

   c. **show ip bgp route**

   d. **debug ip bgp**

9. How many IS-IS areas can be configured in the NSX Edge?

   a. 1

   b. 2

   c. 3

   d. 10

10. What OSPF metric type is assigned to routes redistributed into OSPF by a universal logical router?

    a. Intra-Area

    b. Inter-Area

    c. External Type 1

    d. External Type 2

Foundation Topics

Routing

Let's start by talking about how the logical router and the NSX Edge populate their routing tables. The routing table contains the destination path information the logical router and the NSX Edge use when deciding the egress interface for forwarding packets. The routing table contains a list of routes. A route is defined as a subnet/subnet mask pair, administrative distance and cost, and the next hop. We discuss the administrative distance and cost in the "Administrative Distance and Cost" section that follows. The next hop is defined as an entity that should know how to get traffic delivered to the destination. The subnets and subnet masks configured in the interfaces of the routers, also referred to as *directly connected*, get added by default to the routing table of the logical router and NSX Edge, with the router's interface IP as the next hop. Any other subnet and subnet mask not configured in the interface of the router will have a next hop. The routing entries of NSX Edges for directly connected subnets look similar to Figure 12-1.

```
                                          El Autentico Pirata del Caribe
                                             elver@LabRouter: ~
Captain-0> show ip route

Codes: O - OSPF derived, i - IS-IS derived, B - BGP derived,
C - connected, S - static, L1 - IS-IS level-1, L2 - IS-IS level-2,
IA - OSPF inter area, E1 - OSPF external type 1, E2 - OSPF external type 2,
N1 - OSPF NSSA external type 1, N2 - OSPF NSSA external type 2

Total number of routes: 2

C     10.154.15.0/28      [0/0]        via 10.154.15.4
C     10.154.15.16/28     [0/0]        via 10.154.15.20
Captain-0>
```

Figure 12-1   Command output of **show ip route** in NSX Edge

Both the logical router and NSX Edge Gateway support routing protocols. By saying the logical router supports a routing protocol, it is implied that the protocol runs in the logical router Control VM. If the logical router and the NSX Edge form a routing adjacency, the Edge would be exchanging routing information with the Control VM. You should always consider placing the Control VM in the same cluster as the NSX Edge that it is exchanging routing information with. Table 12-2 shows the protocols supported by each router.

Table 12-2   Routing Protocols

Routing Protocol	Logical Router	Perimeter Edge
Static Routes	Yes	Yes
OSPFv2	Yes	Yes
BGP-4 (iBGP and eBGP)	Yes	Yes
IS-IS	No	Yes

When the logical router or the NSX Edge receives a packet, it reads the destination IP of the packet and finds the most specific subnet and subnet mask match in the routing table for the IP. For example, assume the router has two interfaces with IPs of 192.168.1.2 and 192.168.2.1 and the following four routing entries in the routing table:

- 10.10.0.0/16, via 172.16.1.1

- 10.10.0.0/24, via 192.168.1.1

- 192.168.1.0/24, via 192.168.1.2

- 192.168.2.0/24, via 192.168.2.1

If a packet arrives with a destination IP of 10.10.0.4, the next hop is 192.168.1.1 because it has the most specific route to the destination with a subnet mask of /24. Another thing the routers would do is *recursive routing*. In our example, the destination IP of 10.10.0.4 has a next hop of 192.168.1.1. The router then does another routing lookup, hence the recursive routing, for 192.168.1.1. The router continues doing routing lookups for the next hops in the routing table until it finds the next hop to be the IP of one of its interfaces. For the lookup for IP 192.16.1.1, the next hop for 10.10.0.4, the router turns up the following entry in the routing table:

```
192.168.1.0/24, via 192.168.1.2 <- IP of router's interface
```

The router stops the recursive routing lookup and sends an ARP request for 192.168.1.1's MAC address.

Administrative Distance and Cost

A router can add routing table entries learned by different methods and protocols. Assume a router has a routing table with the following two entries:

- B 192.168.1.0/24, via 172.16.1.1

- C 192.168.1.0/24, via 192.168.1.1

The router has two routing entries to the same destination but with different gateways. The first entry is learned via BGP and the second entry is directly connected to the router. The question the router needs to ask itself is "which of the two entries should I use?" You would be wrong if you suggest we use ECMP, although you may be forgiven for it. The best path for a directly connected subnet will always be the router's interface connected to that subnet. There is no way that selecting the BGP learned path over the directly connected path would be better in this case (or any case). The same would be true if the first routing entry was a static or OSPF learned route.

When the router has multiple paths to the same destination, however, those paths are learned via different methods or routing protocols. The router must make a decision as to which of those paths is the most reliable and only add that path to the routing table. To do so, the router assigns a value to each method or protocol, with the lowest number viewed as more reliable. That number is called the *administrative distance*. Table 12-3 shows the default administrative distance of the different learning methods and routing protocols.

Table 12-3   Administrative Distance

Learning Method	Administrative Distance
Connected Subnet	0
Static Routes	1
eBGP	20
OSPF Intra-Area	30
OSPF Inter-Area	110
IS-IS	115
iBGP	200

Administrative distance only matters to the router if two different learning methods or routing protocols have a path to the same subnet.

In our routing table example, there would be one entry for subnet 192.168.1.0/24, which would appear in the routing table as:

```
C 192.168.1.0/24 [0/0] via 192.168.1.2
```

The first 0 in the brackets represents the administrative distance. The second 0 represents the cost to reach the destination. Cost is a value assigned by the learning method or routing protocol to differentiate which is the best path to a destination. If a learning method or routing protocol with the lowest administrative distance knows of multiple paths to the same destination, the router only adds to the routing table the path with the lowest cost. Each routing protocol uses its own algorithm to calculate cost.

Some routing protocols use metric instead of cost. The application and goal are the same.

Only directly connected routes would have a cost of 0.

ECMP only works for multiple paths to the same destination that have the same cost.

Static Routes

Static routes are manual entries to the routing table. Static routes are easy to implement and once created they are permanent until someone removes them. Static routes do not lend themselves to be flexible in accounting for network changes, which makes them inadequate in many situations. On the upside, static routes do not consume a lot of the router resources, which makes them ideal for smaller scale routers at the edge of the network. Routers at the edge of the network are also called *spokes* or *stubs*. Logical routers are almost always deployed as stubs, and in an NSX environment with a well-planned IP addressing scheme, the Perimeter Edge can be viewed as a stub by the physical network.

Both the logical router and the NSX Edge support static routes. The process to configure a static route is almost identical for both the logical router and the NSX Edge. To create a static route (with the exception of a default route), follow these steps:

Step 1.   From the NSX Edges view, select the NSX Manager that owns the Control VM or NSX Edge and double-click the logical router or NSX Edge that is getting the static route.

Step 2.   Go to **Manage > Routing** and select **Static Routes**.

Step 3.   Click the green + icon and wait for the Add Static Routes Wizard to come up.

Step 4.   Complete the following fields:

- **Network**: The subnet for the static route. It should be in the format X.X.X.X/YY, where YY is the subnet mask.

- **Next Hop**: Enter the IP of the next hop. You can enter multiple IPs as next hop if you have enabled ECMP.

- **Interface**: The outgoing interface for the static route.

- **MTU**: You can change the configured MTU of the interface for traffic going to the subnet identified in the Network field. The MTU must be less than or equal to the MTU configured in the interface.

- **Admin Distance**: The administrative distance for this route. This value is also used as the cost.

- **Locale ID**: This is applicable to universal logical routers only. Enter the Locale ID for this route. Only ESXi hosts with matching Locale ID get this static route.

- **Description**: This field is optional.

Your configuration should look similar to the one in Figure 12-2. Click **OK**.

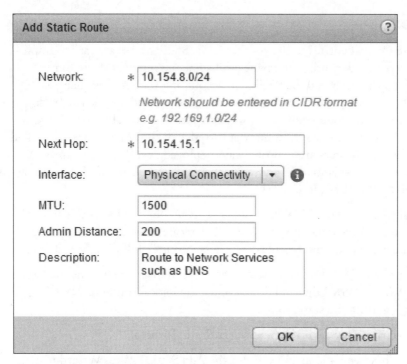

Figure 12-2   Configuring a static route

Step 5.   Click **Publish Changes**.

The default route is created in a different place, the Global Configuration page. The process is also identical for both the logical router and the NSX Edge. To create a default route, follow these steps.

Step 1.   From **Manage > Routing** select **Global Configuration**.

Step 2.   Click **Edit** in the Default Gateway field.

Step 3.   Wait for the Edit Default Gateway Wizard to come up.

Step 4.   Complete the following fields:

- **Interface or vNIC**: The outgoing interface where the default gateway can be found. The logical router has an Interface option; the NSX Edge has a vNIC option.

- **Gateway IP**: The IP of the default gateway.

- **MTU**: You can change the configured MTU of the interface for traffic going to the default gateway. The MTU must be less than or equal to the MTU configured in the interface.

- **Admin Distance**: The administrative distance for this route. This value also is used as the cost.

- **LocaleID**: This is applicable to universal logical routers only (not shown in Figure 12-3). Enter the Locale ID for this route. Only ESXi hosts with matching Locale ID get this static route.

- **Description**: This field is optional.

Your configuration should look similar to the one in Figure 12-3. Click **OK**.

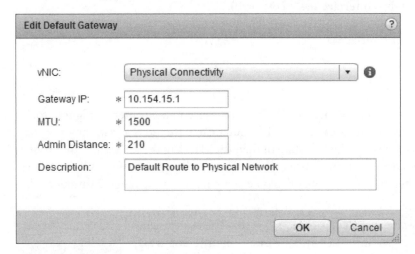

Figure 12-3 Configuring a default route

OSPF

We could jump right in and start configuring OSPF in the logical router and the Edge, but I would be doing you a disservice if I did. There is no point in configuring OSPF without understanding the OSPF basics. For that reason, we spend some pages going over the foundations of OSPF and the features supported by the logical router and the Edge, followed by how to configure OSPF in NSX.

Open Shortest Path First (OSPF) is an open standard Interior Gateway Protocol (IGP) that uses the state of the routers' links to determine a loop-free path to an IP destination. The OSPF protocol has its own transport, and IP Protocol 89 identifies it. An IGP is a routing protocol fully administered by the same organization or Autonomous System (AS). This means that all routing policies for an IGP are made and implemented by the same entity.

A link state is the status of an OSPF configured interface of the OSPF router. Some of the information included in the link state of the interface includes

- The IP of the interface

- The subnet mask of the interface

- The cost of the interface

  The speed is advertised as a cost that gets assigned to the interface. The cost is determined by dividing 10 gig by the interface speed.

  - A 10-Gbps interface has a cost of 1.

  - A 1-Gbps interface has a cost of 10.

- The type of interface

OSPF Areas

OSPF is architectured to work in *areas*. Every interface in the router configured for OSPF must be in a single area. The OSPF router can have interfaces in multiple areas. OSPF routers then share the link state of their interfaces in the area with other routers in the area. An area is identified by a number from 0 through 2^{32}. If the OSPF AS has a single area, then the area number could be any number in the range 0 through 2^{32}.

> **NOTE**   *Intra-area* means entities or things within the same area, such as traffic within the same area. *Inter-rea* means entities or things in different areas.

If there are two or more areas in the OSPF AS, one of those areas must be Area 0, also called the *backbone area*. All other areas in a multi-area OSPF domain must have at least one router with an interface in the backbone. All intra-area traffic must go through the backbone, and two areas can't have the same router connected to each of them unless that router also has an interface in the backbone. A router that has a connection to the backbone and another area is called an *area border router (ABR)*. There is another type of router that redistributes routes into OSPF from another routing process, static routes, or directly connected interfaces. This router is called *Autonomous System Border Router (ASBR)*. An ASBR may or may not have an interface in the backbone area, and all routes redistributed by the ASBR from other routing processes, static routes, or directly connected interfaces are advertised by OSPF as if originating from the ASBR.

Route redistribution is the process of injecting routes to a routing process. The source of the routes could be a static route, another routing process, or directly connected interfaces. Redistributing a directly connected interface's subnet into a routing process is not the same as adding the interface, and its subnet, into the routing process. When redistributing a route, the receiving routing process has no visibility into the true origin of the route. We configure route redistribution at the end of this chapter.

When configuring OSPF in the logical router, the logical router almost always is an ASBR. The logical router's internal interfaces can't participate in a routing process, so the only way to get the internal interfaces' subnets advertised by OSPF is to re-distribute the ASBR connected interfaces.

Figure 12-4 shows four areas, including the backbone area, an ASBR router, and two ABR routers, one of which has connections to three different areas. Intra-area traffic must stay within the area. Inter-area traffic from any non-backbone area must go thru the ABR and the backbone to reach another area.

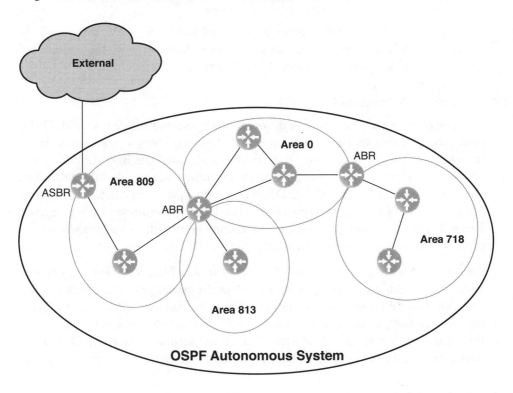

Figure 12-4   OSPF areas, ABR, and ASBR

There are three types of areas. Table 12-4 shows the different OSPF areas and their definitions.

Table 12-4 OSPF Areas

Area Type	Description
Normal	Routers in the area receive all routes from all other areas and external routes. An ASBR can be in a normal area.
Stubby	Routers in the area receive only a default route, and no routes from other areas or external routes. No ASBR can be in a stubby area.
Not So Stubby, NSSA	Routers in the area receive only a default route, and no routes from other areas or external routes from ASBRs in other areas. ASBRs can be in an NSSA.

The logical router and NSX Edge support normal and NSSA areas. If acting as an ABR, the NSX Edge does not support stubby areas; however, both the logical router and the NSX Edge can be members of a stubby area.

OSPF Neighbor Adjacencies

OSPF neighbors exchange routing information by forming adjacencies with OSPF peers, and they only exchange link states with their neighbors if an adjacency has been formed. Link states are used to form the Link State Data Base (LSDB). The LSDB is used by the OSPF router to create a routing table by calculating the shortest path for each network in the LSDB. The shortest path is calculated using an algorithm derived from the Dijkstra's algorithm. Once the shortest path is calculated for each network, an entry is added in the routing table with a cost for the route and the IP of the next hop in the calculated path.

For an OSPF adjacency to be formed there has to be a Neighbor Discovery process first. The Neighbor Discovery process involves the exchange of some parameters with other OSPF routers via a series of multicast and unicast OSPF packets. During these exchanges, some parameters are verified to match between the neighbors. If the parameters don't match, the neighbors won't form an adjacency. Table 12-5 shows some of the parameters exchanged during Neighbor Discovery.

Table 12-5 OSPF Neighbor Parameters

Parameter	Description
Hello Interval	The frequency in which the neighbors check on each other.
Dead Interval	How long to wait to hear back from the OSPF neighbor before declaring it dead and ending the adjacency.
Priority	A number to determine who becomes the DR for the segment, and consequently the BDR. The DR is the router with the highest priority. The highest IP address is the tie breaker. A priority of 0 means this router is not eligible to become the DR or BDR.
Cost	The attractiveness of an interface, the lower the better.

Another parameter exchanged between two OSPF routers while forming an adjacency is the MTU, although it can be disabled in the configurations of the logical router and the NSX Edge. If the MTU of both routers do not match, the OSPF adjacency won't be formed.

One OSPF requirement is that all intra-area routers have the same LSDB. OSPF routers forward link states received from their neighbors to ensure every router in the OSPF area has the same LSDB. To minimize the number of neighbors that an OSPF router needs to form in a broadcast domain, two routers are designated to be the only ones that become neighbors with everyone else in the broadcast domain. Those routers are the Designated Router (DR) and the Backup Designated Router (BDR).

The DR is responsible for collecting all the link state advertisements from everyone in the broadcast domain and floods them out to everyone in the broadcast domain. The BDR has the same neighbor adjacencies as the DR, but it monitors the DR, and when the DR goes down, the BDR becomes the DR.

To provide a level of security and authentication for OSPF neighbors, NSX supports two forms of authentication, besides the None option:

- Password
- MD5

OSPF routers will not become neighbors nor exchange LSAs unless they authenticate each other. With *password authentication*, the password is sent cleartext. *MD5 authentication* is considered more secure because the password is never exchanged between the OSPF routers. Instead, a hash is created from the password and exchanged.

LSA Types

Each OSPF router sends out its link state via packets called Link State Advertisements (LSA). LSAs are sent out when the router gets a new neighbor, when a change occurs in one of the links, or after a certain period of network stability when the LSA ages out. If there are no network changes, LSAs are not sent out frequently.

Each router in the OSPF AS has a unique OSPF Router ID, which it uses to tag each subnet and the link state of each interface the routers advertise in LSAs. The OSPF Router ID is an IP that is unique among the OSPF routers in the OSPF AS. It is typical to use the IP of an interface as the OSPF Router ID.

LSAs are classified by types, and each type carries different information, as shown in Table 12-6.

Table 12-6 OSPF LSA Types

LSA Type	Description	Information Contained
LSA Type 1	Router LSA	The state of each link in the advertising router
LSA Type 2	Network LSA	The routers connected to a broadcast network
LSA Type 3	Summary LSA	The networks in an area
LSA Type 4	Summary ASBR LSA	ASBR reachability
LSA Type 5	Autonomous System External LSA	The external network injected into the OSPF AS and the ASBR that is adding the networks
LSA Type 7	Not So Stubby Area, NSSA, LSA	The external network injected into the OSPF AS and the ASBR that is adding the networks

All routers send out Type 1 LSAs, which are flooded throughout the area, and the DR sends out Type 2 LSAs. All intra-area routers in the area get everyone else's Type 1 LSAs. Type 1 and Type 2 LSAs are never sent outside the area. Type 3 LSAs are generated by ABRs and sent over the backbone area to provide a list of all the subnets from an area. Type 3 LSAs always have the ABR's OSPF Router ID as the owning router of the subnet.

Type 4 LSAs are sent out by the ABR to provide information outside the area in how to reach the ASBR. Type 5 and Type 7 LSAs are originated by the ASBR. Type 5 LSAs are only found in a normal area and are forwarded to other areas by the ABRs. Type 7 is found only in NSSA areas and is turned into a Type 5 LSA by the NSSA ABR before being forwarded to the backbone area.

Routers in a broadcast domain send their LSAs to multicast address 224.0.0.6, which the DR and BDR listen to. The DR forwards all updates to multicast address 224.0.0.5, which all OSPF routers in the broadcast segment listen to. In NSX all OSPF segments are broadcast segments.

Configuring OSPF

To configure OSPF in the logical router or NSX Edge follow these steps:

Step 1. From the NSX Home page click **NSX Edges**.

Step 2. Select the NSX Manager that owns the Control VM or NSX Edge and double-click the logical router or NSX Edge.

Step 3. Go to **Manage > Routing** and select **Global Configuration**.

Step 4. Click **Edit** in the Dynamic Routing Configuration Field.

Step 5.   In the Edit Dynamic Routing Configuration Wizard that opens up, complete the following fields:

- **Router ID**: Select an Uplink interface to use for the OSPF Router ID. Optionally, select Custom and enter an IP address that is unique in the OSPF AS. The primary IP of the Uplink interface is the one used as the OSPF Router ID.

- **Enable Logging**: Check the box if you want to enable logging of routing events.

- **Log Level**: Select the logging level desired.

The configuration should be similar to Figure 12-5. Click **OK**.

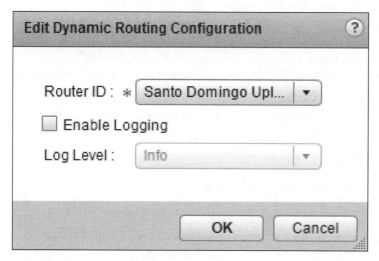

Figure 12-5   Creating OSPF Router ID

Step 6.   Click **Publish Changes**.

Step 7.   Select **OSPF**.

Step 8.   In OSPF Configuration, click **Edit** and complete the following fields in the OSPF Configuration Wizard:

- **Enable OSPF**: Check the box to enable OSPF.

- **Protocol Address**: This is Applicable to the logical router only. Enter the IP to assign the Control VM to use for OSPF Control Plane communication. This IP should be from the uplink segment.

- **Forwarding Address**: This is Applicable to the logical router only. Enter the IP of the Uplink LIF. This IP is used to forward traffic in the data plane by the OSPF neighbors (Type 1 LSA).

- **Enable Graceful Restart**: Check the box to enable Graceful Restart. With Graceful Restart enabled, the Control VM and NSX Edge notify their neighbors that the OSPF process is restarting and not to drop the neighbor adjacency. As a consequence, data plane traffic continues to flow, and the logical router and NSX Edge can resume OSPF control plane quicker.

- **Enable Default Originate**: Check the box to send a default route to the OSPF neighbors. Make sure you fully understand what you are doing before turning this feature on.

Step 9.   Click **OK**.

Step 10.   Under Area Definitions click the green + icon to add an area. Two default areas are available—the Backbone Area and Area 51. You can delete these if you are not going to use them.

Step 11.   In the New Area Definition Wizard that opens up, complete the following fields:

- **Area ID**: The Area number.

- **Type**: Choose the area to be Normal or NSSA.

- **Authentication**: Choose between None, Password, and MD5.

- **Value**: If selecting an authentication, enter the password. This password should be the same for all routers in the Area.

Click **OK**.

Repeat Step 11 for any additional areas.

Step 12.   Under Area Interface Mapping click the green + icon to add an interface to an OSPF area.

Step 13.   In the New Area Interface Mapping that opens up, complete the following fields:

- **Interface or vNIC**: Select the interface to add to the OSPF Area.

  Neighbor discovery runs in this interface.

  The network in this interface is added to the LSDB and sent out in Type 1 LSAs.

- **Area**: The OSPF area to place the interface.

■ **Ignore Interface MTU Setting**: Check this box if you don't want MTU verification to be done during Neighbor Discovery. Be warned that if two routers have MTU mismatch some packets will be dropped.

In the Advanced drop-down menu you can edit the parameters exchanged during Neighbor Discovery. You can edit these settings from their default values:

■ **Hello Interval**: Default value is 10 seconds. This value *must* match with the neighbor.

■ **Dead Interval**: Default value is 40 seconds. This value *must* match with the neighbor.

■ **Priority**: Default value is 128.

■ **Cost**: Default Value is 1; the OSPF routing cost for this interface. This value *must* match with the neighbor.

Click **OK**.

Repeat step 13 for any additional interfaces.

The configuration should be similar to Figure 12-6.

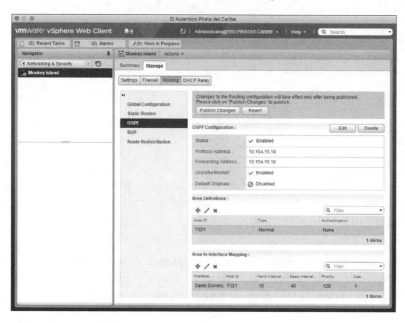

Figure 12-6   OSPF configuration

Step 14.   Click **Publish Changes**.

Remember that the Control VM is the one that handles the Neighbor Discovery, exchanging the OSPF Hello packets with the OSPF adjacencies on behalf of the logical router. In the case of the ULR, you may have multiple Control VMs participating in OSPF. Unless you have *strong* reasons for doing so, you shouldn't allow these Control VMs to be in the same OSPF area. The Control VM needs an IP, the Protocol IP, in the same subnet as the Uplink interface that will be configured for OSPF. Yes, I said *the* Uplink interface because the Control VM supports OSPF only over a single Uplink interface and only a single routing protocol at a time. For the ULR, each Control VM has OSPF configured in different Uplink interfaces.

Verifying OSPF

The best way to verify OSPF is working is to confirm networks are being advertised over OSPF. I (well, NSX, actually) cheated a bit and added some networks to OSPF to get the **show IP route** output in the Perimeter Edge shown in Figure 12-7 (you can also use the command **show IP route OSPF to see only OSPF routes)**. By default, the logical router redistributes connected interfaces into OSPF when you enable it. We cover route redistribution later in this chapter.

```
●  ●  ●                                    El Autentico Pirata del Caribe
                                              elver@LabRouter: ~
Hook-0> show ip route

Codes: O - OSPF derived, i - IS-IS derived, B - BGP derived,
C - connected, S - static, L1 - IS-IS level-1, L2 - IS-IS level-2,
IA - OSPF inter area, E1 - OSPF external type 1, E2 - OSPF external type 2,
N1 - OSPF NSSA external type 1, N2 - OSPF NSSA external type 2

Total number of routes: 8

S       0.0.0.0/0          [1/1]          via 10.154.15.1
C       10.154.15.0/28     [0/0]          via 10.154.15.2
C       10.154.15.16/28    [0/0]          via 10.154.15.17
O   E2  10.154.15.32/28    [110/1]        via 10.154.15.18
S       10.154.16.0/22     [1/1]          via 10.154.15.18
O   E2  10.154.16.0/24     [110/1]        via 10.154.15.18
O   E2  10.154.17.0/24     [110/1]        via 10.154.15.18
O   E2  10.154.18.0/24     [110/1]        via 10.154.15.18
Hook-0>
```

Figure 12-7   Output of command **show ip route**

In Figure 12-7, you can see the type of OSPF route that each subnet represents. OSPF has four different types of routes that can be expressed in the routing table. Table 12-7 lists the four different OSPF route types and their definitions.

Table 12-7 OSPF **show** Commands

Route Type	Routing Table Acronym	Description
Intra-Area	NONE	Defines a network that originates in the local area. The cost (metric) to reach the network source is included in the routing table.
Inter-Area	IA	Defines a network that originates in a different area. The cost (metric) to reach the network source is included in the routing table.
External Type 1	E1	Defines a network redistributed into OSPF by an ASBR. The cost (metric) to reach the ASBR is included in the routing table.
External Type 2	E2	Defines a network redistributed into OSPF by an ASBR. The cost (metric) to reach the ASBR is *not* included in the routing table.

If you don't see the routes you expect or you do not see OSPF routes at all, you can run one of the commands in Table 12-8 to verify OSPF functionality:

Table 12-8 OSPF **show** Commands

Command	Description
show ip ospf	Shows the OSPF Router ID and LSA count information.
show ip ospf database	Shows the OSPF LSDB. There are a number of additional subcommand options to provide a granular view of the LSDB sections.
show ip ospf interface	Shows the interfaces configured with OSPF.
show ip ospf neighbor	Shows the OSPF neighbors discovered and their adjacency status.
show ip ospf statistics	Shows the OSPF areas and the number of times SPF algorithm has been executed.
debug ip ospf	Shows debugging information for OSPF.

BGP

Border Gateway Protocol (BGP), is the de facto routing protocol of the Internet, with a primary goal of avoiding routing loops while exchanging network reachability information. BGP is an External Gateway Protocol (EGP). An EGP differs from an IGP in that multiple autonomous systems may manage an EGP. To differentiate BGP instances managed by different autonomous systems, an Autonomous System Number (ASN) is assigned to each BGP instance. An ASN must be globally unique.

The Internet Assigned Numbers Authority (IANA) is the entity responsible for the maintenance and distribution of BGP ASNs.

BGP ASNs originally consisted of the numbers 1 through 65,534 (2^{16} -2), with numbers 64,512 through 65,534 reserved for private use. ASNs 0 and 65,535 are reserved and should not be used by anyone. Private ASNs are not allowed in the Internet. NSX supports ASNs from 1 through 65,534.

BGP does not do Neighbor Discovery like OSPF. Instead, an administrator must tell the router whom its BGP neighbors, called BGP peers or just peers, should be. The BGP router would then send a series of handshake packets over TCP port 179. This makes BGP unique among routing protocols in that BGP peers do not have to have a connection to the same subnet; they could be worlds apart and still be BGP peers. In the cases where BGP peers are not directly connected to the same subnet, an IGP or static route is needed for the BGP peers to reach each other. BGP supports MD5 authentication to ensure the BGP is exchanging handshake packets with the correct BGP router. Once BGP peers are established, routes are exchanged among them.

BGP makes a distinction in the types of peers it has based on whether the peers are in the same ASN. If the peers are in the same ASN, they are considered internal BGP peers or iBGP. If the peers are in different ASNs, they are considered external BGP peers or eBGP. iBGP and eBGP have slightly different rules for advertising routes and adding routes to the routing table. Figure 12-8 shows a number of ASNs with eBGP and iBGP peers.

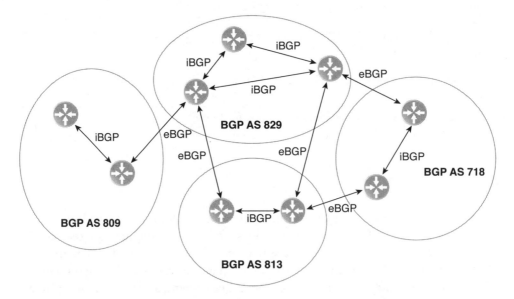

Figure 12-8 iBGP and eBGP peers

iBGP peers exchange routes by assuming that all iBGP peers are peers with all other iBGP peers. Stated in another way, iBGP is expected to be fully meshed. Because of the full mesh requirement, a BGP router shares a route with an iBGP peer only if the following conditions are met:

- The iBGP peer received the route from an eBGP peer.

- The iBGP peer is injecting the route into BGP.

Figure 12-9 shows iBGP peers in AS 829 learning about routes 10.10.11.0/24 and 10.10.20.0/24. The routes are injected into AS 829 from AS 809. Router C learns about the routes from the iBGP peer injecting the routes into AS 829, but Router C will not forward the routes to any iBGP peers.

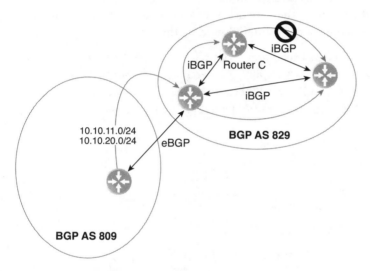

Figure 12-9   iBGP route advertisement

BGP advertisements have a field called the *AS_PATH*. When a route is advertised from one ASN to another, the ASN of the advertising eBGP router is added to the AS_PATH of the route. By default, BGP routers advertise all their routes to all their eBGP peers while following these three rules:

1. Add the advertising eBGP peer's ASN to the AS_PATH of the route before advertising the route.

2. Never send a route to an eBGP peer if the peer's ASN is already in the AS_ PATH.

3. There is an IGP entry in the routing table for the advertised route.

The first two rules are critical in achieving BGP's primary goal: to avoid loops. By adding the ASN to the AS_PATH of the route, each route has an accurate list of every ASN that needs to be crossed to reach the destination. This rule is needed to avoid sending a route back to an ASN that is in the AS_PATH for the route.

In OSPF, a router can have multiple interfaces added to OSPF in different OSPF areas. BGP does not have interfaces added to it. It is the whole router that gets placed in a BGP ASN, and a router can belong to only a single ASN. BGP has networks injected to it, either manually, by redistribution, or route summarization. If an administrator manually injects a network into BGP or redistributes it from a non-EGP routing protocol, IGP is considered the route origin for that network. If the route is redistributed from an EGP routing protocol, the route origin is considered EGP. If the administrator uses route summarization to inject the network into BGP, then BGP lists the origin of the network as unknown. The first entry in the AS_PATH field is always the route origin, followed by the ASNs.

Figure 12-10 shows eBGP peers exchanging routes for network 10.10.11.0/24 and 10.10.20.0/24, which originates in ASN 809. Router F will not forward the route 10.10.11.0/24 or 10.10.20.0/24 to Router B because Router B is in an ASN that is already in the AS_PATH of both 10.10.11.0/24 and 10.10.20.0/24.

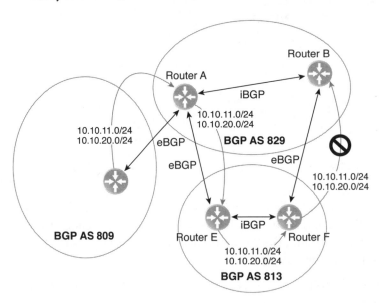

Figure 12-10 eBGP route advertisement

The third BGP route advertisement rule is called *synchronization*. The rule of synchronization says that a BGP router may advertise a route to an eBGP peer only if there is an entry in the routing table for the route. The entry in the routing table could be from OSPF, IS-IS, a static route, or a directly connected subnet.

The number one priority of BGP is to avoid loops among the different ASNs. To avoid the loops, BGP does not natively support ECMP. A BGP router might receive the same route from multiple BGP peers, but it always selects one and only one route to each destination for inclusion to the routing table. BGP follows a straight-forward algorithm to determine which route it adds to the routing table. The algorithm is called BGP Best Path Selection. Table 12-9 lists the BGP Best Path Selection attributes and their priorities. If two routes have a matching attribute, the algorithm proceeds down to the next priority attribute. Once a tiebreaker is found, that best route is added to the routing table.

Table 12-9 BGP Best Path Selection Attributes

Priority	Attribute	Information Contained
1	Weight	A number indicating the importance of routes advertised by a BGP peer. The higher weight is preferred.
2	Local Preference	A number indicating the preference for a route, advertised by the BGP peer. The higher the preference the better the route.
3	Shortest AS_PATH	The route with the least amount of ASN in the AS_PATH is preferred.
4	Lowest Origin Code	Choose the route with the lowest origin code. IGP has a lower origin code than EGP, which has a lower origin code than unknown.
5	Lowest Multi-Exit Discriminator	A number assigned by an AS, typically when it has multiple entry points, to influence the path that a route would take. The lower the Multi-Exit Discriminator, MED, the better the route.
6	eBGP over iBGP	Select eBGP learned routes over iBGP learned routes.
7	Lowest IGP Metric	Prefer the route with the lowest IGP metric to the BGP peer advertising the route.
8	Lowest Router ID	Prefer the route with the BGP peer with the lowest BGP Router ID.

With ECMP enabled, the logical router and the NSX Edge do add multiple BGP paths to the same destination in the routing table.

Configuring BGP

To configure BGP in the NSX Edge follow these steps:

Step 1. From the NSX Home page click **NSX Edges**.

Step 2. Select the NSX Manager that owns the Control VM or NSX Edge and double-click the logical router or NSX Edge.

Step 3. Go to **Manage > Routing** and select **BGP**.

Step 4. Click **Edit** and wait for the Edit BGP Configuration Wizard to pop up.

- **Enable BGP**: Check the box to enable BGP.

- **Enable Graceful Restart**: Check the box to enable Graceful Restart. With Graceful Restart enabled, the Control VM and NSX Edge notify their BGP peers that the BGP process is restarting and not to drop the BGP peering. As a consequence, data plane traffic continues to flow, and the logical router and NSX Edge can resume the BGP control plane quicker.

- **Enable Default Originate**: Check the box to send a default route to the BGP peers. Make sure you fully understand what you are doing before turning this feature on.

- **Local AS**: Enter the ASN for this router.

Step 5. Click **OK**.

Step 6. In Neighbors click the green + icon and wait for the New Neighbor Wizard to pop up.

Step 7. Complete the following fields:

- **IP Address**: The IP Address of the BGP Neighbor.

- **Forwarding Address**: This is applicable to the logical router only. Enter the IP of the Uplink LIF. This is the IP used to forward traffic in the data plane by the BGP neighbors.

- **Protocol Address**: This is applicable to the logical router only. Enter the IP to assign the Control VM to use for BGP control plane communication. This IP should be from the uplink segment.

- **Remote AS**: The ASN of the BGP neighbor.

- **Weight**: Enter the weight. You can enter 0 to ignore the weight.

- **Keep Alive Timer**: The frequency in seconds of the hello packets.

- **Hold Down Timer**: The amount of seconds to wait without receiving hellos from the BGP peer before removing all routes advertised by it from the routing table.

■ **Password**: Enter the password if MD5 authentication is required. This password must match at the BGP neighbor.

Step 8.   If you want to filter the networks advertised to the BGP peer or received from it, click the green + icon under BGP Filters and enter the following values:

■ **Direction**: The direction of the route update the filter will be applied.

■ **Action**: Allow (Permit) or drop (Deny) the route.

■ **Network**: The subnet to filter and the subnet prefix to match.

■ **IP Prefix GE**: The subnet prefix to match. Any prefix greater than or equal to the prefix entered here matches the filter.

■ **IP Prefix LE**: The subnet prefix to match. Any prefix less than or equal to the prefix entered here matches the filter. To match only a single prefix, do not fill in the IP Prefix GE and IP Prefix LE fields.

The New BGP Filter configuration should look similar to Figure 12-11. Click **Save.**

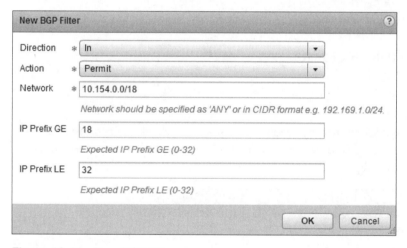

Figure 12-11   New BGP Filter

Step 9.   Repeat step 8 for additional subnets that should be filtered.

The New Neighbor configuration should look similar to Figure 12-12. Click **Save.**

New Neighbour
IP Address : * 10.154.15.1
Remote AS : *
Weight : 60
Keep Alive Time : 60 (Seconds)
Hold Down Time : 180 (Seconds)
(BGP Keep alive timer value needs to be one third of hold down timer)
Password :
BGP Filters :
Filter
Direction Action Network IP Prefix GE IP Prefix LE
In Permit 10.154.0.0/18 18 32
1 items
OK
Cancel

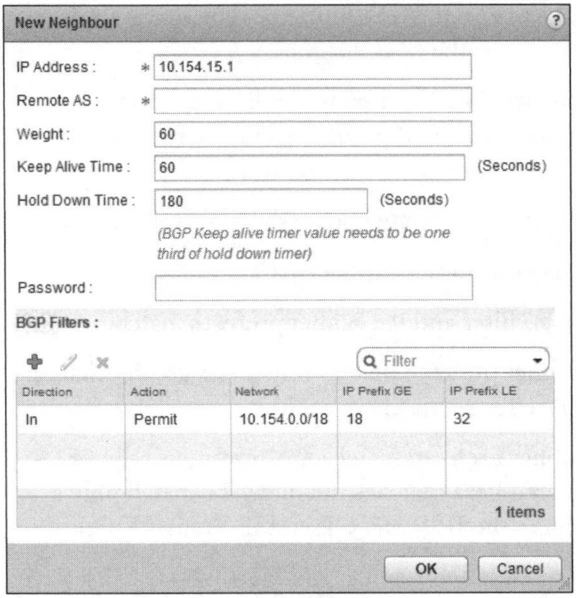

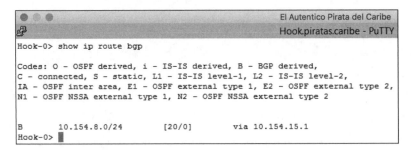

Figure 12-12 New BGP Neighbor

Step 10. Click **Publish Changes**.

Verifying BGP

By now you should know that my recommendation is to check the routing table to make sure we are seeing BGP routes. Figure 12-13 shows the output of the command **show ip route bgp**.

El Autentico Pirata del Caribe
Hook.piratas.caribe - PuTTY
Hook-0> show ip route bgp
Codes: O - OSPF derived, i - IS-IS derived, B - BGP derived,
C - connected, S - static, L1 - IS-IS level-1, L2 - IS-IS level-2,
IA - OSPF inter area, E1 - OSPF external type 1, E2 - OSPF external type 2,
N1 - OSPF NSSA external type 1, N2 - OSPF NSSA external type 2
B 10.154.8.0/24 [20/0] via 10.154.15.1
Hook-0>

Figure 12-13 Output of command **show ip route BGP**

Table 12-10 has a list of commands that can be used to check the status of your BGP peers and BGP table.

Table 12-10   BGP **show** Commands

Command	Description
show ip bgp	Displays BGP route table information
show ip bgp neighbors	Displays the status of your BGP neighbors and peers
debug ip bgp	Displays debugging information for BGP

IS-IS

Interior System to Interior System (IS-IS) is an open standard IGP that exchanges link states with its neighbors like OSPF. IS-IS is similar to OSPF in that it has areas, designated routers, uses the Dijkstra's algorithm to calculate the shortest path to a network, maintains an LSDB, and can be configured with MD5 authentication. However, there are some differences between the two protocols that are worth mentioning before we move to configuring IS-IS in the NSX Edge. The logical router does not support IS-IS.

IS-IS is not part of the TCP/IP stack. IS-IS is a protocol of Connectionless-mode Network Service, CLNS, that resides in Layer 2 of the OSI model. IS-IS is designed to be independent of the protocol for which it is carrying routing information. This makes IS-IS flexible to carry routing information for non-CLNS protocols, such as IPv4, IPv6, and Transparent Interconnection of Lots of Links (TRILL) without having to update the IS-IS standard itself.

IS-IS Areas and IS Types

An IS-IS domain is equivalent to the OSPF AS. In IS-IS every router has to have a 6-byte System ID, which must be unique in the IS-IS domain. The System ID is analogous to an OSPF Router ID. IS-IS places the entire router in an area rather than the router's interfaces, like OSFP does. An IS-IS area must be between 1 byte and 13 bytes in length expressed in hexadecimal. A router can be in multiple areas, and any two areas can send traffic directly between each other without needing to go through a backbone area, like OSPF requires.

Instead of defining an area type, IS-IS defines a router type. Table 12-11 shows the different IS-IS router types and their definitions.

Key Topic

Table 12-11   IS-IS Router Types

Type	Description
Level 1	Intra-area routers. Only exchange link states for routes in the same area and with other Level 1 routers.
Level 2	Inter-area routers, equivalent to backbone routers. Link states are only exchanged with other Level 2 routers.
Level 1-2	An Area Type border router. It exchanges routing information with both Level 1 and Level 2 routers. It serves as the bridge for Level 1 and Level 2 routers.

Instead of LSAs, IS-IS uses Packet Data Units (PDUs). Level 1 routers exchange Level 1 Link State PDUs, and Level 2 routers exchange Level 2 Link State PDUs. Level 1-2 routers exchange both Level 1 and Level 2 Link State PDUs. Like OSPF, all intra-area routers see all Link State PDUs for their level. There are some other PDUs, such as IS-IS Hello PDUs, that are sent by all routers. To connect one area to another area, the connection must be made via two Level 2 routers, Level 1-2 routers, or a combination of the two. Traffic between areas always traverses these connections.

The NSX Edge supports up to three areas and configures different levels in different interfaces. The NSX Edge also supports interfaces joining a Mesh Group. A *Mesh Group* is a group of IS-IS routers that are fully meshed with each other. An advantage of a Mesh Group is that each IS-IS router in the group only receives a single Link State PDU, thus reducing the overhead of processing PDUs by each router. The Mesh Group could have NSX Edges and physical routers. An IS-IS router only exchanges link status updates with members of the same Mesh Group. Authentication can be configured in the Mesh Group to restrict access to the group. The NSX Edge supports multiple Mesh Groups but an interface can only belong to a single Mesh Group.

Configuring IS-IS

To configure IS-IS in the NSX Edge, follow these steps (the logical router does not support IS-IS):

Step 1. From the NSX Home page click **NSX Edges**.

Step 2. Select the NSX Manager that owns the NSX Edge and double-click the NSX Edge.

Step 3. Go to **Manage > Routing** and select **IS-IS**.

Step 4. In IS-IS Configuration click **Edit** and wait for the Edit IS-IS Configuration Wizard to pop up.

Step 5.   Check the Enable IS-IS box and fill out the following fields:

- **System ID**: Enter the NET for the NSX Edge.

- **IS Type**: Select the default Edge IS-IS router type.

- **Domain Password (optional)**: Enter the password for the IS-IS domain.

- **Area Password (optional)**: Enter the password for the area(s) the router will be in.

The configuration should look similar to what is shown in Figure 12-14. Click **OK**.

Figure 12-14   Enabling IS-IS

Step 6.   In Areas, click **Edit** and wait for the Edit IS-IS Areas Wizard to pop up.

Step 7.   Enter up to three different areas and click **Save**. Each area must be between 1 byte to 13 bytes in hexadecimals.

Step 8.   In Interface Mapping click the green + icon and wait for the New Interface Mapping Wizard to pop up.

Step 9.   Select the Interface you want to run IS-IS and complete the following fields:

- **Circuit Type**: Select Router Level to run over the interface.

   In Advanced you can fill out the following fields (or leave them with their default values):

- **Hello Interval**: Enter the frequency to send Hello packets in milliseconds. The default is 10,000 ms.

- **Hello Multiplier**: The number of Hello packets missed before declaring the IS-IS neighbor down. The default is 3 ms.

- **LSP Interval**: The number of milliseconds to wait before sending successive link state packets. The default it 33 ms.

- **Metric**: The cost of the interface. The default is 10.

- **Priority**: The preference for being elected the designated router. The highest priority in the segment wins. The default is 64.

- **Mesh Group** (optional): Enter the Mesh Group number. This number must match for all IS-IS routers in the interface segment.

- **Password** (optional): Enter a password if authentication is required in the Mesh Group.

The configuration should look similar to Figure 12-15. Click **Save**.

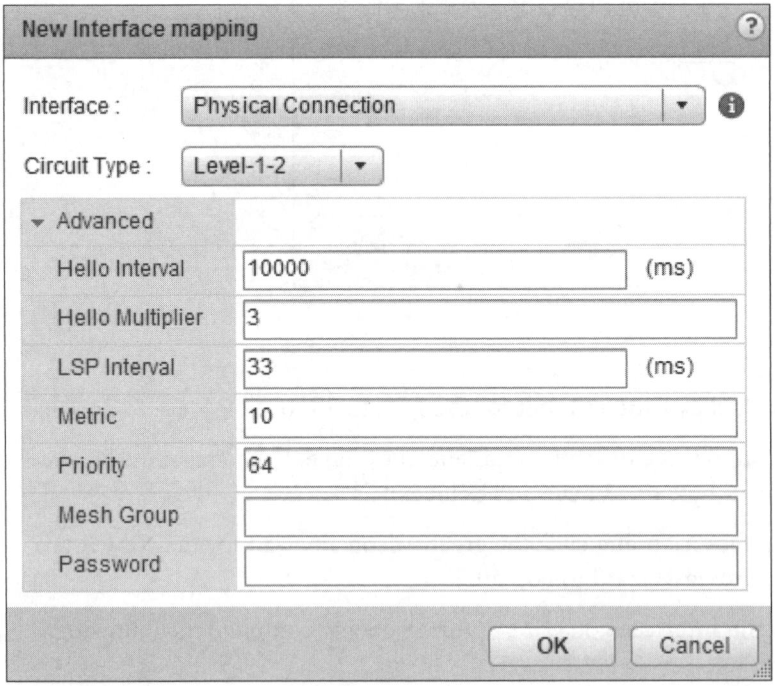

Figure 12-15   New Interface Mapping

Step 10.   Click **Publish Changes**.

Verifying IS-IS

Figure 12-16 shows the output of the command **show ip route isis**. This command lists all the routes learned via IS-IS.

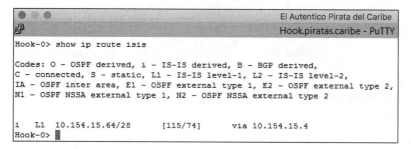

```
Hook-0> show ip route isis

Codes: O - OSPF derived, i - IS-IS derived, B - BGP derived,
C - connected, S - static, L1 - IS-IS level-1, L2 - IS-IS level-2,
IA - OSPF inter area, E1 - OSPF external type 1, E2 - OSPF external type 2,
N1 - OSPF NSSA external type 1, N2 - OSPF NSSA external type 2


i   L1  10.154.15.64/28      [115/74]      via 10.154.15.4
Hook-0>
```

Figure 12-16   Output of command **show ip route isis**

Table 12-12 has a list of commands that can be used to check the status of your IS-IS functionality.

Table 12-12   IS-IS **show** Commands

Command	Description
show isis	Confirms if IS-IS is enabled
show isis neighbors	Shows the status of your IS-IS neighbors
show isis interfaces	Shows the interfaces are configured for IS-IS
show isis database	Shows the IS-IS LSDB
debug ip bgp	Shows debugging information for BGP

Route Redistribution

We conclude this chapter by configuring route redistribution. The process is similar in both the logical router and the NSX Edge. The steps required to redistribute routes into a routing process involve identifying the subnets that will be redistributed into the routing process and from where the subnets would be redistributed. The subnets are identified in an IP prefix. An IP prefix includes the IP prefix name, the subnet, and the subnet prefix.

To configure route redistribution, follow these steps:

Step 1.   From the NSX Home page click **NSX Edges**.

Step 2.   Select the NSX Manager that owns the Control VM or NSX Edge and double-click the logical router or NSX Edge.

Step 3.   Go to **Manage > Routing** and select **Route Redistribution**.

Step 4.   In Route Redistribution Status, click **Change** and wait for the Change Redistribution Settings Wizard to pop up.

Step 5.   Check the box next to the routing protocol(s) you want to enable redistribution for and click **Save**.

Step 6.   In IP Prefix click the green + icon and wait for the New IP Prefix Wizard to pop up.

Step 7.   Enter a name for the IP Prefix, enter the subnet and prefix, and click **OK**. There is a default IP Prefix of *ANY* to include all subnets.

The configuration should look similar to the one in Figure 12-17.

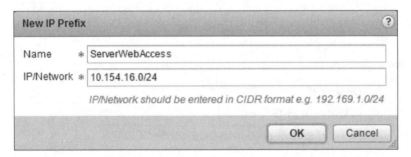

Figure 12-17   New IP Prefix

Step 8.   In Route Redistribution Table, click the green + icon, wait for the New Redistribution Criteria Wizard to pop up, and fill in the following fields:

- **Prefix Name**: Select the IP Prefix to redistribute.

- **Learner Protocol**: The receiving routing protocol.

- **Allow Learning From**: Select the sources from where the networks in the IP Prefix are coming.

Step 9.   In Action, select to **Permit** or **Deny** the routes to be injected to the routing protocol.

The configuration should look similar to Figure 12-18. Click **OK**.

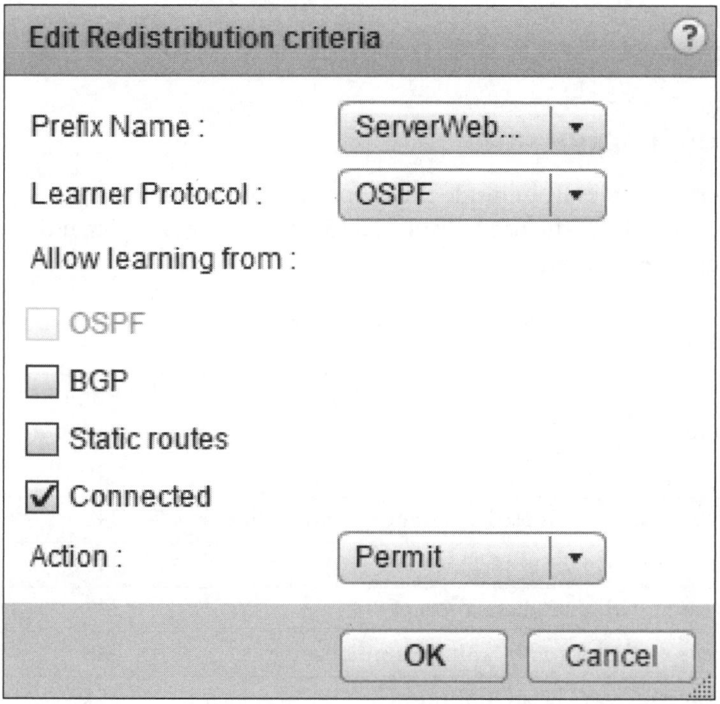

Edit Redistribution criteria   ⑦

Prefix Name :   ServerWeb... ▼

Learner Protocol :   OSPF   ▼

Allow learning from :

☐ OSPF

☐ BGP

☐ Static routes

☑ Connected

Action :   Permit   ▼

OK   Cancel

Figure 12-18   New Redistribution Criteria

Step 10.   Click **Publish Changes**.

The only way get to get the internal logical router interfaces advertised into OSPF is to redistribute them. When redistributing the connected logical router interfaces into OSPF, they show up in the routing table as OSPF external type 2 routes.

Exam Preparation Tasks

Review All the Key Topics

Review the most important topics from inside the chapter, noted with the Key Topic icon in the outer margin of the page. Table 12-13 lists these key topics and the page numbers where each is found.

Table 12-13 Key Topics for Chapter 12

Key Topic Element	Description	Page Number
Table 12-2	Routing protocols.	346
Paragraph	Administrative distance is used as a route selector tiebraker	348
Paragraph	Cost and metric have the same function	348
Paragraph	Directly connected routes have a cost of 0	348
Paragraph	ECMP only works for routes with the same cost	348
Paragraph	The logical router will be an ASBR.	353
Paragraph	The logical router and the NSX Edge support normal and NSSA areas.	354
Paragraph	MTU is one of the parameters that should match between OSPF neighbors.	355
Paragraph	OSPF uses multicast addresses in Ethernet segments.	356
Paragraph	The logical router supports OSPF over a single uplink.	360
Paragraph	The BGP protocol was designed to avoid routing loops.	364
Paragraph	ECMP allows for multiple BGP routes to be added to the routing table	365
Table 12-11	IS-IS Router Types.	370
Paragraph	Redistribute connected is used to advertise internal	375

Complete Tables and Lists from Memory

Download and print a copy of Appendix C, "Memory Tables" (found on the book's website), or at least the section for this chapter, and complete the tables and lists from memory. Appendix D, "Memory Tables Answer Key," also on the website, includes the completed tables and lists so you can check your work.

Define Key Terms

Define the following key terms from this chapter, and check your answers in the Glossary:

administrative distance, cost, Autonomous System (AS), Internal Gateway Protocol (IGP), External Gateway Protocol (EGP), Open Shortest Path First (OSPF), ABR, ASBR, NSSA, Border Gateway Protocol (BGP), iBGP, eBGP, IS-IS

This chapter covers all or part of the following VCP6-NV exam blueprint topics:

- **Objective 6.2**—Configure and Manage Logical Virtual Private Networks (VPN)

- **Objective 9.5**— Administer Logging

CHAPTER 13

NSX Edge VPN Services

No network solution would be complete without the capability of providing secure communications over an untrusted medium, such as the Internet. There are multiple ways to accomplish this, one of which we covered in Chapter 10, "Layer 2 Extensions," when we discussed Layer 2 VPNs. Now how about doing it for Layer 3? NSX can surely do it. NSX provides support for IPsec VPNs and SSL VPNs.

IPsec and SSL VPNs are well-established technologies, and there isn't much new to be said about them. In this chapter we do a high level review of IPsec and SSL VPNs and the features supported by NSX via the NSX Edge. We also cover how to configure those features in the NSX Edges.

Do I Know This Already?

The "Do I Know This Already?" quiz allows you to assess whether you should read this entire chapter or simply jump to the "Exam Preparation Tasks" section for review. If you are in doubt, read the entire chapter. Table 13-1 outlines the major headings in this chapter and the corresponding "Do I Know This Already?" quiz questions. You can find the answers in Appendix A, "Answers to the 'Do I Know This Already?' Quizzes."

Table 13-1 Headings and Questions

Foundation Topic Section	Questions Covered in This Section
IPsec VPN	1-2
IPsec VPN Establishment	3-5
Verifying IPsec VPNs	6
SSL VPN-Plus	7-8
Configure SSL VPN-Plus	9-10

1. Which is not a feature of IPsec VPNs?

   a. Data origin authentication

   b. Data confidentiality

   c. Data integrity

   d. Data replay

2. An NSX Edge is configured with an IPsec site-site VPN tunnel over the Internet to a remote location. The IPsec VPN peer at the remote location only has RFC1918 addresses, and the remote site has a NAT router to connect to the Internet.

   Which requirement must be met for the IPsec VPN to function correctly?

   a. The peer ID of the remote router must be a non-RFC1918 address.

   b. The peer ID of the remote router must be the NAT IP.

   c. The peer endpoint of the remote router must match the Peer ID.

   d. The peer endpoint of the router must be the NAT IP.

3. What is the role of IKE in IPsec VPN?

   a. It provides the encryption mechanism for the IPsec tunnels.

   b. It establishes the conditions for the creation of a secure communication channel.

   c. It establishes data confidentiality.

   d. It establishes the security proposals for the IPsec VPN peers.

4. Which two DH groups does the NSX Edge support? (Choose two.)

   a. DH Group 1

   b. DH Group 2

   c. DH Group 4

   d. DH Group 5

5. Which IKE Phase 2 mode does the NSX Edge support?

   a. Main Mode

   b. Quick Mode

   c. Fast Mode

   d. Secure Mode

6. Which NSX Edge CLI command can be used to verify the subnets allowed over the IPsec VPN tunnel?

    a. **show service vpn sa**

    b. **show service ipsec sp**

    c. **show service ipsec networks**

    d. **show service vpn networks**

7. What is the NSX Edge default port for SSL VPN-Plus?

    a. TCP 443

    b. UDP 443

    c. TCP 636

    d. UDP 636

8. What is the maximum number of SSL VPN-Plus active sessions supported by a single NSX Edge?

    a. 50

    b. 100

    c. 1,000

    d. 6,000

9. Which two components do not need to be configured for Network Access Mode SSL VPN-Plus? (Choose two.)

    a. IP pool

    b. Login script

    c. SSL VPN-Plus server settings

    d. Web resource

10. How does a user get the SSL VPN-Plus client installed?

    a. From VMware's site, http://www.vmware.com/. The user must have a VMware account to download it.

    b. From the NSX Manager, https://NSX-MANAGER-IP_OR_FQDN/VPN-PLUS. The user must have at least NSX Manager Read-Only access.

    c. From the NSX Edge, https://EDGE-IP_OR_FQDN/. The NSX Edge must authenticate the user first.

    d. From a link provided to the user by the NSX administrator. The user must have appropriate rights to access the link.

Foundation Topics

IPsec VPNs

IPsec is an umbrella term for many standards that when cobbled together allow for secure and reliable communication over an untrusted medium. IPsec itself is an Internet Engineering Task Force (IETF) standard. IPsec can provide the security features listed in Table 13-2.

Table 13-2   IPsec Provided Security Features

Feature	Description
Data origin authentication	IPsec validates the traffic's origin to be one of the IPsec peers. The validation can be achieved by using digital certificates, from a CA or self-signed, or pre-shared keys.
Data integrity	IPsec provides a mechanism to guarantee protected traffic has not been altered in transit.
Data confidentiality	IPsec provides for strong encryption to limit the ability for anyone other than the IPsec peers to read the protected traffic.
Anti-replay	IPsec eliminates man-in-the-middle attacks where a third party copies the encrypted traffic, in transit, and resends it.

IPsec provides protection for communications between two endpoints by encapsulating their traffic in an IPsec tunnel. The endpoints may be two routers, in which case it is often referred to as a site-site VPN. Two routers that form an IPsec connection are called IPsec peers, and a router may have multiple IPsec peers. In site-site VPNs, the IPsec peers are told of each other's networks that are reachable over the IPsec tunnel. For example, as shown in Figure 13-1, a remote site in the San Juan office is connecting over the Internet to an NSX Edge in the data center in Santo Domingo. The San Juan office router can be any router that supports IPsec. The NSX Edge is told of the network San Juan user Marcos is connected to. The San Juan router, in turn, is told of the data center network to which a web server is connected. Optionally the San Juan router could be given a default route so all non-local traffic from a San Juan subnet goes to the data center. In the example in Figure 13-1, the NSX Edge may be placed behind a NAT router, which may be a physical appliance or another NSX Edge, in which case the San Juan router uses the NAT IP as its IPsec peer endpoint.

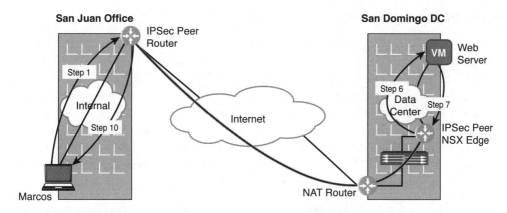

Figure 13-1   Site-site IPsec VPN

Traffic from user Marcos toward the web server goes like this:

1. User Marcos opens a web browser to reach a website in the Santo Domingo Data Center.

2. The traffic is routed internally over to the San Juan router.

3. The San Juan router has an entry for the web server's subnet going over the IPsec VPN toward the Edge IPsec peer.

4. The San Juan router encapsulates the traffic from user Marcos and sends it over the IPsec tunnel, using the NAT router as the IPsec peer endpoint.

5. The NAT router changes the destination IP of the IPsec header.

6. The IPsec Peer Edge receives the IPsec traffic, validates it, decapsulates it, and routes it locally to the web server.

7. The response traffic from the web server is routed locally by the IPsec Peer Edge.

8. The IPsec Peer Edge has an entry for user Marcos's subnet pointing out of the IPsec VPN to the San Juan IPsec Peer router.

9. The IPsec Peer Edge encapsulates the traffic from the web server and sends it over the IPsec VPN.

10. The San Juan router receives the IPsec traffic, validates it, decapsulates it, and routes it locally to Marcos.

The NSX Edge creates a tunnel per each pair of subnets advertised by each of the VPN peers. For example, if the San Juan router is advertising two subnets and the NSX Edge in Data Center Santo Domingo is advertising three subnets, then six VPN tunnels will be established.

IPsec VPN Establishment

If Marcos has any hope of accessing the website in the data center in Santo Domingo, the IPsec VPN must be established between the San Juan router and the NSX Edge. The process of becoming peers involves validating each other's identities, exchanging security parameters, and creating unique keys to encrypt the traffic over the IPsec VPN. This process is handled by a protocol called the Internet Key Exchange (IKE). IKE is a protocol that helps establish secure communication channels. Using IKE, the San Juan and the Edge routers agree on the security parameters for the IPsec VPN. Traffic flows over the IPsec tunnel between the routers only after IKE is successfully completed. IKE has two phases:

- Phase 1 validates the two endpoints that want to be IPsec VPN peers and establishes a secure channel between the two.

- Phase 2 establishes the secure channel for the actual IPsec VPN traffic.

Let's do a walk-through of the IKE process. Figure 13-2 shows the San Juan router and the NSX Edge about to start the process to becoming IPsec VPN peers. Either router can start the negotiations. We assume there is no NAT router between the two and that the IKE negotiations are started by the San Juan router.

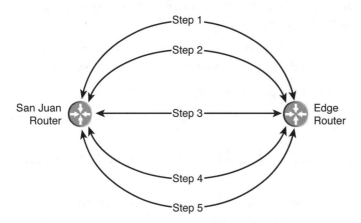

Figure 13-2   Site-site IPsec peer establishment

1. The San Juan router sends an IKE security proposal to the Edge. This traffic is unprotected.

    The proposal includes the following:

    - Router authentication method

    - IPsec VPN encryption algorithm

- Cryptographic hash

- Diffie-Hellman Group

- Security Association (SA) lifetime

2. The Edge responds with either acceptance of the security proposals, a new security proposal, or doesn't accept the security proposals. This traffic is unprotected.

   If the security proposals are not accepted, the Edge sends a *No_Proposal_Chosen* and terminates the negotiations.

3. The routers exchange Diffie-Hellman keys. This traffic is unprotected.

   I'm being oversimplistic here, but Diffie-Hellman (DH) is a mechanism for two parties to create a secret key by exchanging some information over a public medium. Think of the DH key as two pairs of prime numbers randomly generated and agreed upon by each router. The Edge combines the DH key it receives from the San Juan router with a third number that only the Edge knows about to create a secret key. The San Juan router combines the DH keys it receives from the Edge with a third number that only the San Juan router knows about to create the secret key.

   The beauty of Diffie-Hellman is that both routers always come up with the same secret key. As no one knows what the third number is, except for the router that generated it, an eavesdropper cannot calculate the secret key. Diffie-Hellman provides support for different key-size lengths. DH Group 2 supports key lengths of 1024 bit, and DH Group 5 supports key lengths of 1536 bits.

   Up to this point, all traffic between the two routers has been sent in cleartext. Now that Diffie-Hellman has completed its thing, the secret key is used for the next step of the process, which is to authenticate the two routers.

4. The two routers confirm each other's identity by exchanging a pre-shared key or digital certificates. This traffic is encrypted.

   The authentication is proposed in step 1 and agreed upon in step 2.

   If both routers successfully authenticate each other, this concludes IKE Phase 1. At this stage the routers have Security Associations (SA), and IKE Phase 2 begins using the SA.

5. The routers exchange the security parameters they want to use for sending traffic over the IPsec VPN.

   Both sides must have a matching IPsec VPN policy; otherwise IKE Phase 2 will fail and no IPsec tunnel will be created.

The NSX Edge can be deployed to create site-site IPsec VPNs with another Edge or another VPN entity, whether the other entity is physical or virtual. The NSX Edge can be placed behind another Edge doing NAT. Table 13-3 shows the list of features supported by the NSX Edge for IPsec VPN.

Table 13-3   IPsec VPN Support

Feature	Support
Number of remote sites	10
Number of IP VPN tunnels	6,000
Digital certificate authentication	Yes
Pre-Shared Key Mode	Yes
Phase 1 Mode	Main Mode
Phase 2 Mode	Quick Mode
DH Group 2	Yes
DH Group 5	Yes
Perfect forward secrecy	Yes
Static routing	Yes
OSPF	No
BGP	No
IPv4 unicast traffic	Yes
IPv4 multicast traffic	No

Configuring IPsec VPNs

Table 13-3 states that we can use a digital certificate to authenticate IPsec VPN peers. The NSX Edge supports the creation of self-signed digital certificates or from a certificate authority. There is nothing extraordinary on how we go about configuring the Edge to use digital certificates. First we assign a certificate to the NSX Edge and then we enable certificate authentication for IPsec VPN.

Let's go ahead and add a self-signed digital certificate in the NSX Edge in Data Center Santo Domingo:

Step 1.   From the NSX Edges view, double-click the NSX Edge that will be configured for IPsec VPN.

Step 2.   Go to **Manage > Settings** and select **Certificates**.

Step 3. Select **Actions > Generate CSR** and wait for the Generate CSR Wizard to open.

Step 4. Enter a Common Name and Organization Name.

These are the only two required fields.

Step 5. Enter values for the following fields:

- Organization Unit
- Locality
- State
- Country (there is a drop-down with all country names)
- Message Algorithm and Key Size:

RSA and DSA are the algorithm options.

The key size options are 2048 and 3072.

- Enter a description.

Step 6. Your configuration should look similar to the one in Figure 13-3. Click **OK**.

Figure 13-3 NSX Edge digital certificate CSR

Step 7. Select the newly created CSR and click **Actions > Self Sign Certificate**.

Step 8. In the Self Sign window that opens up, enter the number of days the certificate will be valid for.

Step 9.   Click **OK**. You should have a self-signed digital certificate as shown in Figure 13-4.

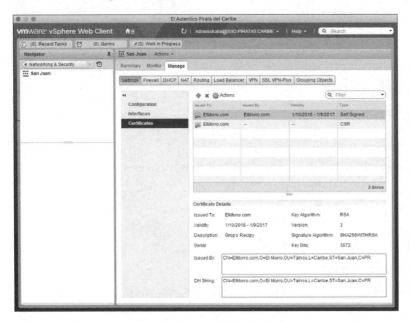

Figure 13-4   NSX Edge self-signed digital certificate

Next, let's turn on the capability to use a digital certificate for IPsec VPN:

Step 1.   Go to **Manage > VPN** and select **IPsec VPN**.

Step 2.   In Global Configuration Status, click **Change** and wait for the Global Configuration window to open.

Step 3.   Check the box **Enable Certificate Authentication**.

Step 4.   Select the Digital Certificate to use and click **OK**.

Step 5.   Click **Publish**.

Now let's configure an IPsec VPN between the NSX Edge and another router by following these steps:

Step 1.   From the NSX Edges view, double-click the NSX Edge that will be configured for IPsec VPN.

Step 2.   Go to **Manage > VPN** and select **IPsec VPN**.

Step 3.   Click the green + icon to create a new IPsec VPN.

Step 4.   Once the Add IPsec VPN Wizard opens, enter the following information:

    a. Uncheck the Enabled box to disable this VPN peer. This is optional as it is checked by default.

    b. Uncheck the Enable Perfect Forward Secrecy (PFS) box. This is optional as it is checked by default.

    PFS is a feature of IKE Phase 1 that ensures that an eavesdropper can't see the identities of those using the IPsec VPN. In Figure 13-1, if the IPsec VPN peers use PFS, no one in the untrusted medium would know Marcos is communicating with the web server.

    c. Assign a name to the IPsec VPN.

    d. Assign a Local ID. This ID is used to identify the Edge with its IPsec VPN peer. If using certification authentication, the Local ID is the common name in the Edge's certificate. If using pre-shared keys, the Local ID can be anything.

    e. Enter the IP for the local endpoint. This is the IP of one of the Uplink interfaces.

    f. Enter the subnets to advertise to the IPsec VPN peer.

    Use Classless Inter-Domain Routing (CIDR) format.

    Use a comma to separate multiple entries.

    g. Enter the Peer ID. This is the ID that identifies the IPsec VPN peer.

    If using certification authentication, the Peer ID will be the common name in the peer's certificate. If using pre-shared keys, the Peer ID can be anything.

    h. Enter the Peer Endpoint IP or type Any.

    This is the destination IP of the IPsec VPN packets. If Any, the IPsec VPN peer must initiate the connection.

    i. Enter the subnets reachable at the IPsec VPN peer.

    Use Classless Inter-Domain Routing (CIDR) format. The NSX Edge adds a static route for this (these) subnet(s).

    Use a comma to separate multiple entries.

    j. Select the Encryption Algorithm. Table 13-4 shows the encryption algorithms supported by the NSX Edge.

Table 13-4   IPsec VPN Encryption Algorithms

Encryption Algorithm	Supported
AES	Yes
AES-256	Yes
AES-GCM	Yes
Triple-DES	Yes

k. Select the IPsec VPN Peer Authentication Method.

The options are Pre-Shared Key (PSK) and Certificates.

If selecting PSK, enter the key. This key must match at the IPsec VPN peer.

If selecting Certificate, the Edge uses the Digital Certificate chosen in Global Configuration. To select Certificate you first have to Enable Security Authentication from the Global Configuration Status in the IPSec VPN view.

l. Select a Diffie-Hellman Group. The options are DH Group 2 and DH Group 5.

m. Enter an Extension to restrict the traffic that may go to this VPN peer over the IPsec VPN tunnels.

The options are *securelocaltrafficbyip=[local IP address]* and *passthroughsubnets=[remote IP or subnet]*.

The *securelocaltrafficbyip* extension determines which local IPs are allowed over the IPsec VPN. This is the default behavior of the NSX Edge for all IPs in the local subnets identified in step 4f.

The *passthroughsubnets* extension overrides the routing table and forces traffic to the destination subnet over the IPsec VPN. It is most useful when overlapping subnets exist in the two VPN peer sites.

Step 5. Your configuration should look similar to the one in Figure 13-5. Click **OK**.

Figure 13-5 shows the Data Center Santo Domingo Edge's IPsec VPN configuration using PSK.

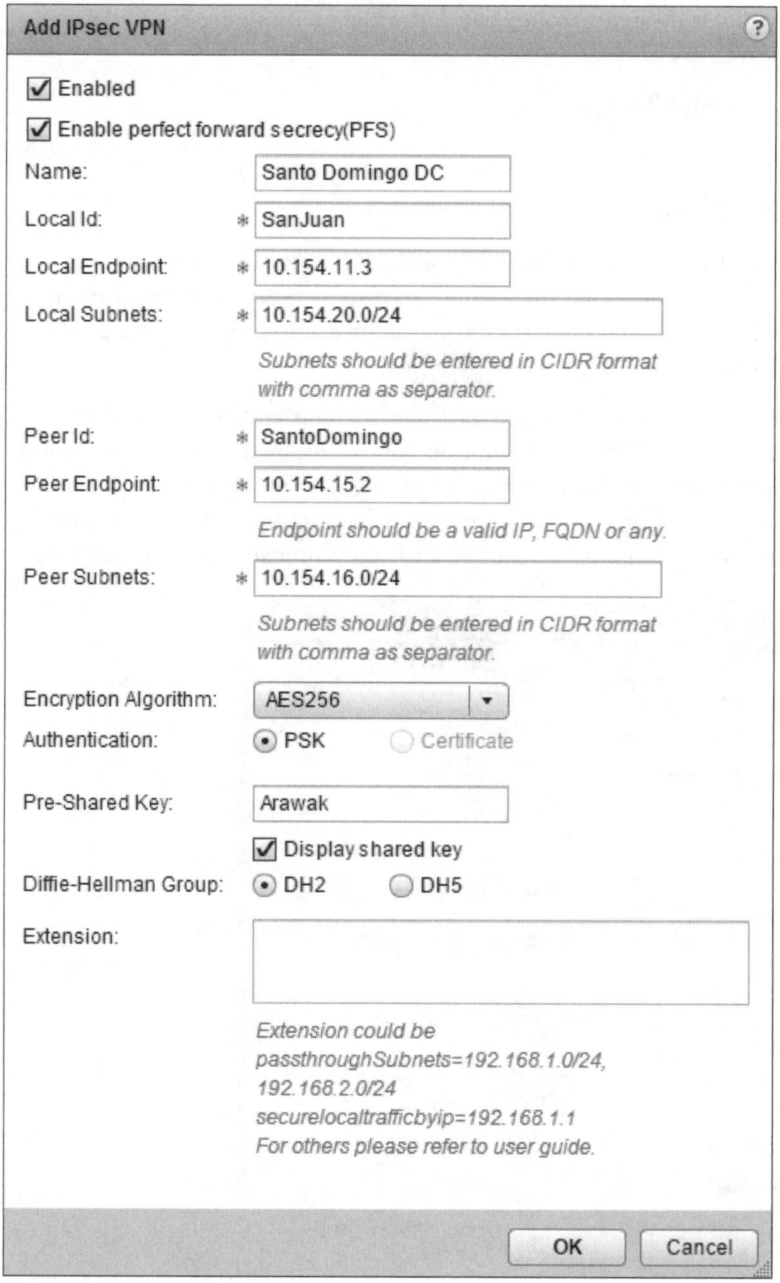

Add IPsec VPN   ⑦

☑ Enabled

☑ Enable perfect forward secrecy(PFS)

Name:	Santo Domingo DC
Local Id:	* SanJuan
Local Endpoint:	* 10.154.11.3
Local Subnets:	* 10.154.20.0/24

Subnets should be entered in CIDR format with comma as separator.

Peer Id:	* SantoDomingo
Peer Endpoint:	* 10.154.15.2

Endpoint should be a valid IP, FQDN or any.

Peer Subnets:	* 10.154.16.0/24

Subnets should be entered in CIDR format with comma as separator.

Encryption Algorithm:	AES256 ▼
Authentication:	⦿ PSK ◯ Certificate
Pre-Shared Key:	Arawak
	☑ Display shared key
Diffie-Hellman Group:	⦿ DH2 ◯ DH5
Extension:	

Extension could be passthroughSubnets=192.168.1.0/24, 192.168.2.0/24 securelocaltrafficbyip=192.168.1.1 For others please refer to user guide.

OK   Cancel

Figure 13-5   Creating an IPsec VPN

Step 6.   In IPsec VPN Services Status, click **Enable**.

Step 7.   Optionally, in Logging Policy check the Enable Logging box and select a Log Level.

Step 8.   Click **Publish Changes**.

Verifying IPsec VPNs

The ultimate test to confirm your IPsec VPN is working between two sites is to ping from one location to the other (assuming there are no security rules in the way that block the traffic). Assuming you don't have the luxury to ping, you can also verify the IPsec VPN directly from the NSX Edge.

The first option to check the functionality is directly from the NSX Edge's IPsec VPN view. Select the IPsec VPN configuration you are interested in and then click the hyperlink **Show IPsec Statistics**. As shown in Figure 13-6, a window opens showing the status of the IPsec VPN connection. Selecting one of the connections shows the status of the subnets that are allowed to communicate via the IPsec VPN.

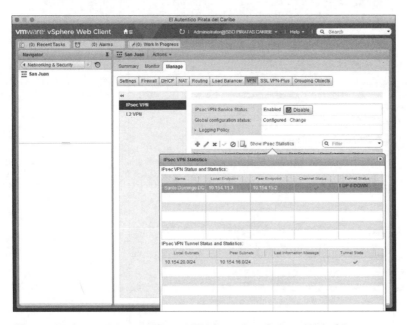

Figure 13-6   Verifying the IPsec VPN from the vSphere Web Client

The second option is directly from the Edge's CLI. Connect to the NSX Edge, via the console or in-band with SSH. Figure 13-7 shows the output of the command **show service ipsec sa**, which shows the security associations of the San Juan router.

```
                                          El Autentico Pirata del Caribe
                                          Hook.piratas.caribe - PuTTY
Hook-0> show service ipsec sa
src 10.154.11.3 ---> dst 10.154.15.2
        esp mode=tunnel spi=20285639(0x013588c7) reqid=16385(0x00004001)
        E: aes-cbc      A: hmac-sha1
        seq=0x00000000 replay=32 flags=0x00000000 state=mature
        created: Jan 10 19:52:02 2016   current: Jan 10 19:54:13 2016
        diff: 131(s)    hard: 0(s)      soft: 0(s)
        last:                           hard: 0(s)      soft: 0(s)
        current: 0(bytes)       hard: 0(bytes)  soft: 0(bytes)
        allocated: 0    hard: 0 soft: 0
src 10.154.15.2 ---> dst 10.154.11.3
        esp mode=tunnel spi=2867420687(0xaae95e0f) reqid=16385(0x00004001)
        E: aes-cbc      A: hmac-sha1
        seq=0x00000000 replay=32 flags=0x00000000 state=mature
        created: Jan 10 19:52:02 2016   current: Jan 10 19:54:13 2016
        diff: 131(s)    hard: 0(s)      soft: 0(s)
        last:                           hard: 0(s)      soft: 0(s)
        current: 0(bytes)       hard: 0(bytes)  soft: 0(bytes)
        allocated: 0    hard: 0 soft: 0
src 10.154.11.3 ---> dst 10.154.15.2
        esp mode=tunnel spi=2964912038(0xb0b8f7a6) reqid=16385(0x00004001)
        E: aes-cbc      A: hmac-sha1
        seq=0x00000000 replay=32 flags=0x00000000 state=mature
        created: Jan 10 19:51:47 2016   current: Jan 10 19:54:13 2016
        diff: 146(s)    hard: 0(s)      soft: 0(s)
        last:                           hard: 0(s)      soft: 0(s)
        current: 0(bytes)       hard: 0(bytes)  soft: 0(bytes)
        allocated: 0    hard: 0 soft: 0
src 10.154.15.2 ---> dst 10.154.11.3
        esp mode=tunnel spi=2628572236(0x9cacd44c) reqid=16385(0x00004001)
        E: aes-cbc      A: hmac-sha1
        seq=0x00000000 replay=32 flags=0x00000000 state=mature
        created: Jan 10 19:51:47 2016   current: Jan 10 19:54:13 2016
        diff: 146(s)    hard: 0(s)      soft: 0(s)
        last:                           hard: 0(s)      soft: 0(s)
        current: 0(bytes)       hard: 0(bytes)  soft: 0(bytes)
        allocated: 0    hard: 0 soft: 0
Hook-0>
```

Figure 13-7   **show service ipsec sa** command output

Figure 13-8 shows the output of the command **show service ipsec sp**, which shows the subnets that are allowed to communicate via the IPsec VPN.

```
                                                    El Autentico Pirata del Caribe
                                                    Hook.piratas.caribe - PuTTY
Hook-0> show service ipsec sp
src 10.154.16.0/24[any]  ---> dst 10.154.20.0/24[any] 255
        out prio high + 1073739480 ipsec
        esp/tunnel/10.154.15.2-10.154.11.3/unique#16385
        created: Jan 10 19:52:02 2016  lastused:
        lifetime: 0(s) validtime: 0(s)
        spid=33 seq=1 pid=30616
        refcnt=1
src 10.154.20.0/24[any]  ---> dst 10.154.16.0/24[any] 255
        fwd prio high + 1073739480 ipsec
        esp/tunnel/10.154.11.3-10.154.15.2/unique#16385
        created: Jan 10 19:51:47 2016  lastused:
        lifetime: 0(s) validtime: 0(s)
        spid=50 seq=2 pid=30616
        refcnt=1
src 10.154.20.0/24[any]  ---> dst 10.154.16.0/24[any] 255
        in prio high + 1073739480 ipsec
        esp/tunnel/10.154.11.3-10.154.15.2/unique#16385
        created: Jan 10 19:51:47 2016  lastused:
        lifetime: 0(s) validtime: 0(s)
        spid=40 seq=3 pid=30616
        refcnt=1
Hook-0>
```

Figure 13-8   show service ipsec sp command output

Let me quickly point out something. The Web Client's Show IPsec Statistics shows you a green check mark for the IPsec Tunnel State and every pair of subnets that should be allowed through the IPsec VPN. The check mark for the IPsec Tunnel State represents the router having all necessary SA, which are shown in the command **show service ipsec sa**. The check in each pair of allowed subnets represents the subnets listed in the command **show service ipsec sp**.

SSL VPN-Plus

In the IPsec VPN section, I emphasized the IPsec tunnel was between two NSX Edges or an NSX Edge and a router. In reality, the IPsec VPN can also be made with an end user if the user has an IPsec VPN client to start the IPsec negotiations. Thus a remote user, say in Bogotá, could use her IPsec VPN client on her MAC and connect back to the Santo Domingo Data Center via the NSX Edge. However, this would require that you configure the user's MAC as a VPN peer of the NSX Edge. One logistical problem with this is knowing up front the MAC's IP. Or what if she doesn't have an IPsec VPN client installed in the MAC? Or she doesn't know the pre-share key to establish the IPsec VPN connection? These are some of the challenges of using IPsec VPN to provide connectivity for remote users. Using IPsec VPNs to provide remote user connectivity many times entails a certain level of technical skill on the user's part. Employees at many companies use many versions of OS in their desktops, laptops, tablets, and smartphones. Managing, installing, and supporting many versions of IPsec VPN clients can be a logistical nightmare.

VMware only supports IPsec VPN for site-site VPN.

Secure Sockets Layer (SSL) VPN was designed to provide a secure communications channel for end users without the need of having to use a VPN client. By default, SSL VPN uses TCP port 443, and the only requirement for a user to establish an SSL VPN is to have access to a web browser. By using the web browser to establish the SSL VPN, the corporate resources the user is allowed to access are displayed as links and shortcuts in a website. The resources are not stored in the remote users' computer thus providing enhanced security.

In case you have not noticed it by now, NSX's implementation of SSL VPN is called SSL VPN-Plus. The NSX Edge can provide web-based SSL VPN access and client-based SSL VPN access, both over IPv4 or IPv6, for up to 50 active sessions.

There are SSL VPN clients that provide additional corporate access beyond what the browser can provide, but these SSL VPN clients are easier to deploy and configure compared to IPsec VPN clients. The NSX SSL VPN client is called the SSL VPN-Plus client. The SSL VPN-Plus client is downloaded from the NSX Edge via the web browser and installed on the user's computer. SSL VPN-Plus supports these operating systems:

- Windows XP and later

- MAC OS Tiger and later

- Linux with TCL-TK for UI, otherwise using CLI

When using SSL VPN without an SSL VPN-Plus client, the user is redirected by the NSX Edge to a web portal that contains the corporate resources the user can access. If using the SSL VPN-Plus client, the user is allowed to access network segments identified in the NSX Edge, similar to how an IPsec VPN is configured to allow certain networks over the IPsec VPN tunnel.

Configure SSL VPN-Plus

Configuring SSL VPN-Plus in the NSX Edge is a bit more involved than configuring an IPsec VPN; however, this is mostly a one-time configuration done by the enterprise or NSX administrator. Configuring web-access mode SSL VPN-Plus is done slightly differently from the way the client-access mode SSL VPN-Plus is configured. Client-access mode SSL VPN-Plus is also called network-access mode. Table 13-5 shows the components that need to be configured for web access mode and network access mode.

Table 13-5   SSL VPN-Plus Components

Component	Description	Web Access Mode	Network Access Mode
Enable SSL VPN-Plus Service	Enables the SSL VPN service in the NSX Edge	Yes	Yes
Create Web Resource	Configures the web page users will be redirected to	Yes	No
SSL VPN-Plus Server Settings	Configures the IPv4/IPv6 and encryption settings for SSL VPN-Plus	Yes	Yes
Authentication	Configures the user authentication methods for SSL VPN-Plus	Yes	Yes
Add Local User	Adds local username accounts	Optional	Optional
Add Login Script	Adds actions to be taken when users log in	Optional	Optional
Portal Customization	Changes the look of the SSL VPN-Plus portal	Optional	Optional
Add Installation Package	Configures the settings for installing the SSL VPN-Plus client	No	Yes
Add IP Pool	Creates an IP pool to assign addresses to the SSL VPN-Plus clients	No	Yes
Add Private Network	Identifies the networks the users have access to with the SSL VPN-Plus client	No	Yes

To configure SSL VPN-Plus, you must configure three things: Server Settings, Web Resources, and Authentication.

SSL VPN-Plus Server Settings

Let's go over the steps needed to configure web access mode SSL VPN-Plus. We mostly cover the mandatory components required to get web access mode to work.

Step 1.   From the NSX Edges view, double-click the NSX Edge that will be configured for IPsec VPN.

Step 2.   Go to **Manage > SSL VPN-Plus** and select **Server Settings**.

Step 3.   Click **Change** and wait for the Change Server Settings Wizard to open.

Step 4.   Select one of the uplink interfaces for the IPv4 address. If using IPv6, select the uplink interface with the IPv6 address.

Step 5.   Select the port number to use. Unless you have strong reasons to change it, leave the TCP port number as 443.

Step 6.   Select the encryption to use. The options are

- AES128-SHA

- AES256-SHA

- DES-CBC3-SHA

Step 7.   Select the digital certificate to use.

Step 8.   The configuration should look similar to Figure 13-9. Click **OK**.

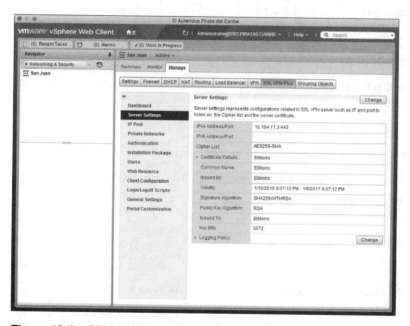

Figure 13-9   SSL VPN-Plus server settings

Creating a Web Resource

A Web Resource is the service that is presented to the SSL VPN-Plus users. To create a Web Resource, follow these steps:

Step 1.   Select Web Resource and click the green **+** icon. This is where you configure the services the SSL VPN users have access to after they authenticate.

Step 2.   Wait for the Add Web Resource Wizard to open.

Step 3.   Enter a name for the web page.

Step 4.   Enter the URL for the web page.

Step 5.   Enter an HTTP Method. The Options are GET and POST.

Step 6.   Enter the HTTP Query to execute against the server hosting the service you are making available to the authenticated users.

Step 7.   Enter a description.

Step 8.   Enable the Web Resource.

Step 9.   Click **OK**.

Step 10.   Repeat steps 1 through 9 for additional Web Resources.

Configuring Authentication

Follow these steps to configure the Authentication method used to authenticate the SSL VPN-Plus users.

Step 1.   Select Authentication and click the green **+** icon.

Step 2.   Wait for the Add Authentication Server Wizard to open.

Step 3.   In Authentication Type select the type of authentication to use:

    a. If using AD or LDAP, complete the fields in Table 13-6.

Table 13-6   AD and LDAP Authentication Fields

Field	Description	Required
Enable SSL	Enables an SSL channel to the Active Directory or LDAP server.	No
IP Address	The IP address of the AD or LDAP server.	Yes
Port	The port number to communicate with the AD or LDAP server. The default port number for LDAP over SSL (LDAPS) is TCP 636. If no SSL is enabled the default port is TCP 389.	Yes
Timeout	The amount of seconds the Edge waits for the AD or LDAP to respond. If left blank, the timeout is set to 0 seconds (no timeout).	No
Status	Enables or disables the authentication method.	Yes
Search Base	The starting location in the Active Directory or LDAP hierarchy for searching.	Yes

Field	Description	Required
Bind DN	The users permitted to search the AD or LDAP within the Search Base.	Yes
Bind Password	The password to authenticate to the AD or LDAP.	Yes
Login Attribute Name	Name attribute against which the user's username is matched.	Yes
Search Filter	AD or LDAP Attributed Operator Value to use to filter searches.	Yes
Use This Server for Secondary Authentication	If checked, the AD or LDAP server is used for secondary authentication.	No
Terminate Session if Authentication Fails	Close the session if the user fails authentication.	No

b. If using RADIUS, complete the fields in Table 13-7.

Table 13-7 RADIUS Authentication Fields

Field	Description	Required
IP Address	The IP address of the RADIUS server.	Yes
Port	The port number to communicate with the RADIUS server. The default port number for TCP 1812.	Yes
Timeout	The amount of seconds the Edge waits for the RADIUS to respond. If left blank, the timeout is set to 0 seconds (no timeout).	No
Status	Enables or disables the authentication method.	Yes
Secret	The password to authenticate to the RADIUS server.	Yes
NAS IP Address	The IP address to be used for RADIUS attribute-4.	No
Retry Count	The number of times to contact a nonresponding RADIUS server before authentication fails.	Yes
Use This Server for Secondary Authentication	If checked, the RADIUS server is used for secondary authentication.	No
Terminate Session if Authentication Fails	Close the session if the user fails authentication.	No

c. If using RSA-ACE, complete the fields in Table 13-8.

Table 13-8   RSA-ACE Authentication Fields

Field	Description	Required
Timeout	The amount of seconds the Edge waits for the RSA server to respond. If left blank, the timeout is set to 0 seconds (no timeout).	No
Configuration File	Upload the sdconf.rec file obtained from the RSA Authentication Manager.	Yes
Source IP Address	The IP address of one of the Edge's uplink interfaces through which the RSA server is reachable.	No
Use This Server for Secondary Authentication	If checked, the RSA server is used for secondary authentication.	No
Terminate Session if Authentication Fails	Close the session if the user fails authentication.	No

> **d.** If using Local, complete the fields in Table 13-9. At least one local user should have been created for this option to work.

Table 13-9   Local Authentication Fields

Field	Description	Required
Enable Password Policy	Enables the password policy options.	No
Password Length	If editable, sets the character length of the passwords.	Yes
Minimum # of character types	Select the minimum number of alphabets, digits, and special characters passwords should have.	No
Password Should not Contain User ID	If checked, passwords can't have the username.	No
Password Expires In	Number of days before password expires.	Yes
Expiry Notification In	Number of days to notify the user the passwords will expire.	Yes
Enable Account Lockout Policy	Enables account lockout policy options.	No
Retry Count	If editable, the number of times a user can enter an incorrect password.	Yes
Retry Duration	The window size, in minutes, in which the user enters the number of incorrect passwords entered in Retry Count.	Yes

Field	Description	Required
Lockout Duration	The number of days the user account will remain locked.	Yes
Status	Enables or disables the authentication method.	Yes
Use This Server for Secondary Authentication	If checked, the RSA server is used for secondary authentication.	No
Terminate Session if Authentication Fails	Close the session if the user fails authentication.	No

Step 4. Figure 13-10 shows a sample configuration for AD authentication, and Figure 13-11 shows a sample configuration for Local authentication. Click **OK**.

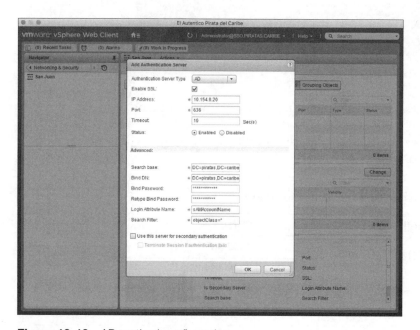

Figure 13-10   AD method configuration

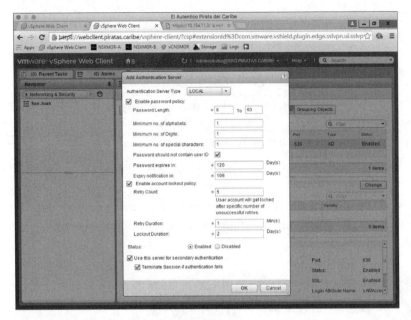

Figure 13-11   Local method configuration

Step 5.   Repeat steps 1 through 4 for additional authentication methods.

Table 13-10 is a bonus table to list the default ports used by the different authentication methods.

Table 13-10   Authentication Methods Default Ports

Authentication Method	Port
Active Directory	TCP 389
LDAP	TCP 389
Active Directory over SSL	TCP 636
LDAP over SSL	TCP 636
RADIUS	TCP 1812

Enable SSL VPN-Plus Service

To enable the SSL VPN-Plus service, select the Dashboard and click **Enabled**.

You are done. The users should be able to open a browser and go to https://YOUR_
EDGE_IP_ADDRESS_or_FQDN/ to reach the login page, as shown in Figure 13-
12. You can make some changes to this portal from the Portal Customization view
in SSL VPN-Plus. We do not cover that section.

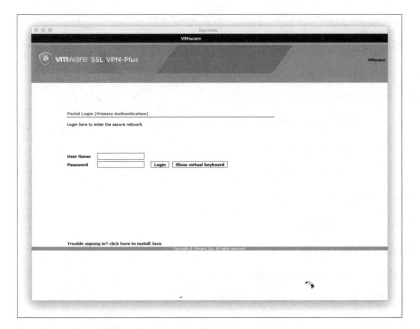

Figure 13-12   SSL VPN-Plus portal

Now let's cover the components required to get network-access mode to work. We do not cover steps already covered in the web-access mode. Review Table 13-5 to see which steps we cover.

Adding the Installation Package

To add the Installation Package, follow these steps:

Step 1.   Go to **Manage > SSL VPN-Plus** and select **Installation Package**.

Step 2.   Click the green **+** icon and wait for the Add Installation Package Wizard to open.

Step 3.   Enter a profile name.

Step 4.   In Gateway, enter the IP of the NSX Edge used to establish the SSL VPN connection.

- This should be the IP of an Uplink interface.

- An FQDN may be used instead of the IP.

- You can change the default port number of 443 for SSL.

Step 5.   Select the OS that is supported:

■ The options are Windows, Linux, and MAC.

■ All three OS can be selected.

Step 6.   Enter a description.

Step 7.   Enable the package.

Step 8.   Choose the Installation Parameter options. The options are

  a. Start Client on Logon

  b. Hide Client System Tray Icon

  c. Allow Remember Password

  d. Create Desktop Icon

  e. Enable Silent Mode Installation

  f. Enable Silent Mode Operation

  g. Hide SSL Client Network Adapter

  h. Server Security Certificate Validation

Step 9.   The configuration should look similar to Figure 13-13. Click **OK**.

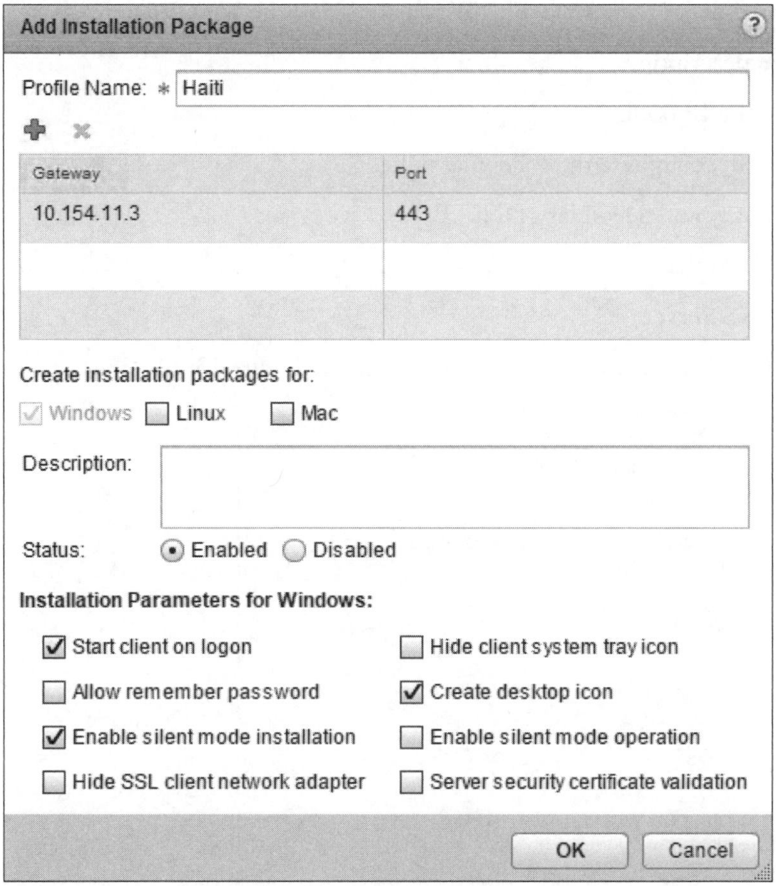

Figure 13-13   SSL VPN-Plus Installation Package

Step 10.   Repeat steps 1 through 9 for additional Installation Packages.

Adding an IP Pool

Follow these steps to add the IP pool:

Step 1.   Select **IP Pool**.

Step 2.   Click the green **+** icon and wait for the Add IP Pool Wizard to open.

Step 3.   Enter the first IP in the IP Pool range.

Step 4.   Enter the last IP in the IP Pool range.

Step 5.   Enter the default Netmask.

Step 6.   Enter the default gateway. This IP is assigned to the NSX Edge.

Step 7.   Enter a description.

Step 8.   Enable the IP pool.

Step 9.   Optionally, complete the following fields:

- Primary and Secondary DNS
- DNS Suffix
- WINS Server

Step 10.   Click **OK**. Your configuration should look like Figure 13-14.

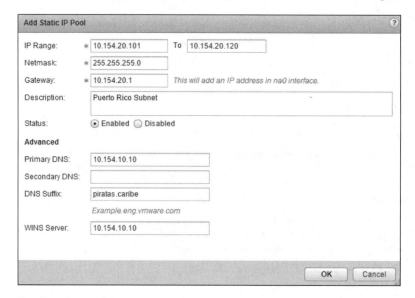

Figure 13-14   Static IP pool

Step 11.   Repeat steps 1 through 10 to add additional IP pools.

Adding Private Networks

Follow these steps to add private networks:

Step 1.   Select Private Networks.

Step 2.   Click the green **+** icon and wait for the Add Private Network Wizard to open.

Step 3.   Enter the subnet and CIDR that should be accessible to the SSL VPN-Plus Client users.

Step 4.   Enter a description.

Step 5.   Select how the subnet should be accessible to the SSL VPN Client users.

- **Over Tunnel**: The network is accessible to the SSL VPN client users over the SSL VPN.

- **Bypass Tunnel**: The network is accessible to the SSL VPN client users outside the SSL VPN. It is locally accessible to the users.

Step 6.   Select whether to use TCP Optimization.

An SSL tunnel encapsulates user traffic with a new TCP/IP header, thus every SSL VPN packet has two TCP/IP headers: the outer nonencrypted SSL VPN header and the inner encrypted header. This is fine and dandy until a packet needs to be retransmitted, which may lead to a condition called TCP-over-TCP meltdown. I won't go into the details here on what it all means, just trust me when I say that it is not a good thing. (Actually, I have never heard of anything with *meltdown* in the name that is a good thing!) The NSX Edge eliminates the problem of the TCP-over-TCP meltdown by using TCP Optimization over the SSL VPN.

Step 7.   If you want to restrict access to the subnet to some number of ports, enter them in the Ports field. If the field is left empty there will be restriction imposed on the user.

Step 8.   Enable the Private Network. Your configuration should look like Figure 13-15.

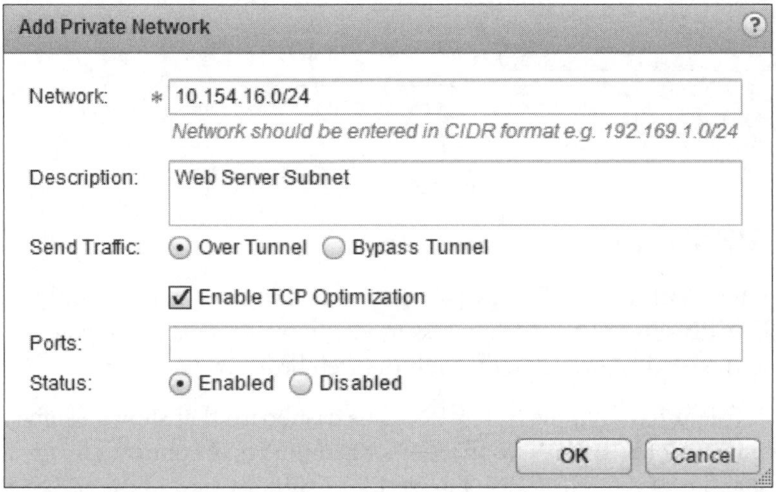

Figure 13-15   Private network

Step 9.   Click **OK**.

Step 10.   Repeat steps 1 through 9 to add more private networks.

We are now all done with network-access mode configuration. The users should be able to open a browser and go to https://YOUR_EDGE_IP_ADDRESS_or_FQDN/ to reach the login page. From the portal, the user goes to the Full Access page to download and install the SSL VPN-Plus client. The installation follows the settings chosen in the Add Installation Package steps. Once the client is installed, the user can connect using it as shown in Figure 13-16.

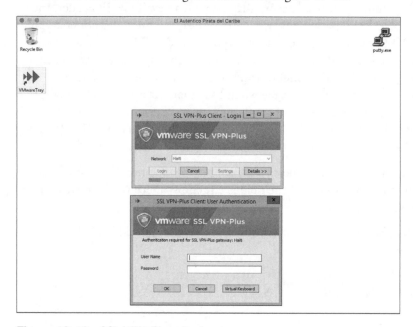

Figure 13-16   SSL VPN-Plus client

Verifying SSL VPN-Plus

Let's get the pinging out of the way first by pointing something out: You can only use pings with SSL VPN-Plus in network-access mode. In web-access mode you only have access to the services available through the web browser.

The vSphere Web Client has a simple SSL VPN-Plus dashboard that shows a summary view of the number of SSL VPN connections, the number of connection failures, and the throughput of the SSL VPN. Figure 13-17 shows a view of the SSL VPN-Plus Dashboard.

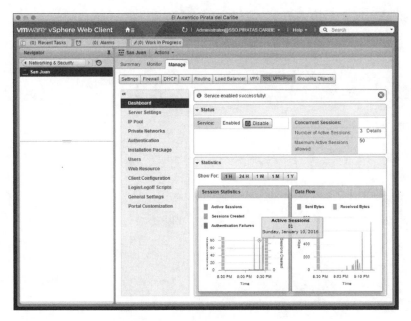

Figure 13-17   SSL VPN-Plus Dashboard

In Status, if you click the **Details** link next to the Number of Active Sessions field, the Active Sessions pane opens where you can see detailed information of the users connected to the SSL VPN-Plus, as shown in Figure 13-18.

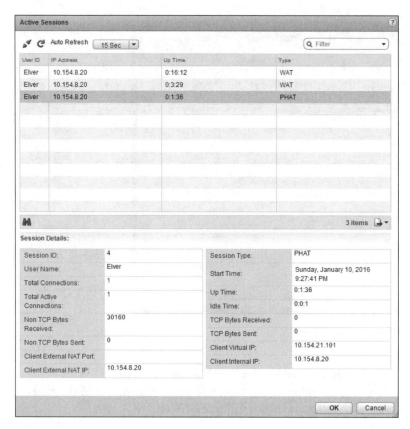

Figure 13-18 SSL VPN-Plus active sessions

From the NSX Edge CLI, you can enter the command **show service sslvpn-plus** to verify that the SSL VPN-Plus is running. The command **show service sslvpn-plus active** shows the number of active sessions, as shown in Figure 13-19.

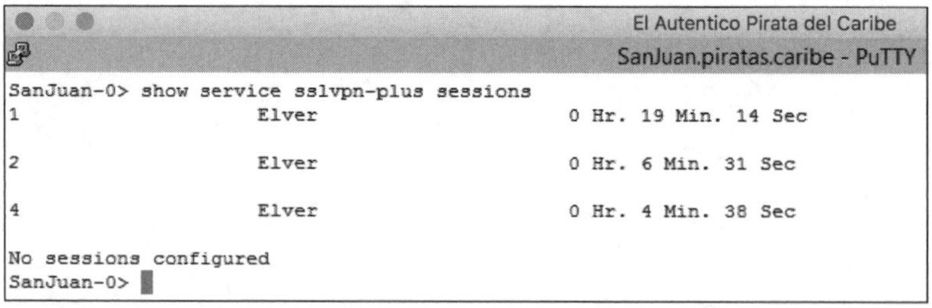

```
                                          El Autentico Pirata del Caribe
                                          SanJuan.piratas.caribe - PuTTY
SanJuan-0> show service sslvpn-plus sessions
1               Elver               0 Hr. 19 Min. 14 Sec

2               Elver               0 Hr. 6 Min. 31 Sec

4               Elver               0 Hr. 4 Min. 38 Sec

No sessions configured
SanJuan-0> █
```

Figure 13-19 Output of command **show service sslvpn-plus active**

Exam Preparation Tasks

Review All the Key Topics

Review the most important topics from inside the chapter, noted with the Key Topic icon in the outer margin of the page. Table 13-11 lists these key topics and the page numbers where each is found.

Table 13-11   Key Topics for Chapter 13

Key Topic Element	Description	Page Number
Table 13-2	IPsec Provided Security Features	382
Paragraph	Tunnels are created per Pair of Subnets	383
List	The items that are part of the security proposal during IKE Phase 1	384
Paragraph	DH creates a unique secret key	385
Table 13-4	IPsec VPN Encryption Algorithms	390
Paragraph	VMware only supports site-site IPSec VPN	395
Paragraph	NSX SSL VPN is called SSP VNP-Plus	395
Paragraph	The SSL VPN-Plus client is downloaded from the NSX Edge	395

Complete Tables and Lists from Memory

Download and print a copy of Appendix C, "Memory Tables," (found on the book's website), or at least the section for this chapter, and complete the tables and lists from memory. Appendix D, "Memory Tables Answer Key," also on the website, includes the completed tables and lists so you can check your work.

Define Key Terms

Define the following key terms from this chapter, and check your answers in the glossary:

IPsec VPN, site-site IPsec VPN, IPsec VPN peers, IKE, Diffie-Hellman, SSL VPN, SSL VPN-Plus

This chapter covers all or part of the following VCP6-NV exam blueprint topics:

- **Objective 6.1**—Configure and Manage Logical Load Balancing
- **Objective 6.3**—Configure and Manage DHCP/DNS/NAT
- **Objective 7.1**—Configure and Administer Logical Firewall Services
- **Objective 9.5**—Administer Logging

CHAPTER 14

NSX Edge Network Services and Security

You have deployed an NSX network using the features covered in this book up to this point. You feel good with yourself. Really GOOD. Now you want to take it up a notch to wow your boss (she is already impressed with you, by the way). You ponder if the best way to go is to use NSX to replace some network functions being done by the other network appliances, such as NAT for the web server. Or would it be best to make the deployments of virtual workloads more dynamic by using the load balancing features of the NSX Edge? Or perhaps do them both plus some firewalling here and there. So many ways you can continue to shine by using NSX. Decisions, decisions…

This chapter covers the additional network and security features that NSX has to offer via the NSX Edge. Similar to Chapter 13, "NSX Edge VPN Services," these features have been a staple in networking and security for years, and there isn't much more that could be added in this book regarding those technologies. This chapter provides a quick overview of the features, as needed, to show how the NSX Edge implements those features and how to configure them.

Do I Know This Already?

The "Do I Know This Already?" quiz allows you to assess whether you should read this entire chapter or simply jump to the "Exam Preparation Tasks" section for review. If you are in doubt, read the entire chapter. Table 14-1 outlines the major headings in this chapter and the corresponding "Do I Know This Already?" quiz questions. You can find the answers in Appendix A, "Answers to the 'Do I Know This Already?' Quizzes."

Table 14-1 Headings and Questions

Foundation Topic Section	Questions Covered in This Section
Network Address Translation	1-3
NSX Edge Load Balancer	4-7
NSX Edge Logical Firewall	8-10

1. What is the name of a NAT that changes the source IP of a packet?
   a. INAT
   b. SNAT
   c. DNAT
   d. PNAT

2. What is the name of a NAT that changes the destination IP of a packet?
   a. INAT
   b. SNAT
   c. DNAT
   d. PNAT

3. Which two NAT rules can be configured in the NSX Edge? (Choose two.)
   a. INAT
   b. DNAT
   c. PNAT
   d. SNAT

4. What is an NSX load balancer virtual server?
   a. The mapping of the VIP with a server pool and an application profile
   b. A virtual machine with an installed operating system
   c. The servers that are members of the NSX load balancer server pool
   d. The servers that are members of the NSX load balancer application profile

5. What type of load balancing is not supported by the NSX Edge?
   a. Load balancing based on the UDP header
   b. Load balancing based on the IGMP header
   c. Load balancing for applications communicating over HTTP
   d. Load balancing for applications communicating over HTTPS

6. What is the load balancing mode the NSX Edge is configured for if an SNAT is done in the user traffic?
   a. Layer 4 load balancing mode
   b. Transparent mode
   c. Layer 7 load balancing mode
   d. Proxy mode

7. Which persistence method is not supported for HTTPS?

    a. Source IP

    b. Destination URI

    c. Cookie

    d. SSL Session ID

8. Which type of security does the NSX Edge firewall provide? (Choose two.)

    a. Layer 2 firewall

    b. Layer 3 firewall

    c. Layer 4 firewall

    d. Layer 7 firewall

9. When processing traffic, where are NSX Edge firewall rules matched against traffic?

    a. NSX Edge firewall rules are matched against ingress traffic of the selected Edge vNIC.

    b. NSX Edge firewall rules are matched against egress traffic of the selected Edge vNIC.

    c. By default, NSX Edge firewall rules are matched against all traffic after any configured NAT rules are applied.

    d. By default, NSX Edge firewall rules are matched against all traffic coming in the Edge.

10. If a firewall rule's source is configured to match a logical switch, how does the NSX Edge match traffic to the firewall rule?

    a. The NSX Edge receives the IP address of all vNICs connected to the logical switch from vCenter and uses these IPs to match traffic to the firewall rule.

    b. The NSX Edge receives the IP address of all vNICs connected to the logical switch from NSX Manager and uses these IPs to match traffic to the firewall rule.

    c. The NSX Edge receives the IP address of all vNICs connected to the logical switch from the ESXi hosts and uses these IPs to match traffic to the firewall rule.

    d. The NSX Edge receives the IP address of all vNICs connected to the logical switch from the NSX Controllers and uses these IPs to match traffic to the firewall rule.

Foundation Topics

Network Address Translation

A Network Address Translation (NAT) device (typically a router) changes either the source or destination IP of an IP packet. If the NAT router changes the source IP, then the NAT is called a *Source NAT (SNAT)*. If the NAT router changes the destination IP, then the NAT is called a *Destination NAT (DNAT)*. The underlying logic in SNAT is rather simple: If an ingress packet arrives in the router matching a particular source IP, the source IP is changed for a predetermined one and then the packet is sent on its way. The same logic applies if doing DNAT. The NSX Edge supports SNAT and DNAT.

The configurations for applying NAT are done via NAT rules. For NAT rules to be effective, an interface must be identified, and the direction of the packet flow is based on this interface. Packets arriving at this interface are considered ingress packets, and packets going out of this interface are considered egress packets. If an SNAT rule is applied to an interface, the source IP address of the ingress packet is changed. If a DNAT rule is applied to an interface, the destination IP of the egress packet is changed. The NAT router keeps a NAT table of all translated IPs so return traffic in the flow can have the NAT reversed. The return traffic must come through the interface that has the NAT rule that was applied to the flow.

NAT is designed to be transparent to the end user. An SNAT rule is usually applied when the source subnet in the packet should remain unreachable by the destination. A typical application of an SNAT rule is to allow a virtual workload to initiate a flow with an entity outside its subnet. A DNAT rule is usually applied when the actual destination of a packet should remain unreachable by the source. A DNAT rule is required for traffic that originates from entities outside the subnet of the virtual workload.

To configure a DNAT rule in the NSX Edge, follow these steps:

Step 1.   From the **NSX Edges** view, double-click the NSX Edge that will be configured with NAT.

Step 2.   Go to **Manage > NAT**.

Step 3.   Click the green **+** icon, select **Add DNAT Rule**, and wait for the Add DNAT Rule Wizard to open.

Step 4.   In the **Applied On** field, select the interface to apply the NAT rule.

Step 5.   In **Original IP/Range**, enter the destination IP or destination IP range to translate.

This is matched against the destination IP in the packets.

This field may include one of the following formats:

- **IP**: Example 10.10.62.3

- **IP Range**: Example 10.10.62.3-10.10.62.31

- **IP Subnet and CIDR**: Example 10.10.62.0/24

- The keyword **Any** to include all IPs

Step 6.   (Optional) In **Protocol**, select the protocol that triggers the enforcement of this NAT rule.

(Optional) If you selected a protocol in step 5, you may enter the port number or range in **Original Port/Range**.

Step 7.   In **Translated IP/Range**, enter the IP or IP range to use for translation.

This field may include one of the following formats:

- **IP**: Example 10.10.62.3

- **IP Range**: Example 10.10.62.3-10.10.62.31

- **IP Subnet and CIDR**: Example 10.10.62.0/24

Step 8.   (Optional) **In Translated Port/Range** enter the ports to translate to.

Step 9.   Enter an optional description.

Step 10.   Check the **Enabled** box to enable the rule.

Step 11.   Check the **Enable Logging** box to enable logging for this rule.

Figure 14-1 shows a sample configuration for a DNAT rule. Click **OK**.

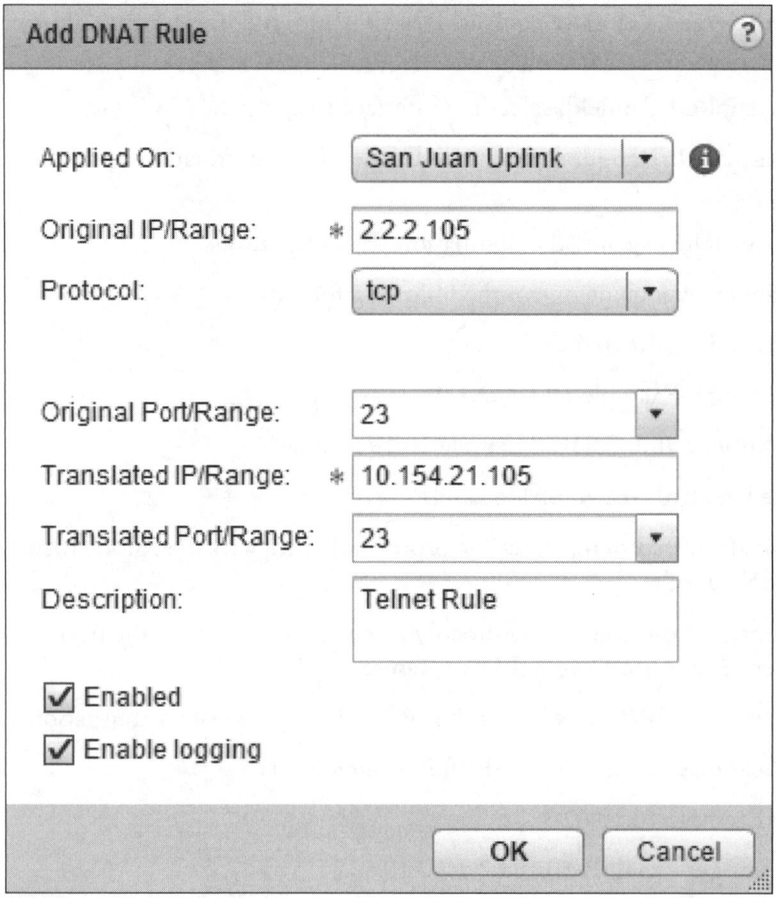

Figure 14-1   New DNAT rule

Step 12.   Click **Publish**.

To configure an SNAT rule in the NSX Edge follow these steps:

Step 1.   Go to **Manage > NAT**.

Step 2.   Click the green **+** icon, select **Add SNAT Rule**, and wait for the Add SNAT Rule Wizard to open.

Step 3.   In the **Applied On** field, select the interface to apply the NAT rule.

Step 4.   In **Original Source IP/Range**, enter the source IP or source IP range to translate.

This is matched against the source IP in the packets.

This field may include one of the following formats:

- **IP**: Example 10.10.62.3

- **IP Range**: Example 10.10.62.3-10.10.62.31

- **IP Subnet and CIDR**: Example 10.10.62.0/24

- The keyword **Any** to include all IPs

Step 5.   In **Translated Source IP/Range**, enter the IP or IP range to use for translation.

This field may include one of the following formats:

- **IP**: Example 10.10.62.3

- **IP Range**: Example 10.10.62.3-10.10.62.31

- **IP Subnet and CIDR**: Example 10.10.62.0/24

If the number of IPs in step 4 is larger than the number of available IPs in step 5, then NAT overload would take place. In NAT overload (also referred to as One to Many or Many to Many NAT), in addition to doing NAT on the Source IP, NAT would be done to the Source Port number. This allows multiple source IP addresses to use the same NAT source IP.

Step 6.   Enter an optional description.

Step 7.   Check the **Enabled** box to enable the rule.

Step 8.   Check the **Enable Logging** box to enable logging for this rule.

Figure 14-2 shows a sample configuration for an SNAT rule. Click **OK**.

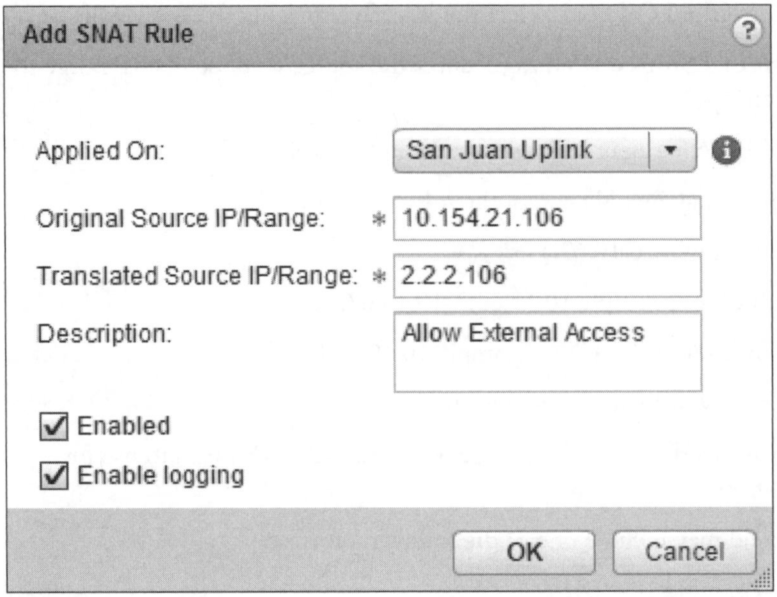

Add SNAT Rule   ?

Applied On: San Juan Uplink   ▾   ⓘ

Original Source IP/Range: * 10.154.21.106

Translated Source IP/Range: * 2.2.2.106

Description: Allow External Access

☑ Enabled
☑ Enable logging

                                    OK   Cancel

Figure 14-2   New SNAT rule

Step 9.   Click **Publish**.

In SNAT, if the number of Original Source IPs is more than the number of Translated Source IPs, the NSX Edge does Port NAT. Port NAT, sometimes referred to as pNAT or NAT Overload, changes the source port number while allowing multiple sources to use the same translated source IP.

NSX Edge Load Balancer

Load balancers started their lives as super-duper NAT entities. They provided a simple load balancing solution for applications. If you had a web server farm hosting the same page, how else do you balance the influx of page requests so that one of the web servers wouldn't be overloaded while you had other web servers with plenty of available capacity to accept new requests? Early load balancers were simple NAT servers or routers doing One to Many DNAT. That is, the destination IP in the packet was changed by the load balancer to one of the translated IPs, which were the IPs of the web servers. New connections were then round robin among the load balanced servers.

Fast-forward to the present day. Load balancers have come a long way from those humble beginnings. They continue to do some sort of DNAT but can be very granular in terms of how traffic flows are apportioned among the balanced workloads and have the capability to look into Layer 7 of the packet to make even more efficient load balancing decisions. In addition, load balancers can also terminate connections on behalf of the workloads. This feature is often used for SSL, where the load balancer offloads the SSL termination from the web servers and establishes a new connection to the web server. The new connection may be an SSL connection or a non-SSL connection.

At the basic level, load balancers work by having a virtual IP (VIP) that is the destination IP of all traffic going to the particular service, such as our web page example. The VIP is mapped in the load balancer to an application that represents the service, called the *application profile*. The application profile is load balanced to a list of servers running the workload, called the server pool. The IPs in the server pool act as the equivalent of the translated destination IPs in a DNAT rule. Traffic that matches the criteria included in the application profile triggers ingress traffic to be load balanced.

Once a VIP is mapped to an application profile and server pool, it is called a *virtual server*. The NSX Edge can have virtual servers that trigger load balancing based on Layer 4 information, TCP and UDP, Layer 7 information, and HTTP and HTTPS. Table 14-2 shows the maximum number of VIPs, server pools, and servers that the Edge supports.

Table 14-2 NSX Edge Load Balancer Support

Object	Maximum Support
Virtual IPs	64
Server pools	64
Servers	2048
Servers (per server pool)	32

Figure 14-3 shows an example of an NSX Edge load balancer. The Edge has a VIP of 10.10.50.4, a server pool that includes IPs 10.10.11.101, 10.10.11.102, and 10.10.11.103, and an application profile that matches destination TCP ports 80 or 8080. In Figure 14-3, any user that wants to reach a web page on ports 80 or 8080 at 10.10.50.4 is redirected to one of the three servers in the server pool. The redirection happens by doing a DNAT on the user packets. The source IP of the packets is not altered.

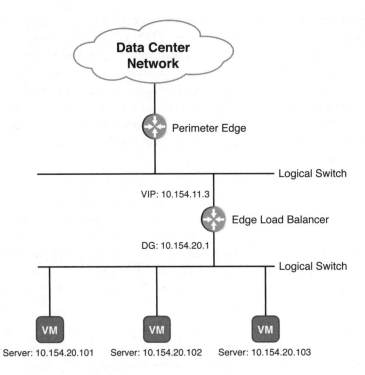

Figure 14-3 NSX Edge load balancer

The load balancer configuration shown in Figure 14-3 is called *In-Line* or *Transparent Mode*. This is the traditional load balancer setup, where one of the load balancer's interfaces is exposed to the "outside" with the VIP, and a second interface is directly connected to the segment where the server pool members reside. By being directly connected to the same segment as the servers in the server pool, they require that the Edge load balancer be their default gateway. Yes, you read that correctly: When deploying the load balancer in Transparent Mode, the Edge must have an interface directly connected to the segment where the members in the server pool are located, *and* the Edge must be the default gateway for the servers.

An alternate deployment to Transparent Mode is *One-Arm* or *Proxy Mode*. In this configuration, the NSX Edge load balancer uses a single interface, and the logical router may be used as the default gateway for the members in the server pool, as shown in Figure 14-4. The VIP is in the same subnet as the server pool servers' subnet.

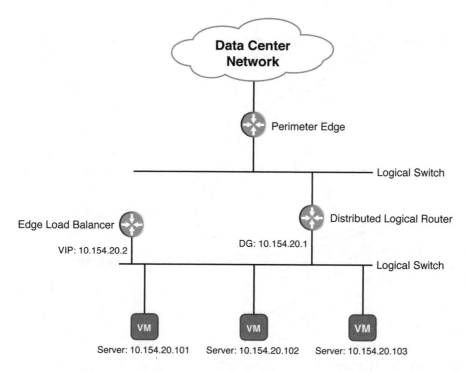

Figure 14-4   NSX Edge load balancer in Proxy Mode

In Proxy Mode a user sends application requests to the VIP, and the Edge does DNAT to redirect the traffic to one of the members in the server pool. However, since the members in the server pool have a default gateway that is not the Edge, the Edge must also do an SNAT on the user traffic to force return traffic from the members in the server pool to go through the Edge. The translated SNAT IP the NSX Edge uses is the VIP. Figure 14-5 shows our friend Marcos from the San Juan office opening a web page being load balanced by the Edge in Proxy Mode in the Santo Domingo Data Center.

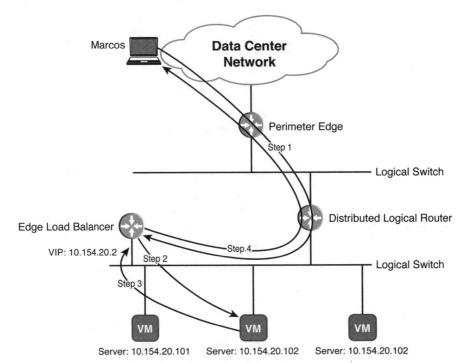

Figure 14-5   Edge load balancer Proxy Mode traffic flow

1. Marcos opens a browser to connect to the website http://blog.senasosa.com. The DNS Server resolves the page to the VIP of 10.10.11.2.

2. The load balancer receives the browser traffic, matches the request to an application profile, and forwards the traffic to the next available server in the server pool.

   a. The Edge does SNAT on Marcos's IP, replacing it for the VIP.

   b. The Edge does DNAT on the VIP, replacing it for the IP of the selected web server.

   c. The decision on which server to select depends on the load balancing algorithm configured in the server pool. The NSX Edge can use six different load balancing algorithms:

      ■ **Round Robin**: New flows are sent to the servers in the server pool in a sequential order.

      ■ **Least Connections**: The server with the least number of connections is selected.

      ■ **IP Hash**: A hash is computed on the user's IP, the source IP of the packet, and used to select a server.

- **Uniform Resource Identifier (URI)**: A hash is computed on the left part of the URI (the left of the question mark), divided by the total weight of the running members in the server pool, and used to select a server. URI load balancing hash is only supported for Layer 7 load balancing.

- **Uniform Resource Locator (URL)**: A hash is computed on the left part of the URL, divided by the total weight of the running members in the server pool and used to select a server. URL load balancing hash is only supported for Layer 7 load balancing.

- **HTTP Header**: A hash is computed based on the HTTP header. HTTP header load balancing is only supported in Layer 7 load balancing.

3. The selected web server receives the traffic and responds.

   a. The web server sees the traffic coming from the VIP.

   b. The load balancer can use the *x-forwarded-for* HTTP header to let the web server know the traffic is not being sourced from the VIP.

4. The Edge receives the return traffic, undoes the SNAT and DNAT, and forwards the traffic to Marcos.

If the NSX Edge is configured with firewall rules and a Layer 4 load balancer, the Layer 4 VIP is processed before the firewall rules, thus no need to add an Allow Firewall rule.

So this covers the basics of what an NSX Edge load balancer does. Now let's talk about other features the NSX Edge load balancer supports. There is this thing called *Service Monitor*, also referred to as *Health Check*, where the load balancer monitors the up state of the members in the server pool. If a particular member is determined to be unavailable, the Edge removes the member from the server pool; actually, the server is not removed from the pool per se, but rather marked as *down*, so it won't be selected for any new traffic flows. Table 14-3 shows the Service Monitor methods the NSX Edge supports for Layer 4 and Layer 7.

Table 14-3 Health Check Methods

Method	Layer 4	Layer 7
TCP	Yes	Yes
UDP	Yes	No
ICMP	Yes	Yes

Method	Layer 4	Layer 7
GET (HTTP and HTTPS)	No	Yes
POST (HTTP and HTTPS)	No	Yes
OPTIONS (HTTP and HTTPS)	No	Yes

If the NSX Edge is configured with Edge HA, the state of the load balancing table, or persistence, is synchronized between the Active Edge and the Standby Edge if the load balancing is being done at Layer 7. Whenever the Active Edge goes down and the Standby Edge becomes the Active Edge, it retains the user session persistence by sending the user traffic to the same server(s). Table 14-4 shows the persistence states that are synced between the Active and Standby Edges.

Table 14-4   Persistence States

Protocol or Application	State
TCP	Source IP Microsoft RDP
UDP	Source IP
HTTP	Source IP Cookie
HTTPS	Source IP Cookie SSL Session ID (If SSL Passthrough is enabled)

The NSX Edge supports throttling to the virtual server and members in the server pool. Table 14-5 shows the methods the Edge can use to throttle access.

Table 14-5   Edge Load Balancer Throttle

Throttle Type	Description
Maximum Number of Connections	Configured per server in the server pool, sets the maximum number of connections to establish to a server
Connection Limit	Configured per virtual server, sets the maximum number of concurrent connections allowed
Connection Rate Limit	Configured per virtual server, sets the maximum number of new connection requests per second

One neat feature of NSX is the capability to use an NSX-registered third party's load balancer. When configured, NSX Manager pushes the load balancer configuration to the third party's load balancer rather than the NSX Edge.

Configuring the Edge Load Balancer

Now we are up to configuring the Edge to be a load balancer. Table 14-6 shows all configuration parts that can be done in the Edge and points out those that are a requirement. In this section we cover the four sections that must be configured to get a working load balancer.

Table 14-6   Edge Load Balancer Configuration Sections

Configuration Section	Description	Required
Global Configuration	Enables the load balancer	Yes
Application Profiles	Creates application profiles	Yes
Service Monitoring	Configures Health Check	No
Pools	Creates server pools	Yes
Virtual Servers	Creates virtual IP and maps to an application profile and server pool	Yes
Application Rules	Creates rules to manipulate the load balanced traffic	No

Application Profile

To create an application profile, follow these steps:

Step 1.   From the **NSX Edges** view, double-click the NSX Edge that will be configured as a **Load Balancer**.

Step 2.   Go to **Manage > Load Balancer** and select **Application Profile**.

Step 3.   Click the green **+** icon and wait for the New Profile Wizard to open.

Step 4.   Give the profile a name.

Step 5.   Select one of the load balancing methods:

   a. TCP: Load balancing is done at Layer 4. A TCP number is required.

   b. UDP: Load balancing is done at Layer 4. A UDP number is required.

   c. HTTP: Load balancing is done at Layer 7.

   d. HTTPS: Load balancing is done at Layer 7.

       i. If the servers in the server pool are terminating SSL, check the box **Enable SSL Pass-through**.

       ii. If **Enable SSL Pass-through** is not checked, the Edge does SSL termination and a digital certificate is required.

Step 6. (Optional) If doing HTTP or HTTPS load balancing, enter the URL to redirect web traffic.

Step 7. (Optional) Select the persistence to use. If cookie is chosen, enter the cookie name and the mode.

Step 8. (Optional) check the box for **Insert-X-Forwarded-For HTTP header**.

Step 9. (Optional) **Enable Pool Side SSL**.

   a. Makes the Edge start an SSL (HTTPS) connection to the selected server in the server pool. If not checked, the Edge starts an HTTP connection to the selected server in the server pool.

   b. This option is only available if the load balancer is doing the SSL termination (see step 5d, ii).

Step 10. In the **Virtual Server Certificates** and the **Server Pool, select the Certificate, CA, and Certificate Revocation List, if any**.

   a. Virtual Server Certificates are available only if the load balancer is doing the SSL termination (see step 5d, ii).

   b. If **Enable Server Pool** is checked, a digital certificate for the server pool must be selected in Pool Certificates.

Step 11. (Optional) Select the cipher to use for the SSL handshake.

   a. If none is selected, the default cipher is used.

   b. This option is only available if the load balancer is doing the SSL termination.

Step 12. (Optional) Choose if the user must authenticate.

   a. If authentication is required, the user must have a digital certificate.

   b. This option is only available if the load balancer is doing the SSL termination.

Step 13. The configuration should look similar to Figure 14-6. Click **OK**.

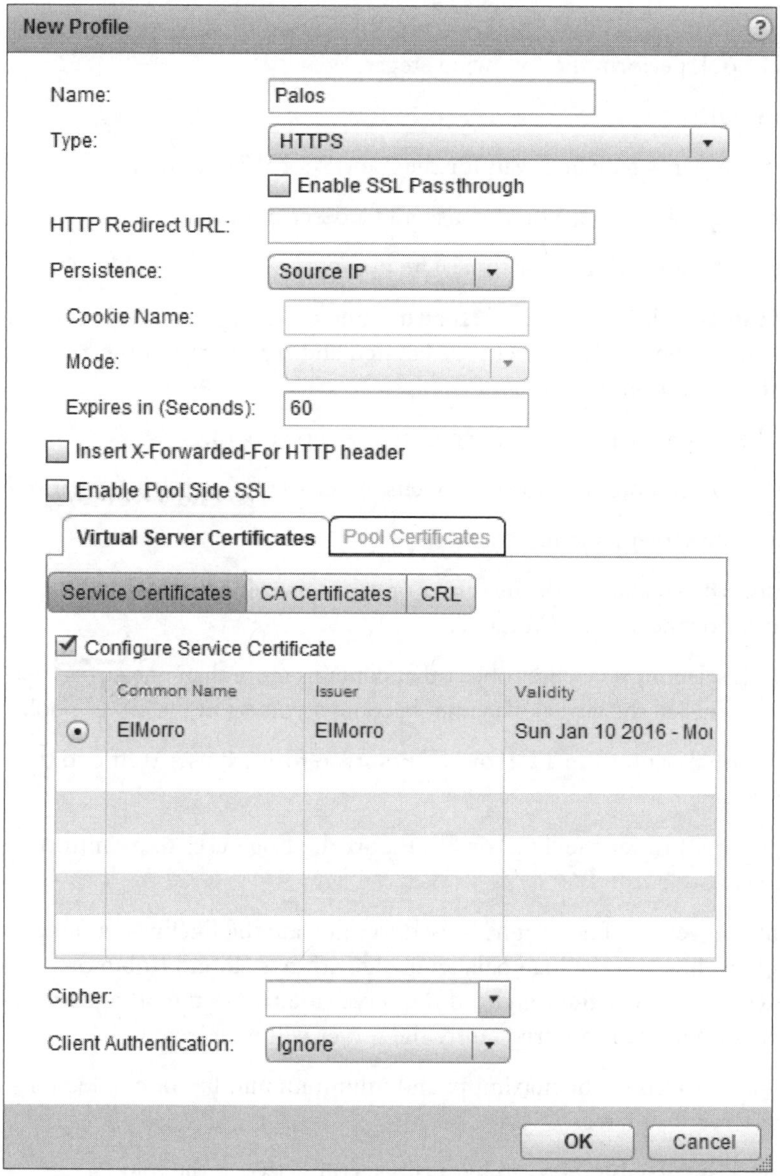

Figure 14-6   Load Balancer application profile

Step 14.   Repeat steps 3 through 13 to add more application profiles.

Server Pools

To create a server pool, perform the following steps:

Step 15.   Select **Pools**.

Step 16.   Click the green **+** icon and wait for the New Pool Wizard to open.

Step 17.   Assign the pool a name. You can also add a description.

Step 18.   Select the load-sharing algorithm. The options are listed in Table 14-4.

Step 19.   In **Monitors**, select the type of **Health Check** to do against the members in the pool. The Health Checks are created and configured in the Service Monitoring section.

Step 20.   Click the green **+** icon to add a server to the server pool.

Step 21.   In the New Member window that opens, enter the following information:

    a. Give the server a name.

    b. Enter the IP address of the server or select a vCenter object, such as a cluster or the actual VM name.

        i. If selecting a vCenter object that contains more than one virtual machine, all the virtual machines become members of the server pool.

    c. (Optional) Enter the TCP or UDP port to forward user traffic to the server.

    d. (Optional) Enter the TCP or UDP port the Edge uses to monitor the server.

    e. Enter a weight. The weight is used to calculate the likeliness a server will be chosen if the load balancing algorithm is Round Robin or URI. The higher the weight of the server relative to the other servers in the pool, the more frequently the server will be selected.

    f. (Optional) Enter the maximum and minimum number of connections the server can have.

    g. Check the **Enabled** box to have this server active in the pool.

    h. Click **OK**.

Step 22.   Repeat step 20 and 21 to add more members to the pool.

Step 23.   (Optional) Check the box for **Transparent**. If the box is checked, the Edge will be in Transparent Mode and only do DNAT on user traffic. If the box is not checked, the NSX Edge will be in Proxy Mode and do DNAT and SNAT on user traffic.

Step 24.   The configuration should look similar to Figure 14-7. Click **OK**.

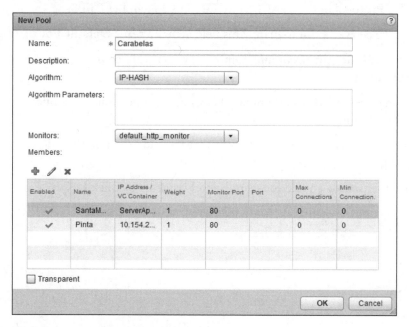

Figure 14-7   Load balancer server pool

Step 25.   Repeat steps 16 through 24 to add more server pools.

Virtual Server

To configure the virtual server, follow these steps:

Step 26.   Select **Virtual Server**.

Step 27.   Click the green **+** icon and wait for the New Virtual Server Wizard to open.

Step 28.   In the General tab, check the **Enabled** box.

Step 29.   (Optional) Enable **Acceleration**. This option is available if acceleration is enabled in the Global Configuration. When this box is checked, load balancing is done using the Layer 4 information of the packet.

Step 30.   Select the **Application Profile** to map.

Step 31.   Give the virtual server a name and description.

Step 32.   In **IP Address**, enter the VIP or select an IP from one of the Edge's interfaces.

Step 33.   Select the Protocol and enter the TCP Port the virtual server is listening to. The Protocol options are TCP, UDP, HTTP, and HTTPS.

Step 34.   Select the **Server Pool** to map. This field actually reads **Default Pool**.

Step 35.   (Optional) Enter the maximum number of concurrent connections in Connection Limit.

Step 36.   (Optional) Enter the maximum number of new connections in Connection Rate Limit.

Step 37.   (Optional) If any application rules were created, add them in the Advanced tab.

Step 38.   The configuration should look similar to Figure 14-8. Click **OK**.

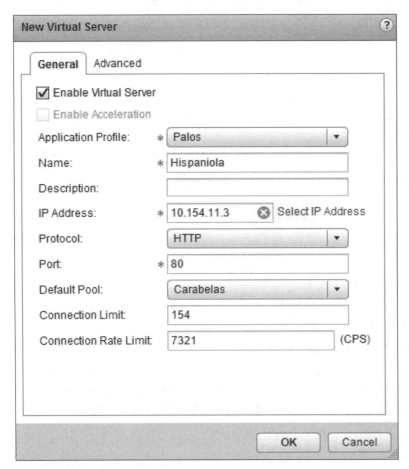

Figure 14-8   Load balancer virtual server

Step 39.   Repeat Steps 27 through 38 to add more virtual servers.

Enable Load Balancer

Finally, we need to enable the load balancer feature in the NSX Edge. To enable load balancing, as well as a few other features, follow these steps:

Step 40.   Select **Global Configuration**.

Step 41.   Click **Edit**.

Step 42.   In the opening window, check the box for Enable Load-Balancer.

Step 43.   Check the box for Enable Acceleration to only use Layer 4 information of the packet for load balancing.

Step 44.   Check the box to enable logging, and choose the log level.

Step 45.   Check the box for **Enable Service Insertion** to redirect traffic to another vendor's load balancer. You need to select the load balancer in the Service Definition, the Service Configuration, and the Service Profile, and choose the Runtime NICs.

Step 46.   Click **OK**.

NSX Edge Protocol and Port Groupings

An NSX Edge Service is a collection of Layer 3 (protocols) and Layer 4 (ports). It is a handy way of grouping related protocols, such as ICMP and IPv6, and ports, such as TCP source and destination ports, which can then be referenced in firewall rules. Examples of supported Layer 3 protocols are ARP, IPv4, IPv6, and IPX (yes, there is still some IPX out in the wild). Examples of Layer 4 protocols are TCP, UDP, and ICMP.

To create a new NSX Edge Service, follow these steps:

Step 1.   From the **NSX Edges** view, double-click the NSX Edge where the Service will be created.

Step 2.   Go to **Manage > Grouping Objects** and select **Service**.

Step 3.   Click the green **+** icon and wait for the Add Service Wizard to open.

Step 4.   Enter a unique name for the service.

Step 5.   Enter an optional description for the service.

Step 6.   In **Protocol**, use the drop-down to select the protocol desired.

Step 7.   If selecting a protocol such as TCP or UDP, enter the Destination port. You can also enter a Source port.

Step 8.   Figure 14-9 shows a sample configuration for TCP ports. Click **OK**.

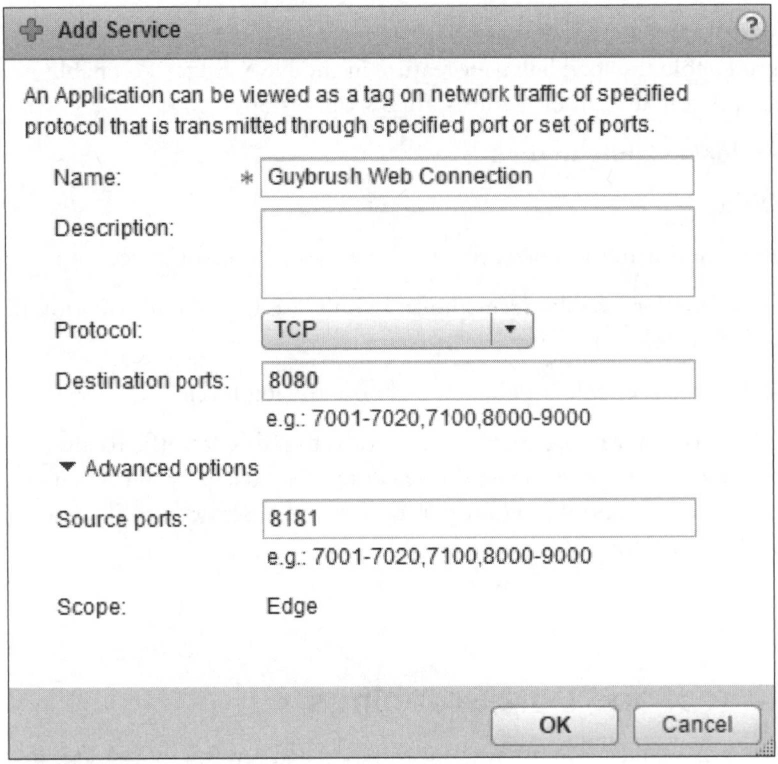

Figure 14-9   New NSX TCP service

Configure NSX Edge DHCP and DNS

The NSX Edge can be a DHCP server for virtual machines or forward DHCP requests to a DHCP server via DHCP Relay. The NSX Edge listens to DHCP discovery on internal interfaces. To configure the NSX Edge as a DHCP server, follow these steps:

Step 1.   From the **NSX Edges** view, double-click the NSX Edge where the service will be created.

Step 2.   Go to **Manage > DHCP** and select **Pools**.

Step 3.   Click the green **+** icon and wait for the **Add DHCP Pool** window to open.

Step 4.   Enter the first and last IPs in the IP pool to use for DHCP.

Step 5.   Enter the domain name.

Step 6.   Enter a Primary and a Secondary DNS server. If you check the box for **Auto Configure DNS**, the default gateway IP is used as the DNS server. You should configure DNS servers in the NSX Edge. Adding DNS servers in the NSX Edge is covered step-by-step after this.

Step 7.   Enter the default gateway IP. If left blank and the IPs in the pool are part of a subnet of an internal interface, the Edge uses the interface's IP as the default gateway.

Step 8.   Enter the lease time. You have an option to have no expiration by checking the box for **Lease Never Expires**.

Step 9.   Click **OK**.

Step 10.   Click **Enable**.

Step 11.   Choose whether to log, and select the logging level.

Step 12.   Click **Publish Changes**.

To configure DHCP Relay, follow these steps:

Step 1.   From the **NSX Edges** view, double-click the NSX Edge where the Service will be created.

Step 2.   Go to **Manage > DHCP** and select **Relay**.

Step 3.   Click **Edit** and wait for the **Modify DHCP Relay Global Configuration** window to open.

Step 4.   Enter the IP sets, IP addresses, or domain names of the DHCP servers.

Step 5.   Click **OK**.

Step 6.   Under DHCP Relay Agents, click the green **+** icon and wait for the **Add DHCP Relay Agent** window to open.

Step 7.   Select the internal vNIC to listen for DHCP discovery and select the Gateway IP. If the vNIC has multiple IPs, you may select any of the IPs to be the source of the DHCP Relay packet sent to the DHCP server.

Step 8.   Click **OK**.

Step 9.   Repeat steps 7 and 8 to add more internal interfaces.

Step 10.   Click **Publish Changes**.

To add DNS servers to the NSX Edge, follow these steps:

Step 1.   Go to **Manage > Settings** and select **Configuration**.

Step 2.   In DNS Configuration click **Change**.

Step 3.   Check the box for **Enable DNS Service**.

Step 4. Enter the IP address of up to two DNS servers.

Step 5. Enter the cache size.

Step 6. Choose whether to log, and select the logging level.

Step 7. Click **OK**.

NSX Edge Logical Firewall

To wrap up the chapter, let's go over the NSX Edge logical firewall, or simply NSX Edge firewall. The NSX Edge firewall is one of two logical firewalls in NSX. The other is the distributed logical firewall or distributed firewall. The NSX Edge can be configured as a Layer 3 and Layer 4 stateful firewall, primarily to provide security for traffic going between the virtual and physical environments, also referred to as North-South traffic. Firewall rules are processed by the Edge from top to bottom, with a default rule at the bottom. The default rule's default action is to block all traffic; however, the default action can be changed during the deployment of the NSX Edge. Figure 14-10 shows the step in the New Edge Wizard where you can change the default action of the default rule to accept all traffic.

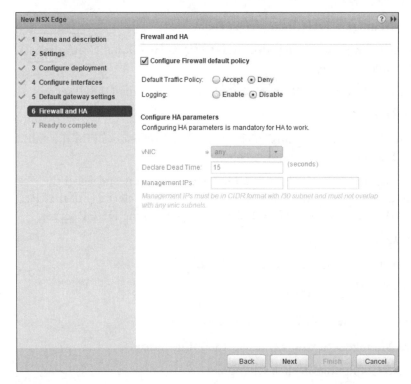

Figure 14-10   Change default rule default action in New Edge Wizard.

The Control VM's firewall is used only for traffic sourced or destined to the Control VM's HA IP, Protocol IP, or Uplink interfaces. The Control VM's firewall rules won't be enforced in internal interfaces.

If you didn't change the default rule's action during the deployment of the NSX Edge, you can change it by going to **Management > Firewall** and clicking the white **+** icon in the Action column of the default rule, as shown in Figure 14-11. In addition to Accept and Deny, you can also choose to Reject the connection. This sends an ICMP destination-unreachable back to the sender of the packet.

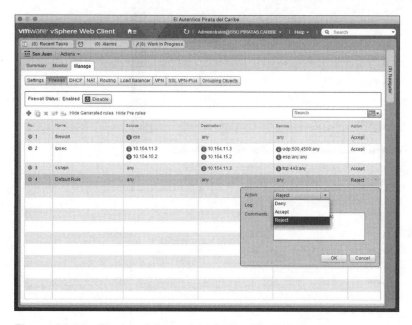

Figure 14-11   Change default rule default action in Edge Firewall view.

Something that I find neat about the Edge firewall is that the Edge can be configured to automatically add firewall rules needed for control traffic functions. For example, if you configure an IPsec VPN, the Edge creates an Allow Firewall rule to permit IPSec traffic between itself and the IPsec VPN peer, as shown in Figure 14-12.

You can configure the Edge to autogenerate firewall rules during the NSX Edge deployment, as shown in Figure 14-13, or by selecting the Edge's **Actions > Change Auto Rule Configuration**, as shown in Figure 14-14.

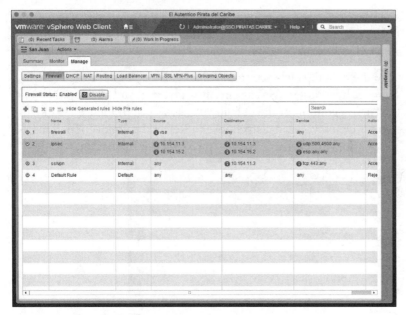

Figure 14-12   Autogenerated firewall rule

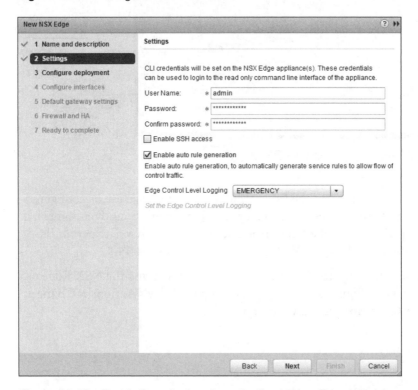

Figure 14-13   Enable firewall rule autogeneration in New Edge Wizard.

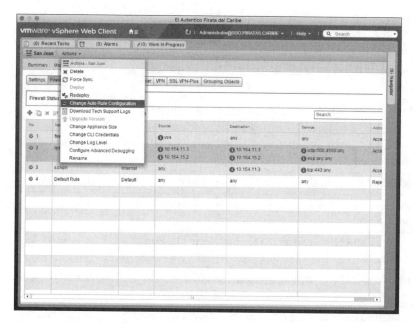

Figure 14-14   Enable firewall rule autogeneration in Edge's Actions menu.

Let me point out one more thing about the Edge firewall rules. The firewall rules are not applied to the Edge interfaces. The rules are applied to all traffic coming into the Edge, and by default they are applied before any NAT is done. You can change this setting on a per-rule basis.

Configuring an Edge Firewall

To configure a firewall rule in the NSX Edge follow these steps:

Step 1.   From the **NSX Edges** view, double-click the NSX Edge that will be configured as a firewall.

Step 2.   Go to **Manage > Firewall**.

Step 3.   Click the green **+** icon. A new empty firewall rule is added.

Step 4.   In the Name column, click the white **+** icon and enter the name of the firewall rule.

Step 5.   In the Source and Destination columns, click the white **+** icon to change the source and destination from the default of *any*. This allows the Edge to use vCenter and NSX Manager objects information to formulate the firewall rule. You can click the red **ip** icon to enter IP addresses.

Table 14-7 shows the container objects that can be referenced in the firewall rule.

Table 14-7   Edge Firewall Rule Source and Destination Containers

Container	Description	Source
Cluster	Includes all vNICs of all virtual machines in the selected cluster(s)	vCenter
Distributed portgroup	Includes all vNICs connected to the selected dvPortgoup(s)	vCenter
Data center	Includes all vNICs of all virtual machines in the selected data center	vCenter
IP sets	Includes all IPs in the selected Edge IP set(s)	NSX Edge
Legacy portgroup	Includes all vNICs connected to the selected standard portgroup(s)	vCenter
Resource pool	Includes all vNICs connected to the selected resource pool(s)	vCenter
Security group	Includes all vNICs belonging to the selected security group(s)	NSX Manager
Logical switch	Includes all vNICs connected to the selected logical switch(es)	NSX Manager
Virtual app	Includes all vNICs of all virtual machines in the selected virtual app(s)	vCenter
Virtual machine	Includes all vNICs of the selected virtual machine(s)	vCenter
vNIC Group	Includes the selected NSX Edge interface(s). Additional selection options include	NSX Edge
	External: Includes all external NSX Edge vNIC(s)	
	Internal: Includes all internal NSX Edge vNIC(s)	
	VSE: Includes all the NSX Edge vNICs	

A single firewall rule source and destination can have multiple entries. For example, a firewall rule's source may have a cluster, a vDS portgroup, and a virtual machine, while the same rule's destination may have a network and an IP, as shown in Figure 14-15. If traffic matches any of the entries in the source and any of the entries in the destination fields of the rule, then the rule will be processed (if it also matches any of the Service entries, as detailed in step 6).

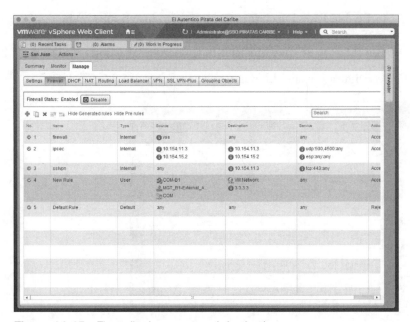

Figure 14-15   Firewall rule source and destination

The Edge processes packets based on the information in the Layer 3 header; thus, it needs the actual IP of every VM that is a member of the objects listed in the source and destination columns for the firewall rule. To get the VM's IPs, NSX Manager queries vCenter for the IPs, which then provides them to the Edge. The IPs are obtained by VMware Tools, DHCP snooping, or ARP snooping.

Step 6.   In the **Service** column, click the white **+** icon to change the default of *any*. As in the **Source and Destination** columns, you can enter multiple Services in the same rule.

Step 7.   In the **Action** column, click the white **+** icon.

   a. A pane opens.

   b. Set the **Action** to **Allow**, **Block**, or **Reject**.

   c. Choose to **Log** or **Do Not Log** when traffic matches the rule.

   d. Enter a comment to describe the rule's function.

   e. Click the **Advance Options** to make visible additional configuration options.

      i. In **Match On**, you can select to match traffic on the translated NAT IP. This causes NAT to be done first before the firewall rule is processed. The default behavior is to match the firewall rule before doing NAT.

> ii. In **Enable Rule Direction**, you can set to match rules on ingress traffic or egress traffic. VMware does not recommend setting this option (I know, I know, why have the option then? Good question ☺).

f. The configuration should look similar to Figure 14-16. Click **OK**.

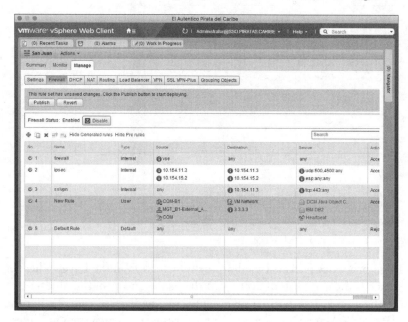

Figure 14-16   Firewall rule action

Step 8.   Click **Publish**.

As of NSX 6.2, NSX Edge firewall rules can also be created from the Firewall page in Network and Security. NSX Edge firewall rules created in the Firewall page of Network and Security are enforced before any firewall rules created in the NSX Edge Firewall page and have a firewall rule type of Pre-Rules. We cover this page in Chapter 15, "Distributed Logical Firewall."

Exam Preparation Tasks

Review All the Key Topics

Review the most important topics from inside the chapter, noted with the Key Topic icon in the outer margin of the page. Table 14-8 lists these key topics and the page numbers where each is found.

Table 14-8   Key Topics for Chapter 14

Key Topic Element	Description	Page Number
Paragraph	SNAT is used to allow virtual workloads to initiate flows. DNAT is used to allow virtual workloads to be the recipients of flows.	416
Paragraph	A mapped VIP to an application profile and a server pool.	421
Paragraph	The NSX Edge must be the default gateway for the servers in the server pool when in Transparent Mode.	422
Paragraph	The NSX Edge performs SNAT, using the VIP as the translated IP, when configured in Proxy Mode.	423
Paragraph	An Allow Firewall rule is not needed when the NSX Edge is configured as Firewall and Layer 4 Load Balancer	425
Paragraph	The NSX Edge supports throttling connections to the servers in the server pool.	426
Paragraph	The Control VM Firewall is applied to Control VM traffic only	437
Paragraph	By default the NSX Edge firewall rules are applied to all traffic that matches the rules, independent of the ingress vNIC.	439
Paragraph	If using a container in the Source or Destination field of the firewall rule, the NSX Edge obtains appropriate IPs from vCenter.	441
Paragraph	Starting in NSX 6.2, NSX Edge Firewall rules can be created in the Firewall page of Network and Security	442

Complete Tables and Lists from Memory

Download and print a copy of Appendix C, "Memory Tables," (found on the book's website), or at least the section for this chapter, and complete the tables and lists from memory. Appendix D, "Memory Tables Answer Key," also on the website, includes the completed tables and lists so you can check your work.

Define Key Terms

Define the following key terms from this chapter, and check your answers in the glossary:

NAT, SNAT, DNAT, VIP,

This chapter covers all or part of the following VCP6-NV exam blueprint topics:

- **Objective 1.1**—Compare and Contrast the Benefits of a VMware NSX Implementation

- **Objective 1.3**—Differentiate Physical and Virtual Network Technologies

- **Objective 7.2**—Configure Distributed Firewall Services

- **Objective 8.1**—Differentiate Single and Cross-vCenter NSX Deployments

CHAPTER 15

Distributed Logical Firewall

We are mostly done with routing, switching, and networking services in NSX. It is time to move on to the next topic in our exam preparation, which happens to be one of my favorite features of NSX. The distributed logical firewall, distributed firewall for short, is nothing short of impressive in my humble opinion. The distributed firewall, together with vSphere's IOChain, makes it possible to take security out of the network and enforce it in its own space.

This chapter covers some of the network design compromises that must be made when doing network security, introduces the distributed firewall, and reviews how enforcing security separate from the network removes the need to compromise in network designs.

Do I Know This Already?

The "Do I Know This Already?" quiz allows you to assess whether you should read this entire chapter or simply jump to the "Exam Preparation Tasks" section for review. If you are in doubt, read the entire chapter. Table 15-1 outlines the major headings in this chapter and the corresponding "Do I Know This Already?" quiz questions. You can find the answers in Appendix A, "Answers to the 'Do I Know This Already?' Quizzes."

Table 15-1 Headings and Questions

Foundation Topic Section	Questions Covered in This Section
Traditional Firewall Design Compromises	1
Distributed Logical Firewall	2-5
Configure Logical Firewall Rules	6-8
NSX Manager and Domains	9
Verifying DFW Functionality	10
SpoofGuard	11

1. Which is not a design compromise that might be made to provide network security to virtual workloads?

   a. Deploy all the tiers of a multitier application in the same Layer 2 broadcast domain.

   b. Span VLANs among multiple ESXi hosts.

   c. Provide multiple IP subnets to support multitier applications.

   d. Allow unrestricted access for virtual workloads in the same Layer 2 broadcast domain.

2. Which statement is true regarding the distributed firewall?

   a. The distributed firewall is a firewall configured on each ESXi host managed by a single vCenter instance. Each ESXi host gets the same distributed firewall configuration.

   b. The distributed firewall is a firewall configured on each NSX-prepared ESXi host. Each ESXi host gets the same distributed firewall configuration.

   c. The distributed firewall is the name of the NSX firewall component applied to each VM.

   d. The distributed firewall is the name of the NSX firewall component applied to every vNIC on every VM.

3. What component(s) contains the distributed firewall?

   a. The NSX Manager

   b. The NSX Controllers

   c. The ESXi hosts

   d. The VMs

4. Which two layers of the OSI model are not protected by the distributed firewall? (Choose two.)

   a. Layer 1

   b. Layer 3

   c. Layer 4

   d. Layer 7

5. How many distributed firewall rules are supported by NSX Manager?

   a. 1,000

   b. 10,000

   c. 100,000

   d. 1,000,000

6. An NSX administrator adds Layer 3 and Layer 4 firewall rules to the distributed firewall for virtual machine **DB_02** with the goal of having the rules processed before an existing Layer 2 firewall rule defined for the same VM.

What must be done to ensure these rules are enforced in the desired order?

    a. Nothing. Layer 2 distributed firewall rules are enforced before any Layer 3 and Layer 4 rules.

    b. Nothing. Existing distributed firewall rules get enforced before any new firewall rules.

    c. Configure the Layer 3 and Layer 4 distributed firewall rules above the Layer 2 rule.

    d. Disable the Layer 2 distributed firewall rule, add the Layer 3 and Layer 4 rules, and then re-enable the Layer 2 rule.

7. Which two are valid options for the Source field of a universal DFW rule? (Choose two.)

    a. vNIC

    b. IP

    c. Universal security group

    d. IP sets

8. What two components/features should be configured/installed for a firewall rule with a destination that includes the name of a virtual machine to be effective? (Choose two.)

    a. VMware Tools should be installed in the VM.

    b. VMware Endpoint Services should be deployed to the ESXi host where the VM is running.

    c. The **Applied To** field should include the VM name.

    d. DHCP snooping.

9. Which statement must be true for a rule that has a source that includes an LDAP group to function properly?

    a. vCenter has been added to the LDAP domain.

    b. The NSX Manager that owns the rule has been added to the LDAP domain.

    c. The ESXi hosts that have a copy of the distributed firewall's rule have been added to the LDAP domain.

    d. The rule is a universal firewall rule.

10. Which ESXi host command shows the vNICs that are not in the exclusion list?

    a. vsipioctl getrules

    b. vsipioctl getaddrsets

    c. vsipioctl getvnics

    d. vsipioctl getfilters

11. What is the configuration of the default SpoofGuard policy?

    a. Include all portgroups and logical switches that are not members of an existing SpoofGuard policy.

    b. Require manual approval of all IPs for VMs added to the policy.

    c. Requires that VMs be manually added to the policy.

    d. Enforce VMware Tools installation to all VMs that get added to the policy.

Foundation Topics

Traditional Firewall Design Compromises

What gets me excited about the distributed firewall (DFW) is that it makes it possible to separate security from the network. The separation of security from the network eliminates some of the routing and switching design compromises that have to be made to provide security. To better explain what I mean by removing security from the network, and how the DFW is implemented, let's take a look at Figure 15-1, which shows a two-tier application that has a web server and a database server. Users access the application by connecting to the web server, and the web server pulls data from the database server. The users do not have direct access to the database server.

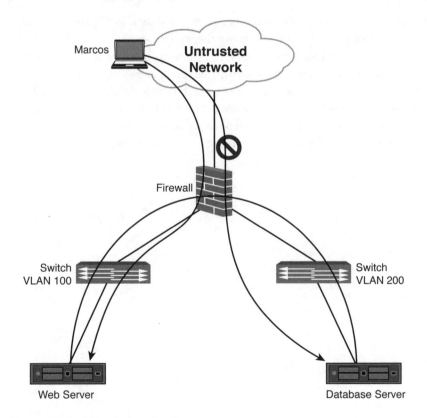

Figure 15-1 Two-tier application

Firewalls traditionally do Layer 3, Layer 4, and Layer 7 (application layer) security. Many Top of Rack (ToR) switches can do some Layer 2 firewalling by using

MAC access lists, but this option is rather cumbersome and hard to manage. Private VLANs can also be configured in ToR; however, this security solution is rather limiting in its extensibility, which renders it insufficient in most cases. Plus, the ToR rarely enforces Layer 3 and Layer 4 security, letting traditional firewalls do that enforcement. It is therefore almost always preferred to place the different tiers of an application in their own Layer 2 domain. By using different Layer 2 domains, traffic between different tiers can be protected by forcing the traffic to go through a firewall, as shown in Figure 15-1. In many instances, the firewall also acts as the default gateway for the application tiers.

To be clear, the design shown in Figure 15-1 provides good security (assuming it is configured and deployed correctly). It prevents users from accessing the database server directly, only allows restrictive access from the users to the web servers, and prevents the web servers from accessing the database server over unauthorized ports.

There are, however, some problems with this design. As shown in Figure 15-2, this design provides no protection for traffic among the web servers nor does it provide protection for traffic among the database servers. A new web server added to the web tier has unrestricted access to the other web servers. A new database server added to the database tier has unrestricted access to the other database servers. This means that if a single web server is compromised, there is not much the network can do in preventing the other web servers from also being compromised. The same happens in the database tier if a single database server is compromised.

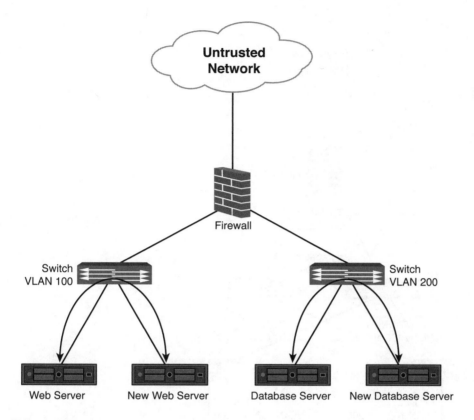

Figure 15-2 Unrestricted intra-tier access

Instead of having a single dedicated Layer 2 and IP segment for all tiers in the multitier application, each multitier application consumes multiple VLANs and multiple subnets. That's one VLAN and one subnet per tier. The use of multiple VLANs per multitier application leads to VLAN sprawl, which greatly reduces the capability of the network to scale (we discussed in Chapter 2, "Network and VMware vSphere Requirements for NSX," the POD network design that tries to address this issue). You also need a different default gateway for each Layer 2 segment, which potentially increases the size of the routing table (there are ways to minimize the increase in size of the routing table by using route summary and careful IP address planning).

In the conversation we have been having, I've assumed the workloads (the web and database servers) are physical. Now let's pretend that we are going to virtualize the physical workloads while maintaining the same level of security. Figure 15-3 shows the same, now virtualized, multitier application from Figure 15-2. Here we see that VMs from the same tier are running in different ESXi hosts. Each ESXi host is running a web server and a database server VM.

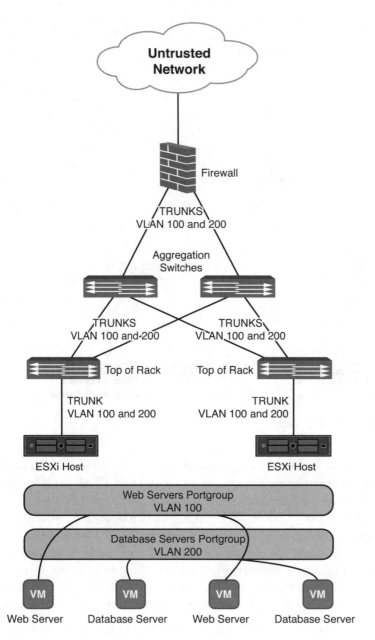

Figure 15-3 Virtualized multitier application

Did you pick up on it? Each ESXi host that runs VMs from the same tier must share the same Layer 2 segment the virtual machines are connected to. Translation: Spanning Tree. Darn it! There are no two ways about it. The moment you have to stretch that Layer 2 past the ToR switches, you must configure STP. Thus we have another design compromise that must be made with virtual workloads: The number of ESXi hosts that can run VMs from the same tier must be managed so as to limit the size of STP tree. These ESXi hosts should also have relatively close physical proximity to each other as Ethernet is designed to be a local area network (LAN). By the way, Figure 15-3 assumed distributed portgroups. The problems discussed in this paragraph are the same if standard portgroups are used.

Remember the ToR switch that could do Layer 2 security? Well, the ToR doing Layer 2 security may be of some use when protecting physical workloads, but not so much with virtual workloads. Existing ToR switches don't have a good mechanism to migrate security policies as VMs vMotion to different ESXi hosts.

Table 15-2 summarizes the design compromises that must be made to enforce network security.

Table 15-2   Design Compromises: Network Security

Compromise	Description
Layer 2	Each multitier application consumes multiple broadcast domains.
Layer 3	Each multitier application consumes multiple subnets, each with a default gateway.
Intra-Tier Security	There is no effective, efficient, and scalable option for providing security for workloads in the same tier.
	For virtual workloads, there is no existing network security available that also works with vMotion.
VLANs	VLANs must be stretched, requiring STP.
vMotion	The diameter of the vMotion zone is reduced.

Distributed Logical Firewall

Have a look at Figure 15-4, which shows virtual workloads (minus the ESXi hosts), and tell me: How many firewalls do you see? (Before you read ahead, you can tweet me the answer @ElverS_Opinion). If you see four different firewalls, you are a winner. (Since you just read ahead before tweeting, you are no longer eligible to be a winner, but you can still send a tweet to say hi.) The four firewalls you see are part of the same *distributed* logical firewall, also referred to as distributed firewall (DFW). The distributed in the name does not imply that a single entity (the firewall) is replicated among multiple hosts the way the vSphere distributed switch or logical router are replicated. Rather the *distributed* in this case is used in the same lingo as distributed computing where multiple ESXi hosts execute some of the firewall rule enforcement against traffic.

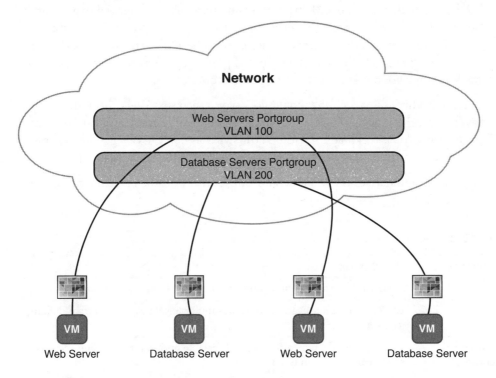

Figure 15-4 How many firewalls do you see?

Next question: Where are these firewalls running? These four firewalls are running in the ESXi host kernel (you should've known that since I've mentioned it through the book a few times now). They are *not* running inside the guest OS, and they are *not* running in the network. The fact that the distributed firewall is completely outside the network allows us to design the network without the same design compromises mentioned in Table 15-2. With the DFW, it is possible to deploy any multitier application in the same Layer 2 broadcast domain for *all* tiers, and have the same subnet and the same default gateway. With DFW, there are no compromises in the diameter of the vMotion range, and if you deploy the application in a logical switch, you don't need to worry about STP. Oh—and yes, you *can* provide security between any two VMs in the same Layer 2 broadcast domain.

The DFW provides the Layer 2, Layer 3, and Layer 4 stateful security to all virtual workloads running in NSX-prepared ESXi hosts, regardless of the virtual switch they connect to. In Chapter 16, "Security Services," we discuss how to provide Layer 7 security and other levels of security to virtual workloads. A VM can be connected to a logical switch, a dvPortgroup, or a standard portgroup. If two VMs connect to the same standard portgroup, you can apply whatever security policy you want between the VMs, and the DFW enforces it.

The DFW kernel module connects itself in slot 2 of the IOChain. This means the DFW will enforce Firewall rules regardless of how the virtual machine connects to the network.

Figure 15-5 shows our multitier application with the only allowed traffic being the one from the users to the web server and the web servers to the database servers. The DFW makes it possible for all tiers in a multitier application to reside in the same Layer 2 broadcast domain and the same subnet.

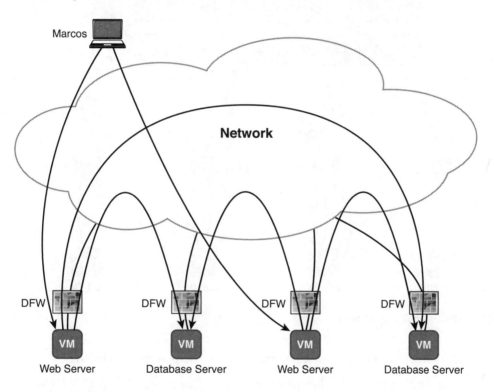

Figure 15-5 DFW enforcing security policies

So how does the DFW actually do its thing? Simple, really! The DFW is composed of firewall rules with source and destination addresses and Ethertypes or Layer 4 protocols, which are then applied to the individual vNIC of a virtual machine. The same DFW rule can be applied to a single vNIC in a VM, all vNICs in the same VM, or the vNICs of multiple VMs. In case the DFW fails, it fails close, blocking all traffic for the impacted vNIC.

Let's do a packet walk of traffic between two VMs. Figure 15-6 shows traffic from one of the web servers toward one of the database servers. The web server and the database server have the same firewall rule that allows traffic from the web server (source) toward the database server (destination).

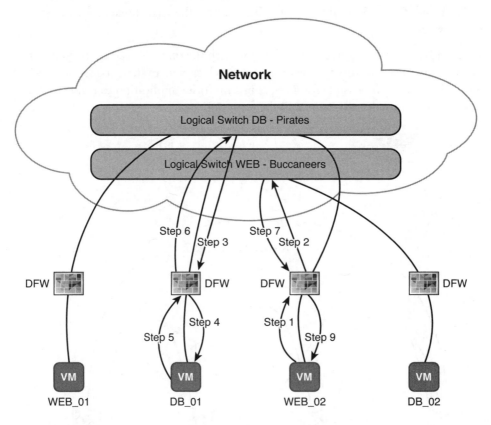

Figure 15-6   DFW packet walk

1. Web server WEB_02 sends some traffic to database server DB_01.

2. Before traffic reaches logical switch Web – Buccaneers, WEB_02's DFW checks the traffic against the firewall rules.

   a. WEB_02's DFW notes the traffic is coming from the direction of the web server WEB_02.

   b. The DFW finds a matching rule allowing the traffic, and the traffic is forwarded to the network.

The first frame/packet in the flow is processed by the ESXi host in user space against the table containing the DFW rules. This table is called the DFW Rule Table. If allowed, the state of the active connection is recorded using the 5-tuple of Layer 3 source/destination address (IP address if IP), Layer 3 Protocol, and Layer 4 source/destination address (port numbers if TCP or UDP), and future frames/packets in the flow are then processed in kernel space. This state table is called the DFW Connection Table. The memory used to record both the DFW rules and the firewall state is attached to the VM's kernel overhead memory. This simple trick allows vMotion to happen without a ping drop, since the DFW state for each of the VMs' vNICs is moved with the VM.

The DFW supports Application Level Gateway (ALG) for the following applications: FTP, CIFS, Oracle, TNS, MS-RPC, and SUN-RPC. ALG support allows the DFW to be aware that the application's return traffic uses different ports from those used to initiate the session. The DFW adds the correct ports to the state tables for the return traffic.

3. Traffic egresses logical switch DB – Pirates toward the database server DB_01.

4. Before the traffic reaches the database server, DB_01's DFW checks the traffic against the firewall rules.

   a. DB_01's DFW notes the traffic is coming from the direction of the network.

   b. The DFW finds a matching rule allowing the traffic, and the traffic is forwarded to DB_01.

The first frame/packet in the flow is processed by the ESXi host in user space, the states and allow decision are recorded, and future frames/packets in the flow are processed in kernel space.

5. Database server DB_01 receives the traffic and responds.

6. Before the traffic reaches logical switch DB – Pirates, DB_01's DFW has an entry in the state table in kernel space for this flow and allows it.

Traffic is now forwarded to the network.

7. Logical switch WEB – Buccaneers forwards the traffic to WEB_02.

8. Before the traffic makes it to WEB_02, WEB_02's DFW processes the traffic using the earlier state entry it made in kernel space and forwards it to WEB_02.

9. WEB_02 receives the traffic.

The ability of the DFW to enforce security granularly at this level on a per vNIC basis is called *microsegmentation*. Microsegmentation is also leveraged to provide Layer 7 and other security services.

One note on the traffic flow we just packet-walked: Each DFW processes traffic starting with the first firewall rule and going down. If the traffic matches a rule, the action in the rule is enforced against the traffic, and no more rules are checked. If the action of the rule is to block, the traffic is dropped without any fanfare. Firewall rules are created in different ways, and these are enforced based in the following order:

1. Firewall rules created by users have the highest priority and are enforced from top to bottom.

2. Firewall rules autogenerated by NSX Edges in support of NSX Edge Services.

3. Firewall rules created by users in the NSX Edges. (We covered these rules in Chapter 14, "NSX Edge Network Services and Security.")

4. Firewall rules created by Service Composer. (We cover Service Composer in Chapter 16.)

5. The default firewall rule. This rule is always present, and it is the last rule. It can't be moved.

Of the five firewall rules mentioned in the preceding list, only numbers 1, 4, and 5 are DFW rules. Numbers 2 and 3 are NSX Edge firewall rules.

The default firewall rule is applied to all instances of the DFW. The default action is to Allow so as not to break any existing connectivity to VMs. You should consider changing the action to either Block or Reject after you have finalized your security plan.

There are two default DFW rules. One for Layer 2, and another for Layer 3 and Layer 4. All Layer 2 DFW rules are processed before any Layer 3 and Layer 4 DFW rules are applied.

That's all there is to it. The DFW concept is deceptively simple yet powerful. Each VM has its own firewall (actually, each vNIC in the VM has its own firewall), and traffic is enforced against the firewall rules for the VM's vNIC in both the ingress and egress. Now you might be thinking, how on Earth is this simpler than what we have today? Well, because it is simpler. The DFW rules for all VMs are configured in the same window. The rules can then be applied to any VM vNIC no matter the ESXi host running it (assuming the ESXi host has the DFW module installed). There is one caveat with the DFW: Just because it is simple doesn't mean that you should go firewall rule crazy. Before applying any DFW rules, you should understand the impact the rules will have on your environment.

DFW Thresholds and Limits

The DFW does consume resources in the ESXi host, and by default the ESXi host monitors DFW resource utilization. There are three default thresholds that if reached or crossed 20 consecutive times in any 200-second interval will raise an alarm. The thresholds are

- **CPU**: 100% of the total physical capacity of the ESXi host.

- **Memory**: 100% of the DFW allocated memory in the ESXi host. Table 15-3 shows the allocated memory based on the total physical memory in the host.

- **Connections per Second (CPS)**: 100,000 CPS by default.

Table 15-3 DFW Allocated Memory

Physical Memory	Total Allocated Memory (This number represents 100% of Allocation)
0 up to 8 GB	160MB
Over 8 up to 32 GB	608MB
Over 32 up to 64 GB	992MB
Over 64 up to 96 GB	1920MB
Over 96 up to 128 GB	2944MB
Over 128 GB	4222MB

The DFW thresholds may be changed via an API call to NSX Manager. The syntax of the API call is listed below. We cover NSX APIs in Chapter 18, "NSX Automation."

```
URL Resource:
          https://[NSX Manager FQDN or IP]/api/4.0/firewall/stats/
          eventthresholds
Request Body:
<eventThresholds>
    <cpu>
        <percentValue>[percent of total physical CPU capacity]
            </percentValue> !This number can't be higher than 100
            percent.
    </cpu>
    <memory>
        <percentValue>[percent of total allocated Memory capacity]
            </percentValue> !This number can be higher than 100
            percent. Refer to Table 15-3.
    </memory>
    <connectionsPerSecond>
        <value>[number of Connections per Second]</value>
    </connectionsPerSecond>
</eventThresholds>
```

Before we cover how the DFW rules are configured and applied to VMs, let me throw out some info that might be of help if you decide to take an exam ☺:

- NSX Manager supports 100,000 DFW rules.

- Each ESXi host supports 100,000 DFW rules.

- A virtual machine can have 1,000 DFW rules.

- The default DFW rule is set to allow by default. (Hey, relax—no need to get excited about this. I'll explain more on the reasons in the next paragraph.)

Exclusion List

Now let me come clean about some details. It is not true that *every* VM gets the DFW. The NSX Edges, the logical router Control VMs, the NSX Controllers, and the NSX Managers do not have a DFW. They are in the DFW Exclusion List by default and can't be removed from the list; however, you may add VMs to the Exclusion List so they won't have any DFW rules enforced. To add a VM to the Exclusion List, follow these steps:

Step 1. From the NSX Manager home page, click **NSX Managers**.

Step 2. Click the NSX Manager where you want to add a virtual machine to the Exclusion List.

Step 3. Go to **Manage > Exclusion List**.

Step 4. Click the green **+** icon and wait for the Add Virtual Machine to Exclusion List window to open.

Step 5. Search for the virtual machine you want to be excluded from the DFW and click **Add**.

Repeat this step for all other virtual machines you want to add.

A virtual machine you might want to consider adding to the Exclusion List is vCenter. If you make a mistake and block all communications to vCenter, you are in for a nice ordeal.

Step 6. Click **OK**.

Logical Firewall Rules

So let's fix us a logical firewall rule and apply it to some VMs. First, take a look and become familiar with Figure 15-7 and Table 15-4, which show the Firewall configuration page in network and security, and learn what each icon means.

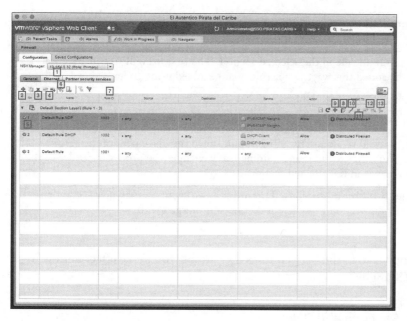

Figure 15-7   DFW Configuration window

Table 15-4   Firewall Configuration Window Icon

Figure 15-7 Index	Description
1	Select Layer 2 (Ethernet), Layer 3, and Layer 4 (General) Firewall view. We cover Partner Security Services in Chapter 16.
2	Add a firewall rule in the selected section. This creates a new rule.
3	Delete a firewall rule.
4	Change the order of the firewall rule. You can move the rule up or down.
5	Processing order of firewall rules. To disable a rule, while leaving it in the configuration, click the green check mark icon next to the order number.
6	Load Saved Configuration. Allows you to restore a saved configuration.
7	Rule ID. Unique ID to identify the firewall rule. This ID is independent of the processing order number. The Default Rule has Rule ID of 1001.
8	Create a Firewall section. This allows the grouping of firewall rules for ease of management and the creation of universal DFW rules by marking the section for universal synchronization. Sections do not impact the enforcement order of firewall rules.

Figure 15-7 Index	Description
9	Add a firewall rule in the selected section. The first firewall rule in a section must be added this way. Other rules can be added using Index 2 above.
10	Rename a firewall section.
11	Delete firewall section. This also deletes the firewall rules in the section.
12	Move firewall section. This moves up or down the placement of the section relative to other sections and automatically changes the processing order of the firewall rules in the affected sections.
13	Merges two firewall sections. This merges two sections. The new section has the name of the section this current section was merged with.

Any changes you make to the firewall rules or sections won't take effect until you click **Publish Changes**.

Creating Firewall Sections and Rules

There are two types of DFW rules:

- **Local DFW rules**: Local DFW rules are created in each NSX Manager, Primary, Secondary, and Standalone.

- **Universal DFW rules**: Universal DFW rules are created only in the Primary NSX Manager and are synchronized with all NSX Managers.

The Primary NSX Manager has read/write access to universal DFW rules with the Secondary NSX Managers having read-only access. Universal DFW rules keep the same rule ID across all NSX Managers.

Universal DFW rules can only be created within a firewall section marked for universal synchronization. There can only be two universal firewall sections, one for Layer 2 (Ethernet) and one for Layer 3 and Layer 4 (General).

To create a firewall section, follow these steps:

Step 1.   From the Network and Security home page, select the Firewall view.

Step 2.   Click either the General or Ethernet tab.

Step 3.   Click the yellow folder icon with the green + sign (refer to Table 15-4, #8).

Step 4.   Give the section a name.

Step 5.   Select where to place the section (above or below the currently selected section).

You can't add a Section below the default section.

Step 6. To make this a universal section, check the box for **Mark this Section for Universal Synchronization**.

Step 7. Click **OK**, and then click **Publish Changes**.

Follow these steps to add a new firewall rule:

Step 1. From the Network and Security home page, select the Firewall view.

Step 2. Click the **General** tab. This creates Layer 3 and Layer 4 DFW rules.

Clicking the **Ethernet** tab allows you to create Layer 2 DFW rules. Layer 2 DFW rules are checked first, before Layer 3 and Layer 4 DFW rules. The configuration of Layer 2, and Layer 3 and Layer 4 rules is identical.

Clicking the **Partner Security Services** tab allows you to integrate third-party security solutions to NSX. We cover this in Chapter 16.

Step 3. Select the NSX Manager where the firewall rule will be added.

If creating a universal firewall rule, you must select the Primary NSX Manager.

Step 4. Click the green **+** icon. A new empty firewall rule is added.

If you want to create a universal DFW rule, you must choose the universal section.

Step 5. In the Name column, click the white **+** icon and enter the name of the firewall rule.

Step 6. In the Source and Destination columns, click the white **+** icon to change the source and destination from the default of **any**. You can click the red IP icon to enter IP addresses.

Table 15-5 shows the container objects that can be referenced in the Source and Destination fields of a local DFW rule.

Table 15-5 Local DFW Rule Source and Destination Containers

Container	Description	Source
Cluster	Includes all vNICs of all virtual machines in the selected cluster(s).	vCenter
vDS Portgroup	Includes all vNICs connected to the selected vDS portgroup(s).	vCenter
Data Center	Includes all vNICs of all virtual machines in the selected data center.	vCenter

Container	Description	Source
Network	Includes all vNICs connected to the selected standard portgroup(s).	vCenter
Resource Pool	Includes all vNICs connected to the selected resource pool(s).	vCenter
Security Groups	Includes all vNICs belonging to the selected security group(s).	NSX Manager
Logical Switch	Includes all vNICs connected to the selected logical switch(es).	NSX Manager
Virtual App	Includes all vNICs of all virtual machines in the selected virtual app(s).	vCenter
Virtual Machine	Includes all vNICs of the selected virtual machine(s).	vCenter
vNIC	Includes the selected vNIC(s).	vCenter
IP Sets	Includes all IPs in the selected NSX Manager IP set(s). This option is only available for Layer 3 and Layer 4 DFW rules.	NSX Manager
MAC Sets	Includes all MACs in the selected NSX Manager MAC Set(s). This option is only available for Layer 2 DFW rules.	NSX Manager
User and Domain Group	AD and LDAP username and/or group. This option is only available for Layer 3 and Layer 4 DFW rules.	AD and LDAP servers

Table 15-6 shows the container objects that can be referenced in the Source and Destination fields of a universal DFW rule.

Table 15-6   Local DFW Rule Source and Destination Containers

Container	Description	Source
Universal Logical Switch	For Layer 3 and Layer 4 DFW rules, includes the IP of all VMs connected to the universal logical switch. For Layer 2 DFW rules, includes the MAC of all VMs connected to the universal logical switch.	Primary NSX Manager
Universal Security Group	Includes Universal IP sets for Layer 3 and Layer 4 DFW rules, Universal MAC sets for Layer 2 DFW rules, or other universal security groups.	Primary NSX Manager

Container	Description	Source
Universal IP Sets	Includes a range of IPs. This option is only available for Layer 3 and Layer 4 DFW rules.	Primary NSX Manager
Universal MAC Sets	Includes a range of MAC addresses. This option is only available for Layer 2 DFW rules.	Primary NSX Manager

Just like the NSX Edge firewall, a single DFW rule source and destination can have multiple entries. When traffic matches one of the entries in the source and destination fields, and one of the entries of the Services field (from step 6 below), the rule will be processed.

The DFW processes packets based on the information in the Layer 2 (Ethernet rules) and Layer 3 (General rules) headers, thus it needs the actual MAC and IP of every VM that is a member of the objects listed in the Source and Destination columns for the firewall rule. For the local DFW rules, to get the VM's MAC and IPs, NSX Manager queries vCenter. A combination of VMware Tools, DHCP snooping, and ARP snooping is used to obtain the VM's IP.

Advanced Options allow you to negate a source or destination entity. The Negate Source and/or Negate Destination option excludes the selected entity(ies) from the rule and applies to all other ports. For example, if you select to Negate Destination Compute Cluster A, then all other VMs, except the ones in Compute Cluster A, will match.

Step 7. In the Service column, click the white **+** icon to change the default of **any**. A service may include Ethertype, IP Protocols, ICMP, and TCP/UDP port numbers. As in the Source and Destination columns, you can enter multiple Services in the same rule.

Universal DFW rules only support universal services and universal service groups. These can be precreated or created by the user.

Step 8. In the Action column, click the white **+** icon.

    a. A pane opens.

    b. Set the Action to **Allow**, **Block**, or **Reject**.

    Reject sends a TCP RST or ICMP message (for ICMP or UDP) for packets not accepted.

      c. Select the direction, relative to the virtual machine, of traffic that this rule will inspect: In, Out, or In/Out.

      d. Select the Packet Type, either IPv4 or IPv6.

      e. Choose to **Log** or **Do Not Log** when traffic matches the rule. For DFW rules, these logs are kept locally in each ESXi host that is running a virtual machine that has this firewall rule.

      f. Enter a comment to describe the rule's function and Click **OK**.

Step 9.   In the **Applied To** column, click the white **+** icon. A pane opens, and this is where the magic happens. This is where you select which vNIC(s) get this rule. Table 15-7 shows the options available for selecting the vNICs in firewall rules and local DFW rules. If multiple vNICs are selected, all the selected vNICs get this rule.

Table 15-7 Firewall Rule Applied To Options

Option	Description
Cluster	All vNICs of all virtual machines in the selected cluster(s) get the rule added to their DFW.
All Edges	All NSX Edges in NSX prepared clusters.
	This option is only available in Layer 3 and Layer 4 DFW rules.
HostSystem	The selected ESXi host.
Edge	The selected NSX Edge(s).
Distributed Portgroup	All vNICs connected to the selected dvPortgroup(s) get the rule added to their DFW.
Data Center	All vNICs of all virtual machines in the selected data center get the rule added to their DFW.
Legacy Portgroup	All vNICs connected to the selected standard portgroup(s) get the rule added to their DFW.
Logical Switch	All vNICs connected to the selected logical switch(es) get the rule added to their DFW.
Security Group	All vNICs of all VMs in the security group.
Virtual Machine	All vNICs of the selected virtual machine(s) get the rule added to their DFW.
vNIC	The selected vNIC(s) get the rule added to their DFW.

Table 15-8 shows the Applied To options for universal DFW rules.

Table 15-8   Firewall Rule Applied To Options

Option	Description
Universal Logical Switch	All vNICs of all virtual machines connected to the universal logical switch.
Distributed firewall	All vNICs in NSX prepared clusters.

Step 10.   Repeat steps 2 through 9 to add more DFW rules.

Step 11.   Click **Publish Changes** to save and apply the configuration.

Table 15-9 shows the other options available after you have finished configuring the DFW rules.

Table 15-9   Rule Change Options

Option	Description
Publish Changes	Saves and applies DFW rule changes. This causes NSX Manager to push a copy of the DFW rule to each ESXi host running a virtual machine listed in the Applied To field. The ESXi host, upon receiving the rule, adds the DFW rule to the corresponding virtual machine's vNIC DFW.
Revert Changes	Undo the changes and do not apply them.
Save Changes	Save changes and do not apply them. Gives an option to preserve the configuration. NSX Manager can store up to 100 saved configurations. When the 100 configurations limit is reached, NSX Manager deletes the oldest configuration that is *not* preserved.
Update Changes	Updates changes. You must first have saved a change to use this option.

Figure 15-8 shows the DFW configuration window with pending changes.

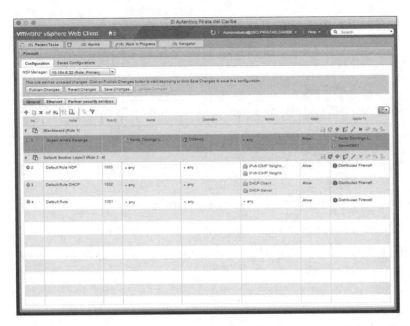

Figure 15-8   Logical firewall with pending changes

So what actually happens when you click **Publish Changes**? I'm glad you asked. NSX Manager reads over the Applied To column of every firewall rule. If the Applied To for a firewall rule includes an NSX Edge, the NSX Manager pushes the firewall rule to the NSX Edge. If the Applied To includes any vCenter object or container, NSX Manager determines:

1. All the vNICs and the powered on virtual machines covered by the Applied To in the DFW rule.

2. The ESXi prepared clusters where the virtual machines are running.

NSX Manager then sends a copy of the DFW rule to each ESXi host in the cluster, via the VSFW daemon. Each ESXi host that gets a copy of the DFW rule then determines which vNIC in the virtual machine the DFW rule should be applied to.

If you don't specify the vNIC of a virtual machine in the Applied To column, all vNICs in the virtual machine get the DFW rule.

Firewall Rules Saved Configurations

Look closely at Figure 15-8. Do you see the Saved Configuration tab? That's where you can manage up to 100 saved firewall configurations. There you can download a configuration, upload a configuration, delete a saved configuration, and... drumroll please… edit a saved configuration. The pencil icon to edit a saved configuration is a bit misleading here. What you can actually edit are the name, description, and preservation of the configuration.

The firewall configuration is saved as an XML file, as shown in Figure 15-9. You can edit the firewall configuration by exporting the firewall configuration's XML file, using your preferred XML editor to make changes and importing it to NSX. From the Configuration page, select to **Load Saved Configuration** (Table 15-4, #6) and select the uploaded firewall configuration.

Figure 15-9 Saved DFW configuration

NSX Manager and Domains

The last entry in Table 15-5 states you can add users or domain groups to the local DFW rule Source and/or Destination field. To do this, you must first add an LDAP domain to NSX Manager. The connection to the LDAP server (could be an AD server as well) can be configured to run over SSL (LDAPS). To add a domain to NSX Manager, follow these steps:

Step 1.   From the NSX Manager home page, click **NSX Managers**.

Step 2.   Click the NSX Manager where you want to add the LDAP domain.

Step 3.   Go to **Manage > Domains**.

Step 4.   Click the green **+** icon and wait for the Add Domain Wizard to open.

Step 5.   In the Name view, enter the FQDN name and the netBIOS name of the domain and click **Next**.

Step 6.   In the LDAP Options view, enter the following information:

- **Server**: The domain controller.

- **Protocol**: LDAP or LDAPS.

- **Port**: The port number to use. LDAP default port is TCP 389, and LDAPS default port is TCP 636. Change these at your own peril ☺.

- **Username and Password**: Enter the credentials NSX Manager will use in the domain.

This account must have AD read permission for all objects in the domain tree.

Click **Next**.

Step 7.   In the **Security Event Log Access** view, enter the following information:

- **Connection Method**: CIFS or WMI.

- **Port**: The port to use. CIFS default port is 445 and WMI defaults to 135.

- **Username and Password**: Enter the credentials NSX Manager will use in the domain. You can use the same credentials entered in step 6 by checking the Use Domain Credentials box.

This account must have read permissions for security event logs.

Click **Next**.

Step 8.   In the **Ready to Complete** view, review the changes and click **Finish**.

Step 9.   Repeat steps 4 through 8 to add more domains.

Verifying DFW Functionality

To verify the DFW rules have been applied, simply look at the Firewall view in the Network and Security page. You see all the DFW rules there. In the Firewall view, you can do a search for objects to narrow the list of visible DFW rules by clicking in the Apply Filter icon in the Configuration tab. For example, if you want to know which rules apply to virtual machine WEB_02, apply a filter for the VM, and only those rules that match the filter show up.

The other way to verify the DFW rules is to go in the CLI of the ESXi host running the virtual machine and running the command **vsipioctl**. Table 15-10 shows the options available for the command.

Table 15-10   **vsipioctl** Command Options

Option	Description
vsipioctl getfilters	Lists the vNICs not in the Exclusion List running the ESXi host
vsipioctl getrules	Lists the DFW rules applied to vNIC(s)
vsipioctl getaddrsets	Lists the MACs and IPs obtained from vCenter to match against the vNICs in the containers used in the Source or Destination fields

Finally, you can also check the DFW logs. There are three places where NSX keeps logs pertaining to DFW. They are the rule message logs, audit logs, and system event logs.

The rule message logs are kept by each ESXi host in the dfwpktlogs.log file located in /var/log/. This file contains information about when sessions start and terminate, and actions of allow, drop, or reject. To collect logs for a particular DFW rule, you must enable logging. To view the rule message logs in the ESXi host, you can SSH into the ESXi host and run the following CLI command:

less /var/log/dfwpktlogs.log | grep *WhatYouAreLookingFor*

Audit logs and system event logs are kept by NSX Manager. Audit logs are in the vsm.log file, and the system event logs are in the system.log file. Both files are in /home/secureall/secureall/logs/ folder. Audit logs record DFW configuration changes and administration logs. System events logs record DFW configuration changes successfully or unsuccessfully published to the ESXi hosts, filters created, virtual machines added to security groups, and so on. To view either audit logs or system event logs, go to the NSX Manager home page from Network and Security and select the Monitor tab.

SpoofGuard

SpoofGuard is an NSX security feature that protects against the spoofing of IPs. SpoofGuard can be configured to trust the IP reported by vCenter to NSX Manager (via VMware Tools) or to have each IP to vNIC mapping verified by an NSX administrator. Upon IP to vNIC policy violation, SpoofGuard blocks the traffic from that vNIC, acting independently of the DFW.

In addition to creating a policy that trusts the IP to vNIC mapping provided by vCenter, SpoofGuard trusts the MAC addresses in the VM's vmx file.

To create a SpoofGuard Policy, follow these steps:

Step 1.   From the NSX Manager home page, go to the **SpoofGuard** view.

Step 2.   Select the NSX Manager where the virtual machine is running, click the green **+** icon, and wait for the Add New Policy Wizard to open.

Step 3.   Give the policy a name.

Step 4.   Enable the rule.

Step 5.   Select one of the two operation modes:

    a. Automatically Trust IP Assignments on Their First Use: This trusts the IP provided by vCenter (using VMware Tools) and an IP assigned to the virtual machine via DHCP. All changes to this IP require manual approval. If the IP is changed, all traffic from the vNIC is blocked until the change is manually approved.

    b. Manually Inspect and Approve All IP Assignments Before Use: It means exactly what it says. No traffic is allowed to leave the vNIC until the IP is manually approved. This includes IPs learned via vCenter and DHCP.

Step 6.   There is a check box to allow IPs in the 169.254.0.0/16 as valid addresses. This is handy if you have an application that does heartbeats using IPs in this subnet range. The configuration should look similar to Figure 15-10.

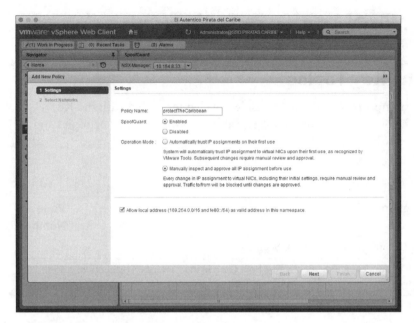

Figure 15-10   SpoofGuard

Step 7.   Click **Next**.

Step 8.   Select the legacy portgroup(s) (standard portgroup), distributed portgroup(s) (dvPortgroup), or logical switch(es) to apply this policy to.

Step 9.   Click **Finish**.

To approve an IP address, return to the SpoofGuard view, select the policy that includes the vNIC, and select the inactive vNICs view. Check the box next to the IP(s) that needs to be approved and click **Approve**.

SpoofGuard comes with a default policy that includes all portgroups and logical switches not already covered by a SpoofGuard Policy.

Exam Preparation Tasks

Review All the Key Topics

Review the most important topics from inside the chapter, noted with the Key Topic icon in the outer margin of the page. Table 15-11 lists these key topics and the page numbers where each is found.

Table 15-11   Key Topics for Chapter 15

Key Topic Element	Description	Page Number
Table 15-2	Design Compromises: Network Security.	453
Paragraph	The DFW functions irrespective of how the virtual machine connects to the network.	455
Paragraph	The DFW's memory is attached to each virtual machine's overhead memory.	457
Paragraph	The enforcement of security policies at the vNIC level.	457
Paragraph	The default DFW rule default action is set to Allow.	458
Paragraph	Layer 2 DFW rules are enforced before Layer 3 and Layer 4 DFW rules.	458
Paragraph	DFW configuration changes do not take effect until you click Public Changes	462
Paragraph	Not specifying a vNIC in the Applied To column will cause the DFW rule too be applied to all vNICs in the virtual machine.	468
Paragraph	SpoofGuard trusts the IP configured in the vNIC and the MAC address in the vmx file.	472
Paragraph	The default policy includes all virtual machines not in a SpoofGuard policy.	473

Complete Tables and Lists from Memory

Download and print a copy of Appendix C, "Memory Tables," (found on the book's website), or at least the section for this chapter, and complete the tables and lists from memory. Appendix D, "Memory Tables Answer Key," also on the website, includes the completed tables and lists so you can check your work.

Define Key Terms

Define the following key terms from this chapter, and check your answers in the glossary:

distributed firewall (DFW), microsegmentation, Exclusion List, local firewall rule, universal firewall rule, SpoofGuard

This chapter covers all or part of the following VCP6-NV exam blueprint topics:

- **Objective 7.3**—Configure and Manage Service Composer

CHAPTER 16

Security Services

The previous chapter covered the distributed logical firewall and how it provides Layer 2, Layer 3, and Layer 4 security. NSX also provides the capability to enforce security at Layer 7 (application layer), and provide IDS and IPS, antivirus, and malware protection. All these are done outside the context of the network, just like the distributed logical firewall. NSX provides some of these security services natively, but others can be provided by integrating with VMware's technological partners, such as Trend Micro, Palo Alto, and Symantec to name a few.

NSX is actually a platform where other security solutions can be integrated with it. Some allow security workflows that permit some level of automation when security threads are identified. This chapter covers how NSX manages to be a platform and allow some security automation by way of Service Composer.

Do I Know This Already?

The "Do I Know This Already?" quiz allows you to assess whether you should read this entire chapter or simply jump to the "Exam Preparation Tasks" section for review. If you are in doubt, read the entire chapter. Table 16-1 outlines the major headings in this chapter and the corresponding "Do I Know This Already?" quiz questions. You can find the answers in Appendix A, "Answers to the 'Do I Know This Already?' Quizzes."

Table 16-1   Headings and Questions

Foundation Topic Section	Questions Covered in This Section
Security Services for NSX	1-4
Service Composer	5-9
Security Tags	10

1. Which component is not a security service facilitated by Guest or Network Introspection?

    a. Data loss prevention

    b. Network Address Translation

    c. Malware protection

    d. Vulnerability management

2. Which security service is not facilitated by Network Introspection?

    a. Intrusion prevention

    b. Data security

    c. Malware protection

    d. Antivirus protection

3. Which statement is a valid example of a security service protecting a virtual machine?

    a. The logical switch sends traffic that leaves the virtual machine and is directed to the security service appliance.

    b. The distributed firewall sends traffic that arrives for the virtual machine from the security service appliance.

    c. The ESXi host redirects virtual machine traffic to the security service module running in the host's kernel.

    d. The ESXi host redirects the virtual machine traffic to the security service appliance using the IOChain.

4. What is the first step in consuming a security service from a provider?

    a. Register the security service with NSX Manager.

    b. Register the security service with vCenter.

    c. Register the ESXi hosts with the security service.

    d. Create a profile with the security service provider.

5. Which is not a dynamic selection option for a security group?

    a. Virtual machine name

    b. Computer OS name

    c. LDAP group

    d. Entity

6. How do you prevent a virtual machine from being a member of a security group?

   a. Do not include the virtual machine in the Define Dynamic Objects view.

   b. Do not include the virtual machine in the Select Objects to Include view.

   c. Add the virtual machine to the Select Objects to Exclude view.

   d. Add the virtual machine to the NSX Manager's Exclusion List.

7. If two security policies are associated with the same security group, which policy gets enforced first?

   a. The security policy that is associated first

   b. The security policy that is associated last

   c. The security policy that has the highest weight

   d. The security policy with the most secure service

8. Which is not a policy that can be configured as part of a security policy?

   a. Guest Introspection Services

   b. Network Introspection Services

   c. Distributed firewall rule

   d. SpoofGuard

9. A security policy named Santa Maria is configured with a distributed firewall rule and then applied to a security group named La Pinta.

   Based on this configuration, which two conditions are true? (Choose two.)

   a. The source or the destination of the distributed firewall rule is La Pinta.

   b. The distributed firewall rule is added below any existing rules, but above the default rule.

   c. Both the source and destination of the distributed firewall rule can be Any.

   d. Santa Maria can be applied to another security group.

   e. The distributed firewall rule is added at the top so it will be enforced before any existing rules.

10. Where are security tags created?

   a. In NSX Manager

   b. In vCenter

   c. In Service Composer

   d. In the security service provider

Foundation Topics

Security Services for NSX

Services providers, in the context of NSX, are NSX registered entities that deliver network and security services beyond those offered natively by NSX. The fact that you can register non-NSX entities with NSX to enhance NSX functionality turns NSX into both a network platform and a security platform.

The nonhardware based services delivery sometimes requires the deployment of a virtual appliance in the ESXi host(s) where the virtual machine(s) that will receive the service is(are) running. In Chapter 10, "Layer 2 Extensions," we touched on hardware-based services with Brocade's Hardware VTEP. Table 16-2 lists the security services that may be delivered by service providers and whether VMware, a VMware Technology Partner, or both make available the service.

Table 16-2 Security Services

Security Service	Provider(s)
Antivirus and malware protection	VMware Technology Partner
Data security	VMware
Data loss prevention	VMware and VMware Technology Partner
Vulnerability management	VMware Technology Partner
Intrusion detection (IDS)	VMware Technology Partner
Intrusion prevention (IPS)	VMware Technology Partner
Layer 2, 3, and 4 security	VMware (via DFW) and VMware Technology Partner

There are two types of security services:

- Guest Introspection, such as malware protection and data security, requires that the virtual machine be running VMware Tools.

- Network Introspection, such as application firewalls and intrusion prevention, are delivered by assigning a slot in the IOChain to redirect traffic to the virtual appliance delivering the security service. When traffic leaves the virtual machine toward the network or when the traffic leaves the network toward the virtual machine, the Network Introspection Service appliance receives the interesting traffic *after* the DFW processes it.

Figure 16-1 shows virtual machine DB_01 with a security service from Trend Micro. The Trend Micro virtual appliance is doing Network Introspection for all interesting traffic from and to DB_01.

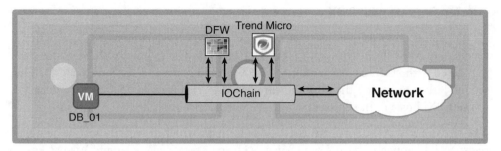

Figure 16-1 Network Introspection service

1. DB_01 sends interesting traffic (it doesn't matter what the destination is).

2. DB_01's DFW enforces the Layer 2, Layer 3, and Layer 4 security policies applied. For simplicity I'm skipping over the fact that the DFW works at the vNIC level and just assuming that DB_01 has a single vNIC.

3. If the DFW allows the traffic, the traffic is then passed to the Trend Micro Deep Security Virtual Appliance, hanging off slot 4 in the IOChain.

   VMware calls this traffic redirection *traffic steering*. The security service appliance has a vNIC, but it is only used for management plane traffic.

4. The Trend Micro virtual appliance performs Network Introspection. If the traffic is allowed, the traffic is sent back to the kernel.

5. The host forwards the traffic to the network. The network entry point can be a standard portgroup, a dvPortgroup, or a logical switch.

6. The host receives the interesting traffic from the network.

7. The host sends the traffic to the DB_01's DFW.

8. DB_01's DFW enforces the Layer 2, Layer 3, and Layer 4 security policies. If the traffic is allowed, the traffic is sent to the next slot in the IOChain.

9. The traffic is given to the Trend Micro Deep Security Virtual Appliance, in slot 4 in the IOChain.

10. The Trend Micro Deep Security Virtual Appliance performs Network Introspection.

11. If Trend Micro Deep Security Virtual Appliance allows the traffic, it is forwarded to DB_01.

Registering Service with NSX

Two tasks need to take place for a security service to be available to NSX. The first task is to register the service with NSX Manager (similar to how NSX Manager was registered with vCenter in Chapter 3, "NSX Architecture and NSX Manager"). The second task is to deploy the nonhardware based service provider's appliance in each of the ESXi hosts in the clusters where the virtual machines are.

The registration of the service varies based on the provider of security service being registered. I happen to have Trend Micro's Deep Security Manager and Virtual Appliance, so I'll be using its security service solution to go over this task. (I won't cover the step-by-step on how to configure the Trend Micro Deep Security Virtual Appliance itself as it's beyond the scope of this book and not part of the exam blueprint.) First, have a look at Figure 16-2. It shows the Service Definition's Service Managers view of NSX. The Service Managers view is where you can find all the service providers registered with NSX. Once Trend Micro is registered with NSX it shows up here.

A service provider may register more than one security service with NSX.

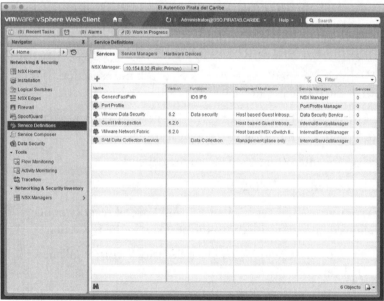

Figure 16-2   Service Definition's Service Managers view

Now let's get started in registering our Trend Micro Service:

NOTE   The Trend Micro screenshots that follow are for Deep Security Manager registering with NSX 6.1.

Step 1.   Connect to the Trend Micro Deep Security Manager. This step varies by service provider.

Step 2.   Enter the vCenter's FQDN or IP and its credentials. You also are asked for NSX Manager's FQDN or IP and its credentials. This also registers Deep Security Manager with NSX as a service, which is what is actually needed.

Step 3.   Wait for the Deep Security Manager's message stating the VMware vCenter has been successfully added, as shown in Figure 16-3. vCenter is listed in the Computer view on the left panel.

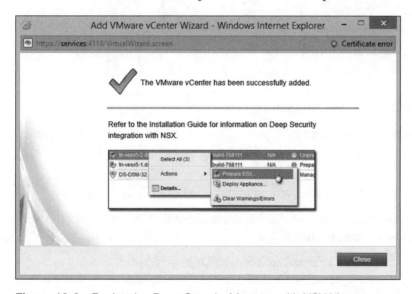

Figure 16-3   Registering Deep Security Manager with NSX Manager

Step 4.   Return to the Service Managers view of Networking and Security, select the NSX Manager that service registered with, and validate that you can see the Trend Micro Manager, as shown in Figure 16-4.

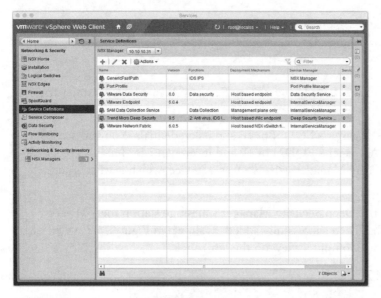

Figure 16-4   Service Definition with Trend Micro security service

Deploying the Security Service Appliance

Our second task is to deploy the appliance to those ESXi hosts that will be running the VMs that use the service. Remember that NSX Manager likes to deploy at the cluster level.

Step 1.   Go to NSX Manager's home page and select the **Installation** view.

Step 2.   Select the NSX Manager that has the registered service and click the **Service Deployments** tab.

Step 3.   Click the green **+** icon and wait for the Deploy Network & Security Services Wizard to open. You see all available service appliances that can be deployed, as shown in Figure 16-5.

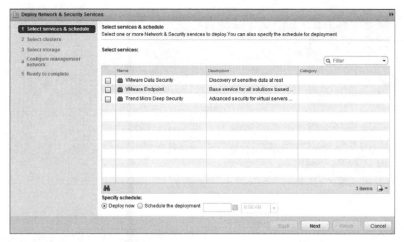

Figure 16-5 Service deployment tab

Step 4. In the **Select Services & Schedule** view, select the service appliance(s) you want to deploy. You can select multiple services if you are going to be deploying them in the same clusters. Further down the window, you have the option to schedule the deployment for a certain date and time.

Step 5. Click **Next**.

Step 6. In the **Select Clusters** view, select the clusters to deploy the security service virtual appliance(s) and click **Next**. You can only do one data center at a time.

Step 7. In the **Select Storage and Management Network** view, select (per cluster), the datastore to deploy the service appliance(s), and the dvPortgroup to connect the management interface of the service appliance(s). You can also select to assign an IP by DHCP or from an IP pool.

Step 8. In the **Ready to Complete** view, review the configuration and click **Finish**.

At this point (or whenever you scheduled the service appliance[s] to be deployed), the following happens:

1. NSX Manager gets the service appliance ovf from the Service Management entity.

2. NSX Manager gives the ovf to vCenter and instructs it where to deploy it, per the instructions you provided.

3. vCenter creates a resource pool in each cluster, deploys the ovf, and adds the service appliance(s) to the resource pool, as shown in Figure 16-6.

   The resource pool has expandable and unlimited CPU and memory reservations.

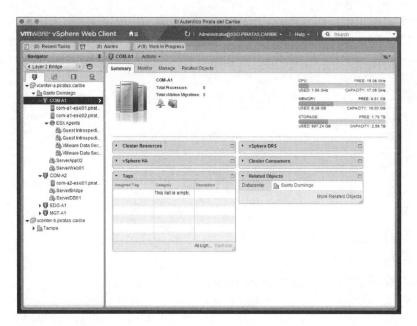

Figure 16-6   Security services resource pool

You are probably wondering: How do I add or configure a VM so that it leverages the security service? First, you need to create service profiles in the service provider manager (which varies by security service provider), which are made available to NSX. You then can apply them via NSX to VMs. The service profiles are the policies the security service appliance enforces. You have two options to apply the security service to a VM: Option 1, via Service Composer, and Option 2, via the logical firewall. In the next section we discuss how to apply the security service's profiles to a VM to do Guest Introspection and Network Introspection.

Service Composer

Service Composer is one of the features that makes it possible for NSX to be a security platform. Service Composer allows for the consumption and enforcement of security services by applying policies to VMs. Service Composer allows for a VM with multiple vNICs to have the same policy applied to all its vNICs or to have different policies applied to each vNIC. Once a VM has been assigned to a policy, NSX enforces the policy on the VM no matter where the VM is running (as long as it runs in an ESXi host that has been prepared).

There are two parts to Service Composer: the security groups that contain a list of VMs and the security policies that get applied to the security groups (and thus the VMs).

Security Groups

A security group is the list of VMs or VMs' vNICs for which you want to provide some security protection. A VM or its individual vNICs can be in a single security group or multiple security groups. A security group's VM inclusion is done dynamically when a VM that is powered on matches the security group's membership criteria. If a VM is powered off, the VM and its vNICs are removed from the security group membership. If the VM is powered on again, vCenter notifies NSX Manager, which then adds the VM and its vNICs into the security group again. A security group can be created before the VM is created.

To create a security group, follow these steps:

Step 1. Go to the Networking and Security page and select the **Service Composer** view.

Step 2. Click the **Security Groups** tab.

You may also go to the NSX Manager's home page from the Networking and Security page, and then go to **Manage > Grouping Objects > Security Groups**.

Step 3. Click the **New Security Group** icon and wait for the New Security Group Wizard to open.

Step 4. Enter the name of the security group and click **Next**. You can also include a description.

If you create the security group from the Primary NSX Manager's home page, you have the option to make this a universal security group by checking the **Mark This Object for Universal Synchronization** box.

Step 5. In the **Define Dynamic Membership** view, enter the criteria that the virtual machine must match for inclusion in the security group and click **Next**. Table 16-3 shows the virtual machine dynamic selection options, whereas Table 16-4 shows the criteria that must be matched for the selection.

VMware does not support dynamic membership for universal security groups.

Table 16-3 Dynamic Selection Options

Entity	Description
Computer OS Name	The Guest OS name.
Computer Name	The name of the server, as configured in the Guest OS.
VM Name	The name of the virtual machine, as recorded by vCenter.
Entity	Object in vCenter or NSX Manager.
Security Tag	Label defined in NSX Manager. It is case sensitive.

Table 16-4 Matching Criteria Options

Entity	Available To
Belongs to	Entity
Contains	Computer OS Name, VM Name, Computer Name, Security Tag
Starts With	Computer OS Name, VM Name, Computer Name, Security Tag
Ends With	Computer OS Name, VM Name, Computer Name, Security Tag
Equals to	Computer OS Name, VM Name, Computer Name, Security Tag
Not Equals To	Computer OS Name, VM Name, Computer Name
Matches Regular Expression	VM Name, Security Tag

- Multiple criteria groups can be created.

- Matching options for criteria groups are **And** and **Or**.

- Each criteria group can have multiple criteria.

- Matching options within a criteria group are **Any** and **All**, as shown in Figure 16-7.

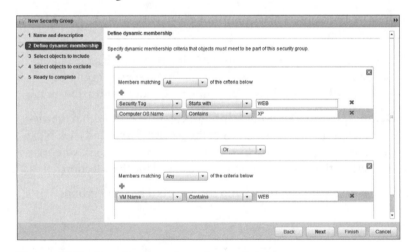

Figure 16-7 Security group dynamic membership

Step 6.   In the **Select Objects to Include** view, manually select any virtual machine(s) that would not be dynamically selected in step 5 and click **Next**.

Multiple objects containing vNICs, IPs, or MAC addresses can be selected. Table 16-5 shows the objects available for inclusion.

Table 16-5 Security Group Object Selection Options

Object	Description
Data Center	A vCenter Datacenter.
Cluster	A cluster prepared for NSX.
Resource Pool	A resource pool in a cluster prepared for NSX.
Security Group	An existing security group.
Logical Switch	An existing logical switch.
Distributed Portgroup	Any vCenter distributed portgroup. The virtual machine must run in an NSX prepared host.
Network	Any standard virtual switch portgroup. The ESXi host must be prepared for NSX.
Virtual App	A vApp in vCenter. The virtual machines in the vApp must run in an NSX prepared host.
Virtual Machine	Any virtual machine running in an NSX prepared host.
vNIC	Any vNIC of any virtual machine running in an NSX prepared host.
Security Tag	Label defined in NSX Manager. It is case sensitive.
IP Sets	An NSX Manager list of IPs.
MAC Sets	An NSX Manager list of MAC addresses.
Directory Group	AD or LDAP groups.

Table 16-5 has a line for security groups. You can select an existing security group, which is then called a *nested security group*. Nested security groups may be used to reference some level for hierarchy among virtual machines for the purpose of policy enforcement. For example, a two-tier application may have a security group for each tier and a third security group that references the two-tier specific security groups.

Universal security groups only support security groups, IP sets, and MAC sets. All three must be universal.

Step 7.   The next view, **Select Objects to Exclude**, is the exact opposite of **Select Objects to Include**. Manually select any virtual machine(s) that you do not want to be included in this security group. Even if the object has been included in steps 5 or 6, the object selected here always excludes from this security group. The options are the same as those in Table 16-5.

Universal security groups only support security groups, IP sets, and MAC sets. All three must be universal.

Step 8.   Click **Next**, review your changes, and click **Finish**. Figure 16-8 shows the
Security Groups tab with some security groups that have been created.

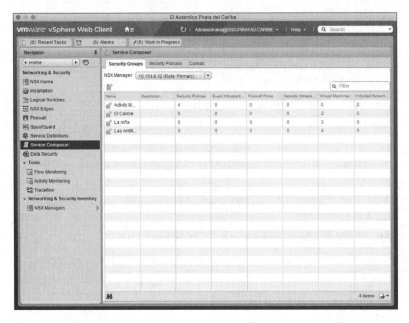

Figure 16-8   Security groups

Now that we have some security groups, let me go on a slight tangent and revisit the
logical firewall (this one is for you, security team). In Chapter 15, "Distributed Logical Firewall," Table 15-5 listed security groups as one of the options for the firewall
rules' Source and Destination fields, and Table 15-7 listed security groups as one of
the options for the firewall rules' Applied To field. One potential advantage of using
security groups in the logical firewall rules is that updates to the security group do
not require that the logical firewall rules be republished. When a security group's
membership is updated, and the security group is being referenced in a logical firewall rule, NSX Manager immediately updates the necessary ESXi hosts about the
membership change.

As cool and useful as using security groups in logical firewall rules sounds, it is not
a panacea. As your environment evolves, security needs will change. Anyone who
works in the data center knows that almost every new application that gets deployed
comes with new security policies that don't quite match the existing ones. This often
requires creating a new firewall rule in the firewall. To allow for granular control of
the enforcement of policies without impacting existing workloads, you want to use
security policies from Service Composer for DFW rules.

Security Policies

Security policies are the security team's NSX best friend. This is where you define exactly what you want happening in terms of security for VMs (and their vNICs). Security policies have one or more of the following:

- Guest Introspection Services

- Distributed firewall rules

- Network Introspection Services

Guest Introspection provides security services at the VM level, such as malware protection. Network Introspection provides security services on the payload of the packet. The same service provider may provide both Guest Introspection Services and Network Introspection Services.

After a security policy is created, you associate it to one or more security groups. The moment you finish the association, the security policy to the security group(s), NSX Manager instructs the ESXi hosts to enforce the policies in the security policy to each and every VM in the security group. As the security group membership changes (VMs get created and/or powered on), the policies in the security policy associated to the security group get enforced on the new security group members. If a VM is removed from a security group, the policies associated with that security group will no longer be enforced on that VM.

To create a security policy, follow these steps:

Step 1. Go to the Networking and Security page and select the **Service Composer** view.

Step 2. Click the **Security Policies** tab.

Step 3. Click the **Create Security Policy** icon and wait for the New Security Policy Wizard to open.

Step 4. In the **Name and Description** view, enter a name and a description.

 a. If you want to use the policies of an existing security policy, check the box for **Inherit Security Policy** and select the security policy.

 b. In the **Advanced** section, you can change the weight of the policy. The weight is used to determine the ranking of the security policies relative to each other. For new security policies, NSX Manager adds a default weight of 1,000 plus the highest weight of any existing security policy.

 c. Click **Next**.

Step 5.   In the **Guest Introspection Services** view, click the green **+** icon to add a Guest Introspection Security Service and wait for the Add Guest Introspection Services Wizard to open.

This is how we call up the service configurations created in the Guest Introspection service provider. At the moment this security policy is applied to a security group, NSX Manager finds out the hosts that are running all the virtual machines in the security group and tells the service provider to push the security service configuration to the security service virtual appliances in the hosts.

   a. Enter a name and description.

   b. Choose whether to apply or block the service. If you block the service, this service won't be enforced on the virtual machines of the Security Group(s) this security policy gets associated with.

   c. If you choose to block the service, select the service type to block.

   d. If you choose to allow the service, select the service name.

   e. If you choose to allow the service, select the service's profile to use. The list of available profiles is provided by the security service provider to NSX Manager. The same service name (step 5d. above) may provide multiple profiles to choose from.

   f. In **State**, select to enable (or disable) the Guest Introspection Service. Disabling the Guest Introspection Service is typically used for staging. You configure the security policy now and turn it on (enable it) at a later time, perhaps during the maintenance window.

   g. Select whether to enforce the service. If enforced, this service can't be overwritten by other security policies.

     This is mostly used when this security policy is inherited by other security policies (step 4a.). When this Guest Introspection Service gets inherited, it will be enforced first before any other Guest Introspection Services the inheriting security policy may have.

   h. Click **OK**.

Step 6.   Repeat step 5 to add more Guest Introspection Services. Click **Next** when done.

Step 7.   In the **Firewall Rules** view, click the green **+** icon and wait for the New Firewall Rules Wizard to open.

This is the alternative I alluded to when I diverted the conversation toward the logical firewall at the end of the security group discussion. You can add DFW rules directly in the security policy. By writing the DFW rules in the security policy, you only impact the virtual machines that belong to the security group where this security policy gets applied.

a. Enter a name or description for the DFW rule.

b. For **Source and Destination**, the options are the Policy's **Security Groups, existing Security Groups,** and **Any**. The Policy's Security Groups means all the security groups this security policy gets associated to. If you select existing security groups you have the option to negate the source or destination.

You can apply the same security policy to multiple security groups. So what happens here is that the DFW rule gets created under a new DFW section named after the security policy. The DFW rules Source and Destination fields are updated to include the security group the security policy gets associated to. For example, have a look at Figure 16-9. It shows a DFW rule that has two security groups in the source. This DFW rule was added because the same security policy, Enriquillo, was applied to both security groups. Security policy Enriquillo had a DFW rule that used the security group as the source. And while we are on the topic, either the source or the destination, or both, *must* be the policy's security group.

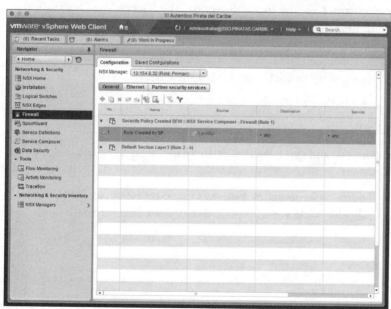

Figure 16-9 DFW rules created by security policy

c. Select the Service(s) for the DFW rule.

d. Select to **Allow** or **Block**.

e. Choose whether to log the rule.

f. Choose whether to enable or disable the rule. If disabled, the rule won't be enforced. This is another good way to stage the security policy.

g. Click **OK**.

Step 8. Repeat step 7 to add more DFW rules and then click **Next**.

Step 9. In the **Network Introspection Service** view, click the green **+** icon and wait for the Add Network Introspection Service Wizard to open.

a. Write down a name and a description.

b. Choose whether to redirect the traffic being defined here to the service's virtual appliance.

c. Select the service and the profile.

d. Select a source and destination to match the interesting traffic. Selection options are existing **Security Groups**, the **Policy's Security Group**, and **Any**. You have the option to negate the **Source and the Destination**. Like the Firewall section, the Source, the Destination, or both must be the policy's security group.

e. Select the service(s) to match the interesting traffic.

f. Choose whether to enable or disable the rule.

g. Choose whether to log the rule.

h. Click **OK**.

Step 10. Repeat step 9 to add more **Network Introspection Services** and then click **Next**.

Step 11. Review your changes and click **Finish**. Figure 16-10 shows the **Security Policies** tab with some security policies that have been created.

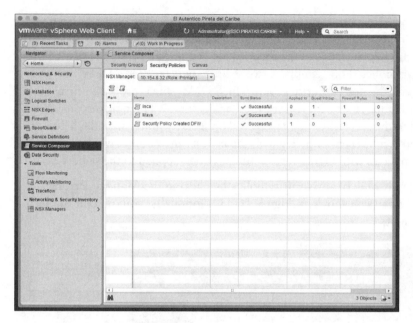

Figure 16-10 Security policies

Let's do a quick recap of what we've done thus far in this chapter:

1. We registered security services with NSX Manager.

2. We deployed the security service's virtual appliances in the clusters.

3. We created security groups.

4. We created security policies.

Now on to the final step to associate a security policy with one or more security groups. While in the **Security Policies** tab, follow these steps to associate a security policy to one or more security groups:

Step 1. Select the security policy to associate.

Step 2. Click the **Apply Security Policy** icon and wait for the **Apply Security Policy** window to open.

Step 3. Select the Security Group(s) to associate.

Step 4. Click **OK**.

Step 5. Repeat steps 1 through 4 to associate other security policies to security groups.

It is possible to associate two security policies to the same security group or have a VM belonging in two different security groups, each with its own security policy association. When this happens, one of the security policies must be enforced first before the other security policy. For example, if two security policies have a DFW rule and are associated with the same security group, which DFW rule is processed first? Have another look at Figure 16-10. Do you see the Rank column? The rank placement is directly related to the security policy's weight. The security policy with the highest weight is ranked 1. The security policy with the lowest rank number will be enforced before security policies with higher rank numbers (when applied to the same VM).

You can change the rank of any security policy by clicking the **Manage Priority** icon to display the screen shown in Figure 16-11. Optionally, you can edit the security policy's weight.

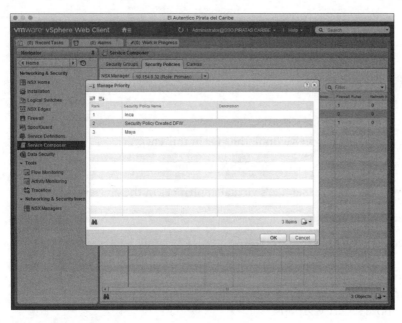

Figure 16-11 Change security policy rank

Logical Firewall Service Redirection

The logical firewall can be configured to redirect interesting traffic to a security service virtual appliance. In the Firewall view of the Networking and Security page is a tab called Partner Security Services. In that tab, you can configure the equivalent of a firewall rule with Source, Destination, and Service fields. However, the Action field gives you slightly different options from a normal firewall rule. The options you have are the following:

- **Action**:

  - **Redirect**: Send traffic that matches this rule to the security service virtual appliance.

  - **Do not Redirect**: Do not send the traffic that matches this rule to the security service virtual appliance.

  - **Balance**: Use the distributed load balancer for traffic that matches this rule.

- **Redirect To**: Select the services' profile and the logical switch or security group that will be bound by this rule. This Redirect To field also serves as the Apply To field in logical firewall rules.

- **Direction**: In, out, or in/out relative to the virtual machine.

- **Log**: To log or not to log (that is the question).

- **Comments**: If desired, add a note or comment.

- **Virtual Server IP**: This option is available only if you select an Action of Balance. This IP will be the distributed load balancer's VIP.

Before you can use the logical firewall service redirection, you must first register the Security Service provider with NSX Manager and deploy the security service virtual appliance.

Rules created in the Partner Security Services tab are enforced after all Ethernet and General rules are processed. This means that a Layer 2 or Layer 3 and Layer 4 rule must allow the interesting traffic identified in the Partner Security Services rule.

Security Tags

A *security tag* is a label that you create in NSX Manager that can be attached to a VM. Security tags can be used as a membership parameter for security groups. So what's so sexy about it since we already have so many other alternatives to add VMs in security groups? For one, a security tag is fully controlled by NSX Manager, so no matter what modifications are done to the virtual machine in vCenter (short of removing the virtual machine from vCenter's inventory or deleting it) the virtual machine membership in the security group will remain. Another benefit of using security tags: You can create security workflows where a security service provider interacts with NSX Manager, triggered by some security event, and instructs NSX Manager to attach a security tag to a particular virtual machine.

As an example, let's go over Figure 16-12, where a virtual appliance is providing a security service to virtual machine WEB_03. The initial conditions are as follows:

■ DB_02 belongs to the security group named Database Servers.

■ A security policy named Protect From Database Servers is associated to Database Servers. Protect From Database Servers has a Network Introspection Service.

■ A security group named Isolated Servers has as a membership criteria of security tag named Isolate Me.

■ A security policy named Isolated is associated to Isolated Servers.

Security policy Isolated has a DFW rule blocking all traffic for the policy's security group.

Security policy Isolated has a higher weight than *security policy* Protect From Database Servers.

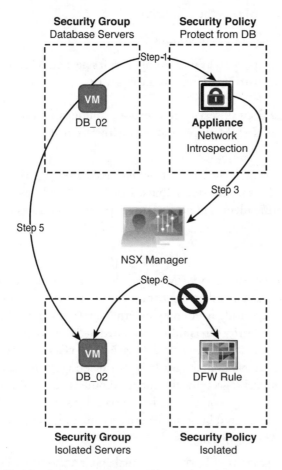

Figure 16-12 Security workflow with security tags

1. DB_02 is sending traffic, which is steered to the Network Introspection virtual appliance.

2. The traffic triggers a security alert in the virtual appliance.

3. The security alert causes the Network Introspection provider to alert NSX Manager, requesting that security tag Isolate Me be placed on DB_02.

4. NSX Manager attaches the security tag Isolate Me to DB_02.

5. DB_02 becomes a member of Isolated Servers.

6. A DFW rule blocks all traffic to and from DB_02.

To create a security tag, follow these steps:

Step 1. From the Networking and Security page, click **NSX Managers**.

Step 2. Click the NSX Manager where you want to add the security tag.

Step 3. Go to **Manage > Security Tags**.

Step 4. Click the green **+** icon and wait for the New Security Tag Wizard to open.

Step 5. Enter the name and description of the security tag and click OK.

Once you have created the security tag, you can manually assign it to one or more virtual machines. To manually assign a security tag, follow these steps:

Step 1. Select the security tag.

Step 2. Click the Assign Security Tag icon and wait for the Assign Security Tag window to open.

Step 3. Select the virtual machines to assign.

Step 4. Click **OK**.

IP Sets and MAC Sets

NSX Manager can have its own list of IPs and MAC addresses, which can be used as Source and Destination in DFW rules, as well as selection criteria for security group membership. NSX Manager IP sets are separate and independent of NSX Edge IP sets.

To create an NSX Manager IP set, follow these steps:

Step 1. From the Networking and Security page, click **NSX Managers**.

Step 2. Click the NSX Manager where you want to add the IP set.

Step 3.   Go to **Manage > Grouping Objects**.

Step 4.   Select IP Sets, click the green + icon, and wait for the New IP Set Wizard to open.

Step 5.   Enter a name and description for the IP set.

Step 6.   Type the IP address to include in the set:

    a. You can enter a single IP address.

    b. You can enter an IP range such as 10.73.21.154-10.73.21.73.

    c. You can enter a subnet, such as 10.73.21.0/24.

Step 7.   Check the **Enable Inheritance to Allow Visibility at Underlying Scopes** box if you want to allow this IP set to propagate to other scopes. This option is not available for universal IP sets.

Step 8.   Check the **Mark This Object for Universal Synchronization** box to make this a universal IP set. This option is only available for the Primary NSX Manager.

Step 9.   Click **OK**.

Step 10.   Repeat steps 4 through 9 to add more IP sets.

To create a MAC set, follow these steps, starting from the Grouping Objects window:

Step 1.   Select **MAC Sets**.

Step 2.   Click the green **+** icon and wait for the **New MAC Set** Wizard to open.

Step 3.   Enter a name and description for the MAC set.

Step 4.   Type the MAC address to include in the set. You can enter multiple MAC addresses separated by commas.

Step 5.   Check the **Enable Inheritance to Allow Visibility at Underlying Scopes** box if you want to allow this MAC set to propagate to other scopes. This option is not available for universal MAC sets.

Step 6.   Check the **Mark This Object for Universal Synchronization** box to make this a universal MAC set. This option is only available for the Primary NSX Manager.

Step 7.   Click **OK**.

Step 8.   Repeat steps 2 through 7 to add more MAC sets.

Exam Preparation Tasks

Review All the Key Topics

Review the most important topics from inside the chapter, noted with the Key Topic icon in the outer margin of the page. Table 16-6 lists these key topics and the page numbers where each is found.

Table 16-6 Key Topics for Chapter 16

Key Topic Element	Description	Page Number
Paragraph	Guest Introspection Services require VMware tools be installed in the virtual machines.	480
Paragraph	Redirecting of traffic to a security service appliance by use of the IOChain	481
Paragraph	Multiple security services may be registered by a security provider	482
Paragraph	Universal Security Groups only support IP-based objects and groups	489
Paragraph	If a security group is referenced in a DFW rule, updating the security group does not require that the DFW rules be published.	490
Paragraph	After configuring a service in a security policy, NSX Manager asks the security service provider to push its security policies to the security service's virtual appliance(s).	492
Paragraph	Adding DFW rules to to a security policy limits the VMs that are impacted by the rules.	492
Paragraph	The security policy with the highest weight gets enforced before lower weight security policies.	496
Paragraph	The Security Service provider must be registered with NSX Manager before using service redirection	497

Complete Tables and Lists from Memory

Download and print a copy of Appendix C, "Memory Tables," (found on the book's website), or at least the section for this chapter, and complete the tables and lists from memory. Appendix D, "Memory Tables Answer Key," also on the website, includes the completed tables and lists so you can check your work.

Define Key Terms

Define the following key terms from this chapter, and check your answers in the glossary:

security service provider, Service Composer, security groups, security policy, security tag

This chapter covers all or part of the following VCP6-NV exam blueprint topics:

- **Objective 9.1**—Configure Roles, Permissions, and Scopes

- **Objective 9.3**—Monitor a VMware NSX Implementation

- **Objective 9.4**—Perform Auditing and Compliance

- **Objective 10.1**—Compare and Contrast Tools Available for Troubleshooting

CHAPTER 17

Additional NSX Features

We are almost done with NSX, at least the parts that pertain to the UI in the vSphere Web Client. We have covered all the SDN foundations of NSX as it pertains to networking and security. By this point, you should feel comfortable with deploying and using NSX.

In this chapter we cover additional features that NSX has to offer, in particular tools that can be used for troubleshooting and alerting of security policy violations. One of these features is Traceflow, which I believe accentuates the benefits of SDN solutions like NSX over your traditional physical network.

Do I Know This Already?

The "Do I Know This Already?" quiz allows you to assess whether you should read this entire chapter or simply jump to the "Exam Preparation Tasks" section for review. If you are in doubt, read the entire chapter. Table 17-1 outlines the major headings in this chapter and the corresponding "Do I Know This Already?" quiz questions. You can find the answers in Appendix A, "Answers to the 'Do I Know This Already?' Quizzes."

Table 17-1 Headings and Questions

Foundation Topic Section	Questions Covered in This Section
VMware Data Security	1-2
Activity Monitoring	3-5
Flow Monitoring	6-7
Traceflow	8
Role Based Access Control	9-10

1. How does VMware Data Security provide its services to virtual machines?

    a. VMware Data Security scans, via an appliance, data stored in protected virtual machines to check against security compliance.

    b. VMware Data Security scans, via NSX Manager, data stored in protected virtual machines to check against security compliance.

    c. VMware Data Security scans, via vCenter, data stored in protected virtual machines to check against security compliance.

    d. VMware Data Security scans, via NSX Edge, data stored in protected virtual machines to check against security compliance.

2. Which two components are required to successfully implement VMware Data Security? (Choose two.)

    a. A data security appliance deployed to the data center where you want to enable Data Security.

    b. An EPSEC-MUX agent deployed to the ESXi host where you want to enable Data Security.

    c. A security policy with Guest Introspection Services of Data Security.

    d. A logical firewall rule that allows Data Security, applied to the virtual machines that require protection.

3. Which two steps are used to enable data collection in a virtual machine? (Choose two.)

    a. Right-click the virtual machine and select **Edit Settings**. In the **VM Options** tab, check the **Enable Activity Monitoring Data Collection** box.

    b. In the virtual machine's **Manage** tab, select **NSX Activity Monitoring**, click **Edit**, and answer **Yes** in the pop-up window.

    c. Add the virtual machine to the **Security Group Activity Monitoring Data Collection**.

    d. From the **Networking and Security** home page, select **Activity Monitoring**. In the **VM Activity** tab, click **Add VM**.

4. What activity is displayed by the Inter Container Interaction activity report?

    a. Activities between virtual machines running on the same ESXi host.

    b. Activities between virtual machines in the same cluster.

    c. Activities between monitored virtual machines.

    d. Activities of users in the selected Active Directory group.

5. What two appliances must be deployed for Activity Monitoring to work? (Choose two.)

   a. VMware Data Security virtual appliance

   b. VMware Activity Monitoring virtual appliance

   c. NSX Data Security virtual appliance

   d. Universal services virtual machine

6. Which entity collects the traffic flow information when Flow Monitoring is enabled?

   a. vCenter

   b. The configured IPFix collector

   c. The NSX Manager

   d. The NSX Edge device(s)

7. Which is not a source exclusion container option for Flow Monitoring?

   a. IP sets

   b. Virtual machines

   c. ESXi host

   d. vNIC

8. Which Traceflow is used when enabling a multicast Traceflow?

   a. Layer 2 Traceflow

   b. Layer 3 Traceflow

   c. Layer 4 Traceflow

   d. A Traceflow where both the source and destination are virtual machines.

9. You are assigning a role to a user. Where does NSX Manager obtain the user information?

   a. From the configured LDAP server in NSX Manager.

   b. From the configured AD server in NSX Manager.

   c. From a list of users manually entered into NSX Manager.

   d. From the list of users known to vCenter.

10. Which of the following is not a role in NSX Manager?

   a. NSX administrator

   b. Security administrator

   c. Read-only

   d. Enterprise administrator

Foundation Topics

VMware Data Security

I remember when the Payment Card Industry (PCI) Data Security Standard came around in the mid-2000s. What a pain! But a necessary one. Credit card fraud was starting to get businesses' (and governments') attention, and something had to be done to stop it (I wonder if they were successful). Those of us in the network and security teams had to create new and segregated segments to connect end systems (servers) that were deemed under the PCI purview. Since almost no one knew for certain which end systems were under PCI compliance, the default behavior was to drop in those segments any device that couldn't be guaranteed 100% that it had nothing to do with credit cards. You see, penalties for failing a PCI audit were stiff, and you didn't want to be *that* guy who didn't do "his job."

A popular (original) solution was to sniff all traffic coming (and going) to the end systems within the PCI zones. Things then got interesting when server virtualization became popular toward the late 2000s. I mean, how were you going to sniff traffic of two VMs within the same ESXi host that are communicating with each other? It turns out that virtualization made it easier to meet PCI compliance rather than more difficult. First, it is easier to identify the virtual machines (VMs) that fall within PCI scope. Second, you install an agent in these VMs (no need to sniff traffic anymore) and scan the data inside the VMs. An advantage of scanning the data in the VMs, rather than sniffing the traffic, is that you can proactively know when a PCI violation is taking place without having to wait for that data to be sent to some bad actors somewhere.

VMware Data Security is a Guest Introspection Service that scans the data stored in the virtual machine for security compliance against government and industry data privacy regulations and standards. The Data Security scan is nonintrusive and only requires of the virtual machine that VMware Tools be installed. Of the ESXi hosts, Data Security requires that the Data Security Virtual Appliance be installed in the ESXi hosts where the virtual machines are running. Data Security works by scanning the files in the virtual machines running in NSX prepared hosts. All compliance violations are reported by NSX.

VMware Data Security supports data privacy regulations and standards for Payment Card Industry (PCI), Protected Health Information (PHI), and Personally Identifiable Information (PII) from industry, state, federal, and national governments around the world.

To use Data Security, the VMware Data Security Virtual Appliance and the Guest Introspection Virtual Appliance, also called Universal Services Virtual Machine (USVM), must be deployed first. The appliances are deployed just as other partner security services get deployed. To deploy VMware Data Security Virtual Appliance and the USVM, follow these steps:

Step 1. Go to the Networking and Security page and select the **Installation** view.

Step 2. Click the **Service Deployment** tab and select the NSX Manager to deploy the VMware Data Security Virtual Appliance.

Step 3. Click the green **+** icon and wait for the Deploy Network & Security Services Wizard to open.

Step 4. Select **VMware Data Security**, the USVM, and click **Next**.

Step 5. In the **Select Clusters** view, select the clusters to deploy the VMware Data Security Virtual Appliance, the USVM, and click **Next**.

Step 6. In the **Select Storage and Management Network** view, select (per cluster), the Datastore to deploy the appliance, the dvPortgroup for the appliance's management interface, and the IP, as shown in Figure 17-1.

The IP options are DHCP and IP Pool.

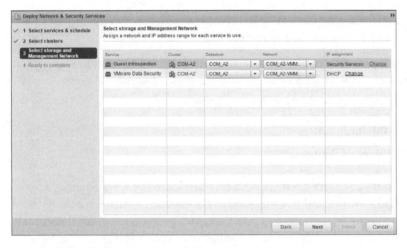

Figure 17-1 Select Storage and Management Network view

Step 7. In the **Ready to Complete** view, review the configuration and click **Finish**.

At this point NSX deploys a copy of the VMware Data Security Virtual Appliance and the USVM, using an OVF, in each ESXi host in the clusters selected. Both appliances are added to a new resource pool called ESX agents.

It turns out that the appliances have a second interface used for local communication with the ESXi host where it is running. A new standard switch, named vmservice-vswitch, is deployed in each ESXi host with no uplinks and two standard portgroups, vmservice-vshield-pg and vmservice-vmknic-pg. The appliances' second interface is connected to standard portgroup vmservice-vshield-pg. A new VMkernel port is added to each ESXi host and connected to the second standard portgroup vmservice-vmknic-pg. The IPs of the appliances' second interface and the VMkernel port are in the 169.254.1.x subnet.

The deployment of the USVM also includes the installation of the EPSEC-MUX agent in each ESXi host in the cluster.

The next step is to select the data privacy regulations that will be used in the Data Security scans. To select the regulation and standards, follow these steps:

Step 1.   Go to the Networking and Security page and select the **Data Security** view.

Step 2.   Click the **Manage** tab.

Step 3.   Click the **Edit** button and wait for the Select Regulations and Standards Wizard to open.

Step 4.   Select all the regulations and standards you want to scan against and click **Next**.

Step 5.   If you selected a regulation or standard that requires a matching data pattern, enter the pattern using regular expressions.

For example, you could enter the following regular expression to match a United States Social Security Number (3 digits-2 digits-4 digits):

^(\d{3}-?\d{2}-?\d{4}|XXX-XX-XXXX)$

Step 6.   Click **Finish**.

Step 7.   Click **Publish Changes**.

The final step to run your Data Security scan is to associate the Data Security regulations and standards with virtual machines. The association to virtual machines is done via Service Composer. You must create a security group containing the virtual machines you want to scan, create a security policy with Guest Introspection Services of Data Security and associate the security policy to the security group. We covered Service Composer in Chapter 16, "Security Services." At the beginning of this section I mentioned that virtualization made it easier to run regulation compliances, and Service Composer is an example of how this is possible. You could create an NSX security tag, for example, PCI-Audit; create a security group that contains the NSX security tag PCI-Audit; and add the NSX security tag to just those VMs that need to be audited for PCI.

You are literally now ready to start your Data Security scan. Just click Start in the Manage tab of the Data Security view and let NSX do its thing. You can see the scan statistics in **Monitor > Dashboard**. The Dashboard also shows the scan history, where you can download the scan reports. To see a report of the latest scan, go to **Monitor > Reports**.

NSX Data Security automatically throttles, per host, the number of concurrent virtual machines getting scanned to minimize impact on host performance.

Returning to the Manage view briefly, at the bottom of the page you can see the list of files that will be scanned by Data Security. You can edit this list by clicking Edit. Your options for file scanning include

- Monitor all files in the virtual machines.

- Monitor only files that match the following criteria.

    You can choose one or more of the following:

    - File Size

    - Last Modified Date

    - File Extension Type

    You can either list the file extensions to scan or the file extensions to skip.

Activity Monitoring

Whereas Data Security checks for security compliance against regulations and standards, Activity Monitoring is a Guest Introspection Service that checks for user access compliance. Activity Monitoring makes it possible to verify that only the intended users are accessing applications. You can even check whether the user is accessing a business application, on the server-side, by using the approved client-side application.

For example, if your company's security policies dictate that only members of the LDAP group Sales Managers are allowed access to the CRM database, you can generate an activity report that can tell whether users not in the Sales Managers LDAP group are accessing the CRM database.

Activity Monitoring only supports Windows as the virtual machine's Guest OS, and VMware Tools and the Guest Introspection driver must be installed.

Before you can create an activity report that shows whether the company's security access policies are being implemented as intended, you need to add NSX Manager to an LDAP domain to match user groups to Windows users (this was covered in Chapter 15, "Distributed Logical Firewall"), deploy the USVM (covered in the "VMware Data Security" section in this chapter), and enable virtual machine data collection for at least five (5) minutes. Data collection enables NSX Manager to log the traffic to/from the virtual machine.

To enable data collection for a single virtual machine, follow these steps:

Step 1.   Go to **Hosts and Clusters** or **Virtual Machine and Templates** view.

Step 2.   Select the virtual machine and go to **Manage > Settings**.

Step 3.   Select **NSX Activity Monitoring**.

Step 4.   Click **Edit** and answer **Yes** in the pop-up window.

The pop-up window asks: **Enable Activity Monitoring data collection for virtual machine** {Virtual Machine's name}**?**, as shown in Figure 17-2.

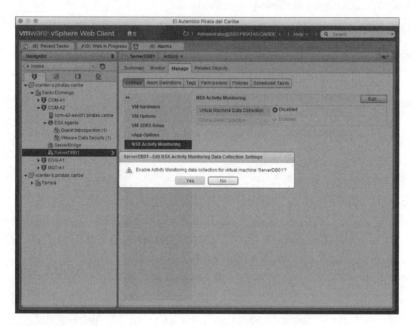

Figure 17-2   Enable data collection in a virtual machine

Enabling data collection one VM at a time could be time consuming. You can also enable data collection in multiple VMs at the same time. In Service Composer there is a security group called Activity Monitoring Data Collection, as shown in Figure 17-3. Simply add in this group the VMs for which you want to have data collection enabled.

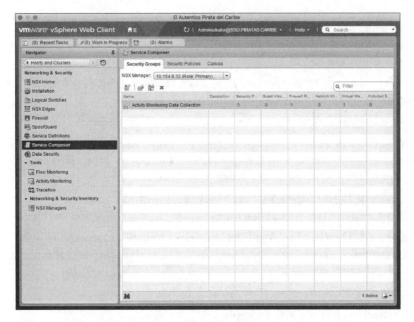

Figure 17-3   Activity Monitoring Data Collection security group

After running data collection for at least five (5) minutes, you can run an activity report for the VMs. We walk through viewing the different activity reports available in Activity Monitoring. We then review how to run a report from the VM's Monitor view.

VM Activity

This report shows traffic between VMs. Both the source and destination VMs must have data collection enabled. To run this report, follow these steps:

Step 1.   Go to the Networking and Security page and select the **Activity Monitoring** view.

Step 2.   Click the **VM Activity** tab and select the **NSX Manager**.

    a. In **Where source**, select to include or exclude one or more source virtual machines.

    b. In **Where Destination**, select to include or exclude one or more of the destination virtual machines.

    c. In **During Period**, select how far back to run the report.

Step 3.   Click **Search** to run the activity report.

Inbound Activity

This report shows traffic coming toward the monitored VMs (ingress). To run this report, perform the following steps:

Step 1.   Go to the Networking and Security page and select the **Activity Monitoring** view.

Step 2.   Click the **Inbound Activity** tab and select the NSX Manager.

 a. In **Outbound From**, select the security groups, AD groups, and/or desktop pools to match in the report. The Outbound From refers to the entity that sent the traffic from the monitored VMs.

 b. In **Where Destination Virtual Machine**, select to include or exclude one or more of the virtual machines that have data collection enabled.

 c. In **Where Destination Application**, select to include or exclude one or more of the applications running in the virtual machines that have data collection enabled.

 d. In **During Period**, select how far back to run the report.

Step 3.   Click **Search** to run the activity report.

You can also run this report for a single virtual machine from the **Virtual Machine's Monitor > Activity Monitoring** view by selecting **Inbound** and entering the source information, as shown in Figure 17-4. However, the **Where Source** must be a virtual machine.

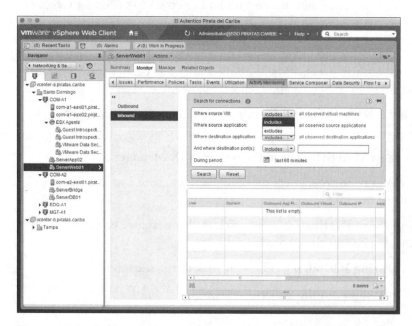

Figure 17-4   Running Inbound Activity Monitoring report for a virtual machine

Outbound Activity

This report shows traffic leaving the monitored virtual machines (egress). To run this report, follow these steps:

Step 1.   Go to the Networking and Security page and select the **Activity Monitoring** view.

Step 2.   Click the **Outbound Activity** tab and select the NSX Manager.

    a. In **Outbound From**, select the security groups, AD groups, and/or desktop pools to match in the report. The Outbound From refers to the entity that sent the traffic from the monitored virtual machines.

    b. In **Where Application**, select to include or exclude one or more destination applications.

    c. In **Where Destination**, select to include or exclude one or more of the destination virtual machines.

    d. In **During Period**, select how far back to run the report.

Step 3.   Click **Search** to run the activity report.

You can also run this report for a single virtual machine from the virtual machine's **Monitor > Activity Monitoring** view by selecting **Outbound** and entering the destination information. However, the **Where Destination** must be a virtual machine, and there is no **Where Application** option.

Inter Container Interaction

This report shows traffic among the monitored virtual machines. To run this report, follow these steps:

Step 1.   Go to the Networking and Security page and select the **Activity Monitoring** view.

Step 2.   Click the **Inter Container Interaction** tab and select the NSX Manager.

    a. In **Outbound From**, select the security groups, AD groups, and/or desktop pools to match in the report.

    The Outbound From refers to the entity that sent the traffic from the monitored virtual machines.

    Only traffic to and from the virtual machines matching this field are shown in this report.

> **b.** In **Where the Destination**, select to include or exclude one or more of the destination virtual machines.
>
> Here **is** and **is not** replace **include** and **exclude** from the other activity reports.
>
> **c.** In **During Period**, select how far back to run the report.

Step 3.   Click **Search** to run the activity report.

Outbound AD Group Activity

This report shows traffic from monitored virtual machines matching the selected AD groups. To run this report, follow these steps:

Step 1.   Go to the Networking and Security page and select the **Activity Monitoring** view.

Step 2.   Click the **Outbound AD Group Activity** tab and select the NSX Manager.

> **a.** In **Outbound From**, select the security groups and/or desktop pools to match in the report.
>
> The Outbound From refers to the entity that sent the traffic from the monitored virtual machines.
>
> **b.** In **Where AD Group**, select to include or exclude one or more of the LDAP groups that sent the traffic.
>
> **c.** In **During Period**, select how far back to run the report.

Step 3.   Click **Search** to run the activity report.

Viewing Activity Report

The activity report can be viewed in the window in which the activity report was configured in **Activity Monitoring** view or directly from the virtual machine's Monitor view. In both views, the activity report can be exported in cvs format by clicking the Export icon at the bottom right of the page.

Flow Monitoring

Activity Monitoring is valuable in monitoring the security compliance of traffic to and from protected VMs, but it is does not provide for in-depth (Layer 7) traffic analysis as other traffic analyzer tools do. However, Flow Monitoring does allow for real-time traffic analysis, at Layer 3 and 4, of VM traffic. Flow Monitoring also has the built-in capability to identify which DFW rule allowed the traffic flow and gives the option to create a DFW rule to block the traffic flow.

Flow monitoring has no restrictions on which Guest OS runs in the virtual machines.

Enabling Flow Monitoring is as easy as enabling Global Flow Collection Status in **Flow Monitoring > Configuration > Flow Exclusion**, as shown in Figure 17-5 (make sure you select the NSX Manager first). When you enable Flow Monitoring, NSX Manager starts collecting traffic flow information from the NSX prepared ESXi hosts for all virtual machines in the NSX domain. NSX Manager collects this information in 15-minute intervals.

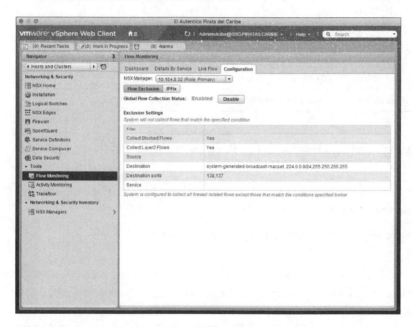

Figure 17-5   Enabling Flow Monitoring

You may, however, restrict the VMs for which NSX Manager collects traffic flow information by following these steps:

Step 1.   After enabling Flow Monitoring, go to the **Exclusion Settings** section of **Flow Monitoring > Configuration**. Any virtual machines identified in this section are excluded from Flow Monitoring.

   a. After selecting **Collect Blocked Flows**, choose **Yes** or **No** in the bottom of the window:

   These are flows blocked by the DFW. Select **No** to exclude blocked flows.

b. After selecting **Collect Layer 2 Flows**, choose **Yes** or **No** in the bottom of the window.

c. After selecting **Source**, enter the IPs to exclude. Select **No** to exclude Layer 2 flows.

You can also choose NSX Manager and vCenter containers and objects to be excluded. Table 17-2 shows the container options available.

Table 17-2   Flow Monitoring Source Exclusion Container Options

Container	Description
IP Sets	NSX Manager IP sets
MAC Sets	NSX Manager MAC sets
Virtual Machine	Virtual machines running in NSX prepared ESXi hosts
vNIC	vNICs of virtual machines running in NSX prepared ESXi hosts

d. After selecting **Destination** or **Port**, enter the IP and Layer 4 ports to exclude.

The containers from Table 17-2 can also be chosen to be excluded in the Destination.

e. After selecting **Service**, enter the service to be excluded.

Step 2. Click **Save**.

To view the collected flows in NSX Manager, head over to the Dashboard tab. There you see the flows NSX Manager has collected (it gets updated in as little as every 15 minutes) showing the Top Flows (consuming most bandwidth), Top Destinations, and Top Sources.

If you go to Details by Service, you can see the flows by Layer 4 ports. There are two view options in this window: Allowed Flows and Blocked Flows. The Allowed Flows were allowed by a DFW rule. The Blocked Flows were blocked by a DFW rule. Regardless of which flow you are looking at, you can select a service, see the flows for that service, and either add a DFW rule to allow or block the flow, or edit the existing DFW rule that allowed or blocked the flow, as shown in Figure 17-6.

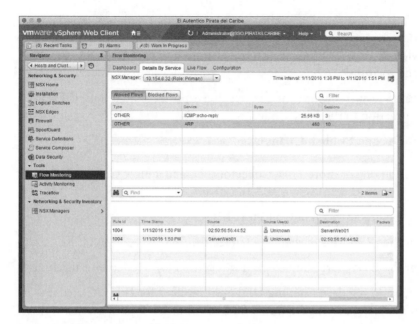

Figure 17-6 Flow Monitoring Details by Service tab

You can change the time interval of the viewed flows by clicking the calendar icon on the top-right and entering the time range to view.

If you want to edit the DFW rule that allowed or blocked the flow, or just add a rule for the flow, select the flow and click either **Add Rule** or **Edit Rule**. If you select **Add Rule**, you get to create a new DFW rule. If you select **Edit Rule**, you get to change the rule's Actions field.

You can export the collected flows to an external collector by enabling Internet Protocol Flow Information Export, IPFix. IPFix is an IETF protocol that enables the exportation of IP flow information. The receiver of the IPFix information is called a Flow Collector.

Flow Monitoring must be enabled to use IPFix, and IPFix information is exported by the ESXi host's DFW.

To enable IPFix, follow these steps:

Step 1.   Go back to the Configuration tab and click **IPFix**.

Step 2.   Click **Edit** to enable IPFix and populate the following fields:

    a. Check the box for Enable IPFix Configuration.

    b. Add an Observation DomainID.

The Observation DomainID is a 32-bit (think IP address) number that uniquely identifies the exporter. However, you only need to provide the first 16 bits here (a number from 0 to 65,335). NSX would add the other 16 bits.

c. Enter how frequently, in minutes, the exporter should send IPFix information to the Flow Collector.

Step 3.   Click **OK** and **Publish Changes**.

Now we need to add one or more Flow Collectors. To add a Flow Collector, follow these steps:

Step 1.   Click the green **+** icon in Collectors IPs.

Step 2.   Enter the IP address of the Flow Collector.

Step 3.   Enter the UDP port number from which the Flow Collector is listening.

There is no standard listening UDP port number for IPFix. Check the Flow Collectors configuration to find out what UDP port number to use.

Step 4.   Click **OK**.

Step 5.   Repeat steps 1 through 4 to add more Flow Collectors.

Step 6.   Click **Publish Changes**.

Finally, you may want to see flows in real time. You may not have 15 minutes to wait for NSX Manager to refresh the view. In this case, you can go to the Live Flow tab and select a single vNIC and capture flows with as little as a 5 second refresh rate. To enable Live Flow, follow these steps:

Step 1.   In the Live Flow tab, select the NSX Manager, and click the **Browse** hyperlink.

Step 2.   In the Select Virtual Machine and vNIC window that opens, select the virtual machine and vNIC.

Step 3.   Click **OK**.

Step 4.   Click **Start**.

Figure 17-7 shows a virtual machine's real-time flows.

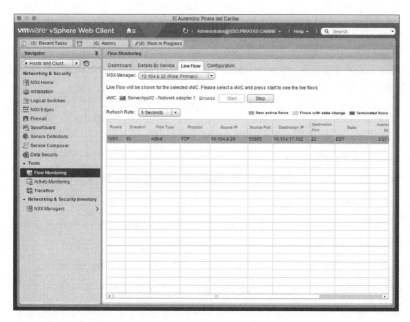

Figure 17-7   Flow Monitoring's live flow

Traceflow

Traceflow is one of the first tools that takes full advantage of the software defined network. Traceflow is a troubleshooting and planning tool that allows you to inject traffic sourced from a virtual machine's vNIC without having to touch the virtual machine. The vNIC must be connected to a logical switch.

When using Traceflow, all ESXi hosts, logical switches, logical routers, distributed firewalls, and NSX Edges along the path to the destination, monitor the frame or packet created. The destination of a Traceflow packet can be a physical device; however, the monitoring of the packet ends at the border of the NSX network and the physical network. Using this information, NSX can determine the path taken by the frame or packet, and if and where the frame or packet is being dropped.

Traceflow supports unicast, multicast, and broadcasts in Layer 2. Traceflow supports unicast in Layer 3.

To configure Traceflow, perform the following steps:

Step 1.   From the Networking and Security page, click Traceflow.

Step 2.   Select the NSX Manager.

Step 3.   Select the Traffic Type: Unicast, Multicast, or Broadcast.

a. If selecting Unicast:

Select the destination VM vNIC or enter the destination IP.

If it is a Layer 2 unicast, you must also enter the destination MAC address.

b. If selecting Multicast, you must enter the multicast group.

c. If selecting Broadcast, you must enter the subnet mask.

Step 4. In Advanced Options:

a. Select the Layer 4 protocol. The options are ICMP, TCP, and UDP.

For ICMP, you may enter the ICMP ID and Sequence Number.

For TCP, you may enter the source and destination port numbers, and the TCP Flags to set.

For UDP, you may enter the source and destination port numbers.

b. Enter the timeout, in milliseconds.

c. Enter the frame size from 128 bytes to 1000 bytes.

d. Enter a Time To Live.

Step 5. Click **Trace** to start TraceFlow.

Figure 17-8 shows the results of a Traceflow. Feel free to stand up and leave if you don't think Traceflow is awesome.

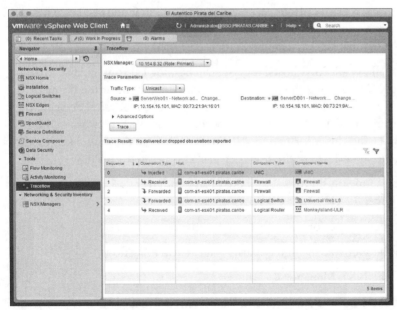

Figure 17-8 Traceflow results

The NSX APIs allow for more header field editing options in Traceflow than is available via the vSphere Web Client.

Role Based Access Control

Role Based Access Control (RBAC) is a method to grant user access to a system based on a role assigned to the user. Each role has a predetermined set of access privileges that get inherited by the users with the role. For example, a user with a role of security administrator can't create a logical switch in NSX Manager. In addition to having a limit in the changes that a user can make in the environment, NSX supports limiting of the scope of what NSX components that user may configure. For example, a user with the security administrator role may be allowed to only make changes to a portgroup or an NSX Edge and nothing else.

NSX has its own RBAC, which is separate from the user permissions employed by vCenter; however, NSX users (except for the default Admin user) and groups must exist in vCenter, whether or not they are authenticated against an external identity source such as LDAP.

However, NSX can integrate with Single Sign On (SSO) to improve the security of user authentication for vCenter users. The SSO must be the same one used by vCenter. SSO authentication enables NSX to authenticate against other identity sources. When integrated with SSO, NSX can leverage users from AD, LDAP, and Network Information Services (NIS) servers. SSO integration also allows NSX to do authentication for REST API calls and other VMware solutions using Security Assertion Markup Language (SAML) tokens from trusted sources. We cover the RESTful NSX APIs in Chapter 18, "NSX Automation."

NSX's RBAC has four roles, shown in Table 17-3. Of the four roles, the Security Administrator and the Auditor can have their scope limited to individual portgroups, NSX Edges, and/or Datacenters. The Auditor has the least privileged role of the four, with read-only access. If you want to completely deny all access to a user, just don't add that user to NSX.

Table 17-3 NSX Roles

Role	Description
Enterprise Administrator	User has read/write access over all NSX deployments, configuration, and administration.
NSX Administrator	User has read/write access over all non-security NSX deployments and administration. For example, deployment of virtual appliances and configuration of portgroups.

Role	Description
Security Administrator	User has read/write access over all security compliance policies. Has read-only access to view reporting and auditing information.
Auditor	User has read (only) access over all NSX system settings and auditing, events, and reporting.

User management for NSX access is separate from the user management for CLI access in NSX Manager, NSX Controllers, NSX Edges, and the Control VM.

A user can only have one role; however, if the user belongs to multiple groups, the user may inherit multiple roles by virtue of being a member of those groups, and the user's rights will be the union of those roles on the overlapping vCenter objects. If a user is assigned to roles because she is a member of two different user groups, each one with a different role, the user inherits the union of the privileges of both roles where the vCenter permissions overlap. For example, user Teresa belongs to two vCenter groups, La Niña and La Santa Maria. La Niña has administrator permissions in Clusters A and B, and a role of Security Administrator. La Santa Maria has administrator permissions for Clusters B and C, and a role of NSX Administrator. Thus Teresa would have the equivalent of Enterprise Administrator privileges for Cluster B, while having Security Administrator role for Cluster A and NSX Administrator for Cluster C.

NSX user access control is most effective when done in coordination with vCenter Permissions. You should plan out the vCenter objects that the user may have permission to and match by assigning the NSX role the user may have.

To integrate NSX Manager with SSO, follow these steps:

Step 1. Log in to the NSX Manager Virtual Appliance home page. The address is https://[NSX_Manager_FQDN_or_IP]/.

Step 2. Go to **Manage > NSX Management Service**.

Step 3. Under Lookup Service, click **Edit** and wait for the Lookup Service window to open.

Both SSO and NSX Manager should have an NTP server configured for accurate time.

Step 4. Enter the IP or FQDN of the server where SSO is installed.

The default port number for vSphere 6.0 is 443, and SSO is integrated with the Platform Services Controller, PSC. If using SSO from vSphere 5.5, the default port is 7444.

Step 5. Enter the administrator credentials for SSO and click **OK**.

Wait for the Lookup Service status to say connected, as shown in Figure 17-9.

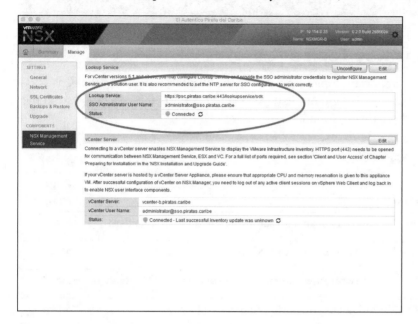

Figure 17-9   NSX Manager connected to Lookup Service

To add a user to NSX and assign it a role using RBAC, follow these steps:

Step 1.   Go to the Networking and Security page, click **NSX Managers**, and se-lect the NSX Manager where the user will be added.

Step 2.   Go to **Manage > Users** and click the green **+** icon.

Step 3.   When the Assign Role Wizard pops up, enter the name of the vCenter user and click **Next**.

The alternative is to enter a vCenter group.

This is a bit misleading. The vCenter user or group may be presented to vCenter by an external identity source.

Step 4.   In **Select Roles**, select the role and click **Finish**.

Exam Preparation Tasks

Review All the Key Topics

Review the most important topics from inside the chapter, noted with the Key Topic icon in the outer margin of the page. Table 17-4 lists these key topics and the page numbers where each is found.

Table 17-4   Key Topics for Chapter 17

Key Topic Element	Description	Page Number
Paragraph	VMware Data Security supports multiple regulations and standards.	506
Paragraph	EPSEC-MUX gets installed with USVM.	508
Paragraph	NSX Data Security throttles the number of concurrent VMs scanned.	509
Paragraph	Activity Monitoring only supports Windows Guest OS.	509
Paragraph	Enable Data Collection by adding VMs to the Activity Monitoring Data Collection security group.	510
Paragraph	Flow Monitoring works with all Guest OSes.	515
Paragraph	Flow Monitoring can be viewed in different time intervals.	517
Paragraph	IPFix requires Flow Monitoring be enabled.	517
Paragraph	Traceflow supports Layer 2 unicast, multicast, and broadcast, and Layer 3 unicast.	519
Paragraph	Traceflow has more options available via the NSX APIs.	521
Paragraph	NSX's RBAC is separate from vCenter's user permissions.	521
Paragraph	NSX Manager's CLI user access is separate from CLI user access to other NSX entities.	522

Complete Tables and Lists from Memory

Download and print a copy of Appendix C, "Memory Tables," (found on the book's website), or at least the section for this chapter, and complete the tables and lists from memory. Appendix D, "Memory Tables Answer Key," also on the website, includes the completed tables and lists so you can check your work.

Define Key Terms

Define the following key terms from this chapter, and check your answers in the glossary:

Universal Services Virtual Machine (USVM), Traceflow

This chapter covers all or part of the following VCP6-NV exam blueprint topics:

- **Objective 1.5**—Understand VMware NSX Integration with vRealize Automation (vRA)
- **Objective 9.2**—Understand NSX Automation

CHAPTER 18

NSX Automation

The days of the CLI are more or less numbered. Why would you want to be typing commands when you can script it and automate it? With automation, one of the main drivers for SDN and NSX, you can deploy hundreds of logical switches before you finish your coffee (or tea if you prefer).

NSX offers a rich open API that is RESTful based. In this chapter we introduce REST, and we work through a few samples of how to consume NSX services by using the NSX APIs via a REST client.

Do I Know This Already?

The "Do I Know This Already?" quiz allows you to assess whether you should read this entire chapter or simply jump to the "Exam Preparation Tasks" section for review. If you are in doubt, read the entire chapter. Table 18-1 outlines the major headings in this chapter and the corresponding "Do I Know This Already?" quiz questions. You can find the answers in Appendix A, "Answers to the 'Do I Know This Already?' Quizzes."

Table 18-1 Headings and Questions

Foundation Topic Section	Questions Covered in This Section
REST	1-4
NSX API Calls for Logical Switch	5
NSX API Calls for Logical Router	6-7
NSX API Calls for NSX Edge	8
vRealize Automation	9-10

1. Which two are entities the consumption plane communicates with? (Choose two.)

   a. NSX Controller

   b. NSX Edge

   c. vCenter

   d. NSX Manager

2. What is the name of a REST entity that has an HTTP URI?

   a. Web page

   b. Resource

   c. End point

   d. REST client

3. Which HTTP method is not supported by NSX APIs?

   a. GET

   b. COPY

   c. POST

   d. PUT

4. Which two Content-Types do NSX APIs support? (Choose two.)

   a. Text

   b. XML

   d. JSON

   d. HTML

5. Which URL can be used to query the existing transport zones in an NSX Manager?

   a. https://NSXMGR-IP/api/4.0/scopes/

   b. https://NSXMGR-IP/api/2.0/vdn/scopes/

   c. https://NSXMGR-IP/api/2.0/scopes/

   d. https://NSXMGR-IP/api.4.0/vdn/scopes/

6. When deploying a distributed logical router, what is the value of the *type* tag?

   a. gatewayServices

   b. distributedRouter

   c. logicalDistributedRouter

   d. distributedLogicalRouter

7. A logical router was deployed via the NSX APIs, but no Control VM was provisioned. What tag and value were used to prevent the Control VM from being deployed?

   a. Tag: deployAppliances, Value: no

   b. Tag: applianceSize, Value: Null

   c. Tag: deployAppliances, Value: false

   d. Tag: applianceSize, Value: noAppliance

8. What XML tag is used to connect an NSX Edge's interface to a logical switch?

   a. connectedToId

   b. type

   c. portgroupId

   d. isConnected

9. Which is not a valid vRealize network profile?

   a. Routed network profile

   b. NAT network profile

   c. Load balancer network profile

   d. External network profile

10. You are a vRA Tenant Administrator for tenant ABC. You want to create a blueprint that deploys a logical router. What must you do to prepare a blueprint to deploy logical routers?

   a. In vRealize Orchestrator, create a workflow that includes the NSX API calls to create a logical router and call the workflow from the blueprint.

   b. In vRealize Orchestrator, create a logical router network profile and add the logical router network profile to the blueprint.

   c. In vRA, create a logical router network profile and add the logical router network profile to the blueprint.

   d. In vRA, create a routed network profile that includes the logical router and add the routed network profile to the blueprint.

Foundation Topics

REST

There is a fourth plane I have not mentioned in this book. It is called the *consumption plane*. Truth be told, it is not really a "plane" in the traditional sense nor does it have much to do with networking (if anything). Think of the consumption plane as that VBS script, the PowerShell script, or that summer intern you used to force to type a bunch of commands into a lot of different devices for you (while passing it off as a teachable moment), but with a lot more "intelligence" to do its job. The consumption plane is a way to describe an external entity, such as vRealize Automation, that consumes resources, whether they are compute, storage, network, or security. The consumption plane typically communicates with the management plane of the resource it will be consuming. The communication takes place over APIs exposed by the management plane. Exactly how the API communication takes place is constrained by the management plane, the owner of the API.

A personal note to those of you not as familiar with APIs or automation: This is the ~~future~~ present state of the infrastructure. It is not sustainable to delay the execution of business projects because a human needs to be engaged to execute some tasks when those tasks can be scripted/orchestrated/automated and done flawlessly within a matter of minutes. As you read the rest of this chapter, keep in mind that this covers but a small portion of what can be achieved with NSX automation, and I hope that you embrace it. Now, back to our regular program...

REpresentative State Transfer (REST) is a design model, or architectural style, for the development of web services that also offers a way to interface with APIs over HTTP or HTTPS. REST works in a client-server model. Over the last few years, REST has gained prominence as a method to use for API communications. Any API that uses REST is referred to as a *RESTful API*. The NSX APIs are RESTful, with the NSX Manager acting as the REST server. NSX APIs support HTTPS over TCP 443.

In Simple Network Management Protocol (SNMP), each entity has a Management Information Base (MIB) associated with it. In REST, each NSX entity has an HTTP URI associated with it, and the entity is called a *resource*. For example, the HTTP URI for NSX resource *Edge-3* would be https://NSX_MGR/api/4.0/edges/edge-3, and the URL for *Edge-3's* HA interface would be https://NSX_MGR/api/4.0/edges/edge-3/mgmtinterface. The URI of each NSX resource has the NSX Manager's IP or FQDN as the address. With knowledge of the resource URI you can use HTTP methods, or verbs, to interact with NSX Manager to create, query, edit, or delete resources. Table 18-2 has a list of the HTTP methods supported by the NSX API.

Table 18-2   HTTP Methods Supported by NSX APIs

Verb	Description
GET	Retrieves information about the resource
PUT	Adds a resource, but primarily used to update an existing resource (as in changing the subnet of a LIF)
POST	Adds a resource, primarily to add resources for a parent (like a LIF in a DLR)
DELETE	Deletes a resource

PUT and POST API calls must have a body (in addition to the header). The body contains the details of the action (create or edit) that you want to execute on an NSX resource.

In a cross vCenter NSX domain, you must use the address of the NSX Manager that owns the resource, such as the distributed logical router. In the case of connecting a VM to a universal logical switch, you must use the address of the NSX Manager associated with the vCenter that owns the VM.

As mentioned earlier, REST works in a client-server model, with NSX Manager taking the role of the server. The client initiates all requests, or API calls, and all API calls to NSX Manager must be authenticated. When the client sends a request, the server responds with an HTTP response message. Table 18-3 lists some of the HTTP response messages used by NSX Manager.

Table 18-3   HTTP Responses

Verb	Codes	Description
Success	200s	Congratulations, your request was accepted.
Redirection	300s	You must take some additional action to complete the request.
Client Error	400s	An error occurred on your side (the client side).
Server Error	500s	An error occurred on the NSX Manager side (the server side).

All API calls to the NSX Manager must have a header that includes details on how the client communicates with the server. The header may have a field for the language (like English or Spanish) or the encodings the client accepts. To make NSX API calls, it is required that two header fields be included in each API call: Authorization and Content-Type. The Authorization field includes the credentials of the client to authenticate against the NSX Manager. The credentials are encoded in Base64 before they are sent to NSX Manager. The Content-Type field specifies the format in which the request is being sent. NSX Manager supports content formatted in XML or

JSON. The exact syntax for the Content-Type field needs to be *Application/XML* for XML or *Application/JSON* for JSON. NSX Manager's response is formatted in XML.

The access granted to the user credentials provided in the Authorization field is determined based on the role assigned to the user in NSX Manager.

Most major browsers support REST client extensions, and a good thing about them is that the Header fields only need to be populated once, and the client reuses them for all API calls sent. Figure 18-1 shows the header of a REST client with the Authorization and Content-Type fields. For the remainder of this topic we use a REST client extension for the Google Chrome browser. We use this REST client to build two universal logical switches, a ULR with two interfaces, and an NSX Edge with two configured interfaces. We have two NSX Managers, NSXMGR-A, the Primary NSX Manager, and NSXMGR-B, the Secondary NSX Manager.

Figure 18-1 REST client header

NSX API Calls for Logical Switch

There are two things we need to know before we can create a universal logical switch. First is the universal transport zone we will put the logical switch in. The second is the Replication Mode we will use (if different from the one in the universal transport zone). We keep things simple and use whatever Replication Mode is configured in the transport zone we are putting the universal logical switch in. We make an API call to the Primary NSX Manager to retrieve the available universal transport zones. The resource URL to query the existing universal transport zone is the same as for global transport zones; it is https://nsxmgr-a.piratas.caribe/api/2.0/vdn/scopes. In Figure 18-2, we see the response to a GET request to retrieve information about the transport zone resources.

Each transport zone has its own <vdnScope></vdnScope> XML tags. In Figure 18-2 we see that there are two pairs of <vdnScope></vdnScope> tags, meaning that NSX Manager has two transport zones, one of which is the universal transport zone. Expanding one of the tags shows all the transport zone's information, including its name, the cluster members, and the Replication Mode. Table 18-4 shows a list of some of the tags included in the NSX Manager's response to the HTTP GET.

Figure 18-2 GET transport zones

Table 18-4 Transport Zone XML Tags

Tag	Description	Parent Tag
vdnScope	Information for a single transport zone.	vdnScopes
objectTypeName	The type of object. For transport zones, the type value is *VDnScope*.	vdnScope
vsmUuid	The UUID of the transport zone, as assigned by NSX Manager.	vdnScope
name	The name of the transport zone.	vdnScope
isUniversal	This value is *True* if this is the universal transport zone.	vdnScope
objectId	The ID of the transport zone. The ID format is vdnscope-# for global transport zones, where the # is assigned by NSX Manager when the transport zone is created. If this is the universal transport zone, the value is *universalvdnscope*.	vdnScope
cluster	The list of all clusters that are part of the transport zone.	vdnScope
objectId	The ID of the cluster belonging to the transport zone.	clusters
controlPlaneMode	The Replication Mode of the transport zone.	vdnScope

To create our two universal logical switches, we use the universal transport zone in the list, the one with an objectId of *universalvdnscope* and name of *Caribbean Zone*. The URL to create a logical switch in transport zone vdnscope-1 is https://nsxmgr-a.piratas.caribe/api/2.0/vdn/scopes/universalvdnscope/virtualwires/, and we use the HTTP POST method. The NSX Controller cluster must be connected to NSX Manager for this API to be successful.

Table 18-5 shows the tags that we include in the body for the first logical switch.

Table 18-5   Transport Zone XML Tags

Tag	First Logical Switch Value	Second Logical Switch Value
Name	Trinidad	Tobago
Description	Created with NSX API	Created with NSX API
tenantId	Antillas	Menores
controlPlaneMode (optional tag)	Not including. The Replication Mode of the transport zone will be used.	Not including. The Replication Mode of the transport zone will be used.

The XML tags are case sensitive.

The following is the full syntax of the POST body to create one of the universal logical switches. NSX Manager supports the creation of one logical switch at a time:

```
<virtualWireCreateSpec>
        <name>Trinidad</name>
        <description>Created with NSX API</description>
        <tenantId>Antillas</tenantId>
</virtualWireCreateSpec>
```

Figure 18-3 shows the response from NSX Manager of a successful API call to create one of the universal logical switches. Notice that the response only includes the logical switch objectId.

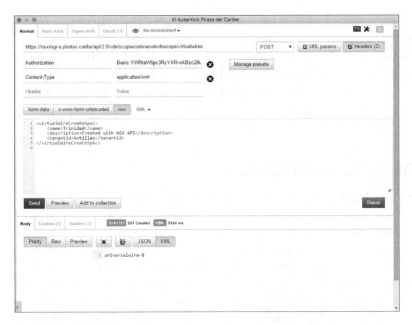

Figure 18-3   Successful API call to create logical switch

Figure 18-4 shows the two new universal logical switches in the Logical Switches view of the vSphere Web Client.

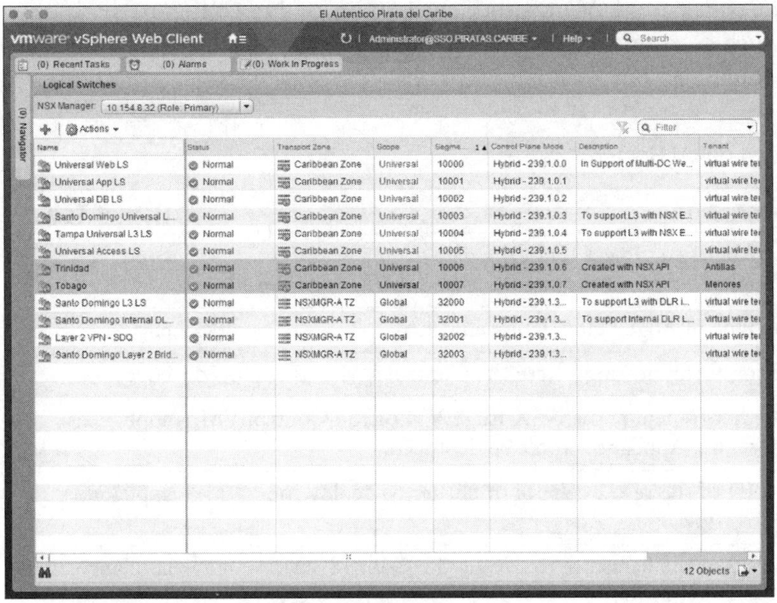

Figure 18-4   vSphere Web Client view of new universal logical switches

Use the DELETE method to delete a logical switch. The URL to use is https://NSX_MGR/api/2.0/vdn/virtualwires/*objectId*, where the objectId is the ID of the logical switch. If you didn't bother to read NSX Manager's response when you created the switch and don't have the logical switch's objectId, you can obtain it by sending an HTTP GET to the URL https://NSX_MGR/api/2.0/vdn/virtualwires. This resource gives a list of all logical switches. This time do read NSX Manager's response to find your logical switch's objectID ☺.

NSX API Calls for Logical Router

Next we create a new ULR. It has two LIFs, one to each of the new universal logical switches we created. The URL to create a new ULR, using the POST method, is https://nsxmgr-a.piratas.caribe/api/4.0/edges, the same URL to create a distributed logical router. Yes, it is also the same URL for an Edge. This is because logical routers are represented by the Control VM, which itself is a modified NSX Edge. What determines whether an Edge acts as a Control VM is the value of *distributedRouter* in the *type* tag. The default value of the *type* tag is *gatewayServices*, which is a regular NSX Edge. What tells the logical router that it is a universal logical router is a value of *True* in the *isUniversal* tag.

Compared to a logical switch, a bit more information is required to create a logical router, such as the cluster and datastore to deploy the Control VM (if we are deploying one). Table 18-6 shows some of the tags we use to create our ULR with two LIFs as well as the tag's parent. Many other tags can be used to configure the ULR during creation, such as tenantId, but we skip those and just let the default values be applied (which could be an *empty* value).

Table 18-6   Distributed Logical Router XML Tags

Tag	Description	Parent Tag
datacenterMoid	The Managed Object ID of the data center where the resource pool or cluster for the Control VM is deployed.	edge
edgeType	The type of Edge being deployed.	edge
appliances	Section for indicating where the Control VM(s) is deployed.	edge
deployAppliances	Whether to deploy the NSX Edge VM or the Control VM. If false, the Appliance won't be deployed.	appliances
resourcePoolId	The ID of the resource pool or cluster to deploy the Control VM.	appliance
datastoreId	The ID of the datastore to deploy the Control VM.	appliance
mgmtInterface	The management interface for the Control VM. This is one of the vNICs in the Control VM.	edge

Tag	Description	Parent Tag
interfaces	The section where the Control VM's interface (vNICs) and the LIFs are configured.	edge
connectedToId	The virtual switch to connect the Control VM's management interface or DLR LIF.	mgmtInterface or interface
portgroupId	The portgroup or virtual switch to connect an NSX Edge's interface.	vnic
type	The type of LIF, Internal or Uplink.	interface
primaryAddress	The IP of the of the Control VM's HA interface or logical router LIF.	mgmtInterface or interface
password	The password for logging on to the appliance.	cliSettings

The following is the full syntax of the POST body to create a new ULR with two LIFs connected to logical switches Trinidad and Tobago, and no Control VM. The tag to not deploy the Control VM is **deployAppliances**, with a value of **false**.

```
<edge>
        <name>Mar Caribe</name>
        <type>distributedRouter</type>
        <isUniversal>true</isUniversal>
                <status>active</status>
        <appliances>
                <deployAppliances>false</deployAppliances>
                </appliances>
        <interfaces>
                <interface>
                        <name>Connection to Trinidad Logical
                           Switch</name>
                        <addressGroups>
                                <addressGroup>
                                <primaryAddress>10.154.15.97
                                   </primaryAddress>
                                <subnetMask>255.255.255.240
                                   </subnetMask>
                                </addressGroup>
                        </addressGroups>
                        <mtu>1500</mtu>
                        <type>internal</type>
                        <isConnected>true</isConnected>
                        <connectedToId>universalwire-8
                           </connectedToId>
                </interface>
```

```
                    <interface>
                        <name>Connection to Tobago Logical Switch
                            </name>
                        <addressGroups>
                                <addressGroup>
                                <primaryAddress>10.154.15.113
                                    </primaryAddress>
                                    <subnetMask>255.255.255.252
                                        </subnetMask>
                                </addressGroup>
                        </addressGroups>
                        <mtu>1500</mtu>
                        <type>uplink</type>
                        <isConnected>true</isConnected>
                        <connectedToId>universalwire-9
                            </connectedToId>
                    </interface>
            </interfaces>
    </edge>
```

Figure 18-5 shows the newly created Mar Caribe ULR in the vSphere Web Client. Notice that we are looking at the Secondary NSX Manager. I'm showing you this view intentionally to demonstrate that the ULR will be synchronized with all Secondary NSX Managers.

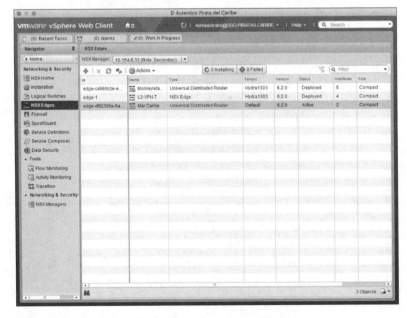

Figure 18-5   vSphere Web Client view of new ULR

Figure 18-6 shows the Configuration view of the Mar Caribe. There is no Control VM.

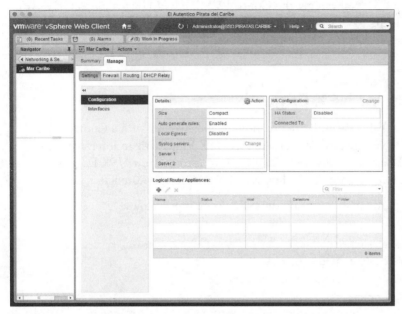

Figure 18-6   Configuration view of Mar Caribe ULR

Figure 18-7 shows the Interfaces view of Mar Caribe. It shows the two interfaces that we created.

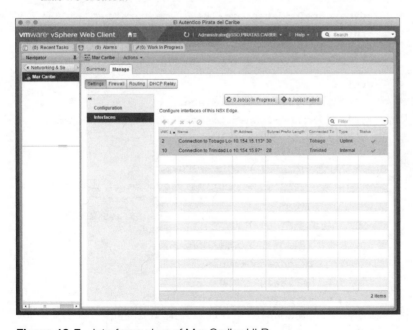

Figure 18-7   Interfaces view of Mar Caribe ULR

To delete a DLR, you need the Control VM's edgeId. Again if you missed it when you created the DLR, you can get the Control VM's edgeId by making a GET API call to the URI https://NSX-MGR/api/4.0/edges. After you have the edgeId for the Control VM, use the DELETE method with the URI https://NSX_MGR/api/4.0/edges/*edgeId*.

NSX API Calls for NSX Edge

Creating an NSX Edge is similar to creating a logical router with a Control VM, which you should've expected. We create this NSX Edge with an interface connected to the Tobago logical switch. The URL to create a new NSX Edge is the same as the one to create the ULR, https://NSX-MGR/api/4.0/edges.

The full syntax of the body to create the NSX Edge is as follows:

```
<edge>
        <datacenterMoid>datacenter-2</datacenterMoid>
        <name>Caribe Edge</name>
                <status>deployed</status>
        <appliances>
                <appliance>
                <deployAppliances>true</deployAppliances>
                <applianceSize>compact</applianceSize>
                <resourcePoolId>domain-c333</resourcePoolId>
                <datastoreId>datastore-184</datastoreId>
                </appliance>
                </appliances>
        <vnics>
                <vnic>
                        <label>vNic_1</label>
                        <name>Connection to Tobago Logical Switch
                           </name>
                        <addressGroups>
                                <addressGroup>
                                    <primaryAddress>10.154.15.114
                                        </primaryAddress>
                                    <subnetMask>255.255.255.252
                                        </subnetMask>
                                </addressGroup>
                        </addressGroups>
                        <mtu>1500</mtu>
                        <type>uplink</type>
                        <isConnected>true</isConnected>
                        <index>1</index>
```

```
                    <portgroupId>universalwire-9</portgroupId>
          </vnic>
      </vnics>
      <cliSettings>
                <remoteAccess>true</remoteAccess>
                <password>SenaSosa7321</password>
      </cliSettings>
  </edge>
```

Figure 18-8 shows the NSX Edge Caribe Edge being deployed.

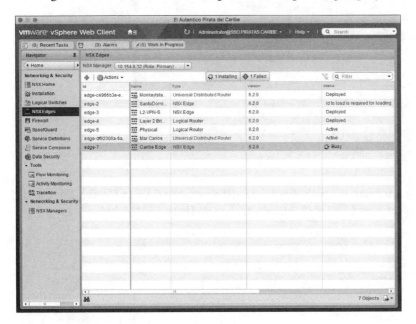

Figure 18-8   Deploying Caribe Edge

Figure 18-9 shows the Configuration view of Caribe Edge after it is successfully created. Notice the Edge Appliance has been deployed.

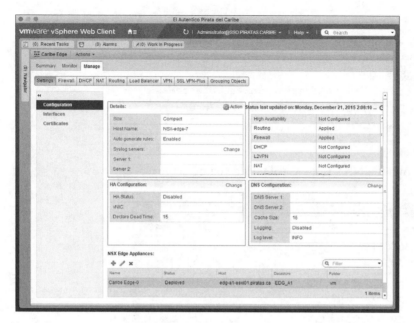

Figure 18-9   Configuration view of Caribe Edge

And now for the moment of truth. Figure 18-10 shows the CLI of Caribe Edge and a successful ping of Mar Caribe's Uplink interface at IP 10.154.15.113.

Figure 18-10   Ping from Caribe Edge to Mar Caribe

To delete the NSX Edge, follow the same steps for deleting a logical router.

vRealize Automation

One of the primary goals of NSX is to allow for the dynamic provisioning and consumption of network and security resources. You should read that to mean *cloud*. vRealize Automation has built-in features that allow you to deploy virtual workloads that consume NSX services. Before I dive into what vRealize Automation interacts with in NSX, let's review what vRealize Automation is.

vRealize Automation (vRA) is one of VMware's cloud solutions. It resides in the consumption plane. vRA allows automated provisioning and consumption of compute, storage, and networking. When a user wants to consume IT resources, she goes to a portal where she is presented with the IT resources that she has the rights to consume. vRA can automate consumption of resources from virtualized environments (vSphere, Hyper-v, and others), public cloud providers (AWS, Azure, and so on), and bare metal servers (HP BladeSystem, Cisco UCS, for example).

The user does not have visibility into the IT infrastructure, so much so that the user may be oblivious as to whether the resource consumption is taking place in a public cloud or a virtual environment (although as the vRA administrator you may elect to provide that insight to the user).

The user's vRA administrator hides the underpinnings of the IT infrastructure by presenting the user a blueprint. A blueprint is what it sounds like: the detailed instructions of how vRA goes about providing the IT resources the user is requesting.

In vRA, a VM in a virtual environment (or the cloud) and a physical server are all called *machines*. For the purpose of this section, we are discussing blueprints to deploy and configure machines that run in a vSphere environment. A blueprint may be created to consume network and security services without deploying or configuring machines.

vRA has a component called a network profile that contains information to pass on to NSX Manager for the purpose of providing network and security services to machines. A network profile gives vRA the power to interact with NSX Manager using the NSX APIs. When putting a blueprint together, you can elect to add network profiles to the blueprint, and when the user calls up the blueprint, vRA executes the API calls to NSX Manager to build the NSX elements in the network profiles.

vRA comes with vRealize Orchestrator (vRO). vRO supports the creation of workflows to make any NSX API call. These workflows can be added to blueprints to augment the interactions of vRA with NSX Manager.

vRA has four types of network profiles, listed in Table 18-7. In the next section we expand on each of the network profiles and some of their use cases.

Table 18-7 vRealize Automation Network Profiles

Network Profile	Description
External	Contains information on how to connect machines to an existing network
Routed	Contains information on how traffic will be routed between machines in the blueprint and the rest of the network
Private	Contains information for deploying an isolated network for the machines
NAT	Contains the information needed to configure NAT and load balancing

External Network Profile

The use of an external network profile allows for the preallocation of an IP range in an existing subnet. The range of IPs is allocated by the blueprint to support network and security services for the machines in the blueprint.

An external network profile must contain a default gateway for the existing subnet, a subnet mask, and an allocation of available IPs from the subnet. You may also add information regarding DNS and WINS servers, and DNS suffixes. Figure 18-11 shows a view of an external network profile.

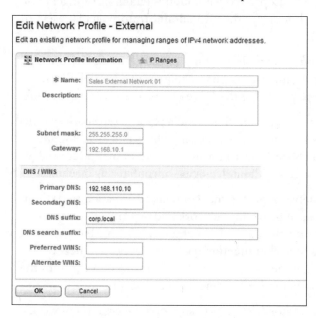

Figure 18-11   External network profile

External network profiles are referenced in routed network profiles and NAT network profiles.

Routed Network Profile

Think of the routed network profile as a fancy name for an NSX Edge with an Uplink interface. The Uplink interface connects to the segment identified in the referenced external network profile. The routed network profile may also have one or more internal interfaces. A routed network profile is used when your blueprint calls for one or more subnets to be used to connect your machines, *and* these subnets need to be externally reachable. When the vRA user deploys a blueprint with a routed network profile, vRA sends an NSX API call to create an NSX Edge *and* a logical switch for every Internal interface in the NSX Edge. The NSX Edge will have as many interfaces (up to 9) as you have subnets in the routed network profile (the tenth interface in the NSX Edge is reserved for the Management interface).

When a routed network profile is created, you must specify the existing network (by referencing an external network profile) that your new NSX Edge connects and one or more internal subnets to connect the machines in the blueprint. Figure 18-12 shows the configuration of a routed network profile.

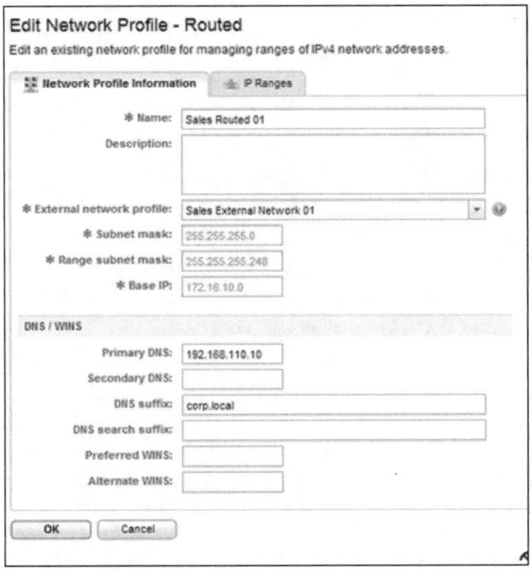

Figure 18-12   Routed network profile

Remember the default gateway in the external network profile? vRA automatically adds static routes in that default gateway for the internal subnets in the routed network profile, and adds a default route in the new NSX Edge pointing to the default gateway. This means one thing to you: The internal routes can't be overlapping with other subnets in the network. If you have overlapping IPs, you need a NAT network profile.

vRA's network profiles do not create distributed logical routers. To create a distributed logical router, create a workflow in vRO and add the workflow to the blueprint.

Private Network Profile

A private network profile is a routed network profile that does not include an external network profile. This is how you create completely isolated networks in the environment. The internal subnets can be whatever you want them to be since there is no way to route to them from the outside, or to route from them to the outside.

A use case for a private network profile is Test/Dev. You can re-create an entire application, including IPs, in the same infrastructure of the production version of the application. This allows the application owner to test for different variables and document results before introducing changes to the production environment. Figure 18-13 shows a sample configuration of a private network profile.

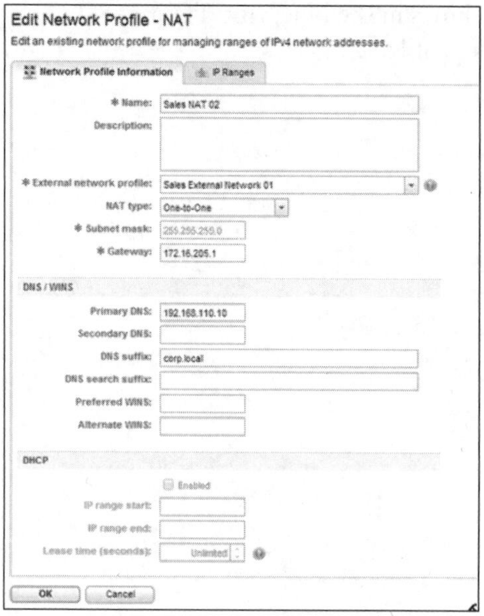

Figure 18-13   Private network profile

NAT Network Profile

There is a fourth network profile called NAT. The NAT network profile is used when the user wants to deploy a blueprint where the subnets used to connect the machines are not routable. Similar to the routed network profile, when the vRA user deploys a blueprint with a NAT network profile, vRealize Automation sends an NSX API call to create an NSX Edge with NAT configured and a logical switch for every Internal interface in the NSX Edge. The NSX Edge is configured with a default route pointing to the default gateway in the external network profile, but the default gateway won't be configured with any static routes.

Figure 18-14 shows a sample configuration of a NAT network profile.

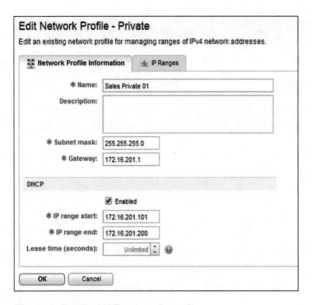

Figure 18-14   NAT network profile

The NAT network profile may also be used to configure the NSX Edge as a load balancer.

Exam Preparation Tasks

Review All the Key Topics

Review the most important topics from inside the chapter, noted with the Key Topic icon in the outer margin of the page. Table 18-8 lists these key topics and the page numbers where each is found.

Table 18-8   Key Topics for Chapter 18

Key Topic Element	Description	Page Number
Paragraph	When making an API call, use the address of the NSX Manager that owns the resource.	531
Paragraph	API calls only have access determined by the NSX role of the credentials used.	532
Paragraph	XML tags are case sensitive.	534
Paragraph	In vRA virtual machines are called machines.	543
Paragraph	vRO supports creation of workflows to make NSX API calls.	543
Paragraph	Routed network profiles and NAT network profiles reference external network profiles.	544
Paragraph	NAT network profiles may be used to deploy Edges as load balancers.	547

Complete Tables and Lists from Memory

Download and print a copy of Appendix C, "Memory Tables," (found on the book's website), or at least the section for this chapter, and complete the tables and lists from memory. Appendix D, "Memory Tables Answer Key," also on the website, includes the completed tables and lists so you can check your work.

Define Key Terms

Define the following key terms from this chapter, and check your answers in the glossary:

REST, NSX APIs, vRealize Automation

This chapter covers all or part of the following VCP6-NV exam blueprint topics:

- **Objective 4.3**—Upgrade Existing vCNS/NSX Implementation

CHAPTER 19

Upgrade to NSX for vSphere 6.2

In this chapter we cover the steps required to upgrade an existing vCloud Network and Security or NSX for vSphere implementation to NSX for vSphere 6.2. This is a brief chapter as the upgrade process is straightforward. If you can find and click the Upgrade button here and there, you should be fine ☺.

Do I Know This Already?

The "Do I Know This Already?" quiz allows you to assess whether you should read this entire chapter or simply jump to the "Exam Preparation Tasks" section for review. If you are in doubt, read the entire chapter. Table 19-1 outlines the major headings in this chapter and the corresponding "Do I Know This Already?" quiz questions. You can find the answers in Appendix A, "Answers to the 'Do I Know This Already?' Quizzes."

Table 19-1 Headings and Questions

Foundation Topic Section	Questions Covered in This Section
Upgrade vCloud Network and Security to NSX for vSphere	1-5
Upgrade NSX for vSphere to NSX for vSphere 6.2	6-10

1. Which versions of vCNS can be upgraded to NSX for vSphere?

    a. vCNS 5.0 and higher

    b. vCNS 5.1 and higher

    c. vCNS 5.5 and higher

    d. vCNS 5.5u3 and higher

2. How is vCNS upgraded to NSX?

    a. Connect to the Networking and Security home page using the vSphere Web Client. Select the Upgrade option in the Installation view. vCNS downloads the vCNS to NSX for vSphere upgrade bundle.

    b. Connect to the Networking and Security home page using the vSphere Web Client. Go to the vShield Manager view and select the upgrade option. vCNS downloads the vCNS to NSX for vSphere upgrade bundle.

    c. Connect to the vCNS's home page and upload the vCNS to NSX for vSphere upgrade bundle.

    d. Connect to the vSphere Web Client and deploy the OVF for the vCNS to NSX vSphere upgrade.

3. What is the first step that should be done to the NSX Manager appliance after vShield Manager is upgraded?

    a. Power up the NSX Manager.

    b. Create a new admin password.

    c. Increase the allocated memory to 8 GB.

    d. Change the number of vCPUs to 4.

4. Which component is upgraded next after vShield Manager is upgraded?

    a. The NSX Controllers

    b. The NSX VIBs in the ESXi hosts

    c. The NSX Edges

    d. The logical switches

5. How are virtual wires upgraded from vCNS to logical switches in NSX?

   a. From the NSX Manager home page, select the **Upgrade** option. You are asked if you want to upgrade virtual wires to logical switches.

   b. From the Networking and Security home page, select the **Installation** view. From the Host Preparation tab click the **Update** option.

   c. From the Networking and Security home page, select the **Logical Switches** view. For each virtual wire listed, select the **Action** menu and choose **Upgrade Version**.

   d. From the Networking and Security home page, select the **Installation** view. From the **Management** tab, click the **Action** menu in the NSX Controllers and select **Upgrade Logical Switches**.

6. What versions of NSX for vSphere can be upgraded to NSX for vSphere 6.2?

   a. NSX for vSphere 5.5 and higher

   b. NSX for vSphere 6.0 and higher

   c. NSX for vSphere 6.0.4 and higher

   d. NSX for vSphere 6.1 and higher

7. Which is a VMware recommendation that should be followed before upgrading an older version of NSX for vSphere to NSX for vSphere 6.2?

   a. Take a snapshot of NSX Manager.

   b. Power off NSX Manager.

   c. Delete the NSX Controllers.

   d. Place the ESXi hosts participating in NSX in maintenance mode.

8. How are logical switches upgraded to version 6.2?

   a. From the NSX Manager home page, select the **Upgrade** option. You are asked if you want to upgrade virtual wires to logical switches.

   b. In the Networking and Security home page, select the **Installation** view. From the Host Preparation tab click the **Update** option.

   c. From the Networking and Security home page, select the **Logical Switches** view. For each virtual wire listed, select the Action menu and choose **Upgrade Version**.

   d. From the Networking and Security home page, select the **Installation** view. From the **Management** tab, click the **Action** menu in the NSX Controllers and select **Upgrade Logical Switches**.

9. Before upgrading NSX Controllers to version 6.2, you notice one of the NSX Controllers is not connected to NSX Manager. What should you do next?

   a. Ensure that All NSX Controllers are in a connected status.

   b. Upgrade the other NSX Controllers. Once the NSX Controller connects to NSX Manager again you may upgrade it.

   c. Delete the NSX Controller and upgrade the other NSX Controllers.

   d. Select the NSX Controller and use the Update Controller State option from the Action menu.

10. How are distributed logical routers upgraded?

   a. From the NSX Manager home page, select the **Upgrade** option. You are asked if you want to upgrade logical routers.

   b. From the Networking and Security home page, select the **Installation** view. From the Host Preparation tab click the **Update** option.

   c. From the Networking and Security home page, select the **NSX Edges** view. For each Logical Router Control VM, select the **Action** menu and choose **Upgrade Version**.

   d. From the Networking and Security home page, select the **Installation** view. From the **Management** tab, click the **Action** menu in the NSX Controllers and select **Upgrade Logical Routers**.

Foundation Topics

Upgrade vCloud Network and Security to NSX for vSphere

If you have an existing vCloud Network and Security (vCNS) installation, you may upgrade it to NSX for vSphere. vCNS is the predecessor of NSX for vSphere and only supports network function virtualization (NFV). With vCNS, it is possible to deploy logical switches (called *virtual wires*), Edges, and some security with the vShield App, Data Security, and some partner integration. Except for Data Security and partner integration, all other vCNS features can be upgraded to NSX without losing their configuration.

Upgrades to NSX are supported for vCNS 5.5. Older versions of vCNS must be upgraded to vCNS 5.5 before upgrading to NSX.

> **NOTE** This chapter assumes that all upgrades are done manually.

Table 19-2 shows the tasks to upgrade vCNS to NSX.

Table 19-2   vCNS to NSX Upgrade Tasks

Task	vCNS Component
Upgrade to NSX Manager	vShield Manager
Upgrade to NSX VIBs	vCNS VIBs
Install NSX Controllers	N/A
Upgrade to NSX DFW	vShield App
Upgrade to NSX Edge	vCNS Edge
Upgrade to USVM	vShield EndPoint

vCNS Data Security and vCNS partner integration can't be upgraded. vCNS Data Security must be uninstalled and NSX Data Security installed. If the third-party product is supported by NSX, partner integration must be reregistered with NSX after the upgrade and the partner service redeployed. Verify with the solutions provider to validate NSX compatibility and any additional requirements that may be needed.

Upgrade to NSX Manager

Upgrading vCNS to NSX Manager has no impact on the data plane. However, no vCNS changes can be made during the upgrade process, and it is strongly recommended that it be performed during a maintenance window. Also, vCenter must be running version 5.5 or higher, and vShield Data Security must be uninstalled.

To upgrade to NSX Manager from vShield Manager, perform the following steps. It is a good idea to take a snapshot of vShield Manager before starting.

> **NOTE**   You should do some benchmark testing before the start of the upgrade (or any changes to production environments) and validate by testing against the benchmark after you are done.

Step 1.   Download the vCNS to NSX for vSphere upgrade bundle from VMware.

Step 2.   Log in to the vShield Manager home page, https://[vShield_MGR_IP_ or_FQDN]/. You can also access this page from **vSphere Client in Home > Solutions and Applications > vShield**.

Step 3.   In **Settings & Reports**, go to the **Updates** tab, as shown in Figure 19-1.

NSX Manager retains the same IP as vShield Manager.

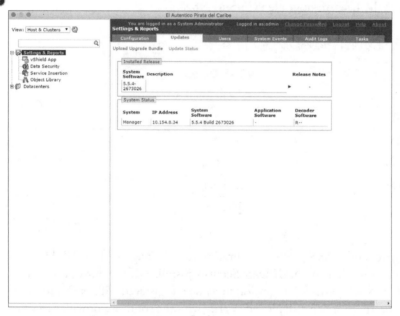

Figure 19-1   vShield Manager Updates tab

Step 4.   Click **Upload Upgrade Bundle**.

Step 5.   Select **Choose File** and select the file you have from step 1.

Step 6. Click **Upload File** and click **OK** in the pop-up window warning you that vShield Manager will be updated with data from the file.

Step 7. After the upload completes, click **Install** followed by **Confirm Install**. Now sit back, relax, and enjoy the show.

vShield Manager reboots and comes back as NSX Manager.

Step 8. After NSX Manager is powered up, log in to the NSX Manager home page, https://[NSX_MGR_IP_or_FQDN]/, and go to the **Summary** tab to confirm the NSX Manager version, as shown in Figure 19-2.

You might want to update DNS to point the old vShield Manager IP to the NSX Manager FQDN.

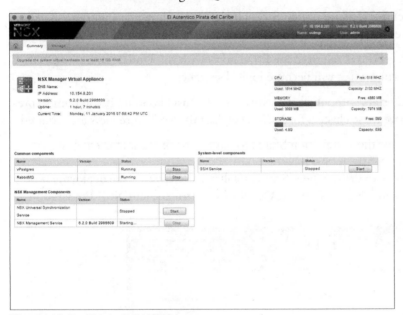

Figure 19-2 Upgraded NSX Manager

Step 9. If you enabled SSH in vShield Manager, start SSH in NSX Manager from the Summary tab.

Step 10. Shut down NSX Manager.

Step 11. Log in to the vSphere Web Client where the NSX Manager Appliance is running and go to Hosts and Clusters.

Step 12. Find the NSX Manager Appliance, and increase the vCPUs to 4 and the memory to 16 GB.

Step 13. Power up NSX Manager.

Don't forget to delete the ~~vShield Manager~~ NSX Manager snapshot once you are done with the upgrade.

Upgrade to NSX VIBs

After you upgrade vShield Manager to NSX Manager, you want to upgrade the vCNS VIBs to NSX VIBs. This step impacts the data plane, thus you should do this upgrade during a maintenance window.

The upgrading to the NSX VIBs requires the removal of the vCNS VIBs. To upgrade virtual wires to logical switches, follow these steps:

Step 1.   Log in to the vSphere Web Client, and go to the Networking and Security home page.

Step 2.   Select the **Installation** view and click the **Host Preparation** tab.

Step 3.   Select the **Update** option for each cluster, as shown in Figure 19-3. All clusters that have virtual wires show the Update option.

   a. A reboot is required for ESXi hosts with the Update option. vCNS virtual wires will become logical switches.

   b. Clusters without virtual wires have the Install option. If you want to prepare these clusters for NSX, click **Install**. No host reboots are required.

Step 4.   Wait for the Installation Status to have a check mark in each cluster.

Now is a good time to deploy the NSX Controllers. We covered the deployment of NSX Controllers in Chapter 4, "VXLAN, NSX Controllers, and NSX Preparation."

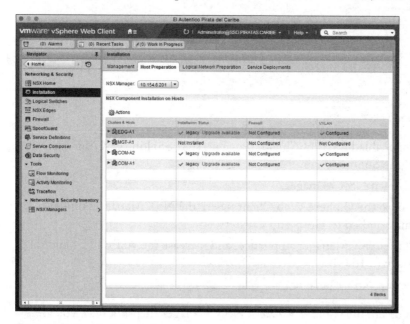

Figure 19-3   Update clusters

Upgrade to NSX DFW

Once you have upgraded the logical switches, you can upgrade the vShield App firewall policies to the DFW. Like the logical switch upgrade, you are updating the VSIP VIB in the ESXi hosts.

To upgrade the vShield App firewall rules to the DFW, perform the following steps:

Step 1.   In the Host Preparation tab, look for the message to update the firewall.

Step 2.   Click **Upgrade**.

Step 3.   After the upgrade, head over to the Firewall view and inspect the DFW rules.

A few things to keep in mind when verifying the DFW rules:

- There is a section for each data center, portgroup, and virtual wire (now logical switch) configured in the vShield App.

- The Applied To field matches the section. For example, a Virtual Wire section has all its rules applied to the ~~Virtual Wire~~ logical switch.

- Portgroup sections go above Virtual Wires sections, which go above Data Center sections, which go above the default rule.

- Any rules with Source ports have the Source ports listed in the service.

  - New applications, with the Source ports, are created for user-defined applications.

  - New applications, with the Source ports, are created for each application in an application group.

Upgrade to NSX Edge

Upgrading the vCNS Edge to the NSX Edge is easy and straightforward. All you are actually doing is upgrading the Edge version from 5.5.

To upgrade to the NSX Edge, follow these steps:

Step 1.   Go to **NSX Edges** view.

Step 2.   For each Edge, click the **Actions** menu and select **Upgrade Version**, as shown in Figure 19-4.

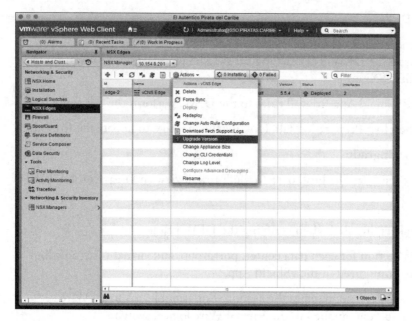

Figure 19-4   Upgrade to the NSX Edge

Step 3.   Wait for the upgrade to finish and confirm the Version column reads 6.2.1.

Upgrade to USVM

The last upgrade that needs to take place is the Universal Service Virtual Machine (USVM). The vShield Endpoint is now called the USVM. To upgrade the USVM, follow these steps:

Step 1.   Go to the **Installation** view.

Step 2.   Select the **Service Deployments** tab.

Step 3.   For each vShield Endpoint, click the arrow next to **Upgrade Available**.

Step 4.   In the pop-up window, select the Data Store and Network to connect the USVM.

Step 5.   Click **OK** and wait for the upgrade to complete.

Upgrade NSX for vSphere to NSX for vSphere 6.2

If you have an NSX 6.0.x or NSX 6.1.x installation, you can upgrade to NSX 6.2. This upgrade is similar but slightly simpler than the upgrade from vCNS. Almost all NSX components can be upgraded except Data Security and the SSL VPN client. You must manually deploy a new Data Security appliance. The old SSL VPN client gets uninstalled the next time a user connects to the NSX Edge 6.2 and the new NSX 6.2 SSL VPN client gets installed.

The SSL VPN version of NSX 6.2 Edges only accept TLS.

The following list outlines the tasks that need to be performed to upgrade to NSX 6.2. Note that these tasks must be done in the order listed.

Step 1.   Upgrade to NSX Manager 6.2.

Step 2.   Upgrade NSX Controllers to 6.2.

Step 3.   Upgrade Host Clusters to 6.2.

Step 4.   Upgrade NSX Edges to 6.2.

Step 5.   Upgrade USVM to 6.2. We covered this step in the vCNS to NSX upgrade section of this chapter.

Step 6.   Reinstall Data Security. We covered this step in Chapter 17, "Additional NSX Features."

Upgrade to NSX Manager 6.2

Upgrading NSX Manager 6.2 has no impact on the data plane; however, no NSX changes can be made during the upgrade process, and it is strongly recommended that it be performed during a maintenance window. Also, vCenter must be running version 5.5u3 or higher, and vShield Data Security must be uninstalled.

To upgrade to NSX Manager 6.2, perform the following steps. Like the upgrade from vCNS, it is a good idea to snapshot the current NSX Manager before starting.

Step 1.   Download the NSX Manager upgrade bundle from VMware.

Step 2.   Log in to the NSX Manager home page, https://[NSX_MGR_IP_or_FQDN]/.

Step 3.   In Manage, go to the **Upgrade** view, as shown in Figure 19-5.

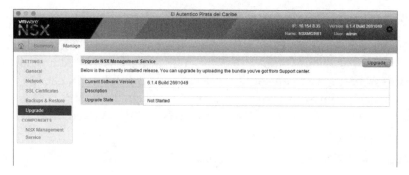

Figure 19-5   NSX Manager Upgrade view

Step 4.   Click **Upgrade**, select **Choose File**, and select the file you have from step 1.

Step 5.   Click **Continue**.

Step 6.   In the next window, confirm the upgrade, choose whether you want SSH to be enabled, and click **Upgrade**.

Step 7.   After the upload completes, NSX Manager reboots with the new version, as shown in Figure 19-6.

Figure 19-6   Upgraded NSX Manager

Step 8.   Shut down NSX Manager.

Step 9.   Log in to the vSphere Web Client where the NSX Manager Appliance is running and go to Hosts and Clusters.

Step 10.   Find the NSX Manager Appliance, and increase the memory to 16 GB.

Step 11.   Power up NSX Manager.

Step 12.   Log out of the vSphere Web Client and go to https://[vCenter_IP_or_FQDN]:5480/ to restart the vSphere Web Client and force the NSX-Plugin to be upgraded.

   If running the vCenter Server Appliance, ssh to vCenter and type the following commands:

```
/bin/service-control --stop vsphere-client
/bin/service-control --start vsphere-client
```

Don't forget to delete the NSX Manager snapshot once you are done with the upgrade.

Upgrade NSX Controllers to 6.2

Next, you need to upgrade the NSX Controllers. Before you upgrade the NSX Controllers, make sure the following are true:

- All NSX Controllers are connected to NSX Manager.

- All NSX Controllers are part of the NSX Controller cluster.

NSX Manager won't upgrade the NSX Controllers if even one NSX Controller is not connected. Just like the NSX Manager, it is a good idea to take a snapshot of the NSX Controllers before starting the upgrade.

The NSX Controllers are rebooted after the upgrade is downloaded to them, but they are rebooted one at a time. Nevertheless, you should assume the control plane will be impacted during the upgrade, and you should schedule this upgrade during a maintenance window.

To upgrade the NSX Controllers, perform the following steps:

Step 1.   From the Networking and Security home page, select the **Installation** view.

Step 2.   Go to the **Management** tab and locate the NSX Manager.

Step 3.   In the Controller Cluster Status column, click **Upgrade Available**, as shown in Figure 19-7.

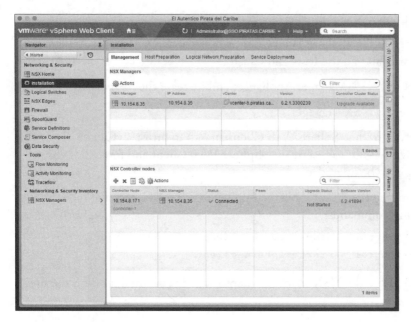

Figure 19-7   NSX Controller upgrade available

Step 4.   Answer **Yes** in the pop-up window asking whether you want to upgrade the NSX Controllers.

Step 5.   After all NSX Controllers have rebooted, the NSX Controller in the Controller Cluster Status column will be gone, and the NSX Controllers all have a status of Connected.

You can remove the snapshot of the NSX Controllers.

Upgrade Host Clusters to 6.2

The next upgrade is the NSX VIBs in the ESXi hosts. The upgrade involves removing the existing VIBs and installing the new ones. This requires the ESXi hosts to be rebooted. But don't worry, NSX Manager tries rebooting the hosts for you. If the cluster has DRS configured, powered on VMs are migrated before the ESXi host reboots. Otherwise, the reboot is halted until the host is placed in Maintenance Mode.

Upgrading the NSX VIBs in the ESXi hosts upgrades the entities that run in kernel: the logical switches, logical routers (data plane), and the logical firewall.

To upgrade the host clusters to 6.2, follow these steps:

Step 1.   In the Installation View, select **Host Preparation**.

Step 2.   For each cluster, click **Upgrade Available** in the Installation Status column, as shown in Figure 19-8. This might take some time, as the ESXi hosts need to be rebooted.

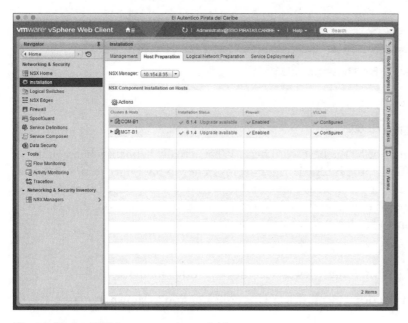

Figure 19-8   ESXi host upgrade available

Step 3.   After the hosts have rebooted, the Installation Status column should show the NSX version, as shown in Figure 19-9.

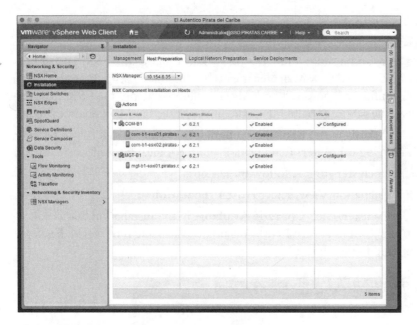

Figure 19-9   Successful ESXi host upgrade

Upgrade NSX Edges to 6.2

Upgrading might not be the best word here. What actually happens when you up-grade the NSX Edge, the NSX Manager deploys a new NSX Edge, version 6.2, and pushes the same configuration as the old Edge. The new NSX Edge has the same VM name as the old one. You should expect a brief service disruption, thus plan on making these upgrades during a maintenance window.

To upgrade to NSX Edge 6.2, follow these steps:

Step 1.   In the **NSX Edge**s view, select the NSX Edge to update.

Step 2.   In the **Actions** menu, select **Upgrade Version** as shown in Figure 19-10.

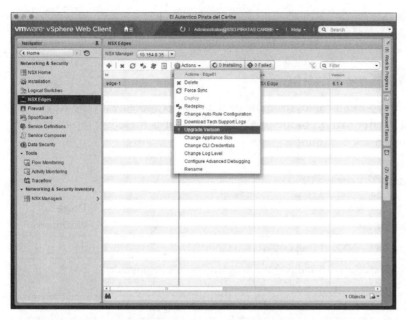

Figure 19-10 Upgrade NSX Edge version

The upgraded NSX Edge should take a few minutes to deploy.

To upgrade the Logical Router Control VM follow the same process as upgrading the NSX Edge.

Exam Preparation Tasks

Review All the Key Topics

Review the most important topics from inside the chapter, noted with the Key Topic icon in the outer margin of the page. Table 19-3 lists these key topics and the page numbers where each is found.

Table 19-3   Key Topics for Chapter 19

Key Topic Element	Description	Page Number
Paragraph	Upgrades to NSX are supported for vCNS 5.5.	555
Paragraph	vCNS Data Security and partner integration can't be upgraded to NSX.	555
Paragraph	NSX Manager keeps the same IP as vShield Manager.	556
Paragraph	NSX Edge 6.2 only supports TLS for SSL VPN.	561
Paragraph	Upgrading the NSX VIBs upgrades the logical switches, logical routers and logical firewall	565
Paragraph	The Logical Router Control VM is upgraded using the same process as the NSX Edge upgrade.	567

Define Key Terms

Define the following key terms from this chapter, and check your answers in the glossary:

vCloud Network and Security (vCNS), vShield Manager, virtual wires

Woohoo! you finished the book—well the parts of the book that matter the most to help you pass the VCP6-NV exam (2V0-641). Now I'm not saying this chapter is not important, but it is not technical. This chapter covers some house cleaning to get you ready to take the exam and offers some preparation tips.

This chapter contains three sections: "Getting Ready," "Taking the Exam," and "Tools for Final Preparation."

CHAPTER 20

Final Preparation

Getting Ready

Before you walk into the testing center, I suggest you do some or all of the following:

- Practice what you've learned in NSX for vSphere. You can build your own little NSX-v environment at home. By having your own lab, you can practice how to install NSX Manager and configure different virtual network environments. If you don't have a home lab, VMware can provide you with temporary ones, after completing free registration, at VMware Hands On Labs, http://labs.hol.vmware.com. VMware Hands On Labs are mini-labs VMware provides you via the browser and without requiring any installation on your computer. These labs do not give you the same freedom you would have with your own personal lab; however, they do allow you to practice most of the topics covered in the exam. There are a few labs you can try for to help you prepare (all free of charge): HOL-SDC-1603 VMware NSX Introduction, HOL-SDC-1625 VMware NSX Advanced, and HOL-SDC-1632 vRealize Automation Advanced: Integration and Extensibility.

- Although the exam is multiple choice, one of its goals is to verify that you have hands-on expertise with software. Be prepared to answer questions aimed at determining whether you know how to use a specific user interface to accomplish a specific task. For example, the correct choice for a question could depend on your knowledge of the exact text that appears on a link or button in the interface. I recommend that you at least practice performing the procedures described in this book.

- VMware may change the requirements for certifications and exams at any time; you should closely examine the requirements on the VMware Certification website at https://mylearn.vmware.com/mgrReg/plan.cfm?plan=88896&ui=www_cert prior to registering for the exam. The following details are accurate at the time of this book's writing but are subject to change at VMware's discretion.

- Candidates who are preparing for any of these exams fall into one of two categories: those who currently hold a VMware Certified Professional (VCP) certification and those who are new to VMware certification (or only hold expired VCP certifications). New candidates are required to take a qualifying course as well as pass the vSphere 6 Foundation Exam.

- Candidates, who are the holders of an earlier certification might be eligible for a delta exam. The stated objectives of both exams are identical, but the following differences exist between the exams:

  - The delta exam is usually more condensed and does not include all the stated sub-objectives as the standard exam.

  - The delta exam is usually a bit shorter at 90 minutes and 65 questions versus 100 minutes and 85 questions.

- On the VMware Certified Professional 6 – Network Virtualization (VCP6-NV) site, https://mylearn.vmware.com/mgrReg/plan.cfm?plan=64294&ui=www_cert, select either the **New Candidate Requirements** tab or the **Existing Candidate Requirements** tab and navigate to the path description that best fits your current status. The path identifies all the requirements for the candidate, such as any qualifying courses and exams. For example, a candidate who holds a current VCP certification for any other VMware solution track, should select **Existing Candidate Requirements** > **Path 2**, which calls for the candidate to pass the standard VCP6-NV exam (2V0-641).

- On the VMware Certified Professional 6 – Network Virtualization Exam site, https://mylearn.vmware.com/mgrReg/plan.cfm?plan=64297&ui=www_cert, use the links provided to examine the details for your required exam. Select the **Exam Topics** tab to view the exam blueprint. You can expand each section and then expand each exam objective to examine the Knowledge items and Tools you can use to additionally prepare for the exam. This book was written to cover all the exam objectives (as of January 2016). Carefully compare the exam objectives and knowledge items in the Table of Contents in this book to identify any items that may have been recently added and are not covered in the book. To address any recently added items, begin by examining the online content for this book, which may include updates and bonus content for premium editions.

- In addition to the exam topics, objectives, and knowledge items, review other exam details. For example, the details for the VCP6-NV Exam are

  Exam Number: 2V0-641

  Duration: 100 minutes

  Number of Questions: 85

Passing Score: 300

Recommended Training: VMware NSX: Install, Configure, Manage [V6.2]

Exam Languages: English, Japanese

Format: Single and Multiple Choice, Proctored

- Use the How to Prepare tab to examine the recommended training details. If you feel your knowledge and skillset are weak, consider some of the provided training courses.

- Use the Additional Resources tab to find links to groups, online training, and other sources of materials that can help you better prepare for the exam.

- Review the following items in each chapter in this book until you have them committed to memory.

  - Do I Know This Already questions at the beginning of each chapter

  - Key Terms and Key Topics that appear throughout and at the end of each chapter

- Prior to registering for the VCP6-NV, you must request authorization. To do so, click on the **Request Exam Authorization** link in the VMware Certified Professional 6 – Network Virtualization Exam site, https://mylearn.vmware.com/mgrReg/plan.cfm?plan=64297&ui=www_cert.

- After VMware provides the requested authorization, you can register for the exam at https://www1.pearsonvue.com/testtaker/signin/SignInPage/VMWAREINC. Sign in with your account (create a new account, if necessary), select the appropriate exam in the Pre-approved Exams section, and use the wizard to schedule the date, time, and location.

- Use the Pearson Cert Practice Test engine to practice. The Pearson Cert Practice Test engine can be used to study using a bank of unique exam-realistic questions available only with this book. The standard edition of this book includes two exams, and the Premium Edition includes two more exams. If you miss any questions, read the provided explanation and the related section in this book. Continue taking the practice exam(s) until you feel you know and can explain each answer. Refer to the "Tools for Final Preparation" section for more information about the Pearson Cert Practice Test engine.

Taking the Exam

Here is a list of considerations and actions for the day of the exam:

- Bring two forms of identification that include your photo and signature. You cannot bring personal items, such as laptops, tablets, phones, watches, pagers, wallets, or notes into the examination room. You may be able to place some of these items into a locker, but you should avoid bringing larger items into the training facility.

- Arrive at the exam center 30 minutes prior to the scheduled start time to provide ample time to complete the sign-in procedure and address personal needs. During the sign-in procedure, you should expect to place personal belongings in a locker, provide credentials, review the test regulations, and sign the agreement.

- Be sure to pay attention to the rules and regulations concerning the exam. For example, follow the venue's protocol for requesting help during the exam and for signaling your completion of the exam. Each venue's rules may be unique.

- The exam format is single and multiple choice, provided via a web-based user interface.

- Pay close attention to the wording of each question and each choice. Some examples of what to expect are

  - Some questions may ask you to select "which statement is correct" and some questions may ask you to select "which statement is incorrect."

  - Most questions call for you to select a single choice from a list of choices. Whenever a question calls for you to select more than one choice, it does so explicitly, by including a phrase such as "(choose two)."

  - Read each question carefully enough to ensure that you successfully interpret feature names and terminology. For example, when a question contains the word *HA*, you need to carefully determine whether it is referring to a vSphere Cluster HA or an NSX Edge HA.

  - Questions tend to be written in a concise manner, where at first glance you may think that insufficient details are provided. For example, the question could provide a symptom and ask you to select three actions that you should take to troubleshoot. Your first thought may be that you would take analytical steps or remediation steps that are not provided as choices for the question. You may even consider the provided choices to be unpractical or insufficient. Do not get frustrated. Just select the appropriate choices that fit the question.

  - Questions that ask you to identify more than one choice to accomplish a specific configuration or troubleshooting task may not always clearly state whether the steps in all the selected choices must be performed or just the steps in any one of the choices must be performed. Although you may wish the question contained better clarity, you should see that only one solution actually fits the question and the specified number of choices that you must select.

- Strive for good time management during the exam. Don't allow yourself to get stuck on a question for too long. If a question is tricky, such as more than one choice seems to fit a question that calls for a single choice, ask yourself, "Which choice is most likely the choice that VMware wants?" You may find some questions easier to solve by focusing on which choices to eliminate.

- Whenever you are unsure of an answer or you are rushed with making a decision, use the web interface to mark the question for review.

- After answering all the questions, a Review Page is provided that identifies all questions that you marked for review and all questions that are incomplete. If sufficient time remains, use the provided links on the review page to return to any questions you marked or any questions identified as incomplete.

Tools for Final Preparation

This section lists some information about the available tools and how to access the tools.

Review Tools on the Companion Website

The companion website for this book includes all the electronic files and review tools. To access this site, follow these steps:

Step 1.   Go to http://www.pearsonitcertification.com/register.

Step 2.   Either log in to your account (if you have an existing account already) or create a new account.

Step 3.   Enter the ISBN of your book (9780789754806) and click **Submit**.

Step 4.   Answer the challenge questions to validate your purchase.

Step 5.   In your account page, click on the **Registered Products** tab, then click the **Access Bonus Content** link.

After you have registered your book, to access the companion website, all you need to do is go to www.pearsonitcertification.com and sign in to your account. From there, select the **Registered Products** tab and click the **Access Bonus Content** link.

Pearson Cert Practice Test Engine and Questions

The companion website includes the Pearson Cert Practice Test engine (software that displays and grades a set of exam-realistic, multiple choice questions). Using the Pearson Cert Practice Test, you can either study by going through the questions in Study mode or take a simulated (timed) VCP6 Foundations exam.

The installation process requires two major steps. The companion website has a recent copy of the Pearson Cert Practice Test engine. The practice exam—the database of VCP6 Foundations exam questions—can be downloaded after you redeem your access code found in the sleeve in the back of the book.

Download and Install the Software

Note If you have purchased another Pearson study guide, you may have already installed the PCPT software. If so, you do not need to install the software again. Skip ahead to the next section to activate your new practice exams.

The software installation process is routine compared with other software installation processes. To be complete, the following steps outline the download and installation process:

Step 1.   Go to the book's companion website (instructions for access are included in the previous section).

Step 2.   Locate the download link for the Pearson IT Certification Practice Test (PCPT) software and download the latest version of the engine to your computer.

Step 3.   When the download is complete, unzip the software and run the installer.

Step 4.   Respond to window prompts as with any typical software installation process.

The installation process gives you the option to activate your exam with the activation code supplied on the paper in the sleeve in the back of the book. This process requires that you establish a Pearson website logon. You need this logon to activate the exam, so please do register when prompted. If you already have a Pearson website logon, there is no need to register again. Just use your existing logon.

Activate and Download the Practice Exam

Once the exam engine is installed, you should then activate the exam associated with this book (if you did not do so during the installation process), as follows:

Step 1. Start the Pearson Cert Practice Test (PCPT) software from the Windows Start menu or from your desktop shortcut icon.

Step 2. To activate and download the exam associated with this book, from the My Products or Tools tab, click the **Activate** button.

Step 3. At the next screen, enter the activation key from the paper inside the cardboard sleeve at the back of the book. Then click the **Activate** button.

Step 4. The activation process downloads the practice exam. Click **Next**, and then click **Finish**.

When the activation process has completed, the My Products tab should list your new exam. If you do not see the exam, make sure you have selected the My Products tab on the menu. At this point, the software and practice exam are ready to use. Just select the exam and click the **Use** button.

To update a particular exam you have already activated and downloaded, simply select the **Tools** tab and click the **Update Products** button. Updating your exams ensures you have the latest changes and updates to the exam data.

If you want to check for updates to the Pearson Cert Practice Test engine software, select the **Tools** tab and click the **Update Application** button. Doing so ensures that you are running the latest version of the software engine.

Activating Other Exams

The exam software installation process, and the registration process, only has to happen once. Then, for each new exam, only a few steps are required. For instance, if you buy another new VMware press Official Cert Guide or Pearson IT Certification Cert Guide, extract the activation code from the sleeve at the back of that book. From there, all you have to do is start the exam engine (if not still up and running) and perform steps 2 through 4 from the previous list.

Premium Edition

In addition to the free practice exam provided with this book, you can purchase additional exams with expanded functionality directly from Pearson IT Certification. The Premium Edition of this title contains an additional two full practice exams and an eBook (in PDF, EPUB, and Kindle formats). In addition, the Premium Edition title also has remediation for each question to the specific part of the eBook that relates to that question.

Because you have purchased the print version of this title, you can purchase the Premium Edition at a deep discount. There is a coupon code in the sleeve in the back of the book that contains a one-time-use code and instructions for where you can purchase the Premium Edition.

To view the premium edition product page, go to www.informit.com/title/9780789756497.

Using the Exam Engine

The Pearson Cert Practice Test engine includes a database of questions created specifically for this book. The Pearson Cert Practice Test engine can be used either in Study mode or Practice Exam mode, as follows:

- **Study mode:** This mode is most useful when you want to use the questions for learning and practicing. In Study mode, you can select options like randomizing the order of the questions and answers, automatically viewing answers to the questions as you go, testing on specific topics, and many other options.

- **Practice Exam mode:** This mode presents questions in a timed environment, providing you with a more exam-realistic experience. It also restricts your ability to see your score as you progress through the exam and view answers to questions as you are taking the exam. These timed exams not only allow you to study for the actual VCP6 Foundations exam, they help you simulate the time pressure that can occur on the actual exam.

When doing your final preparation, you can use Study mode, Practice Exam mode, or both. However, after you have seen each question a couple of times, you will likely start to remember the questions, and the usefulness of the exam database might diminish. So, consider the following options when using the exam engine:

- Use this question database for review. Use Study mode to study the questions by chapter, just as with the other final review steps listed in this chapter. Plan on getting another exam (possibly from the Premium Edition) if you want to take additional simulated exams.

- Save the question database, not using it for review during your review of each book part. Save it until the end, so you will not have seen the questions before. Then use Practice Exam mode to simulate the exam.

Picking the correct mode from the exam engine's user interface is pretty obvious. The following steps show how to move to the screen from which to select Study or Practice Exam mode:

Step 1.   Click the **My Products** tab if you are not already at that screen.

Step 2.   Select the exam you want to use from the list of available exams.

Step 3.   Click the **Use** button.

The engine should then display a window from which you can choose Study mode or Practice Exam mode. When in Study mode, you can further choose the book chapters, limiting the questions to those explained in the specified chapters of the book.

Ta-ta for now. I wish you the best of luck (buena suerte) in your exam. Please send me a tweet once you pass @ElverS_Opinion with the tag #Ipassed. Or if you are not into tweeting, send me a line at elver.sena@hydra1303.com.

Answers to the "Do I Know This Already?" Quizzes

Chapter 1

1. B
2. B
3. A
4. D
5. A
6. B
7. B
8. A
9. C
10. B

Chapter 2

1. B and D
2. A and C
3. A
4. B
5. B
6. C
7. C and D
8. D
9. B
10. D

Chapter 3

1. D
2. B
3. A and D
4. B
5. C
6. D
7. D
8. C
9. D
10. B

Chapter 4

1. D
2. A
3. C
4. D
5. B and D
6. B
7. C
8. A
9. A
10. A

Chapter 5

1. A
2. C
3. B and D
4. C
5. D
6. D
7. B and D
8. C and D
9. C
10. B

Chapter 6

1. B
2. C
3. D
4. A and D
5. C
6. A
7. D
8. B
9. B and D
10. B

Chapter 7

1. C
2. A
3. C
4. C
5. A and D
6. D
7. D
8. A
9. C
10. B

Chapter 8

1. D
2. C
3. A
4. A
5. D
6. C
7. C
8. A
9. C
10. D

Chapter 9

1. C
2. B
3. D
4. B
5. B
6. A
7. B

8. C
9. C
10. C

Chapter 10

1. A
2. B
3. C and D
4. B
5. C
6. C
7. D
8. B
9. B
10. B

Chapter 11

1. A and C
2. D
3. B
4. A
5. B
6. C
7. C
8. C
9. C
10. C

Chapter 12

1. C
2. D
3. D

4. B
5. C
6. D
7. C
8. B
9. C
10. D

Chapter 13

1. D
2. D
3. B
4. B and D
5. B
6. B
7. A
8. D
9. B and D
10. C

Chapter 14

1. B
2. C
3. B and D
4. A
5. B
6. D
7. B
8. B and C
9. C
10. B

Chapter 15

1. A
2. D
3. C
4. A and D
5. C
6. A
7. B and C
8. A and D
9. B
10. D
11. A

Chapter 16

1. B
2. A
3. D
4. A
5. C
6. C
7. C
8. D
9. A and D
10. A

Chapter 17

1. A
2. B and C
3. B and C
4. C
5. A and D
6. C

7. C
8. A
9. D
10. C

Chapter 18

1. C and D
2. B
3. B
4. B and C
5. B
6. B
7. C
8. C
9. C
10. A

Chapter 19

1. C
2. C
3. D
4. B
5. B
6. B
7. A
8. B
9. A
10. B

VCP6-NV Exam 2V0-641 Updates

Over time, reader feedback allows Pearson to gauge which topics give our readers the most problems when taking the exams. To assist readers with those topics, the authors create new materials clarifying and expanding on those troublesome exam topics. As mentioned in the Introduction, the additional content about the exam is contained in a PDF on this book's companion website at http://www.ciscopress.com/title/9780789754806.

This appendix provides you with updated information if VMware makes minor modifications to the exam upon which this book is based. When VMware releases an entirely new exam, the changes are usually too extensive to provide in a simple updated appendix. In those cases, you might need to consult the new edition of the book for the updated content. This appendix attempts to fill the void that occurs with any print book. In particular, this appendix does the following:

- Mentions technical items that might not have been mentioned elsewhere in the book

- Covers new topics if VMware adds new content to the exam over time

- Provides a way to get up-to-the-minute current information about content for the exam

Always Get the Latest at the Book's Product Page

You are reading the version of this appendix that was available when your book was printed. However, given that the main purpose of this appendix is to be a living, changing document, it is important that you look for the latest version online at the book's companion website. To do so, follow these steps:

Step 1. Browse to http://www.ciscopress.com/title/9780789754806.

Step 2. Click the **Updates** tab.

Step 3. If there is a new Appendix B document on the page, download the latest Appendix B document.

NOTE   The downloaded document has a version number. Comparing the version of the print Appendix B (Version 1.0) with the latest online version of this appendix, you should do the following:

- **Same version**: Ignore the PDF that you downloaded from the companion website.

- **Website has a later version**: Ignore this Appendix B in your book and read only the latest version that you downloaded from the companion website.

Technical Content

The current Version 1.0 of this appendix does not contain additional technical coverage.

GLOSSARY

802.1Q   Open standard that defines how multiple VLANs can be shared across a link between two switches.

ABR   OSPF area border router. Connects one or more areas to the backbone area.

administrative distance   A number ranking system to determine the most reliable routing table learning method or routing protocol.

AES-NI   Advanced Encryption Standard New Instructions. CPU technology to allow for the offloading from the OS encryption-based computations.

ARP table   Table created by the Switch Security Module to keep the IP-ARP mappings of each logical switch. The ARP table is populated by doing ARP snooping and DHCP snooping. Each ESXi host's Switch Security Module sends a copy of its ARP entries to the NSX Controller.

ASBR   OSPF autonomous system border router. Injects routes into OSPF from a different routing process or AS.

autonomous system (AS)   A domain under the control of the same administrator or entity.

Border Gateway Protocol (BGP)   Exterior Gateway Protocol (EGP) that is used as the preferred routing protocol for the Internet.

Bridge Instance   The ESXi host doing the Layer 2 bridging.

control plane   The network plane that facilitates, using the configuration provided by the management plane, the information needed to make forwarding decisions for traffic between end systems.

cost Number used to determine the path preference to a destination. The lower the number the better the path.

cross vCenter NSX NSX 6.2 feature to centralize management of NSX and feature configuration of NSX among multiple NSX Managers. In cross vCenter NSX, there is a single NSX dDomain that supports ESXi host clusters from different vCenters.

data plane The network plane that makes the forwarding decision, using information provided by the control plane, for traffic between end systems.

Designated Instance The ESXi host running the copy of the DLR instance responsible for sending ARP requests over the VLAN LIF and sending ARP replies over the VLAN LIF.

Diffie-Hellman Mechanism used for the creation of secret keys over an untrusted medium.

distributed firewall (DFW) Firewall that runs in the ESXi kernel to provide Layer 2, Layer 3, and Layer 4 stateful security to virtual machines.

distributed firewall module Software installed in the ESXi host to enable the distributed firewall.

distributed logical router (DLR) In-kernel NSX router managed by a single NSX Manager that connects to global logical switches.

DNAT Destination NAT. The changing of the destination IP address of a packet.

eBGP External BGP. The type of BGP peers formed by two BGP speakers in the different AS.

Edge HA Two NSX Edges deployed in an Active/Standby state.

Edge VLAN The VLAN the Perimeter Edge connects to.

Equal Cost MultiPath ECMP is the capability of a router to have multiple paths in the routing table to the same destination.

ESXi host A server running the vSphere hypervisor.

exclusion list List of virtual machines excluded from the DFW.

External Gateway Protocol, EGP Term to describe a routing protocol that may be under one or more AS.

hardware VTEP   A physical bridge that can bridge a VXLAN to a VLAN.

iBGP   Internal BGP. The type of BGP peers formed by two BGP speakers in the same AS.

IKE   Internet Key Exchange. Protocol for the creation of secure communications channel over an untrusted medium.

Internal Gateway Protocol (IGP)   Term to describe a routing protocol that is under one AS.

internal LIF   A logical interface where no routing protocol will be configured.

IPsec VPN   Protocol suite that allows for the secure communication between two endpoints over an untrusted medium.

IPsec VPN peers   Two endpoints that have successfully negotiated the creation of an IPsec VPN tunnel.

IS-IS   Intermediate Systems to Intermediate Systems. IGP that exchanges routing information via link state. Similar to OSPF.

Layer 2 bridge   The bridging of a VXLAN and a VLAN by a DLR.

Layer 2 VPN   Mechanism to extend a Layer 2 domain over an untrusted medium.

LIF   Logical Interface. The name of the interface of the logical router.

local firewall rule   DFW rule that is not synchronized among NSX Managers in a cross vCenter NSX domain.

Locale ID   Allows for local egress traffic from universal logical routers.

Logical Router Control VM   In conjunction with the NSX Controller, facilitates the control plane for the distributed logical router.

logical switch   A distributed switch that uses VXLAN Network IDs instead of VLAN Number IDs. Logical switches have the intelligence to know when to forward traffic to the VTEP for VXLAN frame encapsulation. Logical switches are not VTEPs themselves.

MAC learning   A switch function to populate the MAC table by reading the source MAC address of ingress Ethernet frames.

management plane   The network plane that owns configuration and management of network devices.

microsegmentation   Capability of the DFW to enforce security policies at the vNIC level.

MLAG   Multi-Chassis Link Aggregation. Two switches that present themselves as a single switch for the purpose of forming an LACP link.

MTEP   Multicast VTEP. The proxy VTEP for a logical switch configured with Hybrid Replication Mode.

NAT   Network Address Translation. NAT is a method of masquerading the source and/or destination IP and/or port number of a packet.

network function virtualization (NFV)   The virtualization of network and security functions.

network planes A networking layered architecture employed by network devices to deliver traffic between end systems.

NSSA OSPF Not So Stubby Area. Area that allows for an ASBR to be within the area while only receiving a default route from the ABR.

NSX APIs RESTful based APIs to interact with NSX Manager.

NSX Controller Facilitates the NSX control plane for the logical switches and the distributed logical routers.

NSX Controller Master NSX Controller responsible for assigning the NSX Controllers Layer 2 responsibility for logical switches and Layer 3 responsibility for distributed logical routers.

NSX Edge The NSX virtual appliance that provides network and security services such as routing, firewalls, and load balancing.

NSX for Multi-Hypervisors (NSX-MH) The VMware SDN solution that supports vSphere and non-VMware hypervisors.

NSX for vSphere (NSX-V) The VMware SDN solution requiring a vSphere environment.

Open Shortest Path First (OSPF) IGP that uses link state to exchange route information.

Perimeter Edge NSX Edge configured to provide Layer 3 connectivity between the virtual and physical networks.

pMAC A MAC address used by the logical router for some non-ARP traffic. The pMAC will be different in all copies of the logical router instance.

portgroup A logical grouping of ports in the vSS or vDS that contains the configuration to be applied to the virtual ports that connect to the virtual machine's vNIC and the VMkernel ports.

Primary NSX Manager The NSX Manager that owns the management plane of cross vCenter NSX features.

proxy VTEP The VTEP selected by the NSX Controller to forward replicated frames to all other VTEPs in its local VTEP subnet.

Replication Mode Method employed by logical switches to process BUMs.

REST Architectural style used for the development of web services that offers a way to interface with APIs.

routing module Software installed in the ESXi host to enable routing.

Secondary NSX Manager NSX Manager that participates in cross vCenter NSX.

security group Group of virtual machines matching predefined or dynamic criteria.

security policy Collection of Guest Introspection Services, DFW rules, and Network Introspection Services.

security service provider Provides security services to virtual machines by directly interacting with NSX.

security tag   Labels created in NSX Manager that can be attached to virtual machines.

Service Composer   Provides mechanism for the consumption of security services.

sinkport   A dvPort that receives all BUMs in the matching VLAN.

site-site IPsec VPN   IPsec VPN between two routers.

slicing   The process of assigning logical switches and logical routers to different NSX Controllers.

SNAT   Source NAT. The changing of the source IP address of a packet.

software defined data center   A Network solution where the control plane is executed by an entity separate from the one executing the data plane.

software defined network (SDN)   A method of virtualizing the network and security.

SpoofGuard   Protects against IP and MAC spoofing attacks.

SSL VPN   Protocol that allows the secure communication between two endpoints using SSL as the encryption mechanism.

SSL VPN-Plus   NSX's implementation of SSL VPN.

Standalone NSX Manager   NSX Manager that has its role changed from Primary to Standalone while still having some cross vCenter NSX features or objects.

STP   Spanning Tree Protocol. A protocol developed to prevent Layer 2 loops in an Ethernet broadcast domain.

SVI   Switched Virtual Interface. A logical interface in a Layer 3 switch that can have IP and subnet configuration.

Switch Security module   NSX software running in the ESXi hosts' kernel. It maintains the ARP table, per logical switch, in each ESXi host.

ToR   Top of Rack. A switch in a rack that provides uplink connectivity to the end systems in the rack.

Traceflow   Troubleshooting and planning tool that spoofs VMs as the source of traffic.

transit NSX Manager   NSX Manager that is not participating in vCenter NSX.

transport zone   List of ESXi clusters that will be informed of new logical switches or universal logical switches.

TRILL   Transparent Interconnection of Lots of Links. Ethernet technology that natively prevents Layer 2 loops without the use of Spanning Tree Protocol.

ULR   Universal Logical Router. Like the DLR but configured and managed by the Primary NSX Manager. It can only connect to universal logical switches.

undeployed Edge   An Edge that has been staged but not deployed in an ESXi host.

universal firewall rule   DFW rule that is synchronized among NSX Managers in a cross vCenter NSX domain.

universal logical switch A virtual switch that is distributed. It uses VXLAN Network IDs instead of VLAN Number IDs. Universal logical switches support multiple NSX Managers in cross vCenter NSX.

Universal Services Virtual Machine (USVM) Guest Introspection Virtual Machine required to provide data security.

Uplink LIF A logical interface where a routing protocol may be configured.

Uplink port The virtual port connected to a VMNIC. In the vDS the Uplink ports are called dvUplinks.

UTEP Unicast VTEP. The proxy VTEP for a logical switch configured with Unicast Replication Mode.

vCloud Network and Security (vCNS) The network and security predecessor of NSX.

vDS vSphere distributed switch. The virtual switch with the management handled by vCenter.

VIP Virtual IP. In the context of a load balancer, it is the IP used by an external user to access distributed services and applications.

virtual network A network that runs in a virtual environment, such as vSphere.

virtual port A port in a virtual switch. The vDS virtual ports are called dvPorts.

virtual wires vCNS's VXLAN aware virtual switches.

VLAN LIF A logical interface in the distributed logical router that connects to a vDS portgroup.

vMAC The source MAC address used by the logical router to send ARP requests and ARP replies. The vMAC is the same across all copies of the logical router instance.

VMkernel port The logical interface of the ESXi host that provides IP connectivity for the ESXi host.

VMNIC The physical interface in an ESXi host.

VMware tools Code installed in virtual machines to provide updated drivers and allows the ESXi hosts some level of access to the operating system of the virtual machine.

VMX file The instruction set the ESXi host uses to provide the configuration and features needed by the virtual machine on power on.

VNI VXLAN Network ID. Layer 2 number used to uniquely label an Ethernet broadcast domain in an NSX domain.

vNIC Virtual NIC. Ethernet interface of a virtual machine.

vRealize Automation One of VMware's cloud platforms that offers support for NSX APIs.

vShield Manager The entity responsible for the management plane of vCNS.

vSS vSphere Standard Switch. The default virtual switch in the ESXi host. Each host manages its own vSphere Standard Switches.

VTEP   VXLAN Tunnel Endpoint. An entity that can create, encapsulate, or decapsulate VXLAN frames. ESXi hosts may have multiple VTEPs, each represented by a VXLAN VMkernel port.

VTEP table   Table that contains a list of all the VTEPs that have at least one virtual machine's MAC associated with it. The VTEP table is owned and maintained by the NSX Controller.

VXLAN   Virtual Extensible LAN. Overlay technology used to extend Ethernet broadcast domains over IP networks.

VXLAN LIF   A logical interface in the logical router that connects to a logical switch.

VXLAN module   Software installed in the ESXi host to enable logical switches.

Index

Numbers

802.1Q standard, 9

A

ABR (Area Border Routers), OSPF routing, 352-353, 356

access

compliance. *See* Activity Monitoring RBAC, 521

> *assigning roles, 523*
> *NSX Manager/SSO integration, 522*
> *NSX roles, 521-522*
> *user access control, 522*
> *user roles, 522*

Access Layer (networks), 25

collapsed Access Layer design, 30

Spine and Leaf design, 31

access routers, physical networks, 25

access switches. *See* **ToR switches**

activation codes, practice exams (Pearson Cert Practice Test engine), 577

Active mode (LACP), 28

Activity Monitoring, 509

activity reports

> *Inbound Activity reports, 512*
> *Outbound Activity reports, 513*
> *Outbound AD Group Activity reports, 514*
> *running, 511*
> *viewing, 514*
> *VM Activity reports, 511*

data collection, enabling in VM, 510

Inter Container Interaction reports, 513

admin credentials, NSX Manager, 73

administrative distance (routing), 348

AES-NI (Advanced Encryption Standard-New Instructions), 278

Allowed Flows option (Flow Monitoring), 516-517

anti-replay feature, IPsec VPN, 382

API (NSX)

calls for

> *logical routers, 536-540*
> *logical switches, 532-536*
> *NSX Edge, 540-542*

client headers, 531

HTTP responses, 531

supported HTTP methods, 530

application profiles (load balancers), 421, 427-428

areas

IS-IS areas, 369

F

M

S